LICENSE TO GRILL

OTHER BOOKS BY
CHRIS SCHLESINGER AND JOHN WILLOUGHBY

THE THRILL OF THE GRILL
Techniques, Recipes, & Down-Home Barbecue

SALSAS, SAMBALS, CHUTNEYS & CHOWCHOWS
Intensely Flavored "Little Dishes" from Around the World

BIG FLAVORS OF THE HOT SUN
Hot Recipes and Cool Tips from the Spice Zone

LETTUCE IN YOUR KITCHEN
Where Salad Gets a Whole New Spin and Dressings Do Double Duty

License to Grill

CHRIS SCHLESINGER

JOHN WILLOUGHBY

William Morrow and Company, Inc.

NEW YORK

Library of Congress Cataloging-in-Publication Data

Schlesinger, Chris.
    License to grill / Chris Schlesinger and John Willoughby. — 1st
    ed.
        p.   cm
    Includes index.
    ISBN 0-688-13943-4
    1. Barbecue cookery.   I. Willoughby, John.   II. Title.
    TX840.B3S273   1997
641.5'784—DC21   96-46690
                                                                            CIP

Printed in the United States of America

First Edition

1 2 3 4 5 6 7 8 9 10

BOOK DESIGN BY VERTIGO DESIGN

To Susan, Rick, Lizzie, and Tommy,

with love and affection

acknowledgments

FROM CHRIS

In some ways writing a book is like being the chef of a restaurant—that is, there are a lot of people who work really hard to make things happen, but only one person gets the credit. Just like a meal in my restaurant, there is no way this book could have happened without the hard work and diligence of many. To thank them all would be a book in itself.

I'd like to thank my Blue Room chef, Mark Hall, for working his tail off serving outstanding food and keeping the walk-in clean and the customers happy so I could play hooky and work on the book. Wesley Miyazaki, our pastry chef, really helped out with desserts, as did our ombudsperson and secret weapon, Lisa White. Without their help, the only dessert in the book would be fresh fruit. I also want to thank our General Manager, Nick "22" Zappia, and Assistant General Manager, Maureen "Bubbles" Rubino, for their unreal tolerance and good humor on all those early Friday mornings, and the whole kitchen and floor staffs, too.

I was extremely fortunate at this time to have very hardworking, talented, and unique staffs at the East Coast Grill and Jake & Earl's. First, thanks to Jeff Unger. No matter how tired and cranky I was, hanging out with Jeff always cheers me up. Here's to more good years ahead. Thanks also to the Dream Team wait staff anchored by Smiley, Tina, and Taylor. And thanks to Kenton "Jake" Jacobs, the living legend of Northeast barbecue, for not only holding down the fort at Jake & Earl's but also teaching us all a thing or two in the bargain.

Thanks to my business partner, Cary Wheaton, to whom I owe so much I'll never be able to repay—but, Cary, I will try really hard. Thanks also to my special assistant, Kitty Davis at International Headquarters, for her smile, her loyalty, and her hard work.

This is the fifth book that Doc and I have written together and we're starting to figure it out a little, which means we've learned how to get really smart and energetic folks to give us a hand. By all rights Bridget Batson's name should be on the cover of the book along with mine and Doc's. She served as the missing link, deciphering my scribbles and schemes and vague ideas and translating them into hardened, tested recipes—no small feat. Thanks, Bridget.

Thanks, also, to all my buds in the Boston restaurant community. I'm sure you all see familiar stuff in this book—thanks for the ideas. In particular, thanks to Jody Adams, Gordon Hamersley, Lydia Shire and Susan Regis, Todd English and Jasper White—whom I would like to be just like when I grow up.

Also thanks to my amigos Steve "Maurice" Johnson, Bob Kincaid, and Jimmy Burke. It's a beautiful country when guys like us own restaurants. Thanks for your companionship, humor, and free food.

And lastly I'd like to thank my coauthor, Doc. I know it's not always easy, but I wouldn't trade it for anything. I can't think of too many things that are as rewarding as working as a team to create. Thanks for the friendship, the trips, and the cold beers.

CHRIS SCHLESINGER

FROM JOHN (DOC)

After years as a full-time writer, I'm still not totally accustomed to the discipline and concentration that it takes to work at home. So I want to thank my neighbors and friends Rick, Susan, Tommy, and Lizzie for putting up with my idiosyncrasies as I worked on the book. Also, thanks to Maurice for playing with my dog, Sherman, for hours on end so I could work.

Thanks, too, to my friend and colleague Mark Bittman for his advice, friendship, and unfailing willingness to chat on the phone when neither of us felt like working on our respective projects. And thanks to my other friends and colleagues at *Cook's Illustrated* magazine—Pam Anderson, Jack Bishop, Chris Kimball, Stephanie Lyness, and Adam Ried—for their inspiration and their good humor.

And of course, thanks to Chris, my inimitable coauthor. Your sense of humor, your companionship, and your aversion to boredom continue to keep things lively and make what should be work often seem more like play. To my mind, our work is truly a case of the whole being greater than the sum of its parts. Thanks for your constant friendship, your generosity at the beach, and your astounding ability to come up with really bad puns on a moment's notice.

JOHN WILLOUGHBY

ACKNOWLEDGMENTS

viii

FROM BOTH OF US

The photos in this book were taken by Christopher Hirsheimer, and the quality of her pictures is exceeded only by the pleasure of her company. We just hope the food tastes half as good as she makes it look.

To the staff at Morrow, from the person who answers the phone to the person who ships the books, thanks for your consistent professionalism. Special thanks, of course, to our editor, Ann Bramson, who was always a phone call away to listen to our beefs, soothe our egos, or kick our butts, as the occasion demanded. Thanks, Ann, it was a pleasure to work with you.

And none of this would have happened without the help of our own personal impresario, superagent Doe Coover. It's an honor to be associated with you, Doe, not to mention that you're also fun to hang out with.

CHRIS AND JOHN

contents

Eating takes a special talent. Some people are much better at it than others. In that way, it's like sex, and as with sex, it's more fun with someone who really likes it. I can't imagine having a lasting friendship with anyone who is not interested in food.

—ALAN KING

INTRODUCTION

natural-born griller

A special casualness, a thrilling and challenging cooking technique, and some damned tasty eating—to me, that's live fire cooking.

With this book, I want to share the pleasure that I've had while grilling, and to pass on the tips and ideas I've acquired over the past few years. Whether you're a novice looking for your initial license to grill—permission to fool around with live fire, add a wonderful smoky sear to your dinner, and generally turn what could be a chore into one of the most pleasurable parts of the day—or an accomplished griller looking to earn your Ph.G. (Doctor of Grilling) with some recipes that carry a high level of difficulty, I've got your mind in mind. I've even included a few recipes that will put you well on your way to the coveted Ph.B. (Doctor of Barbecue).

Mainly, what I'd like to share with you is my approach to food and cooking. Now, as you know from eating in restaurants and reading cookbooks, different chefs and cookbook authors have different relationships to cooking. Their food and their ideas originate in different places, and they emphasize different aspects of both preparing and eating food.

Some folks will say that technique is the most important—cutting vegetables precisely, getting every tiny lump out of the sauce, creating stunningly beautiful presentations. Others will say that quality of ingredients is paramount—the ripest strawberry, the most tender beef, the best-fed chickens, the oldest balsamic vinegar. To others what really matters is the flavor—aroma, taste, and texture are the big considerations.

I believe that all of these factors (well, at least most of them) are of major significance. But the main question I'll be asking when you're finished cooking something from this book is "Was it fun?" Because to me, that's the most crucial part of any food experience.

That's why I like to cook and eat so much, because it's a blast. It makes me laugh and I like hanging out with other people and doing it—whether cooking or just eating, for work or for pleasure, it's a wonderful quality-of-life activity.

Because I feel this way, I think it's important to remember that what is at the heart of this whole cooking endeavor is good fellowship. The best meals I've ever had were fantastic not only because of the food, but also because of the people I ate it with. Cracking blue crabs and drinking cans of beer at a joint on Maryland's Eastern Shore with a couple of cooking buddies, or slurping oysters, peeling shrimp, and downing margaritas in Florida with my first mentor-chef and his wife—those are truly outstanding meals. For me, no matter how good the food, it doesn't really qualify as a great meal if nobody else is there.

I know that this approach to cooking, eating, and life in general isn't for everybody, but for me having fun is key. And there's no better way to enjoy yourself with food than grilling or barbecuing. This is not some new idea with me, either; I've believed it ever since I can remember.

My first memories of grilling go back to my childhood. My father was a classic dad griller. I remember him coming home from work in the summer and on his way through the door telling me, "We're grilling tonight, get the fire ready." I would go outside, dump out the ashes, and clean the grill, and Dad would then come down in his shorts and observe me as I squeezed on twice as much lighter fluid as was necessary. Then he'd let me light the match and watch as the fireball shot up into the sky.

When the flames had died down, he and I would stand there and cook. When it was ready, we'd deliver the food inside, where he would boast to my mom and sister that we'd "done it again," successfully delivering another fantastic meal from the wilds of the backyard. And each time, as he took the first bite, he would proclaim it "the best meal yet." We're talking heavy bonding here. The food was always good, and somehow, because it was cooked outside, we could relax more.

With this memory in mind, I encourage you to relax and not let yourself get too tied down or intimidated by any specific recipe in this book. If you don't have all the ingredients the recipe calls for, or you don't feel like putting on the spice rub, or you want to combine part of one recipe with part of another, go on ahead, it's okay. Grilling should be a release, not a chore, which means it should at all times be approached in a laid-back, lighthearted direction. Remember, the fun is in the cooking and the eating, not the perfection of the craft.

SO LET'S LIGHTEN UP AND GET GRILLING.

Grilling is the most straightforward of all cooking methods. What could be more basic, after all, than putting something over a fire and cooking it until it's done?

THE BASICS

let the flames begin

Despite this simplicity, though, the constantly changing dynamic of a live fire means grilling is also the most interactive and therefore, in my opinion, by far the most exciting and challenging of all cooking methods. When you bake, you just turn the oven to 350°F, and for sautéing, you twist the dial to medium-high. But there are no such controls in live fire grilling. The cook must make constant, intuitive decisions based on observation and experience. And since no two individual fires are alike, each time you approach the grill you are facing a new culinary landscape, a cooking adventure complete with the possibility of triumph or failure. This provides the uniquely exciting cooking experience that James Beard called "the thrill of the grill."

Rising to this challenge is the joy of grilling, and no matter what you think about your cooking skills, you can become an excellent griller in a few short hours. All it takes is the willingness to spend some time playing with fire out in the backyard, which to my mind sure beats spending time over a stove.

Of course, there are some folks who insist it's not that simple, that only those with an inborn aptitude can master the art of grilling. In fact, people have been saying this sort of thing for a long time. Brillat-Savarin, the famous French gourmand of the nineteenth century, was of the opinion that you were either born with the ability to roast (which in his time meant cooking over an open fire) or you were not. If fate had not smiled upon you in the grilling department, he declared, you might as well just forget about it.

But fortunately Auguste Escoffier, the celebrated nineteenth-century French chef and codifier of Western culinary techniques, disagreed. "One may become a good roaster," he said, "with application, observation, care, and a little aptitude." And Fernand Point, in my opinion the grandfather of nouvelle cuisine, weighed in on the side of Escoffier, saying, "One is not born a roasting chef, as Brillat-Savarin said, but becomes one."

So there you have the classic controversy of the gourmand versus the cook—the gourmand for some reason wanting to make cooking seem like a mysterious art that can be practiced only by those endowed with some innate, near-divine ability, and the cook saying that, while it does take some effort to become a good cook, it's really not that big a deal and anyone can do it.

In this debate I'm definitely on the side of the cook. Whether you're talking about roasting, grilling, or cooking in general, the ability to do it well is less a gift than a product of diligence and an understanding gained through practice. It is possible to look at grilling as a kind of weird, mystical art, but in fact it's a classic culinary technique like any other described by the Escoffier in his earliest works. And as with any other technique, once you experience the thrill, you'll develop the skill through attention to detail and perseverance.

Most Americans come to grilling in the same way that I did, by participating in that unique American experience, the backyard cookout. So to us, grilling is not just a way of cooking food, but the indispensable centerpiece of a culinary rite. This backyard ritual is characterized by the best traits of the American character: genial camaraderie, an air of easy pleasure, and an almost complete lack of pretense. From this American model, grillers can glean what are perhaps the most important aspects of the method—it is relaxing and just plain fun.

But grilling has a previous existence quite apart from its role in American cookouts. To my man Escoffier and his cohorts, for example, grilling was a classic cooking method, to be studied and catalogued just like sautéing, poaching, stewing, or braising. And to cooks around the tropical world, grilling is the daily cooking routine.

As simple as grilling is, knowing how and why it works makes it that much easier to get the results you're looking for. In other words, by realizing that grilling is a bona fide cooking technique governed by certain basic rules, we can begin to have a real understanding of how to do it right every time—or at least most of the time.

So let's take a brief look at fundamentals of the technique.

WHAT IS GRILLING, ANYWAY?

To begin with, we need to get one thing straight: Despite the fact that everybody and his or her brother refers to a cookout as a "barbecue," grilling is not barbecuing. These are two very different techniques and, in fact, are at opposite ends of the live fire cooking spectrum.

To make it simple, barbecuing consists of cooking tough cuts of meat by exposing them to the smoke and indirect heat of a very low fire for a very long time. The idea is not only to infuse the meat with smoky flavor, but also, through long cooking, to break down the tough connective tissues and make the meat tender. Among other cooking methods, barbecuing is most similar to braising.

Grilling, on the other hand, is a high-heat method in which rather tender foods are cooked quickly over the flame of a very hot fire. Grilling is similar to sautéing, with the added benefit of the smoky char that comes from cooking directly over live fire. When food is exposed to the direct heat of the flames, a seared crust develops on its exterior, and it is this flavor-packed crust—rather than the fuel used for the fire, as many believe—that is most responsible for the characteristic grilled flavor.

The flavor the sear provides is created by a process most of us just call browning but that is known to scientists as the Maillard reaction. To put it simply, this reaction occurs when carbohydrates and proteins are heated together. When this happens, the sugar (from the carbohydrates) and amino acids (from the proteins) combine to form new chemical structures. As heat continues to be applied, these compounds in turn break down, producing literally hundreds of by-products, each of which has a distinctive taste and aroma. So food that goes through this process gains new, rich, deep, complex flavors.

Basically, the Maillard reaction can be boiled down to a single rule of thumb: Brown food tastes better.

Anyone who has ever roasted a chicken, for example, knows that the brown stuff stuck to the bottom of the roasting pan is what's righteous, and it is no mistake that the classical sauce system is hinged on the notion of deglazing bits of caramelized food. This same principle gives stews deep character and flavor, because the taste of the initially browned meat permeates the entire dish during its long cooking.

This process happens not just with meat but with fowl, fish, and even vegetables. Consider the difference between the taste of golden-brown crust versus the interior of the bread, for example, or of crusty roasted potatoes versus their boiled cousins, and you will understand browning.

Now, it is true that browning can be accomplished with any cooking process that uses reasonably high heat. But there's no question that grilling rules. It is the hottest of high-heat cooking techniques and the food is usually cooked right over the flames, which means the heat is about as direct as it gets.

So there you have the major principles of grilling. It takes a hot fire, and it is most suitable for ingredients that are tender and cook fairly quickly, since the high heat makes it impossible for food to remain on the fire for very long without being incinerated. The clear implication of all of this is that the key to outstanding grilled food is the relationship between surface sear and interior doneness. In fact, this correlation is at the heart of the matter when it comes to grilling.

SO WHAT SHALL WE EAT?

With some understanding of the fundamentals of the technique of grilling, we can turn to the next question—what are we going to eat? For inspiration in this department we're going to turn to the experts. But in this case we're not talking about technique-driven French chefs, or even about the masters of the American backyard cookout. Instead, we look to the home cooks of the hot-weather world.

It took me a while to fully understand the international scope of grilling. But through consistent and relentless travel to foreign countries that feature beaches and hot weather, I started to realize how truly global grilling really is.

A huge number of people in the warm-weather world rely on grilling and other forms of live fire cooking as an everyday cooking technique. For these folks, cooking over live fire is not a weekend ritual, and it's not a highly defined professional technique: It's just the way they cook. The grill is their stove-top burner, their oven, and their microwave all rolled into one.

From the sidewalk hibachis in Southeast Asian cities to the makeshift grills on the beaches of Mexico to the braziers in the souks of North Africa, cooking over live fire is a truly international cooking technique.

Watching a fisherman grill a mess of shrimp on a beach in the Yucatán, savoring skewers of grilled lamb in a Moroccan bazaar or grilled beef in a market in Saigon, munching on a crisp, flame-marked pappadum in Bombay, or sitting down to a Middle Eastern mezze including platters of grilled peppers, tomatoes, and eggplant, you realize that the range of possibilities for grilled food is virtually endless. As I have begun to understand this relationship between grilling and home cooks around the world, a whole new world of inspiration has opened up to me, and I'm sure that so far I've only scratched the surface.

So here we have three perspectives on grilling: the easy, casual mindset that Americans bring to the cookout, the technical understanding of practiced chefs, and the international range of flavors and foods grilled by the cooks of the hot-weather world. When these three approaches come together, you get it all: interesting new flavors, easy cooking, and a lot of fun along the way.

GETTING TO GRILLING

The Grill Itself

Grilling hasn't changed all that much since the day some really smart cave-guy first introduced food to fire. All you really need is a fire, some food to cook, and something to lay the food on so it doesn't fall into the flames.

That means you need a grill. In this department your options are virtually endless, from flimsy tabletop braziers to slickly designed cast-iron beauties that will set you back almost as much as your first car did. Any of them will work, so which one you select is largely a matter of personal preference and how much room you have.

The first choice is whether to get an open grill or a covered one. I would suggest that you go for the covered option, because with the cover available, you can not only grill, but also do some lower-heat cooking, like smoke-roasting and even a relatively close approximation of barbecuing. Because of this versatility, covered grills have largely taken over the backyard grilling scene and are available just about anywhere.

Some people consider it a disadvantage that on most covered grills the distance between the grill grid and the fuel is fixed. This limits the cook's ability to regulate the heat by moving the grill grid up and down. Personally I don't find that to be too much of a drawback—you can easily regulate the heat by the size of the fire you build, and in my experience it's kind of a drag sliding the grill grid up or down anyway since it tends to stick—but it's a matter of personal preference, so you can decide for yourself.

Open grills come in many variations, the most common being the Japanese-inspired hibachi and the brazier, along with those permanent installations of brick, rock, or cement block built in backyards by truly serious grillers and in thousands of public campgrounds during the WPA work projects of the 1930s.

Whatever type of grill you prefer, the prime directive is the same: Get yourself the one with the largest possible grilling surface. That way, you will have more room to build a two-level fire (described on page 10), and more flexibility in moving food around from hotter to cooler spots as you grill. This makes it much easier to achieve the desired goal of cooking the food through without incinerating the exterior.

I would also encourage you to consider grilling in your fireplace if you have one. It's fun, it keeps the grilling going all year round, and dinner guests almost always find it entertaining. If you want, you can buy a Tuscan grill for fireplace grilling. This handy device consists of a frame that holds an adjustable grill. Or you can just put some bricks in the fireplace to act as supports and use the grid from your regular grill. You should also check out the chapter "Food from the

Ashes," which delves into the mysteries of wrapping food up and cooking it in the depths of the coals.

Other Tools of the Trade

Sure, if you're looking for a way to get rid of excess cash, you can find hundreds of gadgets and gizmos that are supposed to make grilling easier, but they are almost all completely unnecessary. I see no reason to add needless complications to life. You come home from work, you're ready to grill—do you really want to have to haul out a whole lot of equipment? No way. Instead, why not have one part of our life that's still uncomplicated, a throwback to simpler days.

But that said, there are a few tools that will make grilling easier and more fun. Since there are only a handful, you should try to have them around whenever you head out to the grill.

Heavy-duty, long-handled, spring-loaded tongs: Look in a professional cook's hands or back pocket, and you're going to see a pair of these. To me, they are the one indispensable grilling tool. Tongs act like an extra pair of hands, with the added advantage that they don't get burned. Use them to put food on the grill, move it around while it's cooking, pick it up to check for doneness, and take it off the grill, all without dropping anything or burning your arms. Make sure you get tongs that are heavy-duty so they will not bend when you lift big pieces of food, have long handles so you can work over a hot fire without burning your arms, and are spring-loaded so they are always ready for use, rather than having to be manually opened each time.

Stiff wire brush: One of the nice things about grilling is that you use no pots or pans, so you have very little cleanup when the meal is over. But you do need to keep your grill surface clean, and this is the tool for the job. I recommend you brush the grill grid right after you finish cooking, before any grease has congealed and while the hot coals will disintegrate any food residue that falls into them. You can get one of these brushes at any hardware store. I generally go through a couple of them every grilling season, so I suggest you buy two as long as you're at it.

Disposable foil pans: The uses for these pans will multiply as you get used to having them around. They are excellent, for example, for transporting raw ingredients from kitchen to grill and cooked ingredients from grill to table. Despite their name, they can be washed and reused many times over.

Kitchen towels: Those inexpensive white cotton kitchen towels you can buy in restaurant supply stores in batches of twenty or so are very handy for picking up hot dishes or skewers, and it is a lot quicker to grab a couple of towels than to fit your hand into a mitt. They are also very useful for wiping up spills of all sorts and generally keeping your grill area clean and tidy.

Metal pie pans: These come into play when you invoke the "sear and move" technique, described on page 18. They are a nonessential but very useful grilling aid; you can also use the disposable foil version.

Beverage of choice: This might be the most important grilling tool of all. If you want to know why, ask any brain surgeon or air traffic controller. It can get hot over that grill, the pressure is on to make sure you don't ruin everybody's dinner, and sometimes you have to take the edge off. Having your favorite beverage readily at hand will do the trick nicely.

Choosing the Fuel

Just as there are all kinds of grills, so there are many choices for your fuel. Unlike grills, though, there are definitely better and worse fuels.

For most Americans, grilling fuel means just one thing: charcoal briquettes. These little pillow-shaped carbon composites are perfectly acceptable as fuel; they provide a good, hot fire if you use enough of them, and they have the distinct advantage of being available at every supermarket, convenience store, and all-night gas station during the summer months.

But there is one major disadvantage to charcoal briquettes—they are not all charcoal. They are made by taking some powdered charcoal (in this case relatively low quality stuff made from sawdust and scrap lumber) and combining it with binders (so it can be easily formed into those little pillow shapes) and in some cases with chemical additives (so it will light more easily).

The worst thing about this is that until briquettes are completely caught, part of what you are burning is chemicals. This means you don't want to put any food over them until every briquette is totally covered with gray ash. In other words, if you add briquettes to boost or sustain your fire partway through cooking something, you have to wait until the briquettes are all completely caught before you can continue with your cooking.

The better alternative, if you can locate it, is lump hardwood charcoal. This fuel is very simply what its name says it is—irregularly shaped lumps of pure charcoal. It's made by the age-old process of burning hardwood in a closed container with very little oxygen. Because it is almost pure carbon, it lights more easily, is more responsive to changes in oxygen level so you can regulate it more easily, and burns cleaner and hotter than briquettes. Also, since lump charcoal contains no impurities, you can add more of it to the fire at any time and go right on cooking without waiting for it to fully ignite.

The other possible fuels for your grilling fire are all permutations on the true original, wood. Because it is challenging and seems primordial, using wood in any form is great fun. But since wood burns unpredictably and doesn't always yield a uniform bed of coals, a wood-only fire is probably best saved for those occasions when you feel like playing around with the fire more than usual.

But there is a combination wood-charcoal technique that I have started using recently and that I find close to ideal. I call it the "small-log technique" and, as you might suspect, it is very simple. First, build your charcoal fire as you normally would. Then, when the coals are completely lit, take a piece of cord wood (those short logs you burn in the fireplace) and push it into the coals. I like to put it along one edge of the coals, then use the tongs to shove it about one third of the way across the bottom of the grill, bunching up the coals as it goes.

To my mind, this approach is the perfect setup, for a number of reasons. First, even a small wood log will burn longer than charcoal, so if your fire begins to cool down before you have finished cooking, it's simple to just dump more charcoal on top of the burning log and keep the fire going. Second, logs produce more smoke than charcoal; the smoke always creates a nice aromatic atmosphere, and it imparts some degree of wood-smoke flavor on those occasions when you are cooking foods that stay on the grill for a long time. Third, when you shove the log into the fire, you tend to push most of the coals onto one side of the grill, which naturally produces a fire with one hot side and one cool side, a prerequisite for controlled grilling. And finally, while you get all these benefits from using a hunk of wood, you still have the predictable, steady heat of the charcoal, which is your primary fuel. In other words, you get the advantages of both kinds of fuel without their disadvantages.

Where Do I Keep It All? I just keep my grill out in the backyard and stash the charcoal under the deck, but if you don't have that amount of room to devote to grilling, there are many other options. If you need to keep the charcoal inside the house, for example, you can avoid mess by slipping a large plastic garbage bag over the paper bag the charcoal comes in, or by buying a garbage can that you devote to the purpose of storing your fuel. I also know folks who keep their bag of charcoal and their chimney starter in a wheelbarrow in the garage so that it's out of the way but can be brought to the grill quickly and easily. As with just about everything else having to do with grilling, the key is to find some system that makes it easy and fun for you to get that fire lit.

Laying the Fire

Whichever fuel you choose, the two cardinal principles of laying the fire are the same: Don't skimp on the fuel, and build a fire with two levels of heat.

Let's take the fuel issue first. Grilling is basically a high-heat cooking method, and most of that awesome grilled flavor you are after comes from the impact of the heat of the flames on the surface of the food. This is why you can't get real grilled flavor from stove-top grills: they simply don't get hot enough.

Even if you are using hardwood lump charcoal, which is slightly more expensive than charcoal briquettes, the amount you are going to spend on fuel is minimal compared to what you have spent on ingredients. So don't worry about the fuel—go ahead and build yourself a good hot fire.

The reason for the two-level principle is equally straightforward. As I said above, the relationship between exterior sear and interior doneness is at the heart of grilling. If you have a fire with hotter and cooler portions, you can move food around according to whether it needs more sear on the outside (the hot part) or more cooking on the inside without exterior sear (the cool part). The two-level fire is the basis for "sear and move" and "cooking on the edge," two primary grilling techniques described in the Advanced Techniques section on page 16.

With these principles in mind, you can construct your fire. Lay a bed that is about three inches deep on one side, tapers down to about one inch on the other side, and is larger in surface area than the total surface area of the food you are planning to grill. This way, you will end up with a very hot side and a cooler side. As an alternative, you can build the fire in one side of the grill, then shove some of the coals over to the other side after the fire is well lit.

Lighting the Fire

There are several options for igniting this well-laid fire. Despite its present bad reputation, lighter fluid is an acceptable choice. If you wait until the coals are all lit before you start cooking (which you should do in any case), all the fluid will be burned off long before you put anything over the fire, so it won't affect the taste of the food.

The two best options, though, are the electric coil starter and the chimney starter.

An electrical coil starter, which consists of a thick oval electrical coil set into a plastic handle, is available in most hardware stores. Electric coil starters are very reliable and quite consistent, which means you always know how long it will take to get your fuel properly ignited.

To use a coil fire starter, put it right on the fire grate, mound charcoal on top of it, and plug it into a grounded outlet. The coil will soon become red-hot, igniting the charcoal that's in contact with it. At this point, unplug the starter and remove it; the hot coals will ignite the others. Removing the starter from the fire at this point also prolongs its life. Set the starter aside on a fireproof surface, out of reach of dogs and children, until it is cool.

Even better than the coil starter, though, is the chimney starter. Also known as a flue starter, this is one of those great tools that has no moving parts, requires no fuel to make it work, and is totally reliable. It consists of a sheet-metal cylinder, open at both ends, with a ring of ventilation holes around the bottom, a grid located inside the flue several inches from the bottom, and a wooden handle.

To use a chimney starter, just fill the bottom section with crumpled newspaper, set the starter in the middle of the fire grate, fill the top with charcoal, and light the newspaper. The flames will sweep up through the chimney, igniting the charcoal. When the charcoal is red-hot, which should take about fifteen minutes, dump it out and put as much additional charcoal as you want on top of it. The lit coals will light the pieces of charcoal next to them, which will light the ones next to them, and before too long, all of your coals will be glowing hot. Nothing could be simpler, and it works every time.

There is one more benefit to chimney starters: You can make a perfectly acceptable substitute for the real thing by removing both ends from a large coffee can and punching a few ventilation holes along the bottom edge with a can opener.

Once your fire is lit, it will take about forty minutes to work up to the fiery-red stage and then die down until all the coals are covered with a fine gray ash, at which point you're ready to cook.

There's one more fact about fire lighting that may make your job easier. I often see people working and working to get all the charcoal completely lit before they put away their lighter fluid, coil starter, or whatever they happen to be using. This truly is not necessary. All you have to do is get one piece of charcoal even partially lit—just a corner that is white so you know it's really going—and you can stop working at it. So when you see that one or more coals are lit, your fire-starting chores are over.

The Two Big Tests: Temperature and Doneness

Over the years since *The Thrill of the Grill* was published in 1990, I've had literally thousands of conversations with people about grilling. Among other things, I've discovered that there are two aspects of grilling that give folks the most trouble: making sure their fire is the right temperature and figuring out when their dinner is properly cooked.

To make it easier, I've emphasized the fire temperature and the doneness test in most of the recipes in this book. But there are also some general guidelines that I find helpful.

How Hot Is Hot? It's important that you be able to judge the relative temperature of your fire correctly so you have the right type of fire for whatever it is you are going to cook. If you try to cook a steak over a low fire, for example, you won't get that strong surface char you want, and if you put a salmon fillet over a very hot fire, it's going to be incinerated on the outside before it's done on the inside.

First, make sure you don't start cooking until your coals are all uniformly gray. If you want a low-temperature fire, you're looking to catch it on the way down rather than on the way up. Since smoke is mostly unburned particles of fuel, the more completely the fuel is ignited, the cleaner flame you will have.

When the coals are covered with a fine gray ash, it's time to check the fire temperature. The testing method is exactly the same one that all home cooks used in the old days to check the temperature of their wood-fired ovens: You see how hot the fire makes your skin.

Hold your hand about five inches above the cooking surface. If you can hold it there for six seconds (a count of six one-thousand) you have a low fire; five seconds means a medium-low fire; three to four seconds is within the medium range; two seconds means a medium-hot fire; and only one second means you have a truly hot fire.

The Window of Doneness Along with knowing how to use salt, the ability to know when food is done is a cook's greatest skill. When you're cooking, your food spends a long time being underdone and a short time being done just right, then quickly moves on to being overdone, a condition from which there is no recovery. In other words, the window of perfect doneness is a small one, and you need to jump right through it.

This is particularly true with grilling. Since each live fire is unique, cooking times given in grilled recipes are really nothing more than estimates. So a primary technique of the craft is knowing when your dinner is ready to come off the fire.

After you have cooked a thousand chicken thighs or pork chops, you will probably be able to tell just by a poke of the finger when the one that's presently on the fire is ready. In the meantime, though, I suggest you use the method favored by professional chefs—"peek and cheat."

As the name implies, you simply pick up one of whatever you are cooking, nick it slightly with a knife so you can look inside, and check its state of doneness. That's all there is to it. No guesswork, no intricate techniques. It couldn't get much easier—or more accurate.

Despite this, many cooks shy away from this method. One reason is that somehow the idea has taken hold that it is not cool to handle food while it is being cooked. Not true. Check out any professional cook, and you will notice that he or she is constantly touching whatever is cooking. Another reason people avoid the "peek and cheat" method is the belief that cutting into a piece of food automatically lets all the juices run out. Again, not true. Some juices do escape, but it's not like putting a hole in a balloon; the very small amount of juice you may lose pales in comparison to the possibility of serving raw or burned food. This method truly does not harm the food—and if you feel that it mars a perfect appearance, keep the tested portion for yourself.

What you see when you nick and peek will vary according to the food being cooked. Contrary to its reputation, fish is easy in this regard. It is very malleable, so it's easy to get a look inside by bending or otherwise maneuvering it while leaving its appearance untouched. This is fortunate, because fish has a very small window of doneness.

Fish is also one food that many cooks have recently begun to undercook, in reaction to years of overcooking. Although there are some types of fish that are appropriate to serve almost raw, such as very high quality, ultrafresh tuna, in general, fish should be cooked through. What you are looking for is a consistent opacity; that is, the interior flesh should be almost completely opaque, with the very center just changing from translucent. This method will work with any type of fish. With thicker pieces, though, there will be a bit of carry-over cooking after you remove the fish from the heat, so it is best to leave a trace of translucence near the center to avoid overcooking.

With red meat such as steaks and chops, doneness is a matter of taste, with opinions running the gamut from dead-raw to gray throughout. This makes it easy: Simply look inside to see when the meat is done to your liking. Again, remember carry-over cooking; if you want your meat medium-rare, remove it when it still looks almost rare, and so on.

Chicken and other fowl are similar to fish in that you want the flesh to be opaque throughout. (Duck is the exception here, as many people like their duck breast rare.) When cooking chicken parts, simply cut into one and check for opacity.

Of course, if you want to do it the hard way, you can also teach yourself the "hand" method of checking for doneness. This time-honored method is most often used with red meat, and it is based on the fact that meat becomes firmer as it cooks. The technique entails poking whatever you are grilling and judging its degree of doneness by comparing it to the feel of a particular place on your hand. It is presumed to be rare when it has the same feeling as the connective tissue between the ball of your thumb and your index finger, progressing to very well done when it feels like the base of the ball of your thumb. This method can be fun to try, but it is definitely a lot less reliable than the old peek and cheat.

Occasionally when smoke-roasting red meat, you'll need to use a thermometer to test for doneness, because of the size of the cuts that you're cooking. An instant-read thermometer is the easiest to use, and you should remember to poke it into the center of whatever it is you have on the fire.

Whatever method you choose, being able to judge doneness is largely a matter of making cooking an interactive process rather than a means to an end. So go ahead and work with your food as you cook it—poke it, probe it, push it, peer into it. You will have a much better chance of ending up with food done the way you like it, and you'll have more fun cooking, too.

Fire: Friend or Foe?

Never forget that when you're grilling, you're working with live fire, which is at all times to be respected and never underestimated. As long as you take a few simple safety precautions, fire will remain your friend rather than your foe. Mostly these are just common sense. Always set up your grill on level ground in the largest possible open space, away from walls, wooden fences, overhanging eaves or tree branches, or anything else that might easily catch fire. Keep toddlers and pets well away from the grill, and don't let older children run or play too close to the grilling area. Never light your fire with gasoline, and never spray lighter fluid onto lit coals. It's always a good idea to have a fire extinguisher handy. If you don't have a fire extinguisher, try to have a garden hose nearby or, as a last resort, keep a bucket of sand near the grill. After each grilling session, close all the vents on your grill, and never leave it on a wooden deck.

Spices, Shakes, and Rubs

Spices are second only to grilling itself as a way to add deep, satisfying flavors to food. In fact, one of the things I like best about grilled food is that it has enough intrinsic flavor to stand up to the taste intensity of spices.

In order to get the most out of spices, buy them whole and toast and grind them yourself. You're probably familiar with the tremendous flavor difference between preground and freshly ground black pepper. Well, there's just as big a difference with any spice. And toasting the spices before you grind them brings out the volatile oils, further intensifying both flavor and aroma.

Besides, the process doesn't take long. Just put the spices in a sauté pan over medium heat and toast them, shaking frequently to avoid burning, until they release just the first tiny wisp of smoke, about two to three minutes. Let them cool down a bit, then grind them in a mortar with a pestle, or in a spice grinder or electric coffee grinder you keep for that purpose. In the absence of these tools, spices can be crushed by grinding them against a cutting board with the bottom of a small sauté pan.

Since this does take a little extra time, I recommend that you toast and grind more spice than you need for the particular recipe you're making. Even after being stored for a month or two, the spice will still be much fresher and more flavorful than anything you would buy preground in a supermarket. As with all spices, your home-ground stuff should be covered and stored in a relatively cool, dark place.

As you'll see by looking through the book, one of my favorite techniques is to mix a bunch of spices together, then rub the mixture onto the food before it goes on the grill. The spice blends themselves can be as simple as roasted cumin seeds combined with salt and pepper, or as complex as India's garam masala, which may contain a dozen or more spices. Either way, they are a healthful alternative to traditional sauces, adding deep flavor with no fat.

The technique involved in using spice rubs is so simple it's almost embarrassing. Just take small handfuls of the spice mix and rub it over the entire surface of the food you're going to cook, using a bit of pressure to make sure that a good layer adheres to the food (that's why they call it a "rub," after all). Don't bother with brushes; bare hands are the best way to apply these mixtures. This can be done several hours before you begin to cook or five minutes before; the effect will be about the same. As the food cooks, the spices form a deeply browned crust that is packed with complex, concentrated flavors. So you get intense culinary excitement with very little labor, a result I'm always looking for—maximum effect with minimum effort.

In the chapter "Grilling on Skewers," you'll also find several examples of "shakes," another spice-based flavoring technique I've become fond of recently. You simply combine various spices into a mixture that you shake onto the food after it's cooked, like an intensely flavorful version of salt and pepper. This works particularly well with skewered food, since it's easier than rubbing the individual pieces with a spice rub prior to grilling.

But, as always, you should also feel free to do as you please. You can use preground spices or even just skip the rubs or shakes if you want. The recipes will still have plenty of flavor, and sometimes you may just feel like going the easy route. No problem.

ADVANCED TECHNIQUES: MOST FREQUENTLY ASKED QUESTIONS

All right, this section is for those of you who are looking for your Ph.G. (Doctor of Grilling) or Ph.B. (Doctor of Barbecue). I like to keep things simple and give the basic information about live fire cooking, because it's really very straightforward. But, as with any pursuit, there are also more complex aspects to the craft. And, as you probably know, any time you really get into a subject, you come across things that seem contradictory on the face of it. So here we are going to delve into a slightly higher level of live fire knowledge.

In addition to shooting the breeze with my restaurant customers about grilling for the past twelve years, I've also taught grilling classes all over the country. The questions below are the ones that are most frequently asked in my classes. They all concern the proper use of the covered kettle grill and wood chips. I suspect that people have the most questions about these aspects of grilling because the covered grill is a relatively recent innovation. Since it is a slight departure from classic grilling as it has been handed down to us from primeval humanoids, we are still trying to figure out how best to use it. After twenty years of experimentation, I definitely have some opinions on the subject, so I'm passing my ideas on for your consideration.

1. When do you cover the grill and why?

The covered kettle grill was a major breakthrough for grillers. It allows backyard cooks to smoke-roast large items and even to approximate true barbecue. But, like technological advances in other areas of endeavor, the covered grill has been a mixed blessing. Its users are tempted to press it into service not just when it's appropriate, but whenever they can. Sometimes the result is a phenomenon every cook wants to avoid—food that doesn't taste as good as it could.

So here is my general rule about the grill cover: use it only when you want to cook something by smoke-roasting—for a relatively long time with the indirect heat of a fire off to one side of the grill; do *not* use it as a way to deal with flare-ups or uneven cooking when you are actually grilling.

In other words, I don't cover the grill unless I'm cooking something that is so big it can't really be grilled, which is cooking by direct heat, and instead needs to be cooked by the indirect or radiant heat provided by covered cooking. I find it helpful to use the analogy that a covered grill is like an oven and an open grill is like a sauté pan.

The reason I don't like using the cover for regular grilling is that it gives a distinct, unpleasant flavor to food that has been cooked only for a relatively short period of time. The taste is kind of hard to describe, but if you've done any covered grilling of quick-cooking foods such as chicken pieces or hamburgers, I'll bet you recognize it: a little ashy and a little metallic, with a kind of soggy smokiness (it actually reminds me of the inside of the cover).

So generally I put the cover over the flames only when cooking something like a whole chicken, beef brisket, or pork roast that needs to be on the grill for forty-five minutes or longer in order to cook through. Like most cooking times, this three-quarters-of-an-hour rule is somewhat arbitrary. But to my taste buds, that's about how long it takes for the smoke flavor to take over from the dreaded "covered" flavor.

In addition, I never cover anything that cooks directly over the flames. The reason for this has to do with the fat that drips into the fire. When this happens, a chemical called benzopyrene is formed. Just as smoke flavors the food more during enclosed grilling, so it seems logical that benzopyrene may also affect the food more when the cover is on, and while smoke-flavored food is a definite plus to those who like to grill, food flavored with vaporized fat is not nearly so appealing.

Since my advice about the cover flies somewhat in the face of established grilling wisdom, it may make you more comfortable to know that it follows the general precepts laid down by our old buddy Escoffier, who was of the opinion that it was always better to roast over an open flame than in an oven. His reasoning was that, despite any precautions you might take to prevent it, steam always accumulates around anything that's cooking in a closed oven, so that you don't get the same intense flavor produced by cooking in an open, dry atmosphere. I feel the same way about using the cover on the grill—it's an excellent way to add a nice smoky flavor to food, but it is a different technique from straight grilling. When you're cooking relatively small, tender items for short periods of time, the cover is a crutch, not an aid.

2. So how and why do you use the grill cover?

Again, I cover large items that basically need to be roasted, like whole chickens or a roast of beef or pork. And I always use an indirect fire—a fire that is off to one side of the grill—so that the food is never cooking by the direct heat of the fire.

3. But how do you cook fairly large items without using the grill cover?

Thick-cut pork chops, bone-in chicken breasts, thick fish steaks, whole fish— these are the kind of "in-between" items, too large to be cooked directly over the heat of the fire, but too small to qualify for the forty-five minutes on the covered grill that is necessary for the flavor of smoke to overcome the "covered" taste. So these guys fall into the "sear and move" category.

For example, let's say you have a big fat pork chop on the grill that you've nicely seared to a perfect degree of doneness on the outside, but a peek inside shows that the center is totally raw. What do you do? Well, there are a couple of options here.

The #1 option is to move it over to the cool side of the grill (as I explained above, you should always have two sides to your grilling fire, one of which is hot and one of which has only a few coals or no coals) and cover it with a metal pie pan. That way, you stop the cooking on the outside of the food but allow the oven-like radiant heat to continue cooking the inside of the food. What you are essentially doing is forming a mini-oven effect. This method is very effective and is the most common "cheating" technique used by professional cooks. This "sear and cover with a pan" method works really well with bone-in chicken parts, as well as with larger fish like bluefish or thick salmon steaks.

The second option I would consider is taking the food inside and throwing it in the oven, a surefire method. At this point you already have the grilled flavor in the food, and you don't want to risk ruining that by burning the outside. This works particularly well with food like chicken legs or bone-in breasts.

There is also a third method, which I call "cooking on the edge." I use this method with larger items such as rack of lamb or thick fish steaks. In this method you don't go for the big sear up front. (I know I'm kind of going back on past instructions here, but you're on a higher level of understanding at this point, and hopefully can deal with the contradiction.) Instead, you cook the food from beginning to end right on the borderline between the hot and not-so-hot fire, shifting back and forth over this line depending on whether the food is getting too brown or not brown enough. This takes a lot of patience and attention and is a good way to kill forty minutes or so. So grab a couple of cool ones and just kind of nurse whatever you're cooking back and forth over the fire line according to its state of brownedness. The results will justify the effort.

4. How hot is the fire when you cover the grill?

Again, when you cover the grill you're essentially turning it into an oven, and just as with an oven, you can cook at high (350° to 500°F), medium (240° to 350°F), or low (160° to 240°F) temperatures. I generally like to use the higher temperatures for smoke-roasting, because you want to cook the food as quickly as you can while still cooking it evenly all the way through. When you get to barbecuing—which can also be called smoke-cooking—you want a lower fire, with a temperature between 180° and 240°F. That's because the object is to expose the meat to low temperatures for a very long time in order to make it tender, as if you were braising it. With roasting, you cook to a certain temperature that indicates doneness; with barbecuing, you go past the point of doneness to reach true tenderness.

I use the middle temperatures of about 240° to 350°F if I'm really trying to lay some smoke on something but am still roasting instead of barbecuing. In other words, these middle temperatures will put more flavor in the food by leaving it in a smoky environment for a longer time, but at temperatures still hot enough to cook it relatively quickly. Basically I go for either hot smoke-roasting (350° to 500°F) or barbecuing (160° to 240°F).

5. What's the difference between hot smoking, cold smoking, and barbecuing?

While I don't pretend to be super-knowledgeable about smoking, this is my understanding of the different techniques.

Cold Smoking (60° to 90°F): This style of smoking requires a good working understanding of bacterial growth and food technology, as you're working in the very temperature range at which bacteria multiply most quickly. I see this as a technique used primarily for preservation. That is, it's used to create products that can last a long time without refrigeration, such as smoked salmon, sausage, or beef jerky. The food is usually brined in advance to aid in killing bacteria. This method is also used for large items like turkeys and hams, but because of the low temperature, it takes a long time to fully smoke the food.

Hot Smoking (90° to 160°F): This is the smoking method most often used by the home cook. It is used not so much to preserve as to flavor and cook the food with smoke. The danger zone for food is between 45° and 140°F, meaning that when you're hot smoking, you're limited to a maximum of four hours before you either have to cool the food way down (below 40°F) or make sure it's above 140°F. You can still brine for flavor when using this method, but it's not as essential for bacteria inhibition.

Barbecuing (160° to 240°F): Above 160°F, you are smoke-cooking, or barbecuing, a technique that falls between smoking for flavor and just plain cooking with fire. The object of barbecuing is to tenderize the meat as well as flavor it through long, slow, indirect cooking with wood smoke.

6. Why don't you use wood chips when grilling?

I think the characteristic flavor of grilled food results much more from the high heat of the direct flames than from the particular fuel that is used. Smoke is basically unburnt particles of fuel, and I can't see a particular kind of chip or branch making a demonstrative impact on a grilled item that cooks for five minutes per side. That's not to say that I think wood has no impact on grilled food; it's just that to me, chips are silly.

7. Are there any circumstances in which you would use wood chips?

To me, the only time to use wood chips is in a long-term cold-smoking situation, where preservation is key. I will and have argued this point late into the barbecue night on more than one occasion. I far prefer the smoke from a burning/smoldering log to the smoke from chips and, while I cannot articulate exactly why that is, I just trust my feelings on this one. Would I ever use chips? Well, if I didn't have any other wood—fallen branches, logs, chunks, or anything—I might sneak a handful into a covered smoke-roast situation, just so there would be some variety of wood smoke. But that's about it.

FIVE TIPS FOR GRILLING SUCCESS

1. Use plenty of freshly cracked pepper and kosher salt.

There is no comparison between the aromatic power of freshly cracked black pepper and of the preground type you buy in the store. So always use freshly cracked. I also recommend that you always use kosher salt. It seems more flavorful to me than regular table salt, and its larger crystals stick to food better. They are also more fun to sprinkle onto food with your fingers; in addition to pure tactile enjoyment, this gives you a better sense of just how much you are sprinkling, providing at the very least a satisfying illusion of more control over your salting technique. Because of its larger crystals, there is less salt in a tablespoon of kosher salt than in a tablespoon of finely ground table salt, so if you use table salt in the recipes in this book, you should cut down on the amount of salt by 25 or 30 percent.

To make this all easier, I suggest that once a week or so you grind up a big batch of black pepper, mix it with an equal quantity of kosher salt (or whatever proportion you prefer), and keep a dish of the mixture handy at all times when cooking.

2. Hot, hot, hot.

Don't be afraid to work with a good, hot fire, and if you are ever tempted to take something off the grill before it is well seared, remember M. Maillard and just repeat to yourself, "Brown food tastes better." When you get that Maillard browning reaction going, you create all kinds of new, deep, rich flavors in your food—and that's the grilling advantage.

3. Always build a two-level fire.

In other words, a fire with a hotter part and a colder part. With a little bit of practice, you'll know exactly when to move the food from one side to the other so it ends up with a good, strong surface sear and is properly done on the inside.

4. Check frequently for doneness.

It doesn't take much time, and it makes a huge difference if you catch the food in the window of perfect doneness, right between too raw and overcooked. Start checking several minutes before you think the food is going to be done so that you don't overshoot. Remember, it's a small window—jump through it.

5. Be organized.

Before I put that first appetizer on the fire, I like to make sure my grill *mise en place* is all set. It's a lot easier to maintain the proper relaxed attitude if you aren't always having to run back into the house for something you forgot. So I set up a table next to the grill with my tongs, a good supply of my beverage of choice, plenty of kosher salt and freshly ground pepper, some foil trays and kitchen towels, a cutting board or two, and a good, sharp knife. Then all I have to concern myself with is playing with the fire and having a good time with my friends. And that, after all, is what it's all about.

To me, starting a meal with soup seems at once celebratory and calming, which is a pretty unusual combination. Maybe that's because on the one hand formal meals used to invariably begin with what was referred to as "the soup course," and on the other hand when we were sick as children we were very often fed soup as a comforting cure.

STARTERS

soups

Whatever the reasons, I enjoy beginning any meal with soup. Rather than setting it out formally at the dining table, though, I like to put out the big pot and let people dip it out themselves, preferably while I am grilling the main course.

Several of the soups here are variations on or updates of the classic Spanish gazpacho, a soup that is particularly well suited to grilling and the vegetable bounty of summertime. Others include one or more grilled ingredients, which add a smoky flavor undertone that permeates the whole dish. Yet others take their taste cues from the flavor footprints of Southeast Asia, Portugal, and even New England. But any one of them will make an excellent start to a grilled meal.

Grilled Corn Chowder
with Bacon and Thyme

August Tomato and
Cucumber Soup

Grilled and Chilled
Mediterranean-Style
Gazpacho

Avocado Gazpacho with
Corn Bread Croutons

Lisa White's White
Gazpacho

Lime Soup with
Grilled Cumin Chicken

Smoky Chorizo Soup

Collard Soup with
Sweet Potatoes and
Coconut Milk

Grilled Corn Chowder with Bacon and Thyme

SERVES 6

I like corn soups because the flavor of corn really infuses well into broth. Cooking the cobs in the stock adds even more flavor, and in this version the grilled corn adds a hint of smoke. Add more bacon and some white potatoes, and you have your classic chowder ingredients in a new suit. Thyme and corn is a well-established combination, but if you can't get hold of fresh thyme, try substituting fresh basil.

> **6 ears corn, husked, desilked, blanched in boiling water for 2 minutes,**
>   **plunged into ice and water, and drained**
> **8 cups chicken stock**
> **6 slices bacon**
> **2 yellow onions, peeled and diced small**
> **1 large sweet potato, peeled and diced small**
> **¹/₄ cup roughly chopped fresh thyme**
> **Salt and freshly cracked black pepper to taste**

1. Place the corn on the grill over **a medium-hot fire** and cook for 3 to 5 minutes, rolling it around a few times, until golden brown. Remove from the grill and, as soon as the ears are cool enough to handle, cut off the kernels and set them aside; don't throw away the cobs.

2. In a small stockpot over medium heat, combine the chicken stock and the corncobs. Bring to a boil, reduce the heat to low, and simmer for 1 hour.

3. While the stock is simmering, cook the bacon in a small sauté pan over medium heat until brown and crispy, 6 to 8 minutes. Remove the bacon and set it aside on paper towels to drain, then drain off all but about 3 tablespoons of the bacon fat from the pan. Add the onions and cook until soft, 5 to 7 minutes. Add the reserved corn kernels and cook for another 3 minutes, then remove from the heat.

4. Strain the chicken stock, discard the corncobs, and return the stock to the pot. Add the sweet potatoes and the onion-corn mixture, and cook over medium heat, stirring every once in a while, for 45 minutes.

5. Crumble the bacon into the soup, stir in the thyme, and season to taste with salt and pepper. Serve hot. This soup will keep, covered and refrigerated, for 5 days.

For a substantial dinner, try this with Grilled Flank Steak "in the Style of Pastrami" (page 134) and Grilled Shrimp and Black Bean Salad with Papaya-Chile Dressing (page 57).

August Tomato and Cucumber Soup

When tomatoes are plentiful, tasty, and plump, I really enjoy making cold summer soups. This is a variation of the original gazpacho, which was basically a bread and garlic soup. A simple affair, it's easy and healthful, and it tastes great.

> 2 cups 1-inch cubes stale bread (crusts removed)
> 3 cloves garlic, peeled and minced
> 1 quart tomato juice
> 1 cup water
> $^1/_2$ cup red wine vinegar
> $^1/_3$ cup extra virgin olive oil
> $^1/_4$ cup fresh lemon juice (about 1 lemon)
> 2 large tomatoes, cored and diced medium
> 2 cucumbers, peeled, seeded, and diced medium
> $^1/_2$ cup flat-leaf parsley leaves, washed and dried
> Salt and freshly cracked black pepper to taste

1. In a large bowl, combine the bread cubes, garlic, tomato juice, water, vinegar, oil, and lemon juice and allow to stand for 30 minutes so the bread softens and the flavors mingle a bit.

2. In a food processor or blender, puree the bread mixture a few cups at a time until smooth. Place the pureed mixture in a large bowl. Add the tomatoes, cucumbers, and parsley, mix well, and season to taste with salt and pepper. Refrigerate the soup until it is well chilled, and you're ready to go.

For a cold dinner on a hot day, try this with Fava Bean Salad with
Lemon and Shaved Pecorino Romano Cheese (page 318),
Sesame Green Beans with Crispy Fried Shallots (page 281),
and Bridget's Couscous Salad for a Crowd (page 320).

STARTERS

Grilled and Chilled Mediterranean-Style Gazpacho

SERVES 6

Grilled vegetables in tomato juice is a summertime favorite of mine. It makes a very versatile soup and is an excellent way to use last night's leftover grilled vegetables. Make sure the eggplant is thoroughly cooked—it should look moist all the way through, rather than dry, when it is done—and cut the fennel thin so it gets a high proportion of char to flesh. You can use either tomato or Clamato juice for the liquid here; I prefer Clamato because it is thinner.

> 1 large eggplant, cut into rounds about 1 inch thick
>
> 3 fennel bulbs, trimmed, cored, and thinly sliced
>
> 2 red bell peppers, halved and seeded
>
> 1 red onion, peeled and cut into rings about 1 inch thick
>
> $^1/_4$ cup olive oil
>
> Salt and freshly cracked black pepper to taste
>
> 1 quart tomato or Clamato juice
>
> 2 cups chicken stock
>
> 1 tablespoon minced garlic
>
> $^1/_4$ cup fresh lemon juice (about 1 lemon)
>
> $^1/_2$ cup red wine vinegar
>
> 2 tablespoons ground cumin
>
> 2 tablespoons ground coriander
>
> $^1/_4$ cup roughly chopped fresh parsley
>
> $^1/_4$ cup roughly chopped fresh basil
>
> About $^1/_2$ cup freshly grated Parmesan (optional)

1. In a medium bowl, combine the eggplant, fennel, bell peppers, and onion with the olive oil and salt and pepper to taste and toss to coat the vegetables with the oil. Place the vegetables on the grill over **a medium-hot fire.** Grill the fennel and onion until tender and slightly charred, 3 to 4 minutes per side. Grill the eggplant and bell peppers until browned, 4 to 5 minutes per side. As the vegetables are done, remove them from the grill and cut them into small chunks.

2. In a large bowl, combine the grilled vegetables with all the remaining ingredients except the cheese and mix well. Cover and refrigerate until well chilled. Serve sprinkled with Parmesan cheese if you want.

I would serve this with Grilled Delmonico Steak Adobo with Charred Spring Onions and Sweet Corn Relish (page 131) and Chickpea Salad with Cumin and Mint (page 316).

Avocado Gazpacho
with Corn Bread Croutons

This Latin version of the classic Spanish soup has the avocados, cilantro, lime juice, and cumin that are characteristic flavorings of Latin cuisine. We even throw in some mango juice to add to the tropical slant. Easy to prepare, this soup is both refreshing and healthful, a good alternative to the usual salad. You can use either tomato or Clamato juice for the base liquid; I prefer Clamato because it is a lot thinner and I think it gives the soup a better texture.

> 1 quart tomato or Clamato juice
>
> 2 cups mango juice (or substitute pineapple juice)
>
> 1 small red onion, peeled and diced small
>
> 2 small tomatoes, cored and diced small
>
> $^1/_2$ red bell pepper, seeded and diced small
>
> $^1/_2$ green bell pepper, seeded and diced small
>
> 2 avocados, peeled, pitted, and diced small
>
> $^1/_4$ cup chopped fresh cilantro (or substitute parsley)
>
> $^1/_4$ cup fresh lime juice (about 2 limes)
>
> 2 tablespoons ground cumin
>
> Salt and freshly cracked black pepper to taste
>
> 2 slices corn bread (see page 264 for corn bread recipe)

1. Place all of the ingredients except the corn bread in a large bowl and mix well; correct the seasoning. Cover and refrigerate until ready to serve.

2. Cut the corn bread into half-inch cubes, place them on a small baking sheet, and toast in a preheated 350°F oven, tossing once or twice, until nicely browned, 10 to 12 minutes.

3. Serve the soup cold, garnished with the croutons.

I might serve this as a lunch or light supper with Grilled Open-Faced Eggplant Sandwiches with Black Olive Relish and Fresh Mozzarella (page 39).

28

a very fine fennel

TO MY TASTE BUDS, one of nature's really fine flavors is licorice. I don't mean the candy (although that's excellent, too, particularly in the form of the oddly named Good & Plenty), but the kind that comes from, for example, fennel. This is one of those generous plants (the other one that springs to mind is coriander) from which we get several different items useful in cooking. Wild or common fennel provides both leaves and seeds for use as flavorings, depending on whether you are in the mood to use an herb or a spice for your licorice needs.

THE FENNEL THAT WE use as a vegetable, though, is actually a different variety. Known as Florence fennel, it is less than half the height of its seed-yielding cousins, but it makes up for this by the size of the snowy white bulb of overlapping stalks that sits at the base of the plant. Long popular as a vegetable in Italy, this sweet, crunchy, mildly licorice-flavored bulb is now gaining popularity in the United States. When it is cooked, its anise flavor becomes more subtle and mellow, so if you are introducing it to friends who thinks they don't like licorice, try cooking it for them first, then serving it to them raw the next time.

Lisa White's White Gazpacho

This soup is closer to what the original gazpacho looked like than the tomato juice concoction that is so popular today. In Spain, the original home of gazpacho, this famous cold soup started out as a bread and garlic porridge. Later on, some tomatoes were added, and the evolution began. According to Colman Andrews, author of *Catalan Cuisine* (Atheneum, 1988), Spaniards in the southern province of Málaga still make a white gazpacho similar to this version. Although you might think this is an odd combination of ingredients, its time-tested worth will show through as soon as you taste it. This is a super soup for a hot summer evening, best eaten the day it is made.

$^1/_2$ loaf firm white bread, crusts removed and cut into $^1/_2$-inch cubes
    (about 3 cups bread cubes)
$^1/_4$ cup minced garlic
1 cup extra virgin olive oil
$^1/_2$ cup sherry vinegar
3 cups peeled, seeded, and chopped cucumbers
    (about 3 medium cucumbers)
Salt and freshly cracked black pepper to taste
1 $^1/_2$ cups seedless green grapes, halved
$^1/_4$ cup almonds, toasted in a 350°F oven until browned,
    7 to 10 minutes, then roughly chopped, for garnish
$^1/_4$ cup roughly chopped fresh parsley, for garnish

1. Soak the bread cubes in cold water to cover for 30 minutes.

2. Squeeze the water out of the bread, then place it in a food processor or blender along with the garlic, olive oil, and vinegar and puree until smooth. Add 2 cups of the cucumbers and pulse until well combined but still a little bit chunky. (You may need to do this in two batches.)

3. Pour the mixture into a medium bowl and season to taste with salt and pepper. If the soup seems too thick, add a bit of cold water to thin it out. Stir in the grapes and the remaining 1 cup cucumbers, cover, and refrigerate until well chilled.

4. Pour the chilled soup into individual serving bowls, garnish with the toasted almonds and parsley, and serve.

I would serve this alongside Chuletas: Thin Grilled Pork Chops with Simple Tomato Relish (page 147) and Green Apple and Celery Root Salad with Bacon-Buttermilk Dressing (page 306).

Lime Soup with Grilled Cumin Chicken

SERVES 6

That whole thing about hot liquids cooling you off in the summertime heat always struck me as strange. But you need look no farther than the brothy soups of steamy Southeast Asia or the tropical Latin world to confirm this. To check it out, try this soup for lunch on a hot and humid day. We flavor the stock aggressively, then add chunks of cumin-coated grilled chicken and garnish with fresh oregano.

2 tablespoons vegetable oil

1 large red onion, peeled and diced medium

1 tablespoon minced garlic

1 tablespoon minced fresh chile pepper of your choice

1 cinnamon stick (or substitute 1 teaspoon ground cinnamon)

6 cups chicken stock

1 large tomato, cored and diced medium

1/4 cup fresh lime juice (about 2 limes)

1 whole boneless, skinless chicken breast, about 10 to 12 ounces

2 tablespoons ground cumin

1 tablespoon vegetable oil

Salt and freshly cracked black pepper to taste

1/4 cup fresh oregano leaves, for garnish (optional)

4 large tortilla chips, for garnish (optional)

1. In a medium stockpot over medium heat, heat the oil until hot but not smoking. Add the onion and sauté, stirring occasionally, until transparent, 5 to 7 minutes. Add the garlic, chile, and cinnamon and sauté, stirring, for 1 minute.

2. Add the stock, tomato, and lime juice and bring just to a boil. Reduce the heat to low and simmer gently for about 15 minutes.

3. While the stock is simmering, place the chicken in a small bowl along with the cumin, oil, and salt and pepper to taste and toss well to coat. Place the chicken on the grill over **a medium-hot fire** and cook for 7 to 9 minutes on each side. *To check for doneness:* Cut inside and peek to be sure that the flesh is completely opaque, with no pink. Remove the chicken from the grill and, as soon as it is cool enough to handle, cut into bite-sized pieces.

4. Add the chicken to the soup, remove the cinnamon stick if you used it, and let the soup simmer for 5 minutes. Season to taste with salt and pepper, garnish with the oregano leaves and tortilla chips if you want, and serve hot.

As a dinner plan, this goes well with Grilled Jerk Shark with Pineapple Salsa (page 230), with a bowl of Lime-Ginger Chutney (page 326) on the side.

cinnamon impostor

IF YOU ARE A spice purist, you might want to buy cinnamon in stick rather than preground form. If you buy preground, you are very likely buying cassia. This spice, which can be sold under the name cinnamon in the United States, is actually the dried bark of a different Asian evergreen tree, similar to cinnamon but with a somewhat coarser flavor. Its brittle bark does not divide easily into quills like cinnamon bark, but instead breaks into short, flat pieces that are quite difficult to grind. As a result, it is available here only in powdered form, while true cinnamon can be bought either powdered or as quills.

Smoky Chorizo Soup

SERVES 4 TO 6

The grilled sausage adds an undertone of smokiness to this version of the traditional Portuguese kale and potato soup. I also use sweet potatoes instead of the usual white potatoes, since they have more flavor. With some grilled bread and a salad, this makes an easy hearty lunch or light dinner. I like it because it shows that there is often more than one way to cook a particular ingredient and have it come out well. I usually quick-sear kale in a little oil over very high heat, but here it is long-cooked in liquid, and it ends up tasting outstanding.

> $^1/_2$ **pound chorizo sausage, halved lengthwise (or substitute linguiça or kielbasa)**
> **3 tablespoons olive oil**
> **1 red onion, peeled and diced small**
> **2 tablespoons minced garlic**
> **3 cups chicken stock**
> $^1/_2$ **cup red wine vinegar**
> **1 teaspoon red pepper flakes**
> **1 pound kale (1 medium bunch, trimmed), washed and chopped into bite-sized pieces (or substitute collard greens)**
> **2 medium sweet potatoes, peeled and diced medium**
> **Salt and freshly cracked black pepper to taste**

1. Place the sausages on the grill, cut side down, over **a medium fire** and grill for 3 to 5 minutes to brown and render the fat. Be ready with your tongs to move the sausage around if flare-ups occur. Remove from the grill and set aside.

2. In a small stockpot over medium heat, heat the olive oil until hot but not smoking. Add the onions and sauté, stirring occasionally, until transparent, 5 to

7 minutes. Add the garlic and sauté, stirring occasionally, for 1 minute. Add the stock, vinegar, and pepper flakes and bring to a simmer.

3. Add the kale and simmer gently for 40 minutes, giving it a stir every once in a while. Add the sweet potatoes and simmer until they are easily pierced with a fork but still offer some resistance, about 15 minutes. Cut the reserved sausage into bite-sized pieces, add to the soup, and cook for 5 minutes. Season to taste with salt and pepper and serve.

For a substantial dinner, serve this in front of Grilled Double-Thick Pork Chops with Grilled Peaches and Molasses-Rum Barbecue Sauce (page 148) and Romaine and Bulgur Salad (page 319).

sausages: the raw and the cooked

SAUSAGES COME IN HUNDREDS of varieties, but they can all be divided into two camps: those that are precooked and those that are not. In American supermarkets, the most common type of raw sausages are the so-called "Italian sausages," which are relatively small, uncooked pork sausages typically flavored with fennel and, in the hot variety, with red pepper flakes. Among the more readily available precooked sausages, chorizo, linguiça, and kielbasa are perhaps the most flavorful. Chorizo, which is of Spanish descent, comes in many variations but always contains smoked pork and paprika. Be careful, though— the Mexican version of chorizo, which has more chile and a good splash of vinegar, is usually uncooked. Linguiça is a Portuguese sausage very similar to chorizo, while kielbasa is a Polish sausage of smoked pork (and sometimes beef), usually distinguished by its high garlic content. All of these precooked sausages are technically safe to eat without further cooking, but all taste much better when they're seared to add a nice, crusty exterior and to heat the meat through; if you toss them on the grill, they also get the added benefit of smokiness. And by the way, if you can get your hands on andouille sausage, give it a try. This heavily smoked and spiced sausage, a favorite of New Orleans cooks, is made of chitterlings and tripe and has some real flavor on it.

Collard Soup with Sweet Potatoes and Coconut Milk

SERVES 6

This is my version of a classic West Indies soup that is called by many names, most often "callalou" after the Caribbean green of the same name. A simple combination of greens and sweet potatoes, it gains a distinctive tropical flavor from coconut milk. This soup is outstanding when eaten with corn bread and a couple dashes of your favorite hot sauce.

> 2 tablespoons olive oil
> 1 large yellow onion, peeled and diced medium
> 2 tablespoons minced garlic
> 5 cups chicken stock
> 2 cups coconut milk (canned or homemade, page 368)
> 3/4 cup white vinegar
> 2 medium sweet potatoes, peeled and diced medium
> 3 cups collard greens (or substitute kale, chard, or mustard greens)
>   washed, dried, and torn into large pieces
> Salt and freshly cracked black pepper to taste

1. In a medium stockpot over medium heat, heat the oil until hot but not smoking. Add the onion and sauté, stirring frequently, until transparent, 5 to 7 minutes. Add the garlic and sauté, stirring, for 1 minute more.

2. Add the chicken stock, coconut milk, and vinegar, turn the heat to high, and bring the mixture to a boil. Reduce the heat to low and let simmer for 20 minutes.

3. Add the sweet potatoes and collard greens and simmer for another 10 minutes, or until the sweet potatoes are easily pierced with a fork but still offer some resistance. Season with salt and pepper to taste and serve hot. This soup will keep, covered and refrigerated, for up to 5 days.

For a Southern-influenced dinner, serve this in front of Grilled Halibut with Fried Green Apples, Bacon, and Horseradish Sour Cream (page 184) and Cornmeal Mush with Okra and Tomatoes (page 305).

There's something about small courses—call them appetizers, starters, or what have you—that arouses an extra burst of creativity. I'm not sure why this is. Maybe it's because cooks don't feel the same subliminal pressure to fulfill nutritional requirements that they do when making entrées, or maybe it's because there are fewer traditional dishes in this category to clog the mind and inspire slavish imitation. But for whatever reason, it is often easier to let your creative juices flow when you're dealing with small plates.

STARTERS

appetizers and other small dishes

The inspirations for the recipes in this chapter come from just about everywhere, but you can bet that they're more likely to come from my own personal culinary quirks or from flavorful, casual street food than from restaurant dishes, a lineage that increases their playful and adventuresome qualities. My habit of using bread to soak up the remaining dressing in a salad bowl, for example, is incarnated in Grilled Apple and Bread Salad with Arugula, Blue Cheese, and Grapes, while Tortilla Sandwiches of Grilled Shrimp and Corn are descendants of classic Mexican quesadillas, and Grilled Portobellos with Prosciutto and Figs on Seared Greens combine tastes and techniques of the Tuscan countryside. Even when we go a little upscale, as in Grilled Goose Liver with Grapes, Mango, and Port, for example, the antecedent is still a casual one, in this case the grilled foie gras snack sold on the street in Israel.

Informality is also the hallmark of these small dishes, and several are designed to encourage eater participation. Salt-Crusted Grilled Shrimp in Their Shells, for example, require your guests to peel the shrimp themselves, getting salt and lemon juice on their fingers to lick off as they devour the succulent little crustaceans, while "Roll Your Own" Taco Bar sets out a lavish assortment of meats and fresh add-ons for guests to choose from as they create their own "signature" tacos.

You can use the dishes in this chapter any way you like. They are excellent as traditional starters before more substantial entrées, or you can set out several of them for predinner snacking, in the manner of the mezze of the Middle East or the antipasto of Italy. Or you can just combine two or three and make a meal out of them, an approach that has a couple of distinct advantages: You can try more dishes at a single sitting, and you can eat as little or as much as you want without seeming like either a pig or a too-dainty picker.

SO FIRE UP THE GRILL AND LET'S
GET STARTED.

STARTERS

36

Grilled Goat Cheese
Tortilla Sandwiches
with Mango-Lime Salsa

Grilled Open-Faced
Eggplant Sandwiches
with Black Olive Relish
and Fresh Mozzarella

Tortilla Sandwiches of
Grilled Shrimp and Corn
with Goat Cheese and
Pickled Red Onions

"Roll Your Own" Taco
Bar with Lots of
Garnishes

Middle Eastern–Style
Dip

Deviled Egg–Stuffed
Avocados on Lime Slaw

Grilled Black Pepper
Flatbread

Grilled Apple and Bread
Salad with Arugula,
Blue Cheese, and Grapes

Arugula with Pancetta,
Grilled Asparagus, and
White Beans

Grilled Artichoke and
White Bean Salad

Grilled Bread Salad with
Grilled Figs

Grilled Pita Bread Salad
with Cucumbers and
Feta Cheese

Grilled Shrimp and
Cucumber Salad

Grilled Shrimp and
Black Bean Salad with
Papaya-Chile Dressing

Grilled Scallop–Stuffed
Avocados with Papaya
Vinaigrette

Summer Striped Bass
Salad

Grilled Regular
Mushrooms with Sherry

Grilled Chicken and
Mango Salad

Grilled Portobellos with
Prosciutto and Figs on
Seared Greens

Grilled Portobellos with
Creamy Risotto and
Tomato-Bacon Relish

Salt-Crusted Grilled
Shrimp in Their Shells

Fancy Ash-Roasted
Potatoes

Barbecued Oysters in
Their Shells

Grilled Mussels Johnson

Red Snapper Cocktail

Korean-Style Grilled
Chicken Wings

Grilled Chicken Livers
with Green Grape Sauce

Grilled Buffalo Chicken
Hearts

Grilled Goose Liver with
Grapes, Mango, and Port

Raw Beef with Parsley,
Capers, and Hard Cheese

Grilled Lamb and Red
Onion in Grape Leaves

Grilled Sweetbreads
with Herb-Garlic
Crumbs

Grilled Goat Cheese Tortilla Sandwiches with Mango-Lime Salsa

Basically what you've got here is a real grilled cheese sandwich. Goat cheese melts well, and the smoky, crispy tortilla stuffed with the flavorful cheese and topped with a little mango salsa is a most tasty combination. These are easy to make, a good summer appetizer. You want to make sure the cheese melts before the tortillas burn, so the lower the fire, the better. If your fire is too hot, put the stuffed tortillas around the edges to cook.

> $1^1/_2$ cups crumbled goat cheese
> 1 tablespoon minced garlic
> $^1/_4$ cup roughly chopped fresh cilantro or parsley
> 2 tablespoons minced canned chipotles
> 1 tablespoon ground cumin
> Salt and freshly cracked black pepper to taste
> 8 6-inch flour tortillas
> Mango-Lime Salsa (recipe follows)

1. In a small bowl, combine the goat cheese, garlic, cilantro, chipotles, cumin, and salt and pepper to taste and mix well.

2. Spread the goat cheese mixture onto 4 of the tortillas and top them with the remaining tortillas. Place the stuffed tortillas on the grill over **a medium-low fire** and cook until the cheese is melted and the tortillas are golden brown, 3 to 5 minutes per side. Cut into eighths and serve with a generous helping of the Mango-Lime Salsa.

MANGO-LIME SALSA

> 2 mangoes, peeled, pitted, and cut into bite-sized chunks
> 1 red onion, peeled and diced small
> $^1/_2$ red bell pepper, seeded and diced small
> $^1/_3$ cup fresh lime juice (about 2 large limes)
> 1 jalapeño or other fresh chile pepper of your choice, minced
> 1 tablespoon ground cumin
> 3 tablespoons roughly chopped fresh cilantro or parsley
> Salt and freshly cracked black pepper to taste

In a medium bowl, combine all the ingredients and mix well. The salsa will keep, covered and refrigerated, for 2 days.

Try this in front of Basil-Garlic Chicken Breasts with Grilled Balsamic Peaches (page 200) and serve Tomato Risotto with Toasted Pine Nuts (page 302) alongside.

Grilled Open-Faced Eggplant Sandwiches with Black Olive Relish and Fresh Mozzarella

SERVES 4

This is basically grilled eggplant chopped up and put on top of toast along with a loamy, lemony olive relish and some mellow mozzarella. It is excellent as either a hearty hors d'oeuvre or a substantial side dish. If you want to make it more like a canapé, you can grill sixteen thin slices of baguette and spread the mixture on top of those, like crostini.

> 1 large eggplant, cut into rounds about $^1/_2$ inch thick
>
> 2 tablespoons vegetable oil
>
> Salt and freshly cracked black pepper to taste
>
> 2 tablespoons minced garlic
>
> $^1/_3$ cup olive oil
>
> $^1/_4$ cup roughly chopped fresh basil
>
> 1 tomato about the size of a baseball, cored and diced small
>
> 2 tablespoons balsamic vinegar
>
> 4 slices good crusty bread
>
> $^1/_2$ pound fresh mozzarella, cut into slices about $^1/_2$ inch thick
>
> Black Olive Relish (recipe follows)

1. Place the eggplant in a small bowl and toss with the vegetable oil and salt and pepper to taste. Place on the grill over **a medium-hot fire** and cook for 2 to 3 minutes on each side, or until brown and soft on the inside. Remove the eggplant from the grill, roughly chop, and place in a medium bowl. Add the garlic, olive oil, basil, tomato, and vinegar, and toss well. Season to taste and set aside.

2. Place the bread slices on the grill around the outside of the fire where the heat is low, and toast until golden brown, 3 to 4 minutes.

3. Put a piece of toast on each plate, spoon a quarter of the eggplant mixture onto each toast, add a quarter of the mozzarella and a generous spoonful of the Black Olive Relish, and serve.

BLACK OLIVE RELISH

> $^1/_2$ cup pitted Kalamata or other brine-cured black olives, roughly chopped
>
> $^1/_4$ cup fresh lemon juice (about 1 lemon)
>
> 2 tablespoons olive oil
>
> 1 tablespoon red pepper flakes

In a medium bowl, combine all the ingredients and mix well. Keep covered in the refrigerator for three to four days.

Try this as a go-along with a Mediterranean-flavored entrée like Grilled Sausage and Corn over Fettuccine with Tomatoes and Basil (page 99).

Tortilla Sandwiches of Grilled Shrimp and Corn with Goat Cheese and Pickled Red Onions

SERVES 8

You could call these quesadillas, but I like to call them tortilla sandwiches because it makes them seem less intimidating. They are actually very easy to make, and throwing them on the grill for a few minutes after you assemble them adds a nice smokiness. The filling mixture is a little chunky, but if you kind of smash it down on the tortilla, it will work fine. Also, be sure you use the small tortillas, since they are easier to flip on the grill. Once you get a handle on this technique, it's easy to create a lot of different variations. The pickled onions also go very well with all kinds of grilled meats.

> 1 pound medium shrimp (16 to 20 shrimp), peeled, deveined, and tails
> removed
> 1 tablespoon vegetable oil
> Salt and freshly cracked black pepper to taste
> 2 ears corn, husked, desilked, blanched in boiling salted water for
> 2 minutes, drained, and kernels sliced off (about 1 cup kernels)
> $1/4$ cup roughly chopped fresh cilantro
> 2 tablespoons ground cumin
> 1 tablespoon mashed or chopped canned chipotles
> 1 tablespoon minced garlic
> 4 ounces goat cheese
> 16 6-inch corn or flour tortillas
> Pickled Red Onions (recipe follows)

1. In a medium bowl, combine the shrimp, oil, and salt and pepper to taste and toss well to coat the shrimp. Thread the shrimp onto skewers, place them on the grill over **a medium-hot fire,** and cook for 3 to 4 minutes per side. *To check for doneness:* Cut into one of the shrimp and peek inside to be sure it is opaque all the way through.

2. Remove the shrimp from the fire and, as soon as they are cool enough to handle, slide off the skewers, chop into bite-sized pieces, and put into a large bowl. Add all the remaining ingredients except the tortillas, mix well, and season to taste with salt and pepper.

3. Spread a couple of spoonfuls of the shrimp-cheese mixture onto each of 8 tortillas. Place the remaining tortillas on top of the filling, then place these sandwiches on the grill over **a low fire.** You want to cook them until they are golden brown on both sides and the cheese has just melted, about 3 minutes. When they have reached this point, remove them from the grill, cut them into quarters, and serve, garnished with the Pickled Red Onions.

PICKLED RED ONIONS

2 small red onions, peeled and sliced into very thin rings

$^1/_2$ cup white vinegar

$^1/_2$ cup fresh lime juice (about 4 limes)

1 tablespoon sugar

Salt and freshly cracked black pepper to taste

In a small bowl, mix together all the ingredients. Cover and refrigerate until the onions have turned a bright pink color, about 30 minutes. The onions will keep, covered and refrigerated, for about 2 weeks.

These go well with Grilled Veal Chops with Expensive Mushrooms (page 138) and some Pickled Pineapple (page 335). And I'd like to have some Puerto Viejo Rum Punch (page 352) for my beverage.

"Roll Your Own" Taco Bar with Lots of Garnishes

SERVES 10 TO 12

Next time you're having ten or twelve of your nearest and dearest over and are willing to invest a couple of hours in preparation time, this is the recipe for you. It's really
not as difficult as it looks from the long ingredient list: Basically you skewer and grill
several different meats and lay them out with a variety of flavorful condiments. This
does involve a lot of knife work, but that can go slowly or fast depending on your skill
level. And, as long as you're squeezing limes for the salsa anyway, you might as well
squeeze a dozen more for some nice fresh margaritas. Put some salsa music on, sip
on that margarita, and you'll find the work definitely going faster—but watch your
digits as you continue to chop and slice.

If you choose to make this, the results will be unbelievable, with a lavish assortment of spicy flavors, four kinds of meat, and all those fresh add-ons. You can turn
your back porch into the buffet line at the best hotel in the Yucatán. Then it's time to
make your guests do the work as you set all the stuff out and let them roll their own.

1 pound boneless, skinless chicken breasts, cut into $^{1}/_{2}$-inch cubes

2 tablespoons cumin seeds, toasted if you want, or 1 tablespoon
    ground cumin

1 tablespoon coriander seeds, toasted if you want, or $1^{1}/_{2}$ teaspoons
    ground coriander

2 tablespoons olive oil

Salt and freshly cracked black pepper to taste

1 pound boneless pork, cut into $^{1}/_{2}$-inch cubes

$^{1}/_{2}$ cup roughly chopped fresh cilantro

2 tablespoons olive oil

Salt and freshly cracked black pepper to taste

1 pound boneless beef (steak tips are great), cut into $^{1}/_{2}$-inch cubes

3 tablespoons fresh lime juice (about $1^{1}/_{2}$ limes)

1 tablespoon red pepper flakes

2 tablespoons olive oil

Salt and freshly cracked black pepper to taste

20 medium shrimp (about 1 pound), peeled and deveined

2 tablespoons olive oil

1 tablespoon minced garlic

Salt and freshly cracked black pepper to taste

1 pineapple, peeled and sliced into 1-inch-thick rounds

48 medium corn or wheat tortillas

For the Condiments

    3 cups thinly sliced cabbage

    2 red onions, peeled, thinly sliced, marinated in 1 cup fresh lime juice

       (about 8 limes) for 2 hours, and drained

    3 tomatoes, cored and diced medium

    3 avocados, peeled, pitted, and diced medium

    1 cup roughly chopped fresh cilantro

    2 cups sour cream

    4 limes, quartered

    Tomatillo Salsa (recipe follows)

1. In a small bowl, toss the chicken with the cumin, coriander, olive oil, and salt and pepper to taste and mix well. Thread the chicken on skewers and set aside. Follow the same procedure for the pork, tossing it with the cilantro, oil, and salt and pepper and then skewering it; the beef, tossing it with the lime juice, red pepper flakes, oil, and salt and pepper and then skewering it; and the shrimp, tossing it with the oil, garlic, and salt and pepper and then skewering it.

2. Once you have all of the skewers ready, put them on a large platter and head out for the grill. Fortunately, all four types of skewers need **a medium-hot fire.** You can do the different types sequentially or, if you're feeling dexterous and adventurous, put them all on the grill at the same time and pull them off as they are done. Here's how they go: Grill the shrimp for 3 to 4 minutes per side. *To check for doneness:* Cut into one of the shrimp to be sure it is opaque all the way through. Grill the chicken for about 4 minutes per side. *To check for doneness:* Cut into one of the chunks and check to see that it is opaque all the way through. Grill the pork for 4 to 5 minutes per side. *To check for doneness:* Cut into one of the chunks to be sure it is almost completely opaque, with just a bit of pink in the center. Grill the beef skewers for 4 to 5 minutes per side. *To check for doneness:* Cut into one of the chunks and check to see that the meat is just pink inside. As each skewer is done, remove from the grill and set aside.

3. Now put the pineapple slices on the grill and cook for 5 to 6 minutes per side, or until they are well browned. Remove them from the heat and, as soon as they are cool enough to handle, dice medium and place in a small bowl.

4. Place 10 to 12 of your tortillas on the grill to warm, placing them around the edges of the fire, where the heat is low. They should be golden brown and soft when they are ready. Heat more as you need them.

5. When you are ready to serve, slide the meats and shrimp off the skewers and into separate bowls. Place each of the condiments in a separate bowl, and set out the Tomatillo Salsa. What you will end up with is a huge selection of flavors and ingredients that your guests can use to stuff their tortillas any way they like.

continued

TOMATILLO SALSA

3 cups canned tomatillos (about 1 16-ounce can), drained and diced
   medium, or about 1 pound fresh tomatillos (12 to 15), husked, rinsed,
   blanched, and diced medium (see below)

$^1/_2$ cup fresh lime juice (about 4 limes)

2 fresh chile peppers of your choice, minced

1 tablespoon minced garlic

$^1/_2$ cup roughly chopped fresh cilantro

1 teaspoon ground cumin

Salt and freshly cracked black pepper to taste

In a small bowl, combine all the ingredients and mix together well.

**This is pretty much a banquet in itself, but if you want to gild the lily
you could add on Grilled Shrimp and Bacon Skewers with Pickled Onion and
Avocado Salad (page 104). I recommend Puerto Viejo Rum Punch
for a Crowd (page 352) as the beverage of choice here.**

tart tomatillos

TOMATILLOS ARE ONE OF those wonderful, distinctive ingredients that help to define a cuisine—in this case, the cuisine of Mexico. In our recipes we often call for canned tomatillos, since they are easier to locate than fresh, keep forever in the pantry, and are of very good quality. If you can find fresh ones, though, you might enjoy using them. Fresh tomatillos resemble small unripe tomatoes; when on the vine, they are encased in a papery brown husk shaped sort of like a lantern. To use them, husk them and rinse them well, then blanch them in boiling salted water until they are tender and their bright green color has dulled, about 4 minutes. Drain, chop or puree, and you're ready to go. You might also want to check out Rick Bayless's wonderful book, *Rick Bayless's Mexican Kitchen* (Scribner's, 1996), in which he explores all kinds of ways of dealing with these tart little guys.

Middle Eastern–Style Dip

MAKES ABOUT 3 1/2 CUPS

Here's a simple but somewhat unusual dip to substitute for more standard versions at the cocktail hour. It's very easy to put together, as long as you have pomegranate molasses and pine nuts in the house. If you can get hold of a ripe pomegranate too, the bright, juicy, sweet-tart seeds put this dip over the top. Serve it with pita rounds that have been lightly brushed with olive oil, grilled over a medium fire until crisp, just two to three minutes per side, and then cut into eighths.

2 cups plain yogurt

1/2 cup pomegranate molasses

3/4 cup chopped pine nuts, toasted in a 350°F oven for 7 to 10 minutes, or
until golden brown

3 tablespoons cumin seeds, toasted in a sauté pan, stirring, until just
fragrant, 2 to 3 minutes

1/4 cup raisins

Seeds from 1 pomegranate (optional)

In a small shallow bowl, combine the yogurt and pomegranate molasses and mix well. Sprinkle with the pine nuts, cumin, raisins, and the pomegranate seeds if you have them. Serve with lavash or grilled pita bread. This dip will keep, covered and refrigerated, for up to a week.

pomegranate molasses

AS THE NAME IMPLIES, pomegranate molasses is a thick syrup made by boiling down huge quantities of pomegranate juice, along with a bit of sugar and lemon, until the juice is reduced in volume by two thirds or more. Available in most Middle Eastern stores, it has the deep, rich sweetness and tangy sour undertones of the fruit from which it is made. It's one of those "secret weapon" ingredients, like balsamic vinegar, that can give a subtle boost to a wide range of dishes. I like to slip a bit into a vinaigrette or basting sauce, or just paint a very thin coating onto chicken during the last minute or two of grilling. Buy a bottle and keep it in your refrigerator—you'll soon find all kinds of uses for it.

Deviled Egg–Stuffed Avocados
on Lime Slaw

I've encountered the mellow, rich combination of eggs and avocado in a lot of tropical countries. I'm not sure why, but this is a pairing that is inherently complementary; it really works. Here we add some chiles to the egg mixture, then stuff it into avocado halves and put it on a bed of red cabbage slaw with a strong citrus component. If you feel like frying up some tortilla chips, they make a good dipping implement. It's an excellent summer lunch; if I were really hungry, I might grill up a couple of sausages to go with it.

6 large eggs

2 tablespoons pickle relish

2 tablespoons mayonnaise

1 tablespoon mashed canned chipotle pepper (or substitute 1 tablespoon
  minced fresh chile pepper of your choice)

1 medium rib celery, diced small

2 tablespoons roughly chopped fresh cilantro

Salt and freshly cracked black pepper to taste

2 avocados, peeled, pitted, and diced medium

$1/4$ cup vegetable oil

8 flour or corn tortillas (optional)

For the Slaw

2 cups thinly sliced red cabbage

$1/4$ cup olive oil

$1/4$ cup fresh lime juice (about 2 limes)

$1/4$ cup molasses

$1/4$ cup red wine vinegar

Salt and freshly cracked black pepper to taste

1. Put the eggs in a small saucepan and cover with cold water. Bring the water to a boil, reduce the heat to low, and simmer for 12 minutes. Drain and run under cold water to stop the cooking.

2. Peel the eggs and place them in a medium bowl. Add the relish, mayonnaise, chipotle, celery, cilantro, and salt and pepper to taste and mash together with a fork until the mixture is pretty uniform. Stuff one quarter of the mixture into the center of each avocado half and set aside.

3. In a large sauté pan, heat the vegetable oil until hot but not smoking. Place a tortilla in the pan and fry, turning once, until just crisp and lightly browned,

1 to 2 minutes. Remove to a brown paper bag or paper towels to drain and repeat with remaining tortillas. Break the tortillas into chips.

4. Make the slaw: In a large bowl, combine all the ingredients and mix well. Place the slaw on individual serving plates, top with the stuffed avocado halves, and serve, passing the tortilla chips separately.

This makes a nice lunch when served along with Grilled and Chilled Mediterranean-Style Gazpacho (page 27).

the eggshell game

I USED TO AVOID making dishes that included boiled eggs, not because of health concerns about eating eggs, but because I hated peeling the eggs. For some reason, the shells never seemed to come off easily for me, and I was always left picking at tiny little pieces of shell, which inevitably tore away sections of the white. All in all, an annoying proposition.

RECENTLY, THOUGH, I HEARD about a technique for making this process easier. Like many cooking tricks, it sounds a little silly but works really well.

SO HERE IT IS: Cool the eggs a bit after they are done cooking, then tap them lightly on the counter on all sides, slightly cracking the shells all over. Put the eggs back in the saucepan, cover them with cold water, and leave them for an hour or so. When you come back to peel them, the shells will slip off easily in big sections. I think this works because water seeps in between the shell and the egg, but whatever the reason, it makes the task a breeze.

Grilled Black Pepper Flatbread

MAKES 10 ROUNDS

Cooking bread on a grill has a long and varied history in cuisines around the world. If you've never tried it, this is a good place to start—the recipe is easy and it tastes fantastic. The amount of black pepper called for doesn't make the bread very hot, but it does add a strong, deep flavor that matches well with the smokiness the bread soaks up from the fire. This bread is an excellent accompaniment to any kind of grilled food, or you can put it out with cheese or dips for a slightly unusual appetizer platter.

1 package ($\frac{1}{4}$ ounce) yeast

2 cups warm water

$5\frac{1}{2}$ to 6 cups all-purpose flour, sifted

1 tablespoon plus 1 teaspoon kosher salt

2 tablespoons freshly cracked black pepper

$\frac{1}{4}$ cup olive oil plus about 3 tablespoons for brushing

1. In a small bowl, dissolve the yeast in $\frac{1}{2}$ cup of the warm water and set aside.

2. In a large bowl, combine $5\frac{1}{2}$ cups of the flour with the salt and pepper and mix well.

3. In a medium bowl, combine the proofed yeast, the remaining $1\frac{1}{2}$ cups warm water, and the $\frac{1}{4}$ cup olive oil and mix well. Gradually stir these wet ingredients into the dry ingredients, using a wooden spoon, until fully incorporated.

4. Turn the dough out onto a well-floured board and knead, adding all or part of the remaining $\frac{1}{2}$ cup of flour if the mixture is too sticky, until the dough is firm and has some elasticity, 8 to 10 minutes.

5. Place the dough in an oiled bowl, cover with plastic wrap, and set in a warm spot. Allow the dough to rise until doubled in volume, $1\frac{1}{2}$ to 2 hours.

6. Once it has doubled in volume, turn the dough out onto a floured cutting board and divide it into 10 pieces. Roll each piece into a flat round about $\frac{1}{4}$ inch thick.

7. Lightly brush the dough rounds with oil and place them directly on the grill over **a medium fire.** Cook, basting once with olive oil, until the breads are well browned with some dark sear marks, 4 to 5 minutes per side. *To check for doneness:* Tear open one of the breads and make sure it is fully cooked through and no longer doughy inside.

This easy, delicious, flavorful bread is good with just about everything.

Grilled Apple and Bread Salad with Arugula, Blue Cheese, and Grapes

SERVES 4

I'm always the guy at the dinner table who is cleaning out the bottom of the salad bowl with a hunk of bread, going for that last bit of dressing. So between that, the outstanding bread salads of Italy, and the general need to work more grain and bread into our diets, I think bread salads hit on all cylinders. This one's got a fruit and cheese aspect to it, as we complement the oil- and vinegar-soaked bread with some smoky apples, sweet grapes, and—just to make sure no one can claim the dish lacks flavor—a bit of tangy blue cheese. You want to toast the bread just long enough to crisp it up; this salad is also a good use for stale, but not rock-hard, bread.

> 2 Granny Smith apples, halved and cored
>
> 2 to 3 slices good crusty bread
>
> 1 bunch arugula, trimmed, washed, and torn into large pieces
>
> 1 cup seedless red grapes, halved (or substitute seedless green grapes)
>
> $1/2$ cup olive oil
>
> $1/4$ cup red wine vinegar
>
> Salt and freshly cracked black pepper to taste
>
> $1/3$ cup crumbled blue cheese

1. Place the apples cut side down on the grill over **a medium-hot fire** and cook for about 5 to 7 minutes, or until well browned. At the same time, place the bread around the edge of the fire, where the heat is low, and toast for about 5 minutes, or until golden brown. Remove the apples and bread from the grill as they are done.

2. When it is cool enough to handle, cut the bread into large chunks and place them in a large bowl. Cut the apples into thin slices and toss them in with the bread.

3. Add the arugula, grapes, olive oil, vinegar, and salt and pepper to taste and toss well. Just before serving, sprinkle with the blue cheese.

I might serve this in front of Spice-Crusted Pork Tenderloins with Banana-Date Chutney (page 150), along with Grilled Corn with Lime and Chinese Roasted Salt (page 278).

Arugula with Pancetta, Grilled Asparagus, and White Beans

With the combination of arugula, white beans, pancetta, and Parmesan cheese, this is definitely an Italian kind of salad. If you can't get hold of pancetta, you can substitute regular bacon or, as long as the grill is already going, if you've got some prosciutto or salami or ham around, toss that on the grill for just a minute and use it in place of the pancetta. With all the meat and cheese, this is a pretty rich dish, so it's best as a lunch main-course salad or as the predecessor to a light fish or pasta dish.

For the Dressing

$\frac{1}{2}$ cup olive oil

$\frac{1}{4}$ cup red wine vinegar

$\frac{1}{3}$ cup freshly grated good-quality Parmesan cheese

2 cloves garlic

2 tablespoons freshly cracked black pepper

2 tablespoons roughly chopped fresh basil

16 spears asparagus, bottom $\frac{1}{4}$ inch trimmed

1 tablespoon olive oil

Salt and freshly cracked black pepper to taste

2 bunches arugula, trimmed, washed, and dried

1 cup cooked (or canned) white beans (rinsed if canned)

1 small red onion, peeled and diced small

$\frac{1}{2}$ pound pancetta, thinly sliced, cooked in a 350°F oven for 6 to 8 minutes, or until crispy (or substitute bacon), and drained on paper towels

1. Make the dressing: In a food processor or blender, combine all of the ingredients except the basil and puree until smooth. Transfer to a bowl, stir in the basil, cover, and refrigerate. (This dressing will keep, covered and refrigerated, for about a week.)

2. Fill a sink or large pot with ice and water. In a large pot of boiling salted water, blanch the asparagus until just tender, about 3 minutes. Drain, plunge into the ice water to stop cooking, and drain again.

3. Rub the asparagus lightly with the oil, sprinkle with salt and pepper to taste, and grill over **a medium-hot fire,** turning frequently, for 3 to 5 minutes, or until well seared.

4. In a medium bowl, combine the arugula, white beans, and onion. Stir the dressing well, then pour just enough on the arugula-bean mixture to moisten the ingredients (you will probably have some dressing left over). Toss well, place on a serving platter or individual plates, top with the pancetta and asparagus, and serve.

> **I think this goes well with a pasta and seafood dish like Linguine with Grilled Shrimp and Black Olives (page 87), Macaroni with Grilled Squid, Eggplant, and Peppers (page 91), or Perciatelli and Grilled Octopus with Fennel and Lemon (page 93).**

Grilled Artichoke and White Bean Salad

SERVES 4

Grilled artichokes are always a hit and the baby ones are neat because you can eat the whole thing. Here they are grilled and then added to a white bean salad with a zesty lemon vinaigrette. If you can't locate baby artichokes, you can buy the adult version, boil them, and eat the bottom ends of the leaves as usual, then toss the hearts on the grill for a couple of minutes to sear before you add them to this salad. Your other option, of course, is just to buy the hearts.

12 baby artichokes

2 tablespoons vegetable oil

Salt and freshly cracked black pepper to taste

4 cups cooked (or canned) white beans (rinsed if canned)

1 tablespoon minced garlic

$^1/_2$ red bell pepper, seeded and diced small

$^1/_2$ red onion, peeled and diced small

2 tablespoons roughly chopped fresh thyme

For the Vinaigrette

$^1/_4$ cup fresh lemon juice (about 1 lemon)

1 tablespoon Dijon mustard

$^1/_2$ cup olive oil

2 tablespoons chopped pitted black olives

Freshly cracked black pepper to taste

1. Cut off the top third of each artichoke, snip the sharp tips from the remaining leaves, and trim the bottom slightly so that it is even all the way around.

continued

2. In a large saucepan, bring 1¹/₂ quarts of water to a boil. Toss in the artichokes and cook for 7 to 10 minutes, or until you can easily pierce them with a fork but they still offer some resistance. Drain and immediately immerse in cold water to stop the cooking.

3. Cut the artichokes in half lengthwise, sprinkle them with the vegetable oil and salt and pepper to taste, and grill them over **a medium-hot fire,** cut side down, for about 5 minutes, or until the cut sides are well browned.

4. In a medium bowl, combine the artichokes with the beans, garlic, red pepper, onion, and thyme. Toss well, season to taste with salt and pepper, and set aside.

5. Make the vinaigrette: In a small bowl, combine all the ingredients and whisk together well. Pour the vinaigrette over the salad and toss. This can be served right away, but it is much better if allowed to sit for an hour for the flavors to mingle and get acquainted. It will keep, covered and refrigerated, for about 3 days.

Try this with a big meat dish like Grilled Delmonico Steak Adobo with Charred Spring Onions and Sweet Corn Relish (page 131), Grilled Flank Steak "in the Style of Pastrami" with Spicy Tomato-Horseradish Relish (page 134), or Grilled Rack of Lamb with Quick Mint-Apricot Sauce and Blue Cheese–Stuffed Tomatoes (page 139).

artichoke lore

MOST VEGETABLES ARE ANNUALS —you have to plant new ones every year. But artichokes, like asparagus, are perennials; a single artichoke plant may live and yield chokes for as long as ten years. The part of the artichoke plant that we eat is actually a flower head. The individual petals are "bracts," a kind of a hybrid of petal and leaf. And the fuzzy part in the center of the choke that you cut out and discard is in fact composed of thousands of tiny flowers. All in all, a strange (but tasty) vegetable.

Grilled Bread Salad with Grilled Figs

SERVES 4 TO 6

Any excuse for me to grill figs, and I'll do it. The sweet, rich, caramel flavor of these beauties is truly special. Along with the bread and roasted peppers, they create an easy go-along salad.

For the Dressing

1 tablespoon fresh lemon juice

$^1/_2$ cup olive oil

$^1/_4$ cup balsamic vinegar

1 tablespoon minced garlic

Salt and freshly cracked black pepper to taste

1 baguette or other long crusty loaf of bread

6 fresh figs, halved

1 tablespoon olive oil

Salt and freshly cracked black pepper to taste

1 red onion, peeled and diced large

10 basil leaves, cut into long thin strips

2 tablespoons roughly chopped fresh parsley

2 roasted red peppers, diced large (see page 54 for homemade, or use jarred, rinsed)

1. Make the dressing: In a small bowl, combine all the ingredients, whisk together well, and set aside.

2. Cut the loaf of bread in half lengthwise, and place on the grill around the edge of **a medium-hot fire,** where the heat is low, and cook until browned, 5 minutes per side. Don't be impatient—toast the bread slowly on both sides so it dries out and becomes more crusty, which will allow it to absorb some of the dressing without becoming soggy right away. When the bread is well toasted, remove from the grill and cut it into medium-sized chunks. You should have 5 cups.

3. Meanwhile, place the figs in a small bowl with the oil and salt and pepper to taste and toss well. Place the figs on the grill, cut side down, over **the medium-hot fire** and cook, turning once or twice, until browned, 2 to 3 minutes.

4. In a large bowl, combine the toasted bread and grilled figs with the onion, basil, parsley, and roasted red peppers. Stir the dressing well, pour just enough into the bowl to moisten the ingredients, and toss well. Season to taste with salt and pepper, allow to sit about 10 minutes so the bread absorbs some of the dressing, toss again, and serve.

This would make a nice dinner in combination with Grilled Rack of Lamb with Quick Mint-Apricot Sauce and Blue Cheese–Stuffed Tomatoes (page 139).

roasted bell peppers

To ROAST BELL PEPPERS, put them on the grill over a hot fire, rolling around occasionally, until the skin is completely dark and well blistered. Remove from the grill, pop into a brown paper bag, tie the bag shut, and set aside to cool. Remove the peppers from the bag and peel off the skins. Tear the peppers in half, remove the ribs and seeds, and run the peppers gently under cold water to remove any remaining charred pieces of skin. To store for up to 2 weeks, put into a small container, add olive oil to cover, cover, and refrigerate.

Grilled Pita Bread Salad with Cucumbers and Feta Cheese

SERVES 4

Here's a Persian addition to the grilled bread salad family. Easy, healthy, and good-tasting, it features the same cucumber-tomato-mint-parsley combo that has made tabbouleh such a popular salad all over the world. The grilled pita adds a nice crunchy texture. In fact, I like to grill up a double batch of the pita rounds, then pass some around for people to dip into the salad or just eat as additional bread with the meal.

$1/2$ cup extra virgin olive oil

$1/4$ cup red wine vinegar

Salt and freshly cracked black pepper to taste

4 pita bread rounds

2 medium tomatoes, cored and cut into eights

2 cucumbers, peeled, seeded, and cut into bite-sized chunks

1 small red onion, peeled, halved, and thinly sliced

$1/2$ cup crumbled feta cheese

$1/2$ cup Kalamata or other brine-cured black olives, pitted

$1/4$ cup roughly chopped fresh mint

$1/4$ cup roughly chopped fresh parsley

1. In a small bowl, whisk together the olive oil, vinegar, and salt and pepper to taste and set aside.

2. Place the pita bread on the grill over **a medium-hot fire** and toast for 2 to 3 minutes per side or until golden brown. Remove from the grill and, as soon as the pita is cool enough to handle, cut the rounds into eighths.

STARTERS

3. When you are ready to serve, combine the grilled bread with all the remaining ingredients in a large bowl and toss well. Stir the dressing well, add enough just to moisten the ingredients, and serve. This salad will keep, covered and refrigerated, for 3 days, although the pita will not remain crisp.

This is good for dinner with Lamb Shish Kebobs over Fettuccine (page 100) and a bowl of Ginger-Date Chutney (page 328) to pass around.

olive variables

OLIVES COME IN A bewildering variety, from small, smooth-skinned, and light green to large, wrinkled, and deep purple-black. This diversity results largely from two factors controlled by the producers—the point at which the fruits are picked, and the manner in which they are cured.

THE FIRST OF THESE variables is quite simple: green olives are picked when not yet ripened, and black when almost or fully ripe.

WHETHER PICKED GREEN, RIPENING, or dead-ripe, however, all olives have one overwhelming characteristic in common when they come off the tree: a bitterness so intense that anyone foolish enough to bite into one will involuntarily spit it out. This extreme bitterness is caused by a chemical called oleuropein, which makes untreated olives not only ined-

ible but, according to some experts, actually poisonous.

TO RID OLIVES OF oleuropein, they must be cured. This process, which also softens, preserves, and develops flavors in the fruit, can be done in several ways. The major differences are whether or not lye is used in the process and whether the curing is done wet or dry.

ON THE SLEDGEHAMMER END of the subtlety scale, olives may simply be treated in a strong lye solution and then thoroughly rinsed. This does remove the bitterness from the fruit, but it is a rough remedy and tends to break down the flesh, removing some of its flavor as well.

FORTUNATELY, MOST OLIVES ARE treated somewhat less harshly, and are brine-cured. Brine-cured olives may be given a short bath in

lye and then placed in a strong salt solution to ferment or, moving even farther toward the gentle end of the curing continuum, they may skip the lye treatment and simply be slowly fermented in brine.

THE THIRD CHOICE IS to "dry-cure" olives. In this treatment, the fruits are immersed briefly in lye, then packed in salt and dried.

NOT SURPRISINGLY, THE CURING method strongly affects the flavor and appearance of the olive. In general, lye-cured olives are less complex in appearance as well as taste, with very evenly colored skins and a mild flavor with few highlights. Brine- or dry-cured olives have more layers of flavor as well as more residual bitterness. Go for the brine- or dry-cured whenever possible.

Grilled Shrimp and Cucumber Salad

On those not-too-infrequent occasions when I feel as if I've been overindulging in rich food and potent alcohol, I routinely take myself to my neighborhood Japanese restaurant for an antidote. Japanese cuisine has a light freshness that makes you feel cleansed and healthful when you eat it, but at the same time it has a lot of flavors going on, so it's not boring. This easy salad of veggies and shrimp, with its collection of Japanese flavors, is just the thing for those occasions when you want something tasty but not overbearing. Try it for lunch the day after a big party.

> 16 medium shrimp (about 1 pound), peeled and deveined
> 1 tablespoon vegetable oil
> Salt and freshly cracked black pepper to taste

For the Dressing
> 1/2 cup rice wine vinegar (or substitute 1/4 cup each white vinegar
>   and water)
> 2 tablespoons sesame oil
> 2 tablespoons soy sauce
> 2 tablespoons fresh lime juice (about 1 lime)
> 2 tablespoons minced ginger
> 1 tablespoon minced garlic
> 1 small fresh chile pepper of your choice, minced
> 2 tablespoons roughly chopped fresh cilantro
> 2 tablespoons sugar
>
> 2 cucumbers, peeled, halved crosswise, and cut into thin strips
> 1 red bell pepper, halved, seeded, and diced large
> 1 carrot, peeled, halved crosswise, and cut into thin strips
> 4 scallions (white and green parts), roughly chopped

1. Thread the shrimp onto skewers, rub lightly with the oil, and sprinkle with salt and pepper to taste. Place the skewers on the grill over **a medium-hot fire** and cook for 3 to 4 minutes per side. *To check for doneness:* Cut into one of the shrimp and peek inside; it should be opaque all the way through. Remove from the grill, remove from the skewers, and chop into bite-sized pieces.

2. Make the dressing: In a medium bowl, combine all the ingredients and whisk together well. Add the cucumbers, bell pepper, carrot, scallions, and grilled shrimp and toss gently. Adjust the seasoning and serve.

This makes a nice dinner with Eggplant and Tomato Hobo Pack with Lemon and Garlic (page 215) and Spaghetti with Grilled Prosciutto and Figs (page 98).

STARTERS

Grilled Shrimp and Black Bean Salad with Papaya-Chile Dressing

SERVES 4

To me, this is a good example of a dish that uses lots of strong ingredients but ends up being full-flavored rather than what we think of as spicy. It tastes best when just made, so what I sometimes do is prep all the separate ingredients in the morning (make the dressing, chop the tomatoes, peel and dice the avocados—you get the drill) and put them in paper cups (no washing up involved) in the refrigerator. Then when folks are ready to eat, I bring out the paper cups, toss the contents together in a bowl, grill up some shrimp, and still have time to refill everybody's drink before we sit down to eat. This kind of studied casualness makes it easier to enjoy yourself when dinner guests are in the house. This Latin/West Indies–inspired dish is a good starter for a large dinner, or an outstanding lunch by itself.

For the Dressing

1 ripe papaya, peeled and seeds removed

$^1/_2$ cup fresh lime juice (about 4 limes)

$^1/_2$ cup olive oil

1 tablespoon minced garlic

2 tablespoons minced fresh chile pepper of your choice

2 tablespoons cumin seeds, toasted if you want,
    or 1 tablespoon ground cumin

Salt and freshly cracked black pepper to taste

1 cup dried black beans, soaked in water to cover overnight,
    or at least 5 hours, or 1 15-ounce can black beans, drained and rinsed

16 medium shrimp (about 1 pound), peeled, deveined, and tails removed

1 tablespoon vegetable oil

Salt and freshly cracked black pepper to taste

2 avocados, peeled, pitted, and diced medium

2 tomatoes about the size of baseballs, cored and diced medium

1 red onion, peeled and diced small

$^1/_2$ cup roughly chopped fresh cilantro

1. Make the dressing: In a food processor or blender, combine all of the ingredients and puree until smooth. Cover and refrigerate.

2. If using dried beans, drain them, rinse them well, and place them in a medium saucepan with enough water to cover by about 1 inch. Bring to a boil over high heat, reduce the heat to medium, and simmer, adding small amounts of water as needed, for 3 hours, or until just soft to the bite but not mushy. If using canned beans, just drain and rinse them well.

continued

3. Brush the shrimp lightly with the oil, sprinkle with salt and pepper to taste, and thread onto skewers. Grill the shrimp over **a medium-hot fire** for 3 to 4 minutes per side. *To check for doneness:* Cut into one of the shrimp and check to see that it is opaque all the way through. Remove from the grill and, as soon as the shrimp are cool enough to handle, remove them from the skewers and cut each one into 3 pieces.

4. In a medium bowl, combine the shrimp, black beans, avocados, tomatoes, onion, and cilantro. Stir the dressing well, pour in just enough to lightly coat all the ingredients, toss well, and serve. (This salad will keep, covered and refrigerated, for 3 days.)

Serve this in front of any tropical-influenced entrée, such as Grilled
Vietnamese-Style Beef Skewers (page 124).

Grilled Scallop–Stuffed Avocados with Papaya Vinaigrette

SERVES 4

Scallops, papayas, and avocados provide a unique combination of richness, mellowness, and individuality. Each of the ingredients has its own very distinct flavor, but they all share a kind of background mellowness that makes them fit together really well. Here we combine this trio by filling halved avocados with grilled scallops and topping them with a papaya dressing. These are then served on a bed of sliced cabbage; the juice from the scallop mixture should overflow the avocado a bit so it mixes with the dressed cabbage.

> 1 pound (10 to 16) large sea scallops, cleaned
> 1 tablespoon vegetable oil
> Salt and freshly cracked black pepper to taste
> 2 medium tomatoes, cored and diced small
> 1 small red onion, peeled and diced small

For the Vinaigrette
> $^{1}/_{2}$ papaya, peeled, seeded, and cut into small chunks
> $^{1}/_{3}$ cup fresh lime juice (about 2 large limes)
> $^{1}/_{3}$ cup olive oil
> $^{1}/_{4}$ cup roughly chopped fresh cilantro
> Salt and freshly cracked black pepper to taste

2 avocados, halved and pitted (skin left on)
¹/₂ head green cabbage, thinly sliced

1. Blanch the scallops in boiling water for 1 minute. Drain, place in a medium bowl with the oil and salt and pepper to taste, and toss to coat.

2. Thread the scallops onto skewers, place on the grill over **a medium-hot fire,** and cook until well browned on the exterior, 2 to 3 minutes per side. *To check for doneness:* Cut into one of the scallops to see if it is opaque throughout. Slide the scallops off the skewers into a medium bowl, then add the tomatoes and onions.

3. Make the vinaigrette: Combine all of the ingredients in a food processor and puree until smooth. Add about two thirds of the dressing to the scallop mixture, and toss well.

4. Arrange the avocado halves on top of a bed of the sliced cabbage. Fill the avocados with the scallop mixture, drizzle the remaining dressing over the cabbage, and serve at room temperature or chilled.

This makes a good light lunch in combination with
Simple Latin-Style Rice and Beans (page 300).

for scallops, go for the big guys

WE SEE BASICALLY THREE different types of scallops in the United States. Almost all are from the East Coast, with a small amount coming from Mexico.

BAY SCALLOPS, THE SMALLEST type, are harvested from fall to spring in the bays and river mouths of the Atlantic Ocean from New England to North Carolina. A southern cousin of the bay is the calico, which hangs out mostly from Florida south to Brazil, with some action in the Gulf of Mexico. A little larger than the bay, the calico has a more distinct flavor and can be easily identified by its colored shell.

THE THIRD VARIETY IS the sea scallop, the biggest of them all. The largest crop is harvested on Georges Bank off the coast of Massachusetts and brought to shore at the scallop capital of the world, New Bedford. For a long time people have eschewed the mild, salty flavor of these guys in favor of the more subtle flavor of the bays, but the large ones have always been #1 with me. I think it's hard to cook the smaller ones without overcooking them; with sea scallops, you can get a good, hard sear on the outside and still have the inside be tender. Plus, the more pronounced flavor of these bigger scallops stands up to more intense cooking techniques—like grilling.

SO WHEN IT COMES to scallops, I advise you to let others pay the price for subtlety, and go for the big guys.

Summer Striped Bass Salad

I'm lucky enough to be able to spend time at the beach in southern Massachusetts in the summer, and sometimes I'm even fortunate enough to catch some fish down there. If I don't, I can always go on over to the local fish store, which buys the catch of small fishermen. Seeing that this area is a big striped bass hangout, and being that striper in my humble opinion is one of the finest eating fish in the universe (along with pompano and red snapper), I have had the occasion to grill many a striped bass, which means I sometimes have leftovers to use up the next day. So I took the Southeast Asian idea of salads made of fish tossed with lime and herbs and added the smokiness of grilling to boost the flavor dynamism. If you don't have striped bass, you can make this with snapper, tuna, monkfish, swordfish, halibut—or just about any fish or seafood that you can grill.

> 1 pound striped bass fillets, skinned and any bones removed (or use last night's leftover grilled fish)
> 2 tablespoons olive oil
> Salt and freshly cracked black pepper to taste
> 1 large tomato, cored and diced medium
> 1 small red onion, peeled and thinly sliced
> $^1/_2$ cup thinly sliced scallions (white and green parts)
> $^1/_4$ cup roughly chopped fresh basil
> $^1/_4$ cup roughly chopped fresh mint
> $^1/_3$ cup fresh lime juice (about 2 large limes)
> 1 tablespoon minced ginger
> 4 to 6 dashes Tabasco sauce

1. Rub the bass lightly with the olive oil, sprinkle with salt and pepper to taste, and grill over **a medium-hot fire** for 5 to 7 minutes per side. *To check for doneness:* Cut into one of the pieces of fish and check to see that it is just opaque throughout.

2. Remove the fish from the grill and, as soon as it is cool enough to handle, flake the meat from the skin with a fork; the meat will be tossed in with the salad, so don't worry if it comes off in small pieces.

3. Place the fish in a medium bowl, add all remaining ingredients, and season to taste with salt and pepper. Toss lightly and serve. This salad will keep, covered and refrigerated, for 2 to 3 days.

I think this makes a nice combination with something hot and spicy like Grilled Jerk Shark with Pineapple Salsa (page 230) or Grilled Pork, Pineapple, and Jalapeño Skewers with Guava-Lime Sauce (page 238).

striper supply and demand

ALTHOUGH I'M NOT MUCH of a chauvinist, the exclusively American nature of the striped bass somehow enhances its appeal to me—it is the only sport fish that is found nowhere in the world other than the waters off our coasts. Originally stripers hung out only on the East Coast, but in the late nineteenth century some sport fishermen hauled a load of them out to San Francisco. Like true Americans, they adapted well to their new surroundings, so today they can be found on the West Coast too.

UNFORTUNATELY, THE SUPPLY OF wild striped bass is cyclical. Fortunately, we are presently on an upswing. In the waters of southern Massachusetts, where I have done all my striper fishing during the past year or two, the waters are packed with stripers twice a year, during their annual spring and fall migrations from Chesapeake Bay to northern New England and back. So if you like surf fishing and you like cooking deliciously sweet fish, I advise you to get on up to New England in the spring or fall and hook into some of these excellent specimens. After all, you never know when we'll hit another downswing in supply like the last one—which stretched from the late 1930s well into the 1960s.

Grilled Regular Mushrooms with Sherry

I like to serve grilled mushrooms as a first course so folks can munch on them while the rest of dinner is being prepared. They couldn't be easier to make, and the juice is delicious if you have some bread around to sop it up.

The mushrooms are done when the inside has a moist appearance all the way through. Try to pull them off as soon as they reach this point, because if you leave them on longer, they begin to get dry again. Use your longest tongs for this one, as the combination of a hot fire and many things to turn over can make for a hectic four or five minutes.

2 pounds medium mushrooms, stemmed and cleaned

$^1/_4$ cup olive oil

Salt and freshly cracked black pepper to taste

3 tablespoons unsalted butter, cut into small pieces

1 tablespoon minced garlic

$^1/_2$ cup roughly chopped fresh parsley

$^1/_4$ cup sherry

1. In a medium bowl, combine the mushrooms, olive oil, and salt and pepper to taste and toss well.

2. Grill the mushrooms over **a hot fire** until they are brown and soft, 3 to 5 minutes. *To check for doneness:* Cut into one of the mushrooms and see if it looks moist all the way through.

3. Remove the mushrooms from the fire and place in a medium bowl. Add the butter, garlic, parsley, and sherry and mix gently until the butter melts. Season to taste with salt and pepper and serve.

I might serve this as an appetizer combination with
Grilled Mussels Johnson (page 72) and Grilled Pita Bread Salad
with Cucumbers and Feta Cheese (page 54).

Grilled Chicken and Mango Salad

SERVES 4

This is a version of the savory salads common throughout Thailand. These simple but intensely flavored dishes combine a wild range of tastes, including sweet fruit, aromatic herbs, pungent ginger, hot chiles, sour limes, salty fish sauce, and crunchy peanuts. This particular rendition features mangoes, known throughout tropical Asia as the King of Fruits. Of course, in the United States we are lucky to find one variety of mango in our markets; in India, over three hundred and fifty individual varieties of this luscious fruit are cultivated.

2 whole boneless, skinless chicken breasts (each 10 to 12 ounces)
2 tablespoons vegetable oil
Salt and freshly cracked black pepper to taste
2 ripe mangoes, peeled, pitted, and diced medium
1 cup seedless green or red grapes, halved
1 small red onion, peeled and diced large
$^1/_2$ red bell pepper, seeded and diced large
$^1/_4$ cup roughly chopped fresh cilantro (or substitute parsley)
2 tablespoons roughly chopped fresh basil

For the Dressing

6 tablespoons fresh orange juice (about 1 small orange)
$^1/_4$ cup fresh lime juice (about 2 limes)
1 tablespoon fish sauce (optional)
2 tablespoons minced fresh chile pepper of your choice
1 tablespoon minced ginger
Salt and freshly cracked black pepper to taste

$^1/_2$ cup unsalted peanuts, toasted in a 350°F oven until golden brown, about 10 minutes, then roughly chopped

1. Rub the chicken breasts lightly with oil, sprinkle with salt and pepper to taste, and place on the grill over **a medium-hot fire.** Cook for 7 to 9 minutes on each side. *To check for doneness:* Cut into the thickest part and peek inside to be sure they are opaque all the way through, with no pink.

2. As soon as they are cool enough, cut the grilled chicken breasts into bite-sized chunks and place in a large bowl. Add the mangoes, grapes, red onion, bell pepper, cilantro, and basil and set aside.

continued

3. Make the dressing: In a small bowl, combine all the ingredients and whisk together well. Add just enough dressing to the chicken-mango mixture to moisten the ingredients, toss well, and season to taste with salt and pepper. Sprinkle with the chopped peanuts and serve.

I would serve this as a lunch or light dinner with Grilled Eggplant Rounds with Sweet Chile Sauce (page 287).

ripening a mango

IT'S HARD TO FIND a fully ripened mango in the produce market, but that's really no problem. Even in areas where they are grown, mangoes are usually picked when not quite fully ripe and then allowed to ripen off the tree. So go ahead and buy them underripe, and let them mature at home. Don't refrigerate them, though; simply leave them on the dining room or kitchen table and check their progress each day.

THE BEST INDICATION OF mango ripeness is aroma. Leave a mango sitting out on the kitchen table, for example, and you will know it is ready to eat on the morning that you enter the room and notice a rich, flowery perfume that seems to combine the aromas of Concord grapes, peaches, and apricots. Bite into the orange flesh, and you will taste echoes of the flavors of all of those fruits, along with a hint of the sourness of lime and a musky undertone that belongs to mangoes alone. There's nothing quite like it.

Grilled Portobellos with Prosciutto and Figs on Seared Greens

SERVES 4

Grilled portobellos are fantastic. The thick, juicy caps take on a very meaty look when grilled. They get moist and tender and charring creates another layer of deep flavor. We combine the smoky portobellos with grilled prosciutto that gets a little bacon profile going, with some grilled figs for sweetness. We serve all of this on top of some seared greens with garlic and balsamic. With the greens, the key is to use a very large, very hot sauté pan and to get the oil smoking-hot. When the garlic goes in, the greens need to hit the pan at the same time so the garlic doesn't burn. No hesitation here.

> 4 large (about 6 inches in diameter) portobello mushrooms,
> stemmed and cleaned
> 2 tablespoons vegetable oil
> Salt and freshly cracked black pepper to taste
> 4 fresh figs, halved
> 8 thin slices prosciutto (or substitute other very thinly sliced ham)
> 3 tablespoons olive oil
> 1 tablespoon minced garlic
> 1 bunch mustard greens, trimmed and washed
> 3 tablespoons balsamic vinegar
> 1 teaspoon sugar

1. Rub the mushrooms with the vegetable oil and sprinkle lightly with salt and pepper. Grill over **a medium fire** until tender and slightly seared, about 5 minutes per side. *To check for doneness:* Cut into one of the mushrooms; it should appear moist all the way through, rather than dry at the center.

2. At the same time, put the figs on the grill, cut side down, and cook until browned, about 2 minutes per side. Lay the slices of prosciutto on the grill and cook until just seared and a bit wrinkled, about 1 minute per side.

3. As soon as the mushrooms and figs are cooked, heat the oil in your largest sauté pan over high heat until it is so hot it is just about smoking. Add the garlic and cook for about 5 seconds, stirring a bit. Immediately add greens, vinegar, and sugar and toss furiously with your tongs until the greens are just wilted, about 1 minute or so. Remove from the heat and season to taste with salt and pepper.

4. Place the greens on a platter or individual serving plates. Arrange the mushrooms, figs, and prosciutto on top of the greens and serve warm.

I might try this in front of **Grilled Mackerel with Expensive Olive Oil, Lemon, and Oregano (page 192)** with **Grilled Bananas and Pineapple with Rum-Molasses Glaze (page 357)** for dessert.

Grilled Portobellos with Creamy Risotto and Tomato-Bacon Relish

SERVES 4

Here's an Italian-inspired dish that's a rich, smoky treat—and it's even got bacon. The risotto takes a while to cook, so the best plan is to start the rice, then make the relish while the risotto is cooking, and as soon as you take the risotto off the stove, grill the mushrooms. Serving portobellos whole is not uncommon, but grilling gives them a seared aspect that, along with their meaty texture, can make you think you're actually eating steak. If you want to make this dish simpler, you can always skip the relish, but it only takes a couple of minutes to put together and its slightly acidic taste is an excellent complement to the smoky mushrooms and the rich, creamy risotto.

For the Risotto

About 2 cups chicken stock

$^1/_2$ cup white wine

$^1/_2$ cup dry sherry

2 tablespoons unsalted butter

$^1/_2$ white onion, peeled and diced medium

1 tablespoon minced garlic

1 cup arborio rice

Salt and freshly cracked white pepper to taste

4 large (6- to 8-inch) portobello mushrooms (or more if smaller), stemmed and cleaned

$^1/_4$ cup olive oil

Salt and freshly cracked black pepper to taste

1. Make the risotto: Combine 2 cups chicken stock, the wine, and sherry in a medium saucepan and bring to a boil over high heat. Reduce the heat to low and allow to simmer slowly, uncovered.

2. Meanwhile, melt the butter in a medium saucepan over medium heat. Add the onion and sauté, stirring occasionally, until transparent, 5 to 7 minutes. Add the garlic and sauté, stirring occasionally, 1 minute more.

3. Add the rice and stir to coat the kernels. Pour in $^1/_2$ cup of the hot liquid, reduce the heat to low, and cook, stirring very frequently, until almost all of the liquid is absorbed. Add $^1/_2$ cup more of the hot liquid and cook, stirring frequently. Repeat this process, tasting frequently to monitor the texture, until the rice is creamy and firm, neither hard nor mushy; if necessary, add a little more hot chicken stock. Season to taste with salt and pepper, cover to keep warm, and set aside.

4. Grill the mushrooms: In a medium bowl, combine the portobellos, olive oil, and salt and pepper to taste and toss well to coat the mushrooms. Grill over **a medium-hot fire** for 3 to 4 minutes per side, or until still firm to the touch but not hard. *To check for doneness:* Cut into one of the mushrooms; it should look moist throughout rather than dry at the center.

5. Place the risotto on a small serving platter, and place the mushrooms on top. Add the Tomato-Bacon Relish and serve at once.

TOMATO·BACON RELISH

> **6 slices bacon**
> **1 large tomato, cored and diced small**
> **1/4 cup olive oil**
> **1/4 cup balsamic vinegar**
> **1/4 cup roughly chopped fresh basil**
> **Salt and freshly cracked black pepper to taste**

1. Place the bacon in a medium sauté pan over medium heat and cook until crisp, 6 to 8 minutes. Remove from the heat, drain on paper towels or a brown paper bag, and allow to cool.

2. In a medium bowl, combine the remaining ingredients. Crumble the bacon into the mixture, adjust the seasoning, and mix well.

I might try combining this with Grilled Orange-Cumin Mahi Mahi with Smoky Summer Vegetable Hash (page 166) and some Clove-Pickled Peaches (page 332).

portobello family tree

GIANT, FLAVORFUL PORTO-BELLO MUSHROOMS are actually from the same family as the common button mushroom, also known to cooks as the "supermarket mushroom." Partially because portobellos are used when they are older, with the gills in their caps farther open, they have a more distinct flavor than their button mushroom cousins. For both mushrooms, though, one fact remains the same: Their true, deep, rich flavors are only released when they are cooked. And, as long as you're cooking, the best choice is to put them on the grill, which adds another smoky flavor dimension to the whole.

Salt-Crusted Grilled Shrimp in Their Shells

SERVES 4 TO 6

For this recipe, the first thing you need to do is get the biggest shrimp you can possibly find. Then you roll them in salt, cook them over a hot fire, and serve them up with a simple Greek-inspired dipping sauce. The salt and the shells help protect the meat of the shrimp from the hot fire, and most of the salt is removed when you peel off the shells—or, if you're like me, you leave a little shell on just to get some extra salt. It's a fantastic flavor.

> 12 extra-large shrimp (about 1 pound), shells on
> $^1/_3$ cup extra virgin olive oil
> About $^2/_3$ cup kosher salt
> $^1/_4$ cup roughly chopped fresh oregano
> 2 tablespoons fresh lemon juice (about $^1/_2$ lemon)
> 1 tablespoon minced garlic
> 1 tablespoon freshly cracked black pepper
> 1 teaspoon red pepper flakes
> Pinch of ground cinnamon

1. With a sharp knife, make a small slit about $^1/_4$ inch deep down the backs of the shrimp and devein them.

2. Put the shrimp in a large bowl, pour the olive oil over the top, and toss the shrimp to coat them with the oil. Put the salt in a shallow bowl and dredge the shrimp in the salt, making sure that they get completely covered. Set the shrimp aside for a minute.

3. In a small bowl, combine all the remaining ingredients and mix well. Set aside.

4. Grill the salt-crusted shrimp over **a hot fire** for 3 to 4 minutes per side. *To check for doneness:* Cut into one of the shrimp and check to see if it is opaque all the way through. Remove the shrimp from the grill and serve at once, passing the lemon-garlic sauce for dipping.

> **For a dinner that will knock their socks off, serve these with Pepper-Crusted Filet Mignon with Blue Cheese Butter and Roasted Garlic Mash (page 133) and Fava Bean Salad with Lemon and Shaved Pecorino Romano Cheese (page 318).**

STARTERS

Fancy Ash-Roasted Potatoes

SERVES 4

For thousands of years, people around the world have been wrapping food in something and then sticking it in coals to cook. Traditionally, the wrapping has consisted of some kind of readily available and relatively strong leaf, such as a banana leaf, palm frond, or grape leaf, depending on where the cooking was being done. In the United States, of course, our traditional wrapping is aluminum foil.

I think this is an excellent cooking method. In fact, I'm so fond of it that there's a whole chapter in this book devoted to it. But as a foretaste, here's the simplest version of ash cooking, in which you just wrap a single vegetable in foil and plop it into the coals.

My friends Susan Regis and Lydia Shire over at Biba, one of my favorite Boston restaurants, are always coming up with innovative dishes with a unique stamp. This is a variation of a baked potato that I once had there—but theirs had caviar on it.

> **4 medium baking potatoes**
> **$^1/_2$ cup sour cream**
> **4 slices bacon, cooked until crisp (6 to 8 minutes in a sauté pan over**
> **medium heat), drained on paper towels, and roughly crumbled**
> **$^1/_4$ cup finely chopped fresh chives**
> **Salt and freshly cracked black pepper to taste**

1. Double-wrap each potato in heavy-duty foil and place directly in the coals of **a medium-hot fire.** Pile the coals around the potatoes and roast for about 1 hour, depending on the intensity of your particular fire—pull the potatoes out when they are soft but not mushy.

2. Remove the potatoes from the foil and slit open the tops. Spoon on the sour cream, sprinkle with the bacon, chives, and salt and pepper to taste, and serve hot.

For a hearty meal, serve this followed by Grilled Lamb Chops with Pomegranate-Eggplant Relish (page 144) and Latin-Flavored Coleslaw with Grilled Avocados (page 309).

Barbecued Oysters in Their Shells

SERVES 4 TO 8

Not only is this a fantastic oyster recipe, it's also a good way to learn how to open oysters. When the shell of an oyster is heated, it kind of pops and makes the tasty little bivalve quite easy to open. With this recipe, there are two options for taking advantage of this phenomenon. You can cook the oysters on the grill for just a couple of minutes to warm them and then pry them open, which still involves a bit of difficulty; or you can leave them on the grill until they are completely open, three to four minutes, in which case you can just pull off one of the shells from each, and you have yourself a steam-grilled oyster. Either way, the taste is incredible.

I like to make this dish when I have a couple of close friends over and we're hanging outside, so we can just throw a handful of oysters on the grill, eat 'em, and repeat the process as the sun goes down. This prep also works with clams or mussels.

> $^1/_2$ cup (1 stick) unsalted butter
>
> 1 tablespoon minced garlic
>
> 2 tablespoons fresh lemon juice (about $^1/_2$ lemon)
>
> $^1/_4$ cup Tabasco sauce
>
> $^1/_4$ cup Worcestershire sauce
>
> Salt and freshly cracked black pepper to taste
>
> 4 dozen oysters of your choice, washed well
>
> $^1/_4$ cup roughly chopped fresh parsley
>
> 2 lemons, quartered

1. Build **a medium-hot fire** in the grill.

2. In a shallow baking pan, combine the butter and garlic and place at the edge of the fire to melt the butter. When the butter has melted, add the lemon juice, Tabasco, Worcestershire, and salt and pepper to taste and stir everything together.

3. Place the oysters on the grill, directly over the fire, and cook for 2 to 3 minutes. At this point you can pull them off and open them with an oyster knife, or you can leave them on for another 2 minutes until they open themselves. Discard any that do not open.

4. Sprinkle the oysters with the parsley, douse with the butter sauce, and serve in their shells, with the lemon quarters for spritzing.

This makes a good starter in front of Herb-Crusted Pork Loin Roast with Creamy Polenta and Roasted Tomato-Garlic Sauce (page 260), with some Pickled Pineapple (page 335) to go along.

STARTERS

oyster profusion

TO THE UNINITIATED, AN oyster is an oyster is an oyster. Now, there's nothing wrong with that point of view—to my mind, any really fresh oyster is a great eating experience. But there are in fact many varieties of oysters, each with its own distinctive flavor and shape. In the United States, there are four major species: the briny-tasting Atlantic, grown along the East Coast as well as the Gulf Coast; the European, a round flat-shelled species grown in the Northwest and parts of Maine; the Pacific, a species with a very deeply scalloped shell that is grown along the Pacific Coast; and the half-dollar–sized Olympia, grown only in the Northwest.

IF YOU TASTE THESE four species side by side, the difference is nothing short of amazing. In fact, they are so dissimilar that, in the words of Mark Bittman, author of *Fish* (Macmillan, 1994), "'Oyster' is about as helpful in describing them as 'bird' is in comparing turkey, chicken, and duck." As if that weren't enough, within each of the four species there are dozens of individual varieties corresponding to the particular place the oyster was raised, like Bluepoint and Wellfleet, both of which are actually Atlantics. These names are useful (if you can remember them) because oysters get much of their individual flavor from the particular character and temperature of the water where they were grown, as well as from what they eat. But the bottom line is that as long as the oyster is truly fresh and properly shucked, chances are it's going to taste fantastic. So, as with beers, the best oyster for you is probably the one you are enjoying right now.

Grilled Mussels Johnson

SERVES 4

It wouldn't be a Schlesinger/Willoughby cookbook if it didn't contain at least one "Johnson" dish. Recipes so designated gain their name because they are either inspired by or directly stolen from our amigo Steve Johnson, famous Boston chef, close associate, snappy dresser, and all-around good guy. The second requirement for a dish in the Johnson line, and where its true ethos lies, is that the dish must be simple but unique and have outstanding flavor. This one definitely scores there— throw the mussels on the grill, toss them in the pan when they open, and then serve them up and use the bread to soak up the unreal broth. The fire-laying technique is important here. You want to stack the coals high on one side to create a really hot fire and leave the other side free of coals so anything put there will cook by radiant heat.

> 1 cup (2 sticks) unsalted butter
>
> $^1/_2$ cup white wine
>
> $^1/_2$ cup fresh lemon juice (about 2 lemons)
>
> 2 tablespoons minced garlic
>
> 2 teaspoons red pepper flakes
>
> $^3/_4$ cup roughly chopped fresh parsley
>
> 4 dozen mussels, washed well and beards removed
>
> Salt and freshly cracked black pepper to taste
>
> 4 large slices bread, about 2 inches thick

1. Build **a hot fire** on one side of your grill.

2. Find a shallow baking pan that is large enough to hold all the mussels in a single layer and sturdy enough to withstand the heat of a low fire. Put the butter, wine, lemon juice, garlic, pepper flakes, and parsley in the pan and place it on the grill over the side that has no fire. As the butter melts, stir or swirl the mixture around a few times to combine the ingredients.

3. Place the mussels on the high-heat side of the grill and cook until they open, 8 to 10 minutes, depending on the heat of the fire. As the mussels open, place them in the pan with the wine-butter mixture. (Discard any that do not open.)

4. Meanwhile, place the bread around the edge of the fire and toast lightly, about 2 minutes per side. Sprinkle the mussels with salt and pepper to taste and serve in shallow bowls, accompanied by the toast and some of the wine-butter mixture.

Try this as a first-course extravaganza with Barbecued Oysters in Their Shells (page 70), Lisa White's White Gazpacho (page 30), and Peach and Chicken Skewers with Middle Eastern Shake and Simple Raisin Sauce (page 112).

STARTERS

Red Snapper Cocktail

SERVES 4

Ceviche is the Spanish term for seafood cooked by the powerful acids of lime or lemon juice. This may seem odd, but it is actually quite common—wherever fish swim and citrus grows, you're gonna have some ceviche type of thing working. If I were sitting on the beach enjoying this dish, for example, I could be in Mexico, Peru, or anywhere in between. But, in fact, this one comes from a beach restaurant in Puerto Escondido on the southwest coast of Mexico, which also happens to be the home of the Mexican Pipeline, one of the strongest waves on the West Coast. There snappers are plentiful and, along with shrimp and other seafood, are commonly prepared in this way. You can substitute striped bass, grouper, or flounder for the snapper in this recipe.

> $1^1/_4$ cups fresh lime juice (about 10 limes)
>
> 2 tablespoons cumin seeds, toasted if you want, or
>
> 　1 tablespoon ground cumin
>
> 10 dashes Tabasco sauce
>
> 1 pound red snapper fillets, cleaned and cut into thin pieces
>
> 　about the size of a matchbook
>
> 2 small tomatoes, cored and diced medium
>
> 2 avocadoes, peeled, pitted, and diced medium
>
> 1 red onion, peeled and diced medium
>
> 1 teaspoon minced garlic
>
> $^1/_4$ cup roughly chopped fresh cilantro (or substitute parsley)
>
> $^1/_4$ cup green or black olives, pitted
>
> $^1/_4$ cup olive oil
>
> Salt and freshly cracked black pepper to taste

1. In a small bowl, combine 1 cup of the lime juice, the cumin, Tabasco, and snapper. Cover, refrigerate, and allow to sit for no less than 2 but no more than 3 hours. (As it sits, the intense acid in the lime juice will cook the snapper.)

2. While the snapper is marinating, place all remaining ingredients, including the remaining $^1/_4$ cup lime juice, in a medium bowl and mix well. Cover and refrigerate.

3. Drain the snapper and discard the marinade. Add the snapper to the tomato mixture, toss gently, and serve cold.

For a Latin-flavored lunch, serve this along with Simple Latin-Style Rice and Beans (page 300) and some Chile-Coated Grilled Summer Squash and Zucchini with Honey-Lime Dressing (page 239).

Korean-Style Grilled Chicken Wings

SERVES 4 TO 6

I'm a big fan of wings. They're versatile and lend themselves to myriad preparations, they don't take long to grill, they have a high ratio of crisp skin (my favorite) to meat, and, best of all, you get to eat with your hands. I like to grill the wings and then toss them with a sauce, in this case a hoisin-based sauce with lots of Korean flavors.

1 tablespoon vegetable oil

$^1/_2$ white onion, peeled and diced small

2 tablespoons minced garlic

3 tablespoons minced ginger

2 tablespoons minced fresh chile pepper of your choice (optional)

$^1/_2$ red bell pepper, seeded and diced small

$^1/_2$ green bell pepper, seeded and diced small

$^1/_2$ cup hoisin sauce

$^1/_4$ cup fresh lime juice (about 2 limes)

30 chicken wings

Salt and freshly cracked white pepper to taste
   (or substitute black pepper)

$^1/_4$ cup roughly chopped fresh basil

1. In a small saucepan over medium heat, heat the oil until hot but not smoking. Add the onion and sauté, stirring occasionally, until transparent, 5 to 7 minutes. Add the garlic, ginger, and the chile, if you're using it, and sauté, stirring occasionally, for 1 minute. Add the bell peppers and sauté, stirring occasionally, until soft, about 3 minutes. Stir in the hoisin sauce and lime juice, bring to a simmer, and simmer gently for 5 minutes, stirring every once in a while. Remove from the heat and set aside.

2. Separate the chicken wings into three sections each by cutting through both joints. Reserve the tips for making stock. Sprinkle the wing sections with salt and pepper to taste and grill over **a medium-hot fire,** turning occasionally, until golden brown, about 5 minutes. *To check for doneness:* Cut into one of the thicker wings and check to be sure it is opaque all the way through.

3. Remove the wings from the grill and place in a medium bowl. Add the sauce and basil, toss, and serve immediately.

**Try this in front of Simple Grilled Swordfish Skewers
(page 109) and put out some Pickled Ginger Strips (page 333) to munch on.**

STARTERS

Grilled Chicken Livers with Green Grape Sauce

SERVES 4

If you like chicken livers at all, you're really going to love them on the grill. Make sure your grill grid is hot and clean, because sticking is an issue here. Once the livers go on the hot grill, let them stay in place for a minute or two before you try to move them. This allows a sear to develop, providing a barrier between the meat and the grill that makes turning a lot easier. The green grape sauce combines the sourness of vinegar and the sweetness of grapes for that sweet-sour effect that works so well with rich meats like these little morsels.

For the Sauce

> 2 tablespoons olive oil
>
> 1 cup seedless green grapes, halved
>
> 1 tablespoon minced garlic
>
> $^1\!/_4$ cup balsamic vinegar
>
> $^1\!/_4$ cup red wine vinegar
>
> Salt and freshly cracked black pepper to taste
>
> 1 pound chicken livers
>
> 2 tablespoons olive oil
>
> Salt and freshly cracked black pepper to taste

1. Make the sauce: In a large sauté pan over high heat, heat the oil until hot but not smoking. Add the grapes and garlic and sauté, stirring, for 2 to 3 minutes, or until lightly browned. Add the vinegars and cook for 1 minute, stirring occasionally. Season to taste with salt and pepper and remove from the heat.

2. In a small bowl, combine the livers, oil, and salt and pepper to taste and mix well. Place the livers directly on the grill—or, if they're small, thread them on skewers and place on the grill—over **a hot fire** and cook until crusty brown, 2 to 3 minutes per side.

3. Remove the livers from the grill and serve with the warm grape sauce.

> This dish makes a good dinner along with Grilled Monkfish with Sherry, Raisins, and Grilled Asparagus (page 188) and Romaine and Bulgur Salad (page 319).

sour, the sophisticated taste

IN SOME WAYS, SOUR is the simplest of the four basic tastes. Unlike sweet, salt, and bitter, each of which can be evoked by a number of different sense stimuli, the sour taste always comes from an acid.

IN OTHER WAYS, HOW-EVER, sourness is very complicated. In addition to the acids in vinegars, which are created by bacterial action, there are many different organic acids that occur naturally in fruits and vegetables. Lemons and limes contain citric acid, for example, while apples derive their sourness from malic acid, and tamarind gets its tartness from tartaric acid. The variety of sour stimulants, combined with differing concentrations and the way in which the acids combine with other flavor elements, creates a whole range of sour tonalities.

OUR ABILITY TO DETECT sourness in foods is also highly refined, as well as slightly mysterious. While pH is normally used as a measure of acidity, it seems an inadequate indicator when taste buds meet up with organic acids. Going strictly by pH, for example, apples should taste more sour than rhubarb. Obviously this is not the case for most of us. Scientists are still trying to figure this one out, but they generally accept that the receptors in the mouth are simply the more sophisticated detectors of the qualities of acid that cause sourness.

Grilled Buffalo Chicken Hearts

SERVES 4

I know there aren't too many of you out there who are going to try this, but then there are the few, the curious, the brave who will try anything once. Chicken hearts may seem offbeat, but actually they are available at every market, they are cheap, and in many other cultures when you talk about a mixed grill, you are including chicken hearts. A bit like liver, they have the advantage of being small enough to be crisp and tender at the same time.

Now, I'm pretty sure they don't serve chicken hearts at the Anchor Bar in Buffalo, New York, where buffalo chicken wings originated, and even if they did, they probably wouldn't prepare them this way. The lime, garlic, and Tabasco combo is actually closer to the classic South American tradition of grilled and roasted meats than to anything from Upstate New York. But when ingredients are perceived as lowly, it is sometimes necessary to use a little "brand recognition" to sell them. In defense, I can only say, like that classic line from a television ad, "Try them, you'll like them."

1 pound chicken hearts

2 tablespoons olive oil

Salt and freshly cracked black pepper to taste

3 tablespoons fresh lime juice (about 1¹/₂ limes)

3 tablespoons extra virgin olive oil

2 teaspoons Tabasco sauce

2 tablespoons roughly chopped fresh thyme, basil, or oregano

1 teaspoon minced garlic

1. In a small bowl, combine the chicken hearts, olive oil, and salt and pepper to taste and mix well. Thread the hearts on skewers and grill over **a hot fire** until crisp for 4 to 6 minutes, rolling around often.

2. Meanwhile, combine the remaining ingredients in a medium bowl and mix well.

3. Remove the hearts from the skewers and place in the bowl. Mix well, season to taste with salt and pepper, and serve.

These make an interesting dinner when served along with Chickpea Salad with Horseradish-Yogurt Dressing (page 317) and Bridget's Alternative Cold Tuna Plate (page 182).

Grilled Goose Liver with Grapes, Mango, and Port

SERVES 6 TO 8

Grilling might seem like an unusual technique to use on subtly flavored and costly goose liver, but in both France and Israel, two of the largest producers of this delicacy, grilled foie gras is almost commonplace. And it makes sense: The quick high heat of grilling helps keep the foie gras tender and juicy while giving it a pleasant seared flavor. Half-inch-thick medallions of liver work best for this technique. Be prepared to move quickly here, as there will probably be some flare-ups from drips. The sweet-sour sauce is a perfect complement for the ultra-rich liver. In fact, mango and goose liver are a new combination that lots of chefs are using these days, and with the addition of green grapes, it really works.

$^{1}/_{2}$ cup port
$^{1}/_{2}$ cup balsamic vinegar
$^{1}/_{2}$ cup seedless green grapes, halved
$^{1}/_{2}$ cup diced peeled mango (about $^{1}/_{2}$ medium mango)
3 tablespoons roughly chopped fresh thyme, sage, oregano, or parsley
Salt and freshly cracked black pepper to taste
6 to 8 thick slices crusty bread
1 12- to 14-ounce lobe of foie gras, sliced into medallions
    about $^{1}/_{2}$ inch thick
2 tablespoons olive oil

1. In a small saucepan, bring the port to a boil over medium-high heat and allow it to boil until it has been reduced by about half, about 5 minutes. Lower the heat to medium, add the vinegar, and cook for another 5 minutes. Add the grapes and mango and cook, stirring occasionally, for 2 more minutes. Remove from the heat, stir in the herbs, and season to taste with salt and pepper. Set aside.

2. Lightly toast the bread slices over **a medium-hot fire** until just browned, then set aside.

3. Rub the foie gras with the oil, sprinkle with salt and pepper to taste, and grill over **the medium-hot fire** until it has a nice, light sear, 1 to 2 minutes per side. *To check for doneness:* Cut into one of the medallions; it should be pinkish and juicy in the center. Remove the liver from the fire and serve it with the warm fruit relish and the slices of toasted bread.

> **This is a very rich starter, so I might serve it with something like Basil-Garlic Chicken Breasts with Grilled Balsamic Peaches (page 200) and Grilled Potatoes with Yogurt-Parsley Sauce (page 283).**

mango peppers

I ALWAYS WONDERED WHY my grandmother and her gardening friends referred to the bell peppers that they grew in their gardens as mangoes. I saw very little resemblance between those mundane peppers and the luscious tropical fruits properly called by that name, and assumed it was just one of those bizarre turns of phrase I would never figure out. But not long ago, I happened across an explanation in a column written for the *Los Angeles Times* by Charles Perry, an entertaining writer who speaks many languages and has a boundless skill for tracing food history.

PERRY EXPLAINED THAT IN the eighteenth century, mangoes became extremely popular in England. Since ripe mangoes had no chance of making it to London from India in those days of long sea journeys, pickled mangoes became all the rage. But even they were hideously expensive and could only be afforded by the rich. Following the culinary fashion, less-well-off folks began pickling cheaper fruits and vegetables with the same strong spices used for mangoes, calling it "mangoing." Cookbooks soon appeared with recipes for "mangoes" made from, among other things, bell peppers, a name that somehow stuck. So it turns out that my grandmother, bending over her prized pepper plants in her Midwestern garden, was paying unwitting homage to the British raj and the effects it had on European tastes.

Raw Beef with Parsley, Capers, and Hard Cheese

SERVES 4

I love raw beef, whether it's chopped as in steak tartare, or sliced thin for carpaccio. I think the flavor is hard to beat. This is a combination of the two styles that I experienced for the first time at Rialto restaurant in Cambridge, Massachusetts. Chef Jody Adams, my friend and colleague, does a lot with Mediterranean flavors, and I thought her idea of using bite-sized pieces of beef instead of thin slices was a creative way to get that raw meat fix. As with any raw beef dish, be sure that you use only the freshest meat.

> 1 pound very lean sirloin, cut into pieces about the size of grapes
> 1 bunch flat-leaf parsley, cleaned and stemmed
> $1/2$ red onion, peeled and diced small
> $1/3$ cup extra virgin olive oil
> Juice of 1 lemon
> Salt and freshly cracked black pepper to taste
> $1/4$ pound Parmesan cheese

continued

1. In a medium bowl, combine all of the ingredients except the cheese and toss well. Place on a platter, cover, and refrigerate until you are ready to serve—this dish is best when chilled, so you probably want to leave it in the fridge for at least 30 minutes.

2. Just before you are ready to serve, use a vegetable peeler to shave the Parmesan over the top of the mixture.

This goes well with Chicken Hobo Pack with Garlic, Lemon, and Herbs (page 224) and Green Apple and Celery Root Salad with Bacon-Buttermilk Dressing (page 306). For dessert, I might try Gingered Mango Mousse (page 363).

Grilled Lamb and Red Onion in Grape Leaves

SERVES 4

Okay, I'm not going to claim that this recipe is quick and easy—but I will say that it's worth the effort. The combination of lamb, stuffed grape leaves, and a sauce heavily flavored with garlic is a specialty of the Eastern Mediterranean. Make sure you chop the lamb and onions quite small after grilling them, so that when you fold the mixture up in the grape leaves, they will hold together.

For the Sauce

1 large white onion, peeled and diced small

$^1/_4$ cup minced garlic

$^1/_4$ cup unsalted butter

1 cup apple cider

1 cup white wine

Salt and freshly cracked black pepper to taste

2 cups chicken stock

1 tablespoon fresh thyme leaves

2 cups seedless green grapes, halved

1 pound lean lamb, cut into 1-inch cubes

1 large red onion, peeled and cut into rings about $^1/_2$ inch thick

2 tablespoons olive oil

1 tablespoon salt

1 tablespoon freshly cracked black pepper

2 tablespoons roughly chopped fresh mint

2 tablespoons roughly chopped fresh parsley

2 tablespoon minced garlic

1 teaspoon ground cinnamon

1 teaspoon ground cumin

1 teaspoon ground allspice

1 8-ounce jar grape leaves

1. Make the sauce: In a medium saucepan, combine the onion, garlic, and but-ter and cook over very low heat, stirring occasionally, until the onion is very soft and mushy but not brown, 30 to 45 minutes. Add the apple cider and white wine, turn the heat to high, and bring to a boil. Immediately reduce the heat to low and simmer for about 20 minutes, stirring every once in a while. Add the stock and thyme and continue to simmer for another 20 minutes.

2. Pour the mixture into a food processor or blender and puree until very smooth. Return to the saucepan over high heat, add the grapes, and bring just to a boil. Remove from the heat, season to taste with salt and pepper, and set aside.

3. Place the lamb chunks and onion rings in a medium bowl. Add the olive oil, salt, and pepper and toss to coat. Thread the lamb onto skewers.

4. Grill the lamb skewers and the onion rings over **a medium-hot fire** until the lamb is medium-rare and the onions are brown and soft, 2 to 3 minutes per side for the onions and 3 to 4 minutes per side for the lamb. *To check the lamb for doneness:* Cut into one of the chunks to see if it is done to your liking. Remove the onions and lamb from the grill and allow to cool to room temperature.

5. In a large bowl, combine the mint, parsley, garlic, cinnamon, cumin, and all-spice. Chop the lamb and red onions into small pieces and add to the bowl. Season to taste with salt and pepper and toss well.

6. Drain and rinse the grape leaves, setting aside any torn or small leaves. Blot dry and trim off stems, then place shiny side down on a work surface. Place about 1 tablespoon of the lamb mixture in the center of each leaf. Fold the sides in, the bottom up over the filling, and roll up firmly. Set the filled leaves aside seam side down as you finish them.

7. Grill the grape leaves over **a medium fire** until hot all the way through, 3 to 4 minutes on each side. Remove from the grill and serve with the grape sauce. These leaves and sauce will keep, covered and refrigerated, for a couple of days.

This is a good appetizer in front of Grilled Shrimp and Bacon Skewers with Pickled Onion and Avocado Salad (page 104) and Romaine and Bulgur Salad (page 319).

backyard hunting and gathering

USING INGREDIENTS THAT YOU have gathered yourself adds a special dimension of pleasure to the process of cooking—and you don't have to live on a farm to do so. The person who most often reminds me of this is my friend Ihsan Gurdal. Raised in Istanbul, Ihsan spent many pleasurable hours of his youth gathering and processing food on his grandfathers' farm just outside the city. Today, he retains his keen boyhood awareness of the many foods that most of us pass by every day without even noticing. When he came to help me weed my garden, Ihsan ended up making a wonderful salad out of the purslane that I was blithely tossing into the garbage. Walking past a walnut tree a few days later, he paused to pick several handfuls of the green nuts, then spent an hour or so laboriously peeling off the green husks and shells and extracting the delectable white inner meat, which he soaked in water. The bowl of walnut meat we ate that night before dinner was small, but its delicate flavor and crunchy-chewy texture were fantastic. Ihsan also gathers grape leaves whenever he comes across them in the proper conditions. He uses them to wrap some of the cheese he ages for Formaggio Kitchen, the store he and his wife, Valerie, own in Cambridge, Massachusetts. If you find some relatively young leaves that have not been polluted by pesticides, I recommend you use them in this recipe. Just blanch the leaves in boiling salted water for about ninety seconds, plunge them into a cold-water bath, and then follow the directions as if you were using store-bought leaves. The satisfaction you'll get from having gathered part of your meal is guaranteed to make everything taste better.

**Corn Bread-Stuffed
Barbecue Game Hens with
Bourbon-Shallot Sauce,**
page 272

Bridget's Couscous Salad for a Crowd, page 320,
and **Grilled Asparagus,** page 279

**Spice-Crusted Pork Tenderloins with
Banana-Date Chutney,** page 150

**Chile-Ginger Grilled Tuna with
Korean-Style Salad,** page 180

**Linguine with Smoky Lobster, Grilled Corn, and
Roasted Pepper—Garlic Sauce,** page 88

Grilled Shrimp and Bacon Skewers, page 104

Chicken and vegetables on the grill

Chinese-Style Baby Back Ribs with Ginger-Scallion Barbecue Sauce, page 252

Grilled Delmonico Steak Adobo with Charred Spring Onions and Sweet Corn Relish, page 131

Left: **Grilled Spicy
New Potato Salad,** page 313

Below Left: **Sweet-Potato Steak Fries
with Your Own Catsup,** page 284

Below Right: **Chile-Coated Grilled
Summer Squash and Zucchini with
Honey-Lime Dressing,** page 239

**Hobo Pack of Winter Vegetables
with Many Fresh Herbs,** page 221

**Grilled Double-Thick Pork Chops
with Grilled Peaches and Molasses-Rum
Barbecue Sauce,** page 148

Above Left: **Grilled Pineapple,** page 358

Above Right: **Clove-Pickled Peaches,** page 332

Left: **Grilled Bread Salad with Grilled Figs,** page 53

Doc's Chilled Moroccan Mint Tea, page 348

Right, clockwise from top left:
Blue-Green Mangoritas, page 350
Squeezed limes
Lemonade
Rum and Cokes *Estilo Hombre de Negocios,* page 353

**Grilled Swordfish
with Artichokes, Tomatoes,
and Olives,** page 170

Grilled Sweetbreads with Herb-Garlic Crumbs

SERVES 4

I've said it before and I'll say it again, sweetbreads are fantastic on the grill. Even if you find the very idea of sweetbreads off-putting, try them after they've spent some time over the fire and you'll be a convert. I feel so strongly about this that I have a money-back guarantee on all the grilled sweetbread dishes I serve at my restaurants. So far, out of millions of orders (well, okay, maybe a thousand), I've had only three folks take me up on it.

What separates this from other sweetbread dishes is that classically sweetbreads are poached whole, then sliced and sautéed. Instead of doing this, I like to separate the "nuggets" and grill them, because this helps minimize the mealy consistency and provides a contrast in the form of a crispy crust and a creamy, tender interior. It might be hard to find fresh sweetbreads, but they are worth looking for, so try your local high-quality butcher.

For the Bread Crumbs
    1/2 cup toasted bread crumbs
    1 teaspoon minced garlic
    1/4 cup chopped fresh herbs: any one or a combination of parsley, sage, rosemary, thyme, basil, or oregano
    Salt and freshly cracked black pepper to taste

    1 pound very fresh sweetbreads
    Salt and freshly cracked black pepper to taste
    1/4 cup extra virgin olive oil

1. Make the bread crumbs: Combine all the ingredients in a large bowl (you will need the room later when rolling the sweetbreads), mix well, and set aside.

2. Rinse the sweetbreads well, place them in a large saucepan with water to cover, and bring to a boil over high heat. Reduce the heat to low and simmer for 12 to 15 minutes, or until the sweetbreads are firm to the touch (they should feel like the base of your thumb when you press your finger against it). Drain and allow to cool.

3. When the sweetbreads are cool, clean them by gently prying the pieces from the whole and washing well. (They should separate easily into uniform bite-sized white nuggets.) Thread the sweetbreads on skewers, season them with salt and pepper to taste, and grill over **a medium-hot fire** until golden brown, 3 to 4 minutes per side. *To check for doneness:* Cut into one of the nuggets; it should be crisp on the outside and hot all the way through.

4. Remove the sweetbreads from the fire, immediately brush them lightly with the olive oil, and roll them in the reserved crumbs. Then put them back on the fire for just 30 seconds to crisp them up. Serve at once.

This goes well with Grilled Trout in a Smoked Salmon Suit (page 176) and Hobo Pack Italiano (page 223).

what are sweetbreads, anyway?

DON'T BE CONFUSED, AS I was in my youth—sweetbreads are meat, not pastry. In fact, they are one of those inner parts of the animal often shunned in modern American cooking, but actually very rewarding to cook and eat. To be specific, sweetbreads are the thymus glands of young calves or lambs. The sweetbreads you get in the store are almost exclusively from veal. There is no reason to be squeamish about them; it is no more bizarre to eat this piece of the calf than to eat sausages, which are basically ground meat stuffed into a pig intestine. The only down side of sweetbreads is that they are very perishable, so you should be sure to cook them the day you buy them.

Pasta and grilled food have four things in common: They're both quick, easy, healthful, and very tasty. So to me it makes perfect sense to put them together. Plus, the combination of the smoky, slightly charred taste of grilled food and the smooth, satisfying flavor of pasta is a real winner.

FROM THE PASTA BOWL

grilled stuff with pasta

All the recipes in this chapter use what I like to call the "bowl technique." Instead of being cooked or heated together, each of the ingredients is cooked separately, then they're all combined in a big bowl, tossed, and rushed right to the table. That way, each ingredient maintains as much of its individual character and flavor as possible, so the final dish has the range of contrasting flavors and textures that I think makes food exciting. For example, when you make Linguine with Smoky Lobster, Grilled Corn, and Roasted Pepper–Garlic Sauce, you will end up tasting each element distinctly—the rich lobster, the fresh corn, and the smoky sauce—instead of a blend of all of their flavors.

All the recipes here are simple to make, but since you will be grilling outside and boiling the pasta inside, you need to pay a little attention to the cooking sequence. Of course, the two things you should do first for every recipe are to light the fire so it can burn down to the proper coals and then put the pasta water on to boil. After that, I find it works best to do any non–grill cooking first, then the grilling, and finally the pasta. Also, the inside/outside nature of the cooking means that for some recipes, like the Macaroni with Grilled Squid, Eggplant, and Peppers, or the Shells with Grilled Clams, Mussels, and Bacon-Cooked Greens, it's easier if you can enlist one of your guests to give you a hand. That way, one of you can handle the stove-top cooking while the other does the grilling. In my experience, people really enjoy helping you cook, so it's no imposition.

On the other hand, you might be like me and enjoy doing the whole thing yourself. This is, in fact, the way I like to cook, literally running back and forth from the kitchen to the grill. I often do it even when it's not strictly necessary, because it is more fun for me, and my guests seem to find it entertaining.

As always, you should feel free to substitute in these recipes. We have designated a particular type of pasta for each dish, but by all means go ahead and use whatever type seems right to you—or whatever you happen to have around the house.

Linguine with Grilled Shrimp and Black Olives

Linguine with Smoky Lobster, Grilled Corn, and Roasted Pepper–Garlic Sauce

Vermicelli with Grilled Shrimp and Spinach in Saffron Broth

Macaroni with Grilled Squid, Eggplant, and Peppers

Perciatelli and Grilled Octopus with Fennel and Lemon

Penne with Grilled Tuna and Crisp-Fried Capers

Shells with Grilled Clams, Mussels, and Bacon-Cooked Greens

Spaghetti with Grilled Prosciutto and Figs

Grilled Sausage and Corn over Fettuccine with Tomatoes and Basil

Lamb Shish Kebobs over Fettuccine

Linguine with Grilled Shrimp and Black Olives

SERVES 4 AS ENTRÉE, 6 TO 8 AS APPETIZER

This simple combination of Mediterranean flavors will do the trick no matter how often you serve it. It's the kind of thing you can whip up on a few minute's notice when company stops by, or if you just feel like an easy but satisfying lunch or light dinner. If you don't have any shrimp in the house and don't feel like making a trip to the market, you can leave them out and still have an outstanding dish.

24 medium shrimp (about 1½ pounds), peeled and deveined

Salt and freshly cracked black pepper to taste

12 ounces linguine or other dried pasta of your choice

6 tablespoons extra virgin olive oil

4 cloves garlic, sliced lengthwise as thin as possible

5 vine-ripened tomatoes, cored and roughly chopped

¾ cup brine-cured black olives, pitted and roughly chopped

¾ cup chopped fresh basil

½ cup freshly grated hard Italian cheese, such as Parmesan or Asiago

1. Sprinkle the shrimp generously with salt and pepper and thread them onto skewers. Grill over **a medium-hot fire** for 3 to 4 minutes per side. *To check for doneness:* Cut into one of the shrimp and check to be sure it is opaque all the way through. Remove from grill, take off the skewers, and chop each shrimp into 3 or 4 pieces. Set aside.

2. In a large pot, bring about 4 quarts of salted water to a rapid boil over high heat. Add the pasta, return to the boil, and cook until just tender but not mushy, 8 to 10 minutes. Drain and place in a large bowl.

3. While the pasta is cooking, heat the olive oil in a small sauté pan over medium heat until hot but not smoking. Add the garlic and cook, stirring frequently, until it just starts to brown, 2 to 3 minutes. Remove from the heat.

4. Pour the oil and garlic over the pasta, add the tomatoes, olives, the reserved shrimp, and the basil, and toss together. Adjust the seasoning, top with the grated cheese, and serve.

For a Mediterranean-flavored lunch or light dinner, combine this with Grilled and Chilled Mediterranean-Style Gazpacho (page 27).

Linguine with Smoky Lobster, Grilled Corn, and Roasted Pepper–Garlic Sauce

This recipe is a good vehicle to make lobster go a long way, keeping the tab down but still enjoying the rich, sweet taste.

My colleague Jasper White, the dean of Boston chefs, used to serve grilled lobster at his restaurant. Jasper's thing is local East Coast seafood, and his preparations always allow the subtle nature of the seafood to sparkle through. Here I borrow a page from his book and grill the lobster, which is a great way to prepare it. The texture and build of this costly crustacean make it easy to grill, and the smoky char complements the rich meat very well.

In this dish I prepare the ingredients separately and toss everything together in a bowl like a salad. That way, the corn, lobster, sauce, and lemon all retain their individual flavors instead of blending together through cooking. So toss them together at the end, serve it right up, and it's time to eat.

Monkfish is a good substitute for lobster in this dish. And, as good as this dish is hot, try it the next day—it's almost better.

For the Sauce

> 4 roasted red peppers (see page 54 for homemade, or use jarred, rinsed)
>
> 2 heads roasted garlic, pulp squeezed out (see page 89)
>
> $^1/_2$ cup chicken stock
>
> Salt and freshly cracked black pepper to taste

> 2 lobsters, each about 2$^1/_2$ pounds
>
> Salt and freshly cracked black pepper to taste
>
> 3 ears corn, husked, desilked, blanched in boiling salted
>   water for 2 minutes, and drained
>
> 1 tablespoon olive oil
>
> 12 ounces linguine or other dried pasta of your choice
>
> $^1/_2$ cup roughly chopped fresh parsley
>
> $^1/_4$ cup fresh lemon juice (about 1 lemon)

1. Make the sauce: In a food processor or blender, combine the roasted peppers and garlic and puree until smooth. Place in a small saucepan, add the chicken stock and salt and pepper to taste, and bring to a boil over high heat. Reduce the heat to low and simmer for 10 minutes. Remove from the heat, cover to keep warm, and set aside.

2. Split the lobsters in half lengthwise. To do this, place each lobster on its back and insert the point of a large French knife into the head just below the eyes, which should kill it instantly. Bring the knife down through the tail, then cut the other way, up to the head, making sure to cut just through the meat, leaving the shell connected. Lay the lobster open; the two halves should still be slightly attached. Pull off the claws and legs and bash them lightly with the knife handle. You just want to fracture the shell a bit here.

3. Place the lobster claws and legs on the grill over **a medium fire,** cover them with a pie pan, and cook for 5 to 7 minutes, turning once. *To check for doneness:* Peek inside one of the claws to make sure the meat is opaque all the way through.

4. Meanwhile, sprinkle the lobster bodies with salt and pepper to taste and place them flesh side down on the grill over **the medium fire.** Cook for 8 to 10 minutes. (You don't need to turn these guys.) *To check for doneness:* Remove the tail from the shell of one of the lobsters. The exposed meat should be completely opaque.

5. While you are grilling the lobsters, rub the ears of corn lightly with the olive oil, place on the grill and cook them, rolling them around, just until browned, 3 to 4 minutes. When the ears are done, remove them from the grill, cut the kernels off the cobs, and set aside.

6. In a large pot over high heat, bring 4 quarts of salted water to a rapid boil. Add the pasta, bring the water back to a boil, and cook for 8 to 10 minutes, or until tender but not mushy. Drain the pasta well, place it in a large bowl, and add the parsley, lemon juice, the reserved corn, and salt and pepper to taste. Toss well.

7. Remove the lobsters from their shells. (A nutcracker works best for the claws and legs, but if you don't have one, a hammer will do.) Chop the lobster meat roughly, add it to the pasta along with the warm sauce, toss well, and serve.

Combine this with Grilled Asparagus with Garlic Mayonnaise or Simple Vinaigrette (page 279) and you've got an excellent light dinner or substantial lunch.

roasted garlic

RUB A WHOLE HEAD of garlic a bit in your hands to remove some of the papery outer peel. Slice the top ¼ inch off the garlic, exposing the tips of the individual cloves, and place the whole head in the middle of a foot-long sheet of aluminum foil. Pour a couple of tablespoons of olive oil over the top, then wrap up tightly. Place in a 300°F oven and roast for about 1 hour, or until the individual garlic cloves are soft to the touch. To extract the garlic pulp from the roasted head, just squeeze the cloves at the base and the rich, mellow meat will shoot right out. (Or see page 222 for roasting garlic in the ashes.)

Vermicelli with Grilled Shrimp and Spinach in Saffron Broth

SERVES 4 AS ENTRÉE, 6 TO 8 AS APPETIZER

With the orange saffron broth, the green spinach, and the bright pink shrimp, this is a colorful as well as tasty dish. The shrimp cook pretty quickly on the grill, but if you're fast you can fire the shrimp outside, come inside and drop the pasta, get outside to flip and finish the shrimp, then make it back inside in time to drain the pasta. If you're feeling slow, just grill the shrimp and set it aside while the pasta cooks.

If you're not too concerned about fat consumption—or this is your day to splurge—you can enrich this dish by stirring half a stick of butter, cut into small pieces, into the saffron broth right after the spinach. And make sure you have some crusty bread on hand to soak up th-e broth—it's terrific.

> 1 tablespoon vegetable oil
>
> 1 yellow onion, peeled and diced medium
>
> 2 tablespoons minced garlic
>
> 1 cup white wine
>
> 4 saffron threads
>
> 2 tablespoons red pepper flakes
>
> 2 cups spinach—washed, dried, and torn into medium pieces
>
> 24 medium shrimp ($1^1/_4$ to $1^1/_2$ pounds), peeled and deveined
>
> 3 tablespoons olive oil
>
> Salt and freshly cracked black pepper to taste
>
> 12 ounces vermicelli or other dried pasta of your choice
>
> 2 tablespoons fresh lemon juice (about $^1/_2$ lemon)
>
> $^1/_4$ cup extra virgin olive oil

1. In a small saucepan over medium heat, heat the vegetable oil until hot but not smoking. Add the onion and sauté, stirring occasionally, until transparent, 5 to 7 minutes. Add the garlic and cook, stirring occasionally, for 1 minute. Add the wine, saffron, and pepper flakes, reduce the heat to low, and simmer for 10 minutes. Add the spinach, stir, and remove from the heat.

2. In a medium bowl, combine the shrimp, olive oil, and salt and pepper to taste and toss to coat. Thread the shrimp onto skewers and grill over **a medium-hot fire** for 3 to 4 minutes per side. *To check for doneness:* Cut into one of the shrimp; it should be opaque all the way through. Remove from the grill and set aside.

3. Meanwhile, bring 4 quarts of salted water to a boil in a large pot over high heat. Drop in the pasta, bring the water back to a boil, and cook for 5 to 7 minutes, or until the pasta is tender but not mushy. Drain, place in a large bowl, and toss with the lemon juice and extra virgin olive oil.

4. Add the spinach and broth to the pasta. Slide the shrimp off the skewers onto the pasta and toss well. Season to taste with salt and pepper and serve.

I might serve this as an appetizer for a bunch of friends, then follow it up with either Smoky Ratatouille for a Crowd (page 288) or Grilled Eggplant and Bread Salad for a Crowd (page 311).

Macaroni with Grilled Squid, Eggplant, and Peppers

SERVES 4 AS ENTRÉE

As with all the pasta dishes in this book, the various elements are cooked separately and then tossed together at the end so they maintain as much of their individual flavors as possible. So this is one of those inside/outside recipes for which having two people involved makes the process a lot easier. That way one person can handle the stove-top cooking while the other does the grill thing. If you're cooking by yourself, you have to kind of scheme it out so that nothing sits around too long before the other stuff gets done. I would cook the eggplant mixture first, then drop the pasta, then go fire the squid.

When buying squid for grilling, the best bet is to get ones that are at least five inches long, since that makes them easier to deal with. Also, try to dry your squid thoroughly before you put it on the grill, and make sure that the fire is H-O-T. Both of these tricks will help cook the squid as quickly as possible so it doesn't toughen up.

3 tablespoons olive oil

1 medium eggplant, diced small

1 small red onion, peeled, halved, and thinly sliced

$^1/_2$ green bell pepper, seeded and thinly sliced

$^1/_2$ red bell pepper, seeded and thinly sliced

2 tablespoons minced garlic

1 tablespoon red pepper flakes

$1^1/_2$ pounds cleaned squid (bodies and tentacles separated)

2 tablespoons vegetable oil

Salt and freshly cracked black pepper to taste

12 ounces macaroni or other dried pasta of your choice

2 tablespoons fresh lemon juice (about $^1/_2$ lemon)

$^1/_4$ cup extra virgin olive oil

$^1/_2$ cup roughly chopped mixed herbs: any combination of parsley, sage, rosemary, thyme, and/or basil

continued

1. In a large sauté pan, heat the olive oil over high heat until hot but not smoking. Add the eggplant and sauté, stirring, until well browned, about 4 minutes. Add the onion and bell peppers, reduce the heat to medium-high, and cook, stirring frequently, until the onions are softened, about 4 minutes. Add the garlic and red pepper flakes and cook, stirring occasionally, for 1 minute. Remove from the heat and set aside.

2. Dry the squid well, then rub it lightly with the vegetable oil and sprinkle it with salt and pepper to taste. Place the squid bodies on the grill over **a hot fire,** cover them with a clean brick or other heavy large object, and grill for 2 minutes per side. Remove the brick and use your tongs to roll the bodies around on the grill for another 30 seconds to crisp them up, then remove them from the grill. Place the tentacles on the grill and cook for about 2 minutes, or until they are brown and crispy, rolling them around so they cook evenly. Remove from the grill. Cut the bodies into rings and set them aside along with the tentacles.

3. While the squid is cooking, in a large pot, bring 4 quarts of salted water to a rolling boil over high heat. Throw in the pasta, bring the water back to a boil, and cook for 7 to 10 minutes, or until the pasta is tender but not mushy. Drain and place in a large bowl.

4. Add the reserved eggplant mixture and the squid to the pasta. Add the lemon juice, olive oil, herbs, and salt and pepper to taste, toss well, and serve at once.

This goes well with **Fava Bean Salad with Lemon and Shaved Pecorino Romano Cheese (page 318) for a hearty lunch or light dinner.**

proselytizing for squid

DESPITE RECENT GAINS IN popularity, squid is still vastly underappreciated in most of the United States. It's actually an excellent ingredient. Among its virtues are the fact that it is cheap, it is in no danger of being overfished, it is easy to cook, and it has a mild but distinctive flavor that is amenable to all kinds of other complementary flavors.

So WHY ISN'T THIS versatile creature more popular here? Partially, I suspect, because some folks incorrectly associate squid with creepy movies in which giant versions of its fellow cephalopod, the octopus, drag unsuspecting sailors overboard with their lashing tentacles. On a more practical level, squid may also still suffer from the undisputed fact that it is difficult to clean. But here is where yet another

of its many virtues comes into play—it freezes well, and frozen squid is precleaned. So unless you like the satisfaction of preparing your own food from start to finish, you might prefer to buy your squid frozen, which also makes it easier to find, as it's available in many supermarkets. (Just be sure you remember to defrost it in the refrigerator.) Once you try it, you will quickly become a squid convert.

Perciatelli and Grilled Octopus with Fennel and Lemon

SERVES 4 AS ENTRÉE

The octopus, perhaps one of the oddest creatures on this planet, would not make Americans' top ten favorite seafood list. In Asia and throughout the Mediterranean, however, this eight-legged cephalopod is very popular, with the Spanish being perhaps the most devoted octopus lovers.

In our country, the octopus is perhaps as famous for the bizarre methods people have used to tenderize it—my personal favorite being the recommendation that you whack it on rocks for ten to fifteen minutes—as for its flavor. But simple parboiling and proper cooking are really all that are required. Octopus is unsurpassed for surprising dinner guests, because like Sam I Am in the Dr. Seuss story *Green Eggs and Ham,* all folks have to do is try it and they'll be singing the praises of octopus as if they grew up eating it.

The market size for these creatures is usually two to four pounds with tentacles about two feet long. Because it's not always easy to find fresh octopus (try your local Chinatown), you might have more luck finding it frozen. If you can't find it, you can substitute grilled shrimp in this recipe, or even leave the seafood out entirely. You can also substitute any dried pasta for the perciatelli (also called bucatini), which is like thick spaghetti with a hole in the center.

1 cup white vinegar

1^1/$_2$ pounds octopus, cleaned

1 tablespoon olive oil

^{1}/$_4$ cup thinly sliced fennel

2 tablespoons minced garlic

3 tablespoons vegetable oil

Salt and freshly cracked black pepper to taste

12 ounces perciatelli or other dried pasta of your choice

3 tablespoons extra virgin olive oil

^{1}/$_2$ cup roughly chopped fresh basil leaves

2 tablespoons fresh lemon juice (about ^{1}/$_2$ lemon)

^{1}/$_4$ cup roasted red peppers (see page 54 for homemade, or use jarred, rinsed)

1. Bring 1 quart salted water to a boil in a medium saucepan, add the vinegar and reduce heat to low. Add the octopus and simmer for 30 minutes, then drain. Separate the tentacles from the body and divide the tentacles into two sections and cut the body into ^{1}/$_2$-inch-wide strips.

continued

2. Meanwhile, in a small sauté pan over medium heat, heat the olive oil until hot but not smoking. Add the fennel and sauté, stirring, for about 3 minutes to soften. Add the garlic and cook, stirring occasionally, for 1 minute. Remove from the heat and set aside.

3. Lightly sprinkle the octopus with the vegetable oil and salt and pepper to taste and grill over **a hot fire** for 7 to 10 minutes, turning several times. *To check for doneness:* Cut into the largest piece of octopus and peek inside; it should be opaque throughout. Remove from the grill and, as soon as it is cool enough to handle, slice into bite-sized pieces.

4. In a medium pot, bring 4 quarts of salted water to a rolling boil over high heat. Drop the pasta into the water, bring it back to a boil, and cook for 8 to 10 minutes, or until the pasta is tender but not mushy. Drain and place in a large bowl.

5. Add the extra virgin olive oil, basil, lemon juice, red peppers, and the reserved fennel and octopus to the pasta. Toss well, season to taste with salt and pepper, and serve. (This could also be served as a chilled salad.)

Try this with Arugula with Pancetta, Grilled Asparagus, and White Beans (page 50) for a flavorful dinner or a big lunch.

five good uses for extra roasted red peppers

PUT THEM IN A jar, add some sliced garlic, cover with olive oil, and stick in the refrigerator to use on salads or antipastos.

CHOP UP FINE ALONG with some fresh herbs, add some balsamic vinegar, and use as a quick sauce for grilled meats.

PUREE, THEN MIX WITH butter and lemon juice to make roasted red pepper butter for grilled fish.

PUREE, THEN MIX WITH extra virgin olive oil and use as a quick pasta sauce.

THE #1 USE FOR extra roasted red peppers: Get hold of our book *Lettuce in Your Kitchen* (Morrow, 1996) and make some of the salad dressings with roasted red peppers that can also double as sauces for grilled or steamed vegetables!

Penne with Grilled Tuna and Crisp-Fried Capers

SERVES 4 AS ENTRÉE, 8 AS APPETIZER

Here grilled tuna joins with the caper-lemon-garlic-parsley quartet that is so famous all around the Mediterranean. A neat trick is to sauté the capers in butter, which crisps them up nicely. Then save the leftover caper-flavored butter to use on vegetables; I like it as a dip for steamed artichokes. If you're feeling less ambitious, skip the first step below and add the capers along with the tuna and other ingredients in the last step.

^{1}/$_3$ cup capers

^{1}/$_2$ cup (1 stick) unsalted butter

1^1/$_2$ pounds tuna, cut into 1-inch chunks (14 to 16 chunks)

2 tablespoons vegetable oil

Salt and freshly cracked black pepper to taste

12 ounces penne or other dried pasta of your choice

^{1}/$_2$ cup olive oil

^{1}/$_4$ cup fresh lemon juice (about 1 lemon)

2 tablespoons minced garlic

^{1}/$_2$ cup roughly chopped fresh parsley

1. In a small saucepan over medium heat, combine the capers and butter and bring to a simmer—the pan should be big enough so the capers can move around freely in the butter in order for them to fry evenly, which will take 10 to 12 minutes. When they are finished, the capers should be golden brown and very crispy. Drain off the remaining butter (save it to drizzle over grilled vegetables) and place the capers on a paper towel to drain.

2. While the capers are cooking, thread the tuna chunks on skewers, rub lightly with the vegetable oil, and sprinkle with salt and pepper to taste. Place the skewers on the grill over **a medium-hot fire** and cook for 3 to 4 minutes per side. *To check for doneness:* Cut into one of the tuna chunks and peek inside; it should be pink but not red in the center. Remove from the grill and, when they are cool enough to handle, slide the tuna chunks off the skewers.

3. In the meantime, in a large pot, bring 4 quarts of salted water to a boil over high heat. Add the pasta, return the water to a boil, and cook for 8 to 10 minutes, or until the pasta is tender but not mushy. Drain and place in a large bowl.

4. Add the olive oil, lemon juice, garlic, parsley, the grilled tuna, and salt and pepper to taste, toss well, and serve.

This makes a very good light summer dinner or substantial lunch when served with Grilled Corn with Lime and Chinese Roasted Salt (page 278).

Shells with Grilled Clams, Mussels, and Bacon-Cooked Greens

SERVES 4 AS ENTRÉE, 6 AS APPETIZER

Cooking this dish by yourself will give you some sort of idea how a line cook in a restaurant feels about a thousand times over on a Saturday night. Take the pasta out before it's overcooked, make sure the fresh-cooked hot greens are ready at the same time, don't let the clams and mussels sit too long in the broth. . . . It's actually best to cook this as a two-person operation, one person at the grill and the other at the stove. But if you like a challenge, try it solo and try to have it all "come up" (restaurant lingo for "be ready") at the same time.

> $^1/_3$ cup white wine
>
> $^1/_3$ cup extra virgin olive oil
>
> 2 tablespoons minced garlic
>
> 1 medium tomato, cored and diced small
>
> Salt and freshly cracked black pepper to taste
>
> 32 littlenecks or other small clams, washed well
>
> 40 mussels, washed well and beards removed
>
> 8 slices bacon, diced small
>
> 2 cups greens (spinach, arugula, kale, collards, or
> any combination) cut into thin strips
>
> 12 ounces medium shells or other dried pasta of your choice
>
> $^1/_4$ cup fresh lemon juice (about 1 lemon)
>
> $^1/_3$ cup raisins
>
> $^1/_3$ cup pine nuts, toasted in a 400°F oven until golden,
> 5 to 7 minutes
>
> $^1/_2$ cup roughly chopped fresh parsley

1. Build **a medium-hot fire** in your grill. In a large heatproof baking pan, combine the wine, olive oil, garlic, tomato, and salt and pepper to taste and place on the side of the grill, not directly over the fire.

2. While the broth heats, place the mussels and clams on the grill over the fire and cook until they open, 3 to 4 minutes for the mussels and 5 to 7 minutes for the clams. As they open, toss them into the broth.

3. Meanwhile, sauté the bacon over medium heat in a large sauté pan until it just begins to crisp, 4 to 5 minutes. Remove the bacon to paper towels to drain.

4. Drain all but 2 tablespoons of fat out of the pan. Turn the heat to high and heat until the bacon fat is very hot but not smoking. Throw in the greens and toss wildly with your tongs until the greens wilt, which should only take about 1 minute. Place them in a large bowl and set aside.

5. In a large pot, bring 4 quarts of salted water to a boil. Add the pasta, bring back to the boil, and cook for 8 to 10 minutes, or until tender but not mushy. Drain and place in the bowl with the greens. Add the lemon juice, raisins, pine nuts, and the broth, along with the mussels and clams. Season to taste with salt and pepper, toss well, and sprinkle with the reserved bacon and the parsley. Serve at once.

This goes well with Grilled Tomato Halves with Cheesy Bread Crumbs (page 298), and I also like it with Chickpea Salad with Cumin and Mint (page 316).

Spaghetti with Grilled Prosciutto and Figs

SERVES 4 AS ENTRÉE, 6 TO 8 AS APPETIZER

Grilled prosciutto might strike some folks as rather strange, but I think it's really nice because the fat gets cooked and smoked up a little, shrinking the meat but concentrating its flavor so it becomes an intensely crunchy, bacon-type treat. In this dish, the salty prosciutto contrasts with the sweet, slightly mushy figs, which are so excellent that you have to try them even if you don't cook the whole dish.

> $^1/_2$ **pound very thinly sliced prosciutto**
>
> **6 fresh figs, halved**
>
> **1 red bell pepper, halved and seeded**
>
> **2 tablespoons olive oil**
>
> **Salt and freshly cracked black pepper to taste**
>
> **12 ounces spaghetti or other dried pasta of your choice**
>
> $^1/_3$ **cup extra virgin olive oil**
>
> $^1/_3$ **cup chopped fresh sage, oregano, or thyme**
>
> **1 teaspoon minced garlic**
>
> **1 cup freshly grated Parmesan or other hard cheese**

1. Place the prosciutto on the grill over **a medium fire** and cook for 1 minute per side, or until it becomes brown and crisp around the edges. Set aside.

2. Combine the figs, bell pepper, olive oil, and salt and pepper to taste in a small bowl and toss well. Place the figs and pepper on the grill over **the medium fire,** with the figs cut side down, and grill, turning once or twice, until nicely browned, 2 to 3 minutes for the figs and 3 to 4 minutes for the peppers. Remove from the grill and set aside.

3. In a large pot, bring 4 quarts of salted water to a rolling boil. Add the spaghetti, bring the water back to a boil, and cook for 8 to 10 minutes, or until tender but not mushy.

4. While the pasta cooks, roughly chop the prosciutto and bell peppers.

5. Drain the spaghetti and place in a medium bowl. Add the extra virgin olive oil, herbs, garlic, and salt and pepper to taste. Add the prosciutto and bell peppers, along with the figs and toss well. Serve warm, with the cheese sprinkled over the top.

> I like to serve this along with Grilled Open-Faced Eggplant Sandwiches
> with Black Olive Relish and Fresh Mozzarella (page 39) for a big lunch
> or a relatively light dinner.

Grilled Sausage and Corn over Fettuccine with Tomatoes and Basil

SERVES 4 AS ENTRÉE, 6 TO 8 AS APPETIZER

I really like the technique of cooking some pasta, putting it in a bowl, adding a few other flavorful ingredients, tossing it all together, and serving it up. It's quick and easy, and all the flavors of the individual ingredients get a chance to shine. Try to use a good (i.e., expensive) extra virgin olive oil here, since the flavor has a real impact on the dish.

4 pounds sausage links—hot or sweet, your choice

4 ears corn, husked, desilked, blanched in boiling salted water
    for 2 minutes, and drained

2 tablespoons olive oil

Salt and freshly cracked black pepper to taste

12 ounces fettuccine or other dried pasta of your choice

1/3 cup extra virgin olive oil

2 tomatoes about the size of baseballs, cored and diced small

1/2 cup roughly chopped fresh basil

1 tablespoon minced garlic

1 cup freshly grated hard cheese such as pecorino or Parmesan

1. Place the sausages on the grill over **a medium fire** and cook, turning several times, until cooked through, 10 to 12 minutes. *To check for doneness:* Cut into one of the sausages to make sure it is brown all the way through. Remove from the fire and cut each link into 4 pieces.

2. While the sausage is grilling, rub the ears of corn with the oil and sprinkle them with salt and pepper to taste, then place them on the grill and cook, rolling around several times, for 3 to 4 minutes, or until golden brown. Remove from the fire and cut the kernels off the cobs.

3. In a large pot over high heat, bring 4 quarts of salted water to a rapid boil. Add the pasta, return the water to a rapid boil, and cook for 8 to 10 minutes, or until the pasta is tender but not mushy.

4. Drain the pasta well and place in a medium bowl along with the sausage, corn, and all remaining ingredients except the cheese. Toss well, adjust the seasoning, sprinkle liberally with the cheese, and serve at once.

This makes a nice light dinner or a big lunch when served along with Grilled Artichoke and White Bean Salad (page 51).

Lamb Shish Kebobs over Fettuccine

SERVES 6 TO 8 AS ENTRÉE

As you probably know, I'm big into grilled figs. Raw they don't do so much for me, but when they've been on the grill for a few minutes, I can't get enough of them. The heat brings out their inherent sweetness and adds a certain savory aspect that complements it perfectly. To me, fruit and meat are good companions, and here lamb and figs are combined over pasta with the classic trio of lamb seasonings, lemon, garlic, and rosemary.

> 1 pound boneless leg of lamb, cut into 1-inch cubes (12 to 16 cubes)
>
> 2 red bell peppers, halved, seeded, and halves quartered
>
> 2 red onions, peeled and cut into 8 chunks each
>
> $^{1}/_{4}$ cup vegetable oil
>
> Salt and freshly cracked black pepper to taste
>
> 6 fresh figs, halved
>
> 12 ounces fettuccine or other dried pasta of your choice
>
> 3 tablespoons roughly chopped fresh rosemary
>
> 1 teaspoon minced garlic
>
> 1 teaspoon red pepper flakes
>
> $^{1}/_{4}$ cup fresh lemon juice (about 1 lemon)
>
> $^{1}/_{4}$ cup extra virgin olive oil

1. In a large bowl, combine the lamb, bell peppers, onions, 2 tablespoons of the oil, and salt and pepper to taste and toss well. Thread the lamb cubes, peppers, and onions alternately onto skewers and grill over **a medium-hot fire** for 3 to 4 minutes per side for medium-rare. *To check for doneness:* Nick one of the pieces of lamb, which should be well browned on the outside, and look inside to see if it is almost as done as you like it. If you like your lamb more well done, simply continue to cook until the lamb is one degree less done than you want it to be when you eat it. Remove the skewers from the grill and set aside.

2. In a small bowl, combine the figs, the remaining 2 tablespoons oil, and salt and pepper to taste and toss well. Place the figs on the grill over **the medium-hot fire,** cut side down, and cook for 3 to 4 minutes, or until well browned. Remove from the grill and set aside.

3. In a large pot, bring 4 quarts of salted water to a rapid boil over high heat. Add the pasta, bring the water back up to a boil, and cook for 8 to 10 minutes, or until the pasta is tender but not mushy. Drain the pasta.

4. In a large bowl, combine the pasta with the rosemary, garlic, pepper flakes, lemon juice, and olive oil and toss well. Slide the lamb, peppers, and onions from the skewers into the bowl, add the figs, toss well, and serve.

Try this with Arugula with Pancetta, Grilled Asparagus, and White Beans (page 50) for a big lunch or a light dinner.

Kids love skewers. It's cool to string together foods with all different kinds of shapes and colors, plus you get to eat with your hands, which is definitely high on the list of qualities kids look for in food.

THREADING FLAVORS

grilling on skewers

It's pretty high on my list too, so I am also a big fan of skewer grilling. As an adult, though, I can recognize several additional advantages to the method: It's an easy way to cook many different foods at the same time; it keeps small pieces from slipping through the grill grate; it inspires inventive combinations of meats, fish, vegetables, and fruits; and you get unique flavorings at the point on the skewer where two different foods meet.

That last point is particularly important when it comes to deciding how to arrange the food on your skewers. Recently it has become rather fashionable to grill different ingredients on separate skewers—vegetables on one, meat on another, and so on. The advantage of this method is that it's relatively easy to know when to take the skewers from the grill, since you don't have foods with different cooking times on a single skewer.

I recognize this advantage, but it's not strong enough to convince me. After all, part of the fun of skewer grilling is not only the creativity of the combinations, but also the new tastes that you get when different foods are cooked over live fire while pressed tightly up against one another. I believe everybody recognizes the unique flavor of charred lamb and onions that have been grilled up against one another, for example, a taste that cannot be created any other way. The same is true of steak grilled next to apricots or pork grilled right up against apples, just to give a couple more examples.

So I prefer to deal with the situation by using two different techniques. First, I cut the slow-cooking foods into smaller pieces to help even out the cooking times. Second, I try to use the slow-cooking ingredients to protect the fast-cooking ones from the most intense heat. So, for example, when making Grilled Lamb and Fig Skewers with Quince-Ginger Chutney, you want to place the figs on the skewers with the cut sides mashed up against the lamb; this not only helps protect the figs from the heat, it also creates a larger surface area where fig and lamb come into contact.

There is also a lot of talk among grillers as to the best type of skewers. As far as I'm concerned, any variety is fine, from the expensive, intricately decorated metal numbers in upscale kitchen stores to the cheap bamboo models available in any supermarket. The general idea is simply to select a skewer that is large enough and heavy enough to accommodate whatever it is you want to thread onto it.

Let's move on to yet another advantage of skewer grilling—it lends itself very well to different portion sizes. You can serve each person a single skewer as an appetizer, or you can serve several skewers as an entrée. To emphasize this bene-fit, we've designed each of the recipes in this chapter to serve two people as an entrée or four as an appetizer.

You may also notice that several recipes in this chapter use a technique I have recently become fond of: combining various spices into a mixture that you shake onto the food after it's cooked, sort of like an intensely flavorful version of salt and pepper. This works particularly well with skewers, since it's easier than rubbing the many small pieces of food with a spice rub prior to grilling.

**SO GET IN TOUCH WITH YOUR INNER
KID AND LET'S DO SOME GRILLING.**

Grilled Shrimp and
Bacon Skewers with
Pickled Onion and
Avocado Salad

Tommy's Grilled Shrimp
and Red Onion Skewers
with Sour Salad and
Cashew Dipping Sauce

Grilled Shrimp and
Asparagus Skewers with
Lime-Soy Dipping Sauce

Simple Grilled
Swordfish Skewers

Grilled Monkfish and
Apricot Skewers with
Sweet Jalapeño Dressing

Grilled Sesame
Chicken Skewers

Peach and Chicken
Skewers with Middle
Eastern Shake and
Simple Raisin Sauce

Grilled Chicken
Skewers with Coconut-
Ginger Sauce

Grilled Lamb Skewers
with Apricots

Grilled Lamb and Fig
Skewers with Quince-
Ginger Chutney

Grilled Lamb Satay with
Peanut-Mint Relish

Grilled Lamb and
Potato Skewers with
Tomato – Green
Olive Relish

Grilled Vietnamese -
Style Beef Skewers with
Green Mango Slaw

Grilled Sirloin and
Apricot Skewers
with Pomegranate
Vinaigrette

Grilled Pork and Apple
Skewers with Orange-
Balsamic Glaze

Grilled Shrimp and Bacon Skewers with Pickled Onion and Avocado Salad

SERVES 2 AS ENTRÉE, 4 AS APPETIZER

Grilled shrimp is a Mexican standard on both coasts. Here we put the tasty little crustaceans on a skewer with slab bacon that has been blanched first to precook it so you don't have to worry that it won't cook all the way through on the grill. You have to watch these skewers once they get on the grill, though, because the fat from the bacon can easily ignite. If that happens, shift them quickly to a cooler part of the grill until the fire has died down, then move them back over the fire.

For the Salad

> 1 red onion, peeled, halved, and very thinly sliced
>
> 1 cup white vinegar
>
> 2 avocados, peeled, pitted, and diced medium
>
> $1/4$ cup fresh lime juice (about 2 limes)
>
> $1/4$ cup extra virgin olive oil
>
> 1 tomato, cored and diced medium
>
> 1 tablespoon ground cumin
>
> 1 teaspoon minced garlic
>
> $1/4$ cup roughly chopped fresh cilantro (or substitute parsley)
>
> Salt and freshly cracked black pepper to taste

> 1 pound medium shrimp (16 to 20), peeled and deveined, tails left on
>
> $1/2$ pound slab bacon, cut into 16 equal cubes, blanched in boiling water for 1 minute, and drained
>
> $1/2$ red bell pepper, seeded and cut into 8 pieces
>
> 4 scallions (white and green parts), cut into pieces about 1 inch long (about 16 pieces)
>
> 2 tablespoons vegetable oil
>
> Salt and freshly cracked black pepper taste

1. Make the salad: In a small bowl, combine the onion and vinegar and let stand for 1 hour. While the onions are pickling, combine the remaining ingredients for the salad in a medium bowl, toss well, cover, and refrigerate.

2. When the onions have been soaking for an hour, drain them, discard the vinegar, and add to the salad.

3. Thread the shrimp, bacon, bell pepper, and scallions alternately onto skewers. Sprinkle the skewers with the oil and salt and pepper to taste and grill over **a medium fire** for 3 to 4 minutes per side. *To check for doneness:* Cut into one of the shrimp to be sure that it is opaque throughout.

4. Remove the skewers from the grill. Place the salad on a serving platter or individual plates, top with the skewers, and serve.

I might serve this as an appetizer combination lunch along with Grilled Pita Bread Salad with Cucumbers and Feta Cheese (page 54) and Red Snapper Cocktail (page 73).

bacon bits

ALL BACON IS MADE from pork belly, but not all parts of the belly are created equal. The upper portion is relatively lean, which might seem like a positive characteristic but in practice means that bacon made from it has a tendency to be rather tough and inconsistent in texture. The bottom portion of the belly, on the other hand, is very fatty, so bacon made from it has a low proportion of meat to fat. Like the last porridge that Goldilocks tasted, the center of the belly is just right, with the proper blend of fat and meat for the best texture and taste—about two thirds fat to one third meat. "Slab bacon" is simply bacon that has not been presliced; because it is more a specialty item, it is often of higher quality.

Tommy's Grilled Shrimp and Red Onion Skewers with Sour Salad and Cashew Dipping Sauce

SERVES 2 AS ENTRÉE, 4 AS APPETIZER

As my 14-year-old nephew Tommy says, grilled shrimp are "the bomb." Simple to make and blending easily with other flavors, shrimp were undeniably born to be grilled. Because of their quick cooking time, it's easy to get them just right. Here we feature them in an easy Asian-flavored preparation along with a rather spicy cashew-ginger dipping sauce and a refreshingly sour cucumber-pineapple salad. The tart salad is inspired by the cuisine of the Philippines, where sourness is considered a culinary virtue.

For the Dipping Sauce

- 2 tablespoons sugar
- ³⁄₄ cup water
- 1 cup cashews, toasted in a 400°F oven until golden, 5 to 7 minutes, then roughly chopped
- 1 tablespoon creamy peanut butter
- 1 tablespoon rice wine vinegar (or substitute white vinegar)
- 1 tablespoon fresh lime juice (about ¹⁄₂ lime)
- 2 tablespoons finely minced ginger
- 3 tablespoons soy sauce
- 1 tablespoon red pepper flakes
- Salt and freshly cracked black pepper to taste

- 16 medium shrimp (about 1 pound), peeled and deveined
- 1 large red onion, peeled and cut into 16 small chunks
- 3 tablespoons vegetable oil
- Salt and freshly cracked white pepper (or substitute black) to taste
- Pineapple-Cucumber Salad (recipe follows)

1. Make the dipping sauce: In a small saucepan, combine the sugar and water and bring to a boil over high heat, stirring a few times. Remove from the heat, add all the remaining sauce ingredients, and mix well. Set aside to cool.

2. Place the shrimp and onion in a medium bowl with the oil and salt and pepper to taste and toss well to coat. Thread them onto skewers and place them on the grill over **a medium-hot fire.** Cook for 3 to 4 minutes per side. *To check for doneness:* Peek inside one of the shrimp to be sure it is opaque all the way through.

3. Spread the Pineapple-Cucumber Salad on a platter and slide the onions and shrimp off the skewers onto the salad. Serve, passing the cashew sauce in a small bowl for dipping.

PINEAPPLE-CUCUMBER SALAD

ABOUT 3 CUPS

> $^1/_4$ pineapple, peeled, cored, and diced large
>
> 1 medium cucumber, peeled and diced large
>
> $^1/_2$ cup rice wine vinegar (or substitute white wine vinegar)
>
> 2 tablespoons roughly chopped fresh cilantro
>
> 1 teaspoon red pepper flakes
>
> Salt and freshly cracked white pepper (or substitute black) to taste

In a medium bowl, combine all the ingredients and toss well. Refrigerate until ready to serve.

I like to serve several small dishes as a meal, so I would try an appetizer portion of this skewer in combination with Basic Black Beans (page 299), Grilled Eggplant Rounds with Sweet Chile Sauce (page 287), and K. C.'s Bengali-Style Spinach (page 292).

Grilled Shrimp and Asparagus Skewers with Lime-Soy Dipping Sauce

Although we often think of Japanese cuisine as composed mainly of raw fish, the Japanese also have a long tradition of grilling. This is my rendition of an outstanding yakitori skewer that I always get at my local Japanese restaurant. I particularly enjoy the juxtaposition of the rich shrimp and the clean, slightly grassy flavor of the asparagus. It is light and refreshing, and it makes an ideal appetizer for a meal of Asian flavors.

8 spears asparagus, bottom $\frac{1}{4}$ inch trimmed

For the Dipping Sauce

$\frac{1}{3}$ cup soy sauce

1 tablespoon sugar

$\frac{1}{4}$ cup fresh lime juice (about 2 limes)

1 teaspoon red pepper flakes

1 tablespoon freshly cracked white pepper (or substitute black)

16 medium shrimp (about 1 pound), peeled and deveined

1 tablespoon vegetable oil

Salt and freshly cracked black pepper to taste

1. Fill a large bowl with ice and water. In a large saucepan, bring about 6 cups of salted water to a boil over high heat. When the water comes to a full boil, add the asparagus and cook for 2 minutes; the asparagus should be tender but should still retain its bright color and crisp texture. Drain the asparagus and plunge into the ice water to stop the cooking process. When the asparagus is cool, drain it and cut each spear into thirds.

2. Make the sauce: In a small bowl, combine all the ingredients and whisk together well. Set aside.

3. Thread the asparagus and shrimp alternately onto skewers, rub lightly with the oil, and sprinkle with salt and pepper to taste. Grill over **a medium-hot fire** for 3 to 4 minutes per side. *To check for doneness:* Cut into one of the shrimp to be sure it is opaque all the way through. Remove from the grill and serve, passing the sauce on the side for dipping.

This makes an excellent entrée for an Asian-flavored dinner when served with Grilled Eggplant Rounds with Sweet Chile Sauce (page 287), Ginger-Scallion Fried Rice (page 301), and/or Sesame Green Beans with Crispy Fried Shallots (page 281). Malaysian-Style Coconut Pudding (page 366) is a very good dessert choice.

Simple Grilled Swordfish Skewers

SERVES 2 AS ENTRÉE, 4 AS APPETIZER

Swordfish is excellent for grilling and is particularly good for kebobs because of its firm texture. Here we keep it simple—just rub the fish with a spice-herb mixture, thread it onto the skewers with some onion chunks, and grill it up. This goes very nicely with rice pilaf (use boxed rice pilaf if you want); simply pile some pilaf on each plate and slide the fish off the skewers on top. If you want to dress up the skewers a bit, cut a couple of nectarines into quarters and add two quarters to each skewer.

For the Rub

    3 tablespoons olive oil
    3 tablespoons cumin seeds, toasted if you want, or 1$^1/_2$ tablespoons
        ground cumin
    1 tablespoon minced garlic
    $^1/_4$ cup roughly chopped fresh oregano or parsley
    2 teaspoons salt
    2 teaspoons freshly cracked black pepper

    1 pound swordfish, cut into 1-inch chunks (about 12 chunks)
    2 small red onions, peeled and cut into eighths
    2 tablespoons olive oil
    1 lemon, quartered

1. Make the rub: In a small bowl, combine all the ingredients and mix well.

2. Thread the swordfish and red onions alternately onto skewers and sprinkle with the spice rub. Place the skewers on the grill over **a medium-hot fire** and cook for 6 to 7 minutes on each side, or until a peek inside shows that the fish is opaque all the way through. Remove from the fire, sprinkle with the olive oil, and serve with lemon wedges for squeezing.

Serve this as an entrée accompanied by Arugula with Pancetta, Grilled Asparagus, and White Beans (page 50) and Grilled Open-Faced Eggplant Sandwiches with Black Olive Relish and Fresh Mozzarella (page 39).

Grilled Monkfish and Apricot Skewers with Sweet Jalapeño Dressing

SERVES 2 AS ENTRÉE, 4 AS APPETIZER

The smooth, dense texture of monkfish has earned it the moniker of "poor man's lobster." This quality also makes monkfish good for cooking on skewers, because its meaty texture can stand up to the rigors of grilling. Here we combine monkfish with fruit and heat, one of my favorite combinations, in the form of apricots and jalapeños. If you can't locate good-quality monkfish, you can substitute grouper, mako shark, or swordfish in this recipe.

For the Dressing

$^1/_4$ cup fresh lime juice (about 2 limes)

$^1/_4$ cup molasses

2 tablespoons minced jalapeño or other fresh chile pepper of your choice

2 tablespoons roughly chopped cilantro (or substitute parsley)

Salt and freshly cracked black pepper to taste

1 pound monkfish, cleaned and cut into 1-inch cubes
   (10 to 14 pieces)

4 apricots, halved and pitted

1 red bell pepper, halved, seeded, and halves quartered

2 tablespoons vegetable oil

Salt and freshly cracked black pepper to taste

1. Make the dressing: In a small bowl, combine all the ingredients, mix well, and set aside.

2. In a large bowl, combine the monkfish, apricots, bell peppers, oil, and salt and pepper to taste and toss well. Thread the monkfish, apricot halves, and pepper pieces alternately onto 4 skewers and grill over **a medium-hot fire** for 4 to 5 minutes. *To check for doneness:* Cut into one of the pieces of monkfish and check to see that the fish is just opaque at the center.

3. Remove the skewers from the grill, drizzle with the dressing, and serve; or serve the skewers with the dressing on the side.

As an entrée, these go great with Lisa White's White Gazpacho (page 30) in front and Romaine and Bulgur Salad (page 319) on the side.

Grilled Sesame Chicken Skewers

SERVES 2 AS ENTRÉE, 4 AS APPETIZER

In Japan, there is a huge grilling tradition known as yakitori—which, in fact, means "grilled" in Japanese. In this tradition, skewers of meat, fish, or vegetables are grilled in a special rig that resembles a small narrow trench filled with coals. On the menus of Japanese restaurants in the United States, the word *yakitori* has come to mean the grilled skewers themselves. Whenever I go out to get sushi, I always like to have a couple of yakitori to get my appetite ready. Here is my interpretation of this tradition, complete with a sweet-sour soy dipping sauce and a simple but pungent, crunchy coriander shake.

For the Shake

$1/4$ cup coriander seeds

2 tablespoons white peppercorns (or substitute black)

$1/4$ cup sesame seeds

For the Dipping Sauce

$1/3$ cup soy sauce

2 tablespoons fresh lime juice (about 1 lime)

1 tablespoon brown sugar

1 tablespoon Tabasco sauce or other hot sauce of your choice

2 pounds boneless, skinless chicken breasts, cut into about
   20 large chunks

4 scallions (white and green parts), chopped fine

2 tablespoons minced ginger

2 tablespoons sesame oil

2 red bell peppers, halved, seeded, and halves quartered

2 red onions, peeled and quartered

Salt and coarsely ground black pepper to taste

2 limes, quartered, for garnish

1. Make the shake: In a small sauté pan, combine the coriander, peppercorns, and sesame seeds and toast over medium heat, shaking the pan, until the first wisp of smoke appears, 2 to 3 minutes. Remove from the heat and allow to cool.

2. Place the toasted spices on a flat surface and place a small sauté pan on top of them. Holding the handle with one hand, place the other hand palm side down in the center of the pan and apply pressure, rolling the pan over the spices to crack them.

3. Make the dipping sauce: In a small bowl, combine all the ingredients, mix well, and set aside.

continued

4. In a medium bowl, combine the chicken chunks, scallions, ginger, and sesame oil and toss well. Thread the chicken onto 4 skewers alternately with the bell pepper and onion chunks, sprinkle with salt and pepper to taste, and grill over **a medium fire** for 5 to 7 minutes per side. *To check for doneness:* Cut into one of the pieces of chicken and check to be sure it is opaque all the way through.

5. Place the chicken skewers on a platter, sprinkle with the shake, garnish with the lime wedges, and serve with the dipping sauce on the side.

I would serve an entrée portion of these skewers accompanied by Pungent Carrot and Cucumber Salad with Ginger and Garlic (page 308) and Grilled Plums with Spicy Hoisin Glaze (page 296).

Peach and Chicken Skewers with Middle Eastern Shake and Simple Raisin Sauce

SERVES 2 AS ENTRÉE, 4 AS APPETIZER

The idea for the "shake" that I use in this dish came from the Rendezvous restaurant in Memphis, Tennessee, where Charley Vergo sets out saltshakers of his secret barbecue rub on the table so you can add it to his barbecued baby-back ribs. If you double or triple the recipe for the simple shake used here, you can do the same for your guests.

When you are cooking on skewers, it's crucial always to check the food for doneness before you take it off the grill. If you pack the food onto the skewers too tightly, it may not cook through in the estimated time—a particular downer when the skewered food is chicken, because most people are really not into rare chicken.

For the Raisin Sauce
> ¹⁄₃ cup olive oil
> ¹⁄₄ cup raisins, roughly chopped
> ¹⁄₄ cup fresh lime juice (about 2 limes)
> Salt and freshly cracked black pepper to taste

For the Shake
> 2 tablespoons cumin seeds, toasted if you want, or
>> 1 tablespoon ground cumin
> 2 tablespoons ground coriander, toasted along with the
>> cumin seeds if you want, or 1 tablespoon ground coriander

Pinch of ground cinnamon

1 tablespoon kosher salt

1 tablespoon freshly cracked black pepper

3 tablespoons vegetable oil

1 tablespoon minced garlic

$1/4$ cup roughly chopped fresh cilantro

Salt and freshly cracked black pepper to taste

1 pound boneless, skinless chicken breasts, cut into large
  chunks (about 16 chunks)

2 red bell peppers, halved, seeded, and halves quartered

2 peaches, pitted and cut into eighths

1. Make the sauce: In a small bowl, combine all the ingredients. Whisk together well and set aside.

2. Make the shake: In a small bowl, combine all the ingredients, mix well, and set aside.

3. In a medium bowl, combine the oil, garlic, cilantro, and salt and pepper to taste. Add the chicken chunks and toss well so the chicken becomes well coated. Thread the chicken onto 4 skewers alternately with the peaches and pepper pieces, place the skewers on the grill over **a medium fire,** and cook for 5 to 7 minutes per side. *To check for doneness:* Cut into one of the pieces of chicken and check to be sure it is opaque all the way through.

4. Remove the skewers from the grill and place them on a platter. Pour the sauce over the top, sprinkle with the shake, and serve hot.

I might serve an appetizer portion of these skewers along with Chickpea Salad with Horseradish-Yogurt Dressing (page 317) and Grilled Corn with Lime and Chinese Roasted Salt (page 278) for a kind of "small dish lunch."

Grilled Chicken Skewers with Coconut-Ginger Sauce

When we travel in the United States we find ourselves eating lots of hot dogs, because you can get them anywhere and they always hit the spot. When we traveled in Southeast Asia, outstanding grilled skewers of various sorts, known as satays, were available everywhere—street corners, bus stations, train depots, in the stands of the kickboxing or badminton arenas. We ate them every day, and began to refer to them as the "hot dogs of Southeast Asia." Fortunately, they're just about as easy to cook as hot dogs, too.

Here the chicken is grilled and the slightly spicy, sweet, and pungent coconut dipping sauce is complemented by the traditional peanuts, not in the usual sauce but in a shake that goes on after grilling. You'll probably have some shake and coconut sauce left over, but don't worry—both go really well with grilled pork or lamb skewers too.

For the Sauce

- 1 teaspoon sesame oil
- 2 tablespoons minced ginger
- 1 tablespoon minced garlic
- 1 tablespoon minced fresh chile pepper of your choice
- 1 12-ounce can unsweetened coconut milk
- 2 tablespoons fresh lime juice (about 1 lime)
- 2 tablespoons roughly chopped fresh cilantro

For the Shake

- $1/4$ cup sesame seeds, toasted in a sauté pan over medium heat, shaking frequently, until fragrant, 2 to 3 minutes
- $1/4$ cup unsalted roasted peanuts, roughly chopped
- 2 tablespoons red pepper flakes
- 1 teaspoon curry powder

- 1 whole boneless chicken breast (10 to 12 ounces), cut into 12 chunks
- 1 tablespoon vegetable oil
- Salt and freshly cracked black pepper to taste

1. Make the sauce: In a medium saucepan over medium-high heat, heat the sesame oil until hot but not smoking. Add the ginger, garlic, and chile and sauté, stirring, until soft, about 2 minutes. Add the coconut milk and lime juice and bring to a boil. Reduce the heat to low and let simmer for about 20 minutes, or until the liquid has reduced by about half. Once the sauce has reduced, remove it from the heat, stir in the cilantro and chile pepper, and cover to keep warm.

2. Meanwhile, make the shake: In a small bowl, combine all the ingredients, mix well, and set aside.

3. Thread the chicken chunks onto 4 skewers, sprinkle lightly with the oil and salt and pepper to taste, and grill over **a medium-hot fire** for 3 to 4 minutes per side. *To check for doneness:* Cut into one of the pieces of chicken and check to be sure it is opaque all the way through.

4. Remove the skewers from the fire, sprinkle a bit of the shake over them, and serve with the warm ginger-coconut sauce.

I would serve these as an entrée along with K. C.'s Bengali-Style Spinach (page 292) for a light lunch or dinner.

coconut milk

ALTHOUGH WE AMERICANS TEND to think of coconut as an occasional flavor accent, it is actually a daily staple for more than one third of the world's population. It plays a central role in the diets of almost all peoples living in a broad band around the earth's equator, from Asia to coastal India to tropical Africa to Brazil and the Caribbean.

IN THESE AREAS, BY far the most prevalent culinary use of coconut is to make coconut milk. A simple preparation, coconut milk is made by steeping fresh coconut meat in hot water and then straining it,

pressing against the meat until all the liquid is extracted.

AS WITH OLIVE OIL, the first pressing is the most expensive and desirable, the second less so, and so on. In Malaysia, for example, the milk pressed from grated coconut meat without the addition of water, called *pati,* is used sparingly in cooking, as we use cream. The first pressing of coconut meat and water, the first *santan,* is slightly less rich; it is usually stirred into a dish at the end of the cooking time in order to preserve its creamy texture. The second pressing (second

santan), thinner and less flavorful, is almost always added at the beginning of cooking.

WHILE IT IS QUITE easy to make your own coconut milk (see page 368), many of the canned versions found in Asian or Caribbean markets are as good as or better than anything you can make from the second-rate fresh coconuts found in American produce markets. The canned coconut milks imported from Thailand are generally of higher quality than the others, but Goya is quite acceptable.

Grilled Lamb Skewers with Apricots

This combination of grilled lamb and exotic spices could come from many different parts of the world—India, the Middle East, parts of Asia. The spice rub, which combines dry spices with fresh garlic and ginger, creates a super crust on the outside of the lamb. The parboiled, then grilled garlic provides another strong flavor element to the dish, as do the sweet grilled apricots. After grilling, everything is combined with a minty, sweet-sour vinaigrette and tossed like a salad, which creates a lot of really fine juices; I recommend you serve this with couscous, rice, or bread to soak up 'em up.

For the Vinaigrette

$^1/_2$ cup extra virgin olive oil

$^1/_4$ cup fresh lemon juice (about 1 lemon)

1 tablespoon molasses

$^1/_4$ cup roughly chopped fresh mint

Salt and freshly cracked black pepper to taste

For the Rub

1 tablespoon minced fresh chile pepper of your choice

2 tablespoons minced ginger

2 tablespoons minced garlic

$^1/_4$ cup roughly chopped fresh cilantro (or substitute parsley)

2 tablespoons cumin seeds, toasted if you want, or 1 tablespoon ground cumin

1 teaspoon ground cardamom (optional)

1 teaspoon ground cinnamon

1 pound boneless lamb leg, cut into $^1/_2$-inch cubes (about 16 pieces)

4 ripe but firm apricots, quartered and pitted

16 large cloves garlic, peeled, blanched in boiling water for 2 minutes, and drained

1. Make the vinaigrette: In a small bowl, combine all the ingredients and whisk together well. Set aside.

2. Make the rub: In a medium bowl, combine all the ingredients and mix well.

3. Add the lamb chunks to the rub and toss well to coat. Thread the lamb chunks onto 4 skewers, alternating the lamb with the apricots and garlic, and grill over **a medium-hot fire** for 5 to 7 minutes per side. *To check for doneness:* Cut into one of the lamb chunks and peek inside; the meat should be pink and still juicy.

THREADING FLAVORS

4. Remove the skewers from the grill and slide the lamb, apricots, and garlic off the skewers into a large bowl. Pour the vinaigrette over the top and toss well. Serve with couscous, rice, or crusty bread.

Try serving these in an appetizer portion as part of an appetizer collection along with Salt-Crusted Grilled Shrimp in Their Shells (page 68) and Raw Beef with Parsley, Capers, and Hard Cheese (page 79).

lump charcoal
the return of the real thing

LIKE THE INTERSTATE HIGHWAY system, backyard grilling is a post–World War II phenomenon, born of America's mass purchase of automobiles and subsequent migration to the suburbs. The suburbs supplied the yards that made outdoor grilling possible, and the profit-hunting ingenuity of Henry Ford supplied the fuel of choice—a new product known as charcoal briquettes.

LOOKING FOR A WAY to sell the wood remaining from forms used to assemble automobile bodies, Ford hooked up with scientist Charles Kingsford. Kingsford converted the scrap wood into a convenient, compressed form of charcoal that also contains sawdust, camphor, petroleum products, and binders. First sold only at Ford dealerships, these briquettes became so popular that they soon were available everywhere. To most baby boomers, Kingsford's briquettes—and their imitators— are synonymous with charcoal.

"REAL" CHARCOAL, HOW-EVER, HAS been made for millennia and is quite a different product. Produced by burning hardwood slowly in a low-oxygen atmosphere until ninety percent of the wood's solids have been converted to pure carbon, it contains no additives or fillers. The resulting charcoal is a lightweight, clean-burning, good-smelling fuel, consisting of irregularly shaped lumps that produce a pleasant clink when two pieces strike each other.

Grilled Lamb and Fig Skewers with Quince-Ginger Chutney

SERVES 2 AS ENTRÉE, 4 AS APPETIZER

Lamb and figs grilled together is a wonderful combination. The sweet caramelized figs perfectly complement the rich, slightly gamy taste of the lamb. Since the figs cook more quickly than the lamb, some folks like to put them on separate skewers for grilling. The problem with this is that the place where the fig and the lamb touch during grilling is very special, with a unique flavor. So what we like to do is put the figs on so the cut face is mushed up against the lamb chunk, rather than facing the grill surface, then kind of push the lamb chunks firmly together. This helps protect the figs from the heat of the fire, and also creates a larger surface area where fig and lamb come into contact.

If you can't find good quinces, you can substitute pears or even apples in the chutney. It won't be quite as aromatic, but it will still be excellent.

For the Rub

$^1\!/_4$ **cup vegetable oil**

1 tablespoon ground cumin

2 tablespoons grated lemon zest

2 tablespoons roughly chopped fresh mint

2 tablespoons roughly chopped fresh parsley

1 tablespoon minced garlic

Salt and freshly cracked black pepper to taste

$^1\!/_2$ **pound boneless lamb leg, cut into 1-inch chunks**

1 red bell pepper, halved seeded, and halves quartered

1 red onion, peeled and cut into eighths

4 fresh figs, quartered

Quince-Ginger Chutney (recipe follows)

1. Make the rub: In a small bowl, combine all the ingredients and mix well. Add the lamb chunks and toss to coat well.

2. Thread the lamb onto 4 skewers, alternating it with the bell peppers, onions, and figs. Place the skewers on the grill over **a medium-hot fire** and cook for 5 to 7 minutes on each side. *To check for doneness:* Cut into one of the pieces of lamb; it should be juicy and still pink inside. Remove the skewers from the grill and let them stand 5 minutes, then serve along with the Quince-Ginger Chutney.

QUINCE-GINGER CHUTNEY

2 tablespoons olive oil

1 red onion, peeled and diced small

2 quinces, peeled, cored, and diced small (or substitute pears or apples)

1/2 red bell pepper, seeded and diced small

2 tablespoons minced ginger

1/2 cup sugar (omit if using pears or apples)

3/4 cup balsamic vinegar

Salt and freshly cracked black pepper to taste

In a small saucepan over medium heat, heat the olive oil until hot but not smoking. Add the onions and sauté, stirring occasionally, until transparent, 5 to 7 minutes. Add the quinces, bell pepper, and ginger and sauté, stirring occasionally, for 5 minutes. Add the sugar and vinegar and let cook for 12 to 15 minutes, stirring frequently, until the quinces are tender and most of the liquid has evaporated. Remove from the heat and season to taste. This chutney will keep, covered and refrigerated, for about 1 week.

I might serve this as an entrée accompanied by Grilled Garlicky Eggplant
Planks with Yogurt-Mint Sauce (page 286), with
Ginger Limeade (page 347) as a beverage.

quince comeback

YOU GOTTA LOVE QUINCES. Here's a fruit that has a knobby, uneven appearance; that even when fully ripe is harder and drier than an unripe green apple; that develops almost no sugar during ripening; and that can't be eaten raw. It's a wonder, you might say, that anyone ever bothered to eat the thing. But then you smell it, and you understand its appeal. The aroma of quince is musky, exotic, and tropical, a kind of combination of apples, honey, lilacs, and spice.

FORTUNATELY, WHEN YOU COOK quinces with some sugar, they turn a beautiful golden color and develop a flavor equal to their perfume. Because of this, the quince has remained popular in the Near and Middle East, where perfumy flavors are highly valued. Once equally popular in the United States—until the early 1800s, there were more quince trees in this country than either apple or pear trees—it fell out of favor until recently because it always has to be cooked. Now, however, quinces are making a comeback, and the knobby, aromatic little fruits can be found with increasing ease in produce markets. Try them, they're worth the effort.

Grilled Lamb Satay with Peanut-Mint Relish

SERVES 2 AS ENTRÉE, 4 AS APPETIZER

This recipe is inspired by one of those travel mishaps that turn into a fond memory. Traveling from Singapore to Kuala Lumpur, Malaysia, we got stranded for two days in Johur Bahru, a city at the southern tip of Malaysia. We were none too happy about this, because the city's main claim to fame is that it is the terminus for all the truck lines that go up and down the east and west coasts of Malaysia. That, and the fact that there is a steady stream of Singaporeans coming across the bridge to escape the strait-laced rules of their city-state and let off some steam—in other words, Johur Bahru was kind of like a giant combination truck stop and massage parlor.

But it turned out to be a fine experience because, as everybody knows, truck stops have great food. At night the parking lot around the town's main square was transformed into a giant food court, where scores of vendors dispensed excellent Malay, Chinese, Indian, and Nonya-Baba food from pushcarts to the crowds packed around the card tables that occupied the middle of the square. A few beers and a couple of plates of food, and we were happy just to be there.

Among the many dishes we enjoyed in this sprawling, makeshift, kaleidoscopic food emporium were succulent grilled lamb skewers with a hot peanut relish. As we discovered over the following weeks, the Muslim population of Malaysia has a great lamb-cooking tradition, and we were fortunate enough to participate in it often. So this dish is a tribute to the talented Malay cooks whose lamb we enjoyed in Johur Bahru and all the way up the west coast of the country. As is appropriate for a dish we first tasted in a food stall, it's quick and easy, and it still has a lot of flavor going for it.

For the Relish

$^{1}/_{2}$ cup unsalted peanuts, toasted in a 350°F oven until golden brown, about 7 minutes, then roughly chopped

$^{1}/_{4}$ cup fresh lime juice (about 2 limes)

1 teaspoon to 1 tablespoon minced fresh chile pepper of your choice

1 tablespoon minced ginger

$^{1}/_{4}$ cup roughly chopped fresh mint

2 tablespoons molasses

2 tablespoons soy sauce

Salt and freshly cracked black pepper to taste

$1^{1}/_{2}$ pounds boneless lamb leg, cut into long strips about 1 inch thick

Salt and freshly cracked black pepper to taste

1. Make the relish: In a small bowl, combine all the ingredients, mix well and set aside.

2. Sprinkle the lamb with salt and pepper to taste, thread onto skewers, and grill over **a medium-hot fire** for about 4 minutes per side for medium-rare. *To check for doneness:* Cut into one of the lamb strips and peek inside; the center meat should be pink. Remove from the grill and serve, topped with several table-spoons of the relish.

This makes an excellent entry in a spicy appetizer bonanza along with Ginger-Soy Marinated Grilled Shrimp with Most-Hot Lime-Chile Booster (page 229), Chile-Coated Grilled Summer Squash and Zucchini with Honey-Lime Dressing (page 239), and Lime-Pickled Mangoes with Ginger and Chiles (page 336). To keep the Malaysian theme going, try Malaysian-Style Coconut Pudding (page 366) for dessert.

Grilled Lamb and Potato Skewers with Tomato–Green Olive Relish

Lamb is a great-tasting meat. Unfortunately, in our country, it is kind of neglected, with many families enjoying it only once a year, at Easter. But in a semicircle around the Eastern Mediterranean, from Greece through the Middle East and back around across the top of Africa to Morocco, lamb is the meat of choice. That means that there are whole cultures with centuries of experience in using this savory meat in all kinds of ways, rather than occasionally roasting a celebratory leg. Here we combine chunks of lamb with small potatoes, put them over the fire to crisp them up, and serve them with a relish that features a whole range of Mediterranean flavors. Try this with some grilled pita and a light salad, and you'll soon be a lamb convert.

> 8 red Bliss potatoes about the size of golf balls
> 1 pound boneless lamb leg, cut into 1-inch chunks (16 chunks)
> 1/4 cup olive oil
> Salt and freshly cracked black pepper to taste
> Tomato-Green Olive Relish (recipe follows)

1. Bring a large pot of salted water to a full boil over high heat. Add the potatoes and cook until they are easily pierced with a fork but still offer some resistance, about 10 minutes. Drain the potatoes and immediately put them in a bowl of ice water to stop the cooking process. Drain again and cut in half.

2. In a medium bowl, combine the halved potatoes, lamb chunks, olive oil, and salt and pepper to taste and toss well. Thread the lamb and potatoes alternately onto 8 skewers; each skewer should have 2 potato halves and 2 pieces of lamb.

3. Place the skewers on the grill over **a medium-hot fire** and cook for 3 to 4 minutes on each side for medium-rare. *To check for doneness:* Cut into one of the lamb chunks and see if the center is slightly less done than you want it to be when you eat it, since the meat will continue to cook a bit more after you remove it from the grill. Remove the skewers from the grill and serve warm, accompanied by the Tomato-Green Olive Relish.

THREADING FLAVORS

TOMATO–GREEN OLIVE RELISH

2 large tomatoes, cored and diced large

$^1/_2$ red onion, peeled and diced small

1 cup pitted and roughly chopped green olives

$^1/_4$ cup roughly chopped fresh oregano (or substitute parsley or basil)

1 tablespoon minced garlic

1 teaspoon ground cinnamon

$^1/_4$ cup extra virgin olive oil

2 tablespoons fresh lemon juice (about $^1/_2$ lemon)

Salt and freshly cracked black pepper to taste

In a medium bowl, combine all the ingredients and mix well. This relish will keep, covered and refrigerated, for 2 to 3 days.

I would serve these as an entrée with Chipotle Mashed Sweet Potatoes (page 282) and Grilled Tomato Halves with Cheesy Bread Crumbs (page 298) on the side.

Grilled Vietnamese-Style Beef Skewers with Green Mango Slaw

Wandering down the narrow alleys and broad boulevards of Ho Chi Minh City (or Saigon, as its residents still call it) is a vivid and intensely exotic experience, particularly set against memories of the city as seen on television every night during the war. As in many developing countries, the best food available to strangers is on the streets, and that's okay with me. On a typical blistering-hot day, sitting on the small stools of the street stands drinking the cheapest beer in Southeast Asia and working your way through a couple of beef skewers is as good a meal as you can ask for. The meat is grilled and served with a side of what I can best describe as a green mango slaw. Its aromatic quality really sets the beef off well. You can use the same cuts of beef that you would for any other type of grilling, but I prefer sirloin tips or top round because they are reasonably priced.

For the Vinaigrette

8 stalks lemon grass (inner portion of bottom third only), minced

1 cup rice wine vinegar (or substitute white wine vinegar)

2 tablespoons sugar

$1/4$ cup fresh lime juice (about 2 limes)

2 tablespoons minced fresh chile pepper of your choice

2 tablespoons fish sauce (optional)

For the Slaw

2 green mangoes, peeled, pitted, and cut into matchsticks

1 carrot, peeled and grated

$1/2$ cup mung bean sprouts (optional)

$1/2$ red onion, peeled and thinly sliced

2 tablespoons roughly chopped fresh mint

2 tablespoons roughly chopped fresh cilantro

2 tablespoons roughly chopped fresh basil

1 pound sirloin, top round, or sirloin tips, cut into strips about $1/2$ inch thick and 4 to 5 inches long

2 tablespoons peanut oil

Salt and freshly cracked black pepper to taste

1 lime, quartered, for garnish (optional)

1. Make the vinaigrette: In a small saucepan, bring the lemon grass, vinegar, and sugar to a boil over high heat. Reduce the heat to medium and boil until the liquid is reduced by about half, 20 to 25 minutes. Remove from the heat and strain, discarding the lemon grass. Add the remaining vinaigrette ingredients, mix well, and refrigerate until ready to serve.

2. Make the slaw: In a small bowl, combine all the ingredients and toss well. Cover and refrigerate until ready to serve.

3. In a small bowl, combine the beef chunks with the oil and salt and pepper to taste and toss to coat. Thread the beef onto skewers and grill over **a medium-hot fire** for 2 to 3 minutes per side for rare to medium-rare. *To check for doneness:* Cut into one of the beef chunks and peek inside.

4. Remove the beef skewers from the grill. Add about three quarters of the vinaigrette to the slaw and toss well. Lay the slaw out on a platter, place the beef skewers on top, drizzle them with the remaining vinaigrette, and serve, garnished with the lime quarters if you want.

To keep the Asian feeling going, serve this as a light lunch along with Pungent Carrot and Cucumber Salad with Ginger and Garlic (page 308) and Grilled Plums with Spicy Hoisin Glaze (page 296).

fish farming, vietnam style

IT IS IMPOSSIBLE TO visit Vietnam, a beautiful and totally fascinating country, without being constantly reminded, in ways both predictable and unexpected, of how the long years of war still affect every aspect of life.

ONE DAY WE WERE taken to Co Chi, a village about thirty kilometers outside Ho Chi Minh City. There we were to visit the entrance to the amazingly complex underground tunnel system used by Vietnamese fighters, first against the French and then the Americans. As we drove to the village, gritty tin-shacked suburbs gave way to classic scenes of rice paddies with rows of farmers in conical hats cutting rice. They could have been taken from a travel poster—or from the evening news in 1968.

"HAS THIS ALWAYS BEEN rice paddy land?" I asked our government-assigned guide, Mr. Truan.

"WELL," HE REPLIED IN a matter-of-fact tone, "it was before, but then it was a free-fire zone during the war. Now it is rice paddy land again, but it also has lots of fish farms, since the bomb craters make very good ponds."

WITH RESOURCEFULNESS LIKE THAT, it is no wonder the country is considered a good prospect to rise to prominence in the region once again.

Grilled Sirloin and Apricot Skewers with Pomegranate Vinaigrette

Middle Eastern cooking, and particularly the cuisine of ancient Persia, now Iran, has always been partial to ingredients with very aromatic flavors, almost like perfumes. Quince, rose water, dried limes, and saffron, for example, all have flowery overtones that have made them very popular in that region. Here we take two such ingredients — tender apricots and the wonderfully sweet-tart syrup made from pomegranate seeds — and combine them with sirloin steak for very flavorful skewers. Part of the fun of skewer grilling, after all, is the creativity of the combinations and the unique flavors that result when different foods are cooked over the fire while pressed up against one another. For this dish, you want to push the steak and apricots tightly together to protect the apricots a bit from the heat of the fire.

For the Vinaigrette

$^1/_2$ cup pomegranate molasses (or substitute a mixture of $^1/_3$ cup
   molasses and 2 tablespoons fresh lime juice — about 1 lime)

$^1/_2$ cup fresh lemon juice (about 2 lemons)

$^1/_4$ cup balsamic vinegar

$^1/_2$ red onion, peeled and diced small

1 tablespoon minced garlic

2 tablespoons roughly chopped fresh parsley

Salt and freshly cracked black pepper to taste

1 pound sirloin tips, cut into 1-inch chunks

1 red onion, peeled and cut into eighths

1 red bell pepper, halved, seeded, and halves quartered

4 apricots, pitted and halved (or substitute 2 peaches,
   pitted and quartered)

2 tablespoons olive oil

Salt and freshly cracked black pepper to taste

1. Make the vinaigrette: In a small bowl, combine all the ingredients and mix well. Set aside.

2. Thread the beef onto skewers, alternating with the onions, bell peppers, and apricots. Rub lightly with the olive oil, sprinkle with salt and pepper to taste, and grill over **a medium-hot fire** for about 5 minutes per side for rare. *To check for* *doneness:* Cut into a piece of beef to be sure it is cooked one degree less than you like to eat it. Remove the skewers from the grill and place on a serving platter or individual plates. Drizzle generously with the vinaigrette and serve.

**I like this with Chickpea Salad with Cumin and Mint (page 316)
and Grilled Potatoes with Yogurt-Parsley Sauce (page 283).
For a really sweet ending to the meal, try
Caramelized Banana and Lime Tart (page 374).**

taking turns

LOTS OF TIMES WHEN you are making a grilled dish, you have more than one item to grill. This makes sense, since as long as the fire is going, you might as well take full advantage of it. However, this can also lead to some confusion, since you can't always grill everything simultaneously.

THERE ARE A COUPLE rules of thumb that help out here. First, remember that if you are grilling meat, it usually needs to rest a few minutes after cooking, and you can use that time to grill other items that only take a couple of minutes. Second, since grilled vegetables taste outstanding at room temperature as well as hot off the grill, you can always cook them first and set them aside until you're ready to serve.

Grilled Pork and Apple Skewers with Orange-Balsamic Glaze

SERVES 2 AS ENTRÉE, 4 AS APPETIZER

Pork and apples have a long history as a happy couple. Here we grill both of them, then add a simple sweet-sour glaze. When you're reducing the glaze, the size of the pan has a big influence on how fast the process goes. The larger the pan, the faster the reduction; but keep a close eye on the liquid to be sure it doesn't burn. You want to reduce it only until it's thick enough to coat the back of a spoon. Also keep a careful watch on the pork and apples after you paint them with the glaze at the last minute—any time you add a sweet sauce or glaze to something on the grill, it can go from a golden brown treat to a blackened cinder in a heartbeat. So glaze 'em and get 'em off. By the way, you might want to make a double or triple batch of the glaze while you're at it; it keeps well and is very tasty brushed on any grilled meat.

For the Glaze

> 2 cups orange juice
>
> $^1/_2$ cup balsamic vinegar
>
> 1 teaspoon kosher salt
>
> 2 tablespoons freshly cracked black pepper
>
> 1 pound boneless pork loin, cut into 1-inch cubes (12 to 16 cubes)
>
> 2 Granny Smith apples, cored and cut into 8 wedges each
>
> 2 tablespoons olive oil
>
> Salt and freshly cracked black pepper to taste

1. Make the glaze: In a small saucepan, combine all the ingredients and bring to a boil over high heat. Reduce the heat to medium-low and simmer vigorously until the liquid is reduced by half, about 20 minutes. Remove from the heat and set aside.

2. In a medium bowl, combine the pork cubes, apples, olive oil, and salt and pepper to taste and toss well. Thread the pork and apples alternately onto skewers and grill over **a medium-hot fire** for 5 to 7 minutes, turning several times. *To check for doneness:* Cut into one of the pieces of pork; it should be just pink in the center. During the last 30 seconds of cooking, brush the skewers with some of the glaze.

3. Remove the skewers from the fire, drizzle with the remaining glaze, and serve.

Serve this one up with Jícama-Apple Salad with Orange-Mustard Dressing (page 307) and maybe a pitcher of Blue-Green Mangoritas (page 350).

THREADING FLAVORS

Meat is made for grilling. You can bet that when the first ingenious cave dweller figured out that food tastes better after it spends some time interacting with fire, it wasn't vegetables or fruit that was the subject of the experiment, it was meat.

STRICTLY ENTRÉES

the original: grilled meat

Today, meat still tastes best when exposed to the direct high heat and searing flame that come with live fire grilling. When you sink your teeth into a piece of meat that has a good, strong char on the outside and is still tender and juicy on the inside, there's just nothing better.

Not every cut of meat is ideal for grilling, though. Since meat cooks on the grill by direct exposure to a hot fire, you need to choose a relatively small cut that will cook through on the inside before it turns to cinders on the outside. You also want to look for a relatively tender cut, so it doesn't need to spend a lot of time cooking in order to break down tough collagens. Steaks, chops, and tenderloin are the type of cuts we're talking about here, along with burgers and sausages.

When choosing meat to cook on the grill, it might be helpful to keep in mind that grilling is similar to broiling or sautéing, so, in general, you're looking for the kind of cuts you might consider cooking in a broiler or sauté pan.

With its deep, rich taste, meat can handle a lot of intense flavor accompaniment, so I like either to rub it with a flavor-packed spice mixture or just sprinkle it with salt and freshly cracked pepper, grill it, and then serve it up with a strongly flavored accompaniment or two. For example, I match Grilled Lamb Chops with Pomegranate-Eggplant Relish, while Spice-Crusted Pork Tenderloins are paired with Banana-Date Chutney, and Grilled Delmonico Steak Adobo shares the plate with both Sweet Corn Relish and Charred Spring Onions. The recipes are varied in inspiration, but each one provides lots of tastes, with the uniquely satisfying flavor of meat at the center.

Grilled Delmonico Steak Adobo with Charred Spring Onions and Sweet Corn Relish

Pepper-Crusted Grilled Filet Mignon with Blue Cheese Butter and Roasted Garlic Mash

Grilled Flank Steak "in the Style of Pastrami" with Spicy Tomato-Horseradish Relish

Rosemary-Grilled New York Strip with Smoky Eggplant Relish

Spice-Rubbed Grilled Top Round with Tomatoes, Herbs, and Chiles

Grilled Veal Chops with Expensive Mushrooms

Grilled Rack of Lamb with Quick Mint-Apricot Sauce and Blue Cheese–Stuffed Tomatoes

Grilled Lamb Chops and Sausage on Arugula and Mint

Grilled Lamb Chops with Pomegranate-Eggplant Relish

Tandoori-Style Roasted Whole Leg of Lamb

Chuletas: Thin Grilled Pork Chops with Simple Tomato Relish

Grilled Double-Thick Pork Chops with Grilled Peaches and Molasses-Rum Barbecue Sauce

Spice-Crusted Pork Tenderloins with Banana-Date Chutney

Quixotic Mixed Grill with Vegetable Skewers and Four Sauces

Grilled Delmonico Steak Adobo with Charred Spring Onions and Sweet Corn Relish

SERVES 4

If you have ever seen green onions (aka spring onions), you know that they look like large scallions with a bulb about the size of a golf ball. These babies are just plain awesome on the grill. In Mexico, where they are constant companions to tacos *al carbón,* they are charred and served up with a little coarse salt and pepper and a squeeze of lime. If you ever see them in a market, buy them; they will rock your world.

The other parts of this dish are not so shabby either. The sweet, smoky corn relish works nicely with the crispy, charred, super-flavor-packed crust of the tender, juicy Delmonico, aka rib-eye steak. The Mexican-inspired paste that we use to cover the steak is known as adobo and, as with all spice rubs, it crusts up beautifully. If you can't get hold of Delmonico for this dish, New York strip steak makes a fine substitute.

For the Spice Paste

2 tablespoons minced garlic

¼ cup roughly chopped fresh oregano

2 tablespoons paprika

2 tablespoons cumin seeds, toasted if you want, or 1 tablespoon ground cumin

3 tablespoons grainy mustard

¼ cup olive oil

⅓ cup red wine vinegar

4 12- to 16-ounce Delmonico (rib-eye) steaks

Salt and freshly cracked black pepper to taste

8 spring onions, roots trimmed off

2 limes, quartered

Sweet Corn Relish (recipe follows)

1. In a small bowl, combine all of the paste ingredients and mix well. Sprinkle the steaks with salt and pepper. Reserve about ¼ cup of the spice paste, and rub the steaks generously with the remaining amount.

2. Place the steaks on the grill over **a hot fire** and cook for 5 to 7 minutes per side for rare. If you like your meat more well done, cook it until it is almost the way you like it but not quite there, since it will cook a little more after you take it off the heat. *To check for doneness:* Cut into a steak and check to see if the center is slightly less done than you like it.

3. Remove the steaks from the grill, brush on the reserved spice rub, and allow to rest for 5 minutes. Meanwhile, sprinkle the spring onions lightly with salt and pepper and place them on the grill. Cook for 3 to 4 minutes, rolling over several times, or until the outsides are brown.

4. Remove the spring onions from the grill and slice in half lengthwise. Serve each of the steaks with a halved spring onion, a squeeze or two of lime, and a big spoonful of the Sweet Corn Relish.

SWEET CORN RELISH

> 4 ears corn, husked, desilked, blanched in boiling salted water for 2
>   minutes, and drained
> $^1/_2$ red bell pepper, seeded and diced small
> $^1/_2$ green bell pepper, seeded and diced small
> 1 small red onion, peeled and diced small
> 1 to 2 tablespoons minced fresh chile pepper of your choice
> 1 cup red wine vinegar
> $^1/_3$ cup olive oil
> 3 tablespoons molasses
> $^1/_2$ cup roughly chopped fresh parsley
> Salt and freshly cracked black pepper to taste

1. Place the corn around the edges of **a hot fire,** where the heat is lower, so it is just barely over the coals. Cook the corn, rolling it around frequently, for about 3 minutes, or until well browned. Remove from the grill.

2. As soon as the ears are cool enough to handle, slice the kernels from the cobs into a small bowl. Add the remaining ingredients and toss well.

I'd serve this along with Lisa White's White Gazpacho (page 30) in front and Coconut Flan (page 364) for dessert.

Pepper-Crusted Grilled Filet Mignon with Blue Cheese Butter and Roasted Garlic Mash

SERVES 4

You can cook this dish any time of year, but I like its rich, heavy, strong flavors best in the winter, so I set up a grill in my fireplace and cook the steaks close to the fire. If you can get hold of oak logs, the flavor is incomparable. The blue cheese butter is strong but not overbearing, and the garlic mash spread on the toasts works very well with the black pepper. Try to get really thick steaks for this one, so you can get the strong sear on all sides without overcooking the middle.

> 4 8- to 10-ounce beef fillet steaks, 2 to 3 inches thick
>
> $^1/_4$ cup kosher salt
>
> 1 cup freshly cracked black pepper, plus more to taste
>
> $^1/_4$ cup unsalted butter, at room temperature
>
> 2 ounces blue cheese
>
> 4 heads roasted garlic (see page 89)
>
> $^1/_4$ cup olive oil
>
> $^1/_4$ cup fresh thyme leaves
>
> Salt to taste
>
> 4 slices crusty bread

1. Rub the steaks with the salt and pepper, using the full amount. Grill them over **a hot fire** for 6 to 8 minutes on each side for medium-rare. *To check for doneness:* Cut into one of the steaks to see that it is about one degree less done in the center than you want, since it will cook a little more after you take it off the fire. Remove from the fire and let it rest for about 5 minutes.

2. While the steaks are resting, combine the butter and blue cheese in a small bowl, mix until well combined, and set aside.

3. Squeeze the roasted garlic pulp out of the peels into a small bowl. Add the olive oil, thyme, and salt and pepper to taste, mix well, and set aside.

4. Place the bread on the grill over the edge of the fire, where the heat is low, and toast for about 2 minutes on each side, until golden brown.

5. Spread the garlic mash on the toast, slice the steaks thin and place on top of the toast, then put a spoonful of the butter on each and serve.

This goes well with **Simple Lentils (page 304)**. **Grilled Pineapple with Sweet Lime–Black Pepper Sauce (page 358)** makes a good dessert.

Grilled Flank Steak "in the Style of Pastrami" with Spicy Tomato-Horseradish Relish

Flank steak has a ton of flavor, and if you grill it quickly over high heat and slice it very thin against the grain, it also gets reasonably tender. Here the flank is rubbed with a mixture of sweet and savory spices imitating a pastrami cure, then grilled, sliced very thin, and served on top of toasted rye bread with a tomato-horseradish relish—like a summer deli sandwich. I like to cut the rye bread thick and use it to soak up the juices from the relish. The pungent horseradish goes smoothly with the crusty, sweetly spiced exterior of the steak.

For the Relish

> 2 tomatoes about the size of baseballs, cored and diced small
>
> 1 medium red onion, peeled and diced small
>
> $^1/_3$ cup red wine vinegar
>
> $^1/_4$ cup horseradish
>
> 2 tablespoons Dijon mustard
>
> Salt and freshly cracked black pepper to taste

For the Rub

> 2 tablespoons minced garlic
>
> 2 tablespoons ground coriander
>
> 1 tablespoon ground cinnamon
>
> 1 teaspoon ground cloves
>
> 1 teaspoon ground allspice
>
> $^1/_4$ cup kosher salt
>
> 2 tablespoons freshly cracked white pepper (or substitute black)
>
> 2 tablespoons freshly cracked black pepper
>
> 1 teaspoon red pepper flakes
>
> 1 16-ounce flank steak
>
> 4 thick slices hearty rye bread

1. Make the relish: In a medium bowl, combine all the ingredients and mix well. Set aside.

2. Make the rub: In a small bowl, combine all the ingredients and mix well. Cover the flank steak generously with the rub and grill over **a hot fire** for 5 to 7 minutes on each side for medium-rare. *To check for doneness:* Cut into the steak and peek to see if it is one degree less done than you like.

3. While the steak is grilling, place the rye bread around the sides of the grill—when the steak is done, the bread should be nicely toasted.

4. Remove the steak from the grill, allow it to rest for 5 minutes, slice it as thin as you possibly can, and serve on top of the rye bread, accompanied by the spicy relish.

Try this with Grilled Regular Mushrooms with Sherry (page 62) as an appetizer, Jícama-Apple Salad with Orange-Mustard Dressing (page 307) on the side, and Maple Bread Pudding with Oven-Dried Pears and Homemade Raisins (page 367) for dessert. Uh-huh.

Rosemary-Grilled New York Strip with Smoky Eggplant Relish

SERVES 4

With all the health concerns these days about eating too much red meat, it makes sense to really enjoy it when you do eat it. In other words, if I'm eating steak, I want to know it. That means I want to go with a prep that features the rich, savory flavor of the meat itself. To me, both rosemary and smoky eggplant help bring out the true nature of grilled beef rather than obscuring it.

If you go to a butcher for your meat, try to get thick steaks cut from a smaller loin, which will give you a more tender product. In any case, make sure you get steaks that are really thick, so they can get a good, strong sear on the outside and still be rare at the center.

> $^1/_2$ cup minced fresh rosemary
> 3 tablespoons minced garlic
> $^1/_3$ cup kosher salt
> $^1/_2$ cup freshly cracked black pepper
> 4 12- to 16-ounce sirloin steaks, about $1^1/_2$ inches thick

For the Relish
> 2 medium eggplants, cut into rounds about 1 inch thick
> 1 red onion, peeled and cut into rings about 1 inch thick
> $^1/_3$ cup vegetable oil
> Salt and freshly cracked black pepper to taste
> 1 tablespoon minced garlic
> $^1/_2$ cup balsamic vinegar
> $^1/_4$ cup extra virgin olive oil
> 2 tablespoons roughly chopped fresh parsley

continued

1. In a small bowl, combine the rosemary, garlic, salt, and pepper and mix well. Rub the steaks all over with this mixture and grill them over **a hot fire** for 5 to 7 minutes per side for medium-rare. *To check for doneness:* Cut into one of the steaks to see that it is about one degree less done in the center than you want, since it will cook a little more after you take it off the fire. When the steaks are done to your liking, pull them off the grill and let them rest for about 3 minutes.

2. Meanwhile, make the relish: Rub the eggplant and onions with the oil, sprinkle with salt and pepper to taste, and grill around the edge of the fire, just barely over the flame (you are looking for **a medium-hot fire** for these vegetables), until they are well browned and soft throughout, 3 to 4 minutes per side. Pull them off the grill, dice them into medium chunks, and place them in a medium bowl. Add the garlic, vinegar, olive oil, parsley, and salt and pepper to taste and toss well.

3. By this time the steaks should be just right, so serve them up with a few heaping spoonfuls of the relish.

Try this with Lisa White's White Gazpacho (page 30) and, as a side dish, Grilled Asparagus with Garlic Mayonnaise or Simple Vinaigrette (page 279).

Spice-Rubbed Grilled Top Round with Tomatoes, Herbs, and Chiles

SERVES 4

This dish is inspired by the many grilled beef salad dishes I enjoyed in Thailand and Vietnam. At first I was surprised to see the juxtaposition of rare beef and classic Southeast Asian spices and flavorings, but it quickly became my standard order.

In this dish, everything is raw but the meat, which is grilled over a hot fire to give it a good sear, then sliced into small pieces and tossed with everything else, salad-fashion. That way, the flavors are all direct and individual, the taste dynamic that I like best.

With so many tastes going on this dish, you can leave out some of the more exotic ingredients, like fish sauce or bean sprouts, if you don't have them or don't like them. As a matter of fact, you can even forget the spice rub and just grill up the top round with salt and pepper. The important factors here are the hard sear, the fresh lime juice, and the fresh herbs.

For the Rub

    2 tablespoons minced ginger

    2 tablespoons minced garlic

    2 tablespoons minced fresh chile pepper of your choice

    4 scallions (white and green parts), minced

    $1/4$ cup sesame oil

    $1/4$ cup freshly ground white pepper (or substitute black)

    Salt to taste

    2 pounds top round, cut into slices about 2 inches thick

    2 tomatoes, cored and roughly chopped

    1 bunch scallions (white and green parts), thinly sliced

    1 cup bean sprouts (optional)

    2 tablespoons roughly chopped fresh mint

    2 tablespoons roughly chopped fresh basil

    2 tablespoons roughly chopped fresh cilantro or parsley

    2 tablespoons minced ginger

    2 tablespoons minced lemon grass (inner portion of bottom third of
        the stalk only; optional)

    1 tablespoon minced garlic

    $1/4$ cup fresh lime juice (about 2 limes)

    2 tablespoons fish sauce (optional)

    1 to 2 tablespoons chile-garlic paste or minced fresh chile pepper
        of your choice

    Salt and freshly cracked black pepper to taste

    $1/2$ cup unsalted peanuts, toasted in a 350°F oven for 10 minutes,
        or until golden brown, then roughly chopped, for garnish

1. Make the rub: In a medium bowl, combine the ingredients and mix well. Add top round and toss well so the meat is covered on all sides with the rub. Set aside.

2. In a large bowl, combine remaining ingredients except peanuts and set aside.

3. Place the meat on the grill over **a hot fire** and cook for about 5 minutes per side, or until well seared on the outside but still pink on the inside. *To check for doneness:* Cut into a piece and check to see that it is one degree less done than you want it to be, since carry-over cooking will take it the rest of the way.

4. Remove meat from the grill and allow to rest for 5 minutes, slice very thinly against the grain, and cut into bite-sized pieces. Add the meat to the bowl with vegetables and toss well. Serve in large bowls, garnished with toasted peanuts.

> **For a really hot start to this, I'd go with Chile-Grilled Squid on Sesame Spinach (page 233), then cool it out a bit with Sesame Green Beans with Crispy Fried Shallots (page 281) on the side, and finish up with Grilled Pineapple with Sweet Lime–Black Pepper Sauce (page 358).**

getting to know fish sauce

TO MOST OF US, the barrier to appreciating fish sauce is not so much the taste as the process by which the product is made. You basically take a lot of anchovies or other small fish, pack them in salt, and allow them to ferment for three months or more, drawing off the liquid as it seeps out. Truth is, it's not all that appetizing.

THIS MEANS THAT TO appreciate fish sauce, you need to open your mind and your mouth in that order, so that tasting is done with unprejudiced taste buds. Get rid of that mental image of fermenting fish and instead think of flavorings like ketchup or soy sauce, or even seasonings like salt and pepper—which is the way Asian cooks think of fish sauce. It's also important to know that the aroma of fish sauce is its most uncompromising property, outpacing its actual taste by several degrees of intensity. Don't take a whiff and decide you don't like it—try it in a dish. You'll find that the flavors of the food are mysteriously deepened and you won't actually taste the fish sauce as a separate ingredient at all.

ON THE OTHER HAND, you may not like it—but at least you'll know that you gave it a try.

Grilled Veal Chops with Expensive Mushrooms

SERVES 4

Usually I'm a downtown cook, preferring to use the more reasonably priced ingredients that are also a bit more challenging to cook. But that's not to say that I won't go uptown every once in a while—and if you're going uptown, you might as well really do it up. First take out a second mortgage on your home, then go to the butcher and tell him you want four first-cut veal rib chops. If he says he can't possibly get those for you, tell him you'll take second-cut chops, but no end cuts, please. That's because there are a couple of chop cuts toward the leg end of the rack that would make you think I was crazy for recommending this cut of meat at all. So make sure your rib chops are from the loin end. Loin chops are good, too, but they look like pork chops, whereas the rib chops look like mini–prime ribs and tend to have a bit more delicious fat on them.

So with a really good—read expensive—ingredient like this, the cook's goal is to do as little as possible to screw up the delicate nature of the meat. So we just salt and pepper it and grill it at a little lower temperature than red meat, being careful not to oversear or dry the veal.

The mushrooms are also expensive, but they are fantastic. Use any one or a mixture of whichever wild mushrooms most appeal to you. I'll tell you a secret—you

STRICTLY ENTRÉES

can use button mushrooms too, either mixing them in or going all the way with buttons. The mushrooms take different amounts of time to cook, so as each type is done, bring it off the grill; a mushroom is done when you look inside and it's all moist.

> 4 12- to 14-ounce bone-in veal rib chops
> 1/4 cup olive oil
> Salt and freshly cracked black pepper to taste
> 2 pounds fancy mushrooms (porcini, portobellos, chanterelles, morels, shiitakes, etc.), cleaned
> 3 tablespoons unsalted butter
> 2 tablespoons minced garlic
> 1/3 cup sherry
> 1/4 cup roughly chopped fresh sage or oregano

1. Rub the veal chops with about 2 tablespoons of the olive oil and sprinkle with salt and pepper to taste. You want **a medium fire** for the chops, since searing is not as important with white veal meat as it is with red meat. Cook the chops for 8 to 10 minutes per side. *To check for doneness:* Nick one of the chops and peek at the interior—it should be slightly pink for medium, which is how I like to cook veal.

2. While you are cooking the veal, place the mushrooms in a medium bowl with the remaining 2 tablespoons or so of oil and salt and pepper to taste and toss well. Place the mushrooms on the grill and cook, turning once or twice, for 4 to 5 minutes, or until golden brown. *To check for doneness:* Cut open one of each type of mushroom; it should look moist all the way through. Remove from the grill.

3. In a small saucepan over medium heat, melt the butter. Add the garlic and sauté for 1 minute, stirring once or twice, to soften. Add the sherry and cook for 5 minutes to cook off the alcohol. When the mushrooms are cooked, toss them with the butter mixture, add the herbs, and toss again.

4. Pull the chops off the fire and let them rest for 5 minutes, then serve them topped with the mushrooms.

This is a super-special dish, so I might serve Grilled Mussels Johnson (page 72) in front of it, Romaine and Bulgur Salad (page 319) alongside it, and Maple Bread Pudding with Oven-Dried Pears and Homemade Raisins (page 367) as a dessert.

Grilled Rack of Lamb with Quick Mint-Apricot Sauce and Blue Cheese–Stuffed Tomatoes

SERVES 4

A perfectly grilled rack of lamb is a standard qualification in all graduate grilling programs. So if you're looking to earn a Ph.G. (Doctor of Grilling), you're going to have to master this one.

This is a fairly heady recipe. It's not really that complex, but grilling a large piece of meat takes a certain "griller instinct," as there is a lot of jockeying back and forth on the edge of the fire. In addition, this is not a piece of chicken or pork here; two racks of lamb are going to set you back a bit costwise, and there is a high degree of danger involved because of the fat layer that covers one side of the lamb. But it's worth the added vigilance. If you've never had a "grill-roasted" rack of lamb before, the taste is going to blow you away, along with the lucky people you've invited to share the grilled rack experience.

Since the mass of the lamb makes it too large to grill directly over the fire (the surface would be torched beyond recognition while the interior was still dead raw), we first wrap the bones tightly with foil to keep them from burning, then cook the lamb at the edges of a medium to medium-hot fire.

If you have a meat thermometer, this is a good place to use it. You're looking for an internal temperature of around 125°F for rare to medium-rare, which is the way I like lamb. If you're checking doneness by touch, the lamb should be about the same texture when you press on it as the base of your thumb. If you're going to miss it, though, miss it on the rare side, because then you have the option of cutting the underdone racks into chops, sprinkling them with salt and pepper, and refiring them on the grill for about thirty seconds or so per side to finish them up.

But if you hit it right on, make sure you carve the racks in front of your guests, because a perfectly done lamb rack being sliced is truly a sight to behold. The blue cheese–stuffed tomatoes add richness to the mix, and the sweet-sour apricot mint sauce is a throwback to the green jelly that was inseparable from roast lamb in my house when I was a kid. This is the one for those special occasions, a slightly challenging prep for an outstanding meal.

2 tablespoons minced garlic

2 tablespoons olive oil

$^1/_2$ cup roughly chopped fresh herbs: rosemary, oregano, thyme, and/or parsley

2 tablespoons kosher salt

$^1/_4$ cup freshly cracked black pepper

2 racks of lamb, Frenched

For the Sauce

> $^1/_2$ cup apricot jam
> $^1/_4$ cup balsamic vinegar
> $^1/_4$ cup roughly chopped fresh mint
> Salt and freshly cracked black pepper to taste

1. In a small bowl, combine the garlic, olive oil, herbs, salt, and pepper and mix well. Rub this mixture generously over the outside of the lamb racks, then cover the bones with foil to prevent burning.

2. Build a small fire on one side of your grill, using about enough charcoal to fill a shoe box. Allow all of the fuel to become completely engulfed in flames and then, when the flames have died down to flickering coals and the fire temperature is **medium to medium-hot,** place the lamb racks on the grill over the flames but near the edge of the fire, with the fat side up. As soon as the down side browns (about 15 minutes), flip the racks—now the fat side is down, so beware! Watch for flare-ups caused by dripping fat and, when they occur, move the rack in question off the fire until the flare-up dies down, then move it back. Cook for about 15 minutes on this side, or until well browned. *To check for doneness:* Insert an instant-read meat thermometer into the center of the rack; it should read 125°F for rare to medium-rare. Or press against the lamb; it should have some give but be about as firm as the base of your thumb.

3. Meanwhile, make the sauce: In a small saucepan over medium heat, melt the apricot jam, stirring frequently to prevent burning. Add the balsamic vinegar and cook, stirring frequently, for 3 minutes, then remove from the heat and stir in the mint and salt and pepper to taste.

4. Remove the lamb racks from the grill. Take the foil off the lamb and slice the racks in between the ribs. Remove the tomatoes from the foil. Serve the lamb racks with the mint-apricot sauce, which can be either warm or cold, and the Blue Cheese–Stuffed Tomatoes.

BLUE CHEESE–STUFFED TOMATOES

> 4 large ripe tomatoes
> 1 cup crumbled good-quality blue cheese
> $^1/_2$ cup fresh bread crumbs, toasted
> 2 tablespoons roughly chopped fresh parsley
> Salt and freshly cracked black pepper to taste

continued

1. Core the tomatoes and hollow out their centers with a small spoon, digging down almost to the bottom and taking some meat out. Loosely stuff the tomatoes with the blue cheese.

2. In a small bowl, combine the bread crumbs, parsley, and salt and pepper to taste and mix well. Cover the tops of the tomatoes with this mixture. Wrap the tomatoes in foil and set them on the grill over the side with no flames; you want the indirect heat of a medium fire here. Cook for about 15 minutes, or until the tomatoes are soft but not mushy.

For a really fantastic dinner, try serving this with **Red Snapper Cocktail (page 73)** as a starter, **Grilled Asparagus with Garlic Mayonnaise or Simple Vinaigrette (page 279)** on the side, and **Spanish Olive Oil and Wine Cake (page 372)** at the end.

Grilled Lamb Chops and Sausage on Arugula and Mint

SERVES 4

Ask a bunch of chefs about their top five favorite dinners, and I'd be willing to bet that you would find more than a few surprising entries. One of my favorite haunts is a place in East Boston called San Tarpio's. The place is best known for its pizza, but I go for the lamb-sausage combo platter. This hulking plate of food consists of chunked-up and skewered lamb shoulder (maybe a little chewy, but the texture is more than compensated for by the increased lamb flavor) and an Italian sausage, both cooked over hardwood charcoal, then served on a platter with crusty bread and a handful of hot cherry peppers. That and a couple of beers, and I'm loving life. It might not sound like a memorable dining experience, but I think it talks to the point of food being food. It's not art, it's not a religious experience, it's food, and sometimes rustic and straightforward and plentiful is exactly what you want.

In any case, that was the inspiration for this dish. In my stepped-up version, I use shoulder chops instead of lamb shoulder (less chewy but almost as flavorful), rub them with herbs and red pepper flakes, and serve them over an aromatic salad of arugula and whole mint leaves. I grill the bread, but leave the cherry peppers just as they are in the original dish.

I'm not sure that Lefty, the grill man at San Tarpio's, would recognize this dish as a version of what he cooks daily, but I'd like to dedicate it to him anyway. Thanks, Lefty, for all the great food.

4 10- to 12-ounce shoulder lamb chops, about 1¹/₂ inches thick

Salt and freshly cracked black pepper to taste

¹/₃ cup plus 3 tablespoons olive oil

2 tablespoons roughly chopped fresh rosemary

1 tablespoon minced garlic

1 tablespoon red pepper flakes

4 links of your favorite sausage, 4 to 6 ounces each

4 thick slices bread

2 bunches arugula, trimmed, washed, dried, and torn into large pieces

1 cup fresh mint leaves

1 small red onion, peeled and thinly sliced

¹/₄ cup fresh lemon juice (about 1 lemon)

12 pickled hot cherry peppers (optional)

1. Sprinkle the lamb chops with salt and pepper to taste. In a small bowl, combine the 3 tablespoons olive oil, the rosemary, garlic, and red pepper flakes and mix well. Cover the chops generously with this rub, and grill over **a medium fire** for 6 to 7 minutes per side for medium. *To check for doneness:* Cut into one of the chops and check to see that the meat is slightly less done than you want it to be when you eat it, since it will continue to cook a bit after you remove it from the grill.

2. While the lamb is cooking, poach the sausage in boiling salted water to cover for 5 minutes. Drain and place on the grill around the edge of the fire, where the heat is low. The sausages should warm through and crisp up on the outside in about the same amount of time as it takes the lamb to finish cooking.

3. Place the bread slices on the grill around the edges of the fire and toast until golden brown on both sides, 3 to 4 minutes.

4. In a large bowl, combine the arugula, mint, and onion and toss to mix. Add the remaining ¹/₃ cup olive oil, the lemon juice, and salt and pepper to taste and toss again. Place a portion of this salad mixture on each plate and place the lamb chops over the greens, along with a piece of sausage and a slice of grilled bread. Garnish with the peppers if you want, and serve warm.

Put this alongside **Sweet-Potato Steak Fries with Your Own Catsup**
(page **284**), or with **Grilled Buffalo Chicken Hearts** (page **77**)
in front, and try **Grilled Bananas and Pineapple with Rum-Molasses Glaze**
(page **357**) for an ending.

Grilled Lamb Chops with Pomegranate-Eggplant Relish

Lamb and live fire are a natural combination. But you have to be careful when you join them, because the fat is prone to causing flare-ups. As usual, you should arrange your fire so that a portion of the grill rack is not over any coals. That way, if and when flare-ups occur, you can move the chops without taking them completely away from the heat. Also, be sure you check the doneness of the chops before you remove them from the fire because, especially when they are really thick, they tend to appear done before they really are.

The relish here is a little sweet, which I like with lamb, and the tart-sweet pomegranate molasses it calls for is well worth having on hand. You can pick it up in any Middle Eastern store.

For the Relish

$^1/_3$ cup olive oil

1 large eggplant, diced large

1 red onion, peeled and diced medium

2 tablespoons minced garlic

2 tablespoons minced ginger

1 cup tomato juice

$^1/_3$ cup pomegranate molasses

1 teaspoon cayenne pepper

$^1/_2$ cup chopped fresh mint

Salt and freshly cracked black pepper to taste

8 6-ounce lamb loin chops, about 2 inches thick

1 tablespoon ground coriander

1 tablespoon ground cumin

Salt and freshly cracked black pepper to taste

Mint sprigs for garnish

1. Make the relish: In a large sauté pan, heat the oil over high heat until hot but not smoking. Add the eggplant and cook, stirring, until well seared and quite soft, 5 to 7 minutes. Reduce the heat to medium, add the onion, and cook, stirring, for 2 to 3 minutes. Add the garlic and ginger and cook, stirring, for 1 minute. Add the tomato juice, pomegranate molasses, and cayenne and bring just to a boil. Reduce the heat to low and simmer, stirring occasionally, for 5 minutes. Remove from the heat, stir in the mint, and season to taste with salt and pepper.

2. Sprinkle the lamb chops with the coriander, cumin, and salt and pepper to taste. Place the chops on the grill over **a medium-hot fire** and cook for 6 to 7 minutes per side for medium. *To check for doneness:* Cut into one of the chops and check to see that it is one degree less done than you want it to be, since it will continue to cook after you remove it from the fire.

3. Serve the chops with the relish on the side and sprigs of mint for garnish.

I might serve this with Hobo Pack Italiano (page 223), Grilled Portobellos with Prosciutto and Figs on Seared Greens (page 65) in front, and Minted Melon with Caribbean Elixir (page 361) as the dessert.

Tandoori-Style Roasted Whole Leg of Lamb

SERVES 8 TO 10

When you make this dish, you'll start to get an idea of the complex palette of flavors that Indian cooks work with on a daily basis. First the lamb is cleaned and pounded to a uniform thickness of about three inches. Then it is rubbed with a mixture of spices, with an emphasis on sweet ones such as cinnamon, cloves, and cardamom, along with ginger and yogurt. The mixture resembles the marinades used on meat chunks before they are threaded on skewers and cooked in the traditional charcoal-fire roasting pits of India, known as tandooris. Because of the thickness of the meat, you want to cook it over a medium to medium-low fire. This way the lamb cooks slowly, allowing the elaborate, complex flavors of the crust to develop without burning.

> 1 4- to 5-pound boneless leg of lamb
> Salt and freshly cracked black pepper to taste
> $^1/_2$ cup roughly chopped fresh cilantro
> $^1/_4$ cup minced ginger
> $^1/_4$ cup minced garlic
> $^1/_4$ cup ground cumin
> $^1/_4$ cup cayenne pepper
> 2 tablespoons ground coriander
> 2 tablespoons ground cardamom
> 1 tablespoon ground cinnamon
> 1 tablespoon ground cloves
> $^1/_4$ cup kosher salt
> $^1/_4$ cup olive oil
> $^1/_2$ cup plain yogurt

continued

1. Trim off any excess fat from the lamb leg. Now take a mallet or heavy frying pan and whack the lamb at the thicker points until it is about 3 inches thick all over. Your object here is not only to achieve a uniform thickness so the lamb cooks evenly, but also to make it somewhat flatter so it cooks more quickly.

2. In a medium bowl, combine all the remaining ingredients and mix well. Rub the lamb all over with this spice mixture, place it in a roasting pan, cover it with plastic wrap, and refrigerate for 1 to 3 hours.

3. When you are ready to cook the lamb, build a fire off to one side of a covered grill, using about enough coals to fill a shoe box. When the flames have died down and the coals are covered with gray ash, spread them out evenly so that you have **a medium to medium-low fire.** Place the lamb leg over the coals and cook for about 15 minutes per side for medium-rare. *To check for doneness:* If you have an instant-read meat thermometer, push it into the center of the lamb; when it registers 124°F, the lamb is medium-rare. If you don't have a meat thermometer, slice into the lamb and check the appearance at the center, removing it from the fire when it is one degree less done than you want it to be.

4. Remove the lamb from the grill and allow it to rest for about 15 minutes, then thinly slice and serve.

> **I might serve this with a couple of side dishes inspired by the same spice palette, such as Indian-Style Sweet Potato Salad (page 315) and K. C.'s Bengali-Style Spinach (page 292), then put some Lime-Pickled Mangoes with Ginger and Chiles (page 336) out as a relish, and finish the meal with Saffron-Cardamom Poached Pears with Cranberry-Currant Relish (page 359).**

sweet spices: not just for baking

CINNAMON, CLOVES, AND NUTMEG, which are thought of by most American cooks primarily as flavorings for sweet baked goods, are in fact used throughout much of the world as ingredients in savory cooking. They are particularly prevalent in spice blends used in tropical cooking. Earlier in their history, these highly aromatic spices were used in even more unusual ways. For example, cloves were used by the elite in parts of Asia as a breath freshener, nutmeg was a key ingredient in the mummifying formula of ancient Egyptians, and the infamously profligate Emperor Nero created bonfires of cinnamon bark to perfume the streets of Rome for his sister's wedding.

Chuletas: Thin Grilled Pork Chops with Simple Tomato Relish

SERVES 4

When you eat pork chops in Latin America, the cut of choice is paper-thin. Most cooks rub these chops with a little garlic and lime, throw them on a super-hot grill, and cook them fast. It's a sublime experience. Chops as thin as you can find and a fire as hot as you can get it are the two keys to success with this method. The relish is a nice complement, but the *chuletas* are fantastic even without it. Dust off the margarita recipe for a good beverage pairing.

8 to 12 4- to 5-ounce thin-cut pork chops

Salt and freshly cracked black pepper to taste

For the Rub

2 tablespoons minced garlic

1 tablespoon minced fresh chile pepper of your choice

$^1/_4$ cup roughly chopped fresh oregano (or substitute cilantro)

$^1/_4$ cup fresh lime juice (about 2 limes)

3 tablespoons olive oil

1 tablespoon achiote powder (or substitute paprika)

For the Relish

2 tomatoes about the size of baseballs, cored and diced small

2 tablespoons cumin seeds, toasted if you want, or 1 tablespoon
   ground cumin

1 small red onion, peeled and diced small

2 tablespoons red wine vinegar

$^1/_4$ cup extra virgin olive oil

1 teaspoon minced garlic

Salt and freshly cracked black pepper to taste

1. Sprinkle the chops with salt and pepper to taste.

2. Make the rub: In a small bowl, combine all the ingredients and mix well. Cover the chops generously with the rub.

3. Make the relish: In a small bowl, combine all the ingredients, toss well, and set aside.

4. Grill the chops over **a hot fire** for about 3 minutes per side. *To check for doneness:* Cut into one of the chops; there should be just a little pink showing inside. Pull the chops off the grill and serve with the relish.

I'd try this with Basic Black Beans (page 299) on the side, and with Coconut Pancakes with Caramelized Bananas (page 369) for dessert.

annatto, the coloring spice

ACHIOTE POWDER, ALSO CALLED annatto, is a powder made from the dried seeds and pulp of the fruit of the annatto tree. This small tree, native to Latin America, is a brilliant red, and the powder made from its fruit is a kind of neon burnt orange. While it does give some flavor to foods in which it is used, the main purpose of the powder is to provide color. (Like other spices, of course, the fresh version is several times more powerful; if you can get hold of some achiote seeds and grind them yourself, you'll find that this spice does indeed have a distinctive, if mild, flavor.) Many Latin American recipes call for sautéing a little achiote in hot oil at the beginning of the cooking process, and folks who are used to these recipes say the food just doesn't taste the same if the achiote is left out. One thing for certain, it sure doesn't look the same! If you can't find achiote, paprika is a suitable substitute.

Grilled Double-Thick Pork Chops with Grilled Peaches and Molasses-Rum Barbecue Sauce

SERVES 4

Ah, the joys of eating a double-thick pork chop. These days a pork chop weighing almost a pound is an anomaly in a supermarket, but when you tell your butcher to cut you four really fat ones, he's likely to ask what time he should be at your house for dinner. If there's a choice, I prefer the rib chops, because they look a little neater. These chops are going to be really thick, so we use the "sear 'em hard and quick and then move 'em to the side" method. If we left them over the flames, they would surely burn prior to being cooked through. Unless you have highly developed griller instincts, you're going to have to nick, peek, and cheat several times to know when these chops are done, which is no problem, since it does not hurt the chops at all. Use the glaze at the last minute to add an extra caramelized crust. The grilled peaches are not only excellent with pork but they go well with just about any other grilled meat, too.

4 14- to 16-ounce double-thick rib or loin pork chops
2 tablespoons vegetable oil
Salt and freshly cracked black pepper to taste

For the Sauce

  2 tablespoons vegetable oil

  1 large yellow onion, peeled and diced medium

  2 tablespoons minced ginger

  2 tablespoons minced garlic

  1 cup rum of your choice

  $1/2$ cup red wine vinegar

  1 cup catsup

  $1/2$ cup molasses

  $1/4$ cup lightly packed brown sugar

  1 tablespoon ground allspice

  Pinch of ground mace

  Salt and freshly cracked black pepper to taste

  4 ripe peaches, halved and pitted

1. Build a small fire in one side of the grill, using enough charcoal to fill a shoe box.

2. Rub the chops lightly with the oil, sprinkle with salt and pepper to taste, and set aside while you begin the sauce.

3. In a small saucepan over medium heat, heat the oil until hot but not smoking. Add the onions and sauté, stirring occasionally, until transparent, 5 to 7 minutes. Add the ginger and garlic and sauté, stirring, for 1 minute. Add the rum, vinegar, catsup, molasses, sugar, allspice, and mace and bring just to a boil. Reduce the heat to low and simmer gently for 20 minutes, then remove from the heat, season to taste, and set aside.

4. Once the sauce is at the final simmering stage, place the chops on the grill directly over **the hot fire** and cook for 3 to 4 minutes per side to sear them well. When they are nicely seared, move them to the side of the grill with no fire and let them cook slowly for about 10 minutes per side. *To check for doneness:* Cut into one chop to make sure it is cooked through and slightly pink at the center.

5. Shortly before the chops are done, place the peaches on the grill just at the edge of the fire, cut side down, and grill for 3 to 4 minutes on each side, or until they are seared and tender.

6. During the last minute of cooking, brush both the chops and peaches with the sauce. Allow to cook for 1 minute more, then remove from the grill and serve with the extra sauce on the side.

Try this with an appetizer portion of Grilled Shrimp and Bacon Skewers with Pickled Onion and Avocado Salad (page 104) to start, Grilled Corn with Lime and Chinese Roasted Salt (page 278) on the side, and Grilled Bananas and Pineapple with Rum-Molasses Glaze (page 357) at the end.

Spice-Crusted Pork Tenderloins with Banana-Date Chutney

SERVES 4

Most people think of pork as high in fat, but a pork tenderloin actually has no more fat per ounce than a boneless, skinless chicken breast. Because of its weight and thickness, the best grill treatment for this cut of meat is to sear it over a hot fire until it looks good (golden brown) on the outside, then pull it to a cooler section of the grill and let it finish cooking from radiant heat, as opposed to direct heat.

Here we rub the tenderloin with spices before cooking, then serve it with an intense chutney. The dates in the chutney make it very rich, so you don't need to use a lot—a couple of tablespoons per serving should do it.

3 12- to 14-ounce pork tenderloins

Salt and freshly cracked black pepper to taste

3 tablespoons olive oil

2 tablespoons minced garlic

3 tablespoons fennel seeds

3 tablespoons cumin seeds

1 tablespoon ground cinnamon

Banana-Date Chutney (recipe follows)

1. Sprinkle the pork tenderloins generously with salt and pepper.

2. In a small bowl, combine the olive oil, garlic, fennel seeds, cumin seeds, and cinnamon and mix well. Coat the tenderloins generously with this mixture, then grill over **a hot fire,** turning once or twice, for about 5 minutes, long enough to develop a nice brown, crusty sear on the outside. Once the tenderloins are well seared, move them to the side of the grill, where the heat is low, and cook, turning occasionally, for 10 to 12 minutes. *To check for doneness:* Cut into one of the tenderloins at its thickest part; it should be just light pink at the center.

3. Remove the pork from the grill and let it rest for 5 minutes. Slice the pork on the bias and serve with a generous spoonful of Banana-Date Chutney.

BANANA-DATE CHUTNEY

2 tablespoons vegetable oil

1 medium red onion, peeled and diced small

2 tablespoons minced ginger

$^1/_2$ cup roughly chopped pitted dates (about 10 medium dates)

2 ripe but firm bananas, peeled, halved lengthwise, and sliced into half-
   circles about $1/2$ inch thick
2 teaspoons red pepper flakes
$1/2$ cup molasses
$1/2$ cup fresh lemon juice (about 2 lemons)
$1/4$ cup roughly chopped fresh mint
Salt and freshly cracked black pepper to taste

Heat the oil in a small saucepan over medium heat until hot but not smoking. Add the onions and sauté, stirring occasionally, until soft, 3 to 4 minutes. Add the ginger and dates and sauté, stirring a couple of times, for 1 minute more. Add the bananas, red pepper flakes, molasses, and lemon juice, bring to a boil, and simmer until most of the liquid has evaporated, 7 to 10 minutes. Remove from the heat, stir in the mint, and season to taste with salt and pepper. This chutney will keep, covered and refrigerated, for about a week.

This makes an excellent Asian-flavored dinner in combination with Basic Black Beans (page 299) and Grilled Eggplant Rounds with Sweet Chile Sauce (page 287). Papaya Ice with Sweet Hot Pepper Sauce (page 362) makes a nice dessert.

dates to remember

ON A TRIP TO Tunisia a couple of years ago, we were treated to a meal in a Berber village in the southern area of the country, a landscape so strange and forbidding that George Lucas used it as the set for *Star Wars*. Laid out on giant tables in front of us were bowls of spicy carrot salad, platters of oranges, mounds of couscous, and flattish baskets filled with more than a dozen varieties of dried dates. There were round dark ones as sweet and sticky as molasses; elongated green ones with a layer of astringency under the sweetness; and the exotic *degla tnoor,* or "fingers of light," translucent enough to see the pit right through the flesh, mellow and caramelish in flavor, with less cloying sweetness than other dates.

TO AN AMERICAN RAISED to think that a date was a date, this meal was a revelation. I later learned from our hosts that they were familiar with over one hundred date varieties, each with its own particular attributes. And this is only the tip of the iceberg: In Iran today, there are over four hundred and fifty individual types of dates in commercial production. Far from being an occasional treat, dates are a staple food for the people of the Saharan regions, including not only Tunisia but also Morocco, Algeria, Egypt, the Sudan, Arabia, and Iran.

ONE CHARACTERISTIC ALL DATES share is their sweetness. When fresh, dates contain about 55 percent sugar, and as they dry, that percentage increases considerably. For desert cultures in which food is sparse, this makes them an ideal source of energy.

Quixotic Mixed Grill with Vegetable Skewers and Four Sauces

Webster defines *quixotic* as "romantic and slightly unrealistic," and this mixed grill is exactly that. Understand that when I say a mixed grill is romantic, I'm not suggesting that it's an ideal meal for an amorous rendezvous. Instead, I mean romantic in the sense of adventurous, swashbuckling, devil-may-care. It reminds me of a rowdy medieval banquet or the Brazilian churrasco, where every kind of meat you can imagine is grilled over a roaring fire, then brought to the table on huge skewers that look like swords. I grew up eating steaks and chops and sausages, and later became a big fan of offal, such as sweetbreads, livers, and heart. So I guess you could say that I love meat of all kinds, and to me a mixed grill, with its variety of tastes, flavors, and textures, is a romantic meat adventure.

Now we get to the slightly unrealistic part. First of all, it's no small feat to gather together the variety of meats that are called for, not to mention having the grill skills to cook each one well. Beyond that, the number of people who are willing to sit down these days to a big meat dinner that includes a lot of offal is a select and fortunate few. But being a cook and having some odd friends, I do this dinner once a year. If you're like me and have an appreciation for the romance and excitement of the mixed grill, this dish is for you.

For the Red Wine Vinegar–Shallot Sauce

- $1/2$ cup red wine vinegar
- $1/4$ cup roughly chopped fresh parsley
- $1/4$ cup shallots, peeled and minced
- 1 fresh chile pepper of your choice, minced
- Salt to taste
- $1/2$ tablespoon freshly cracked black pepper

For the Mango Chutney

- 1 tablespoon vegetable oil
- $1/2$ red onion, peeled and diced medium
- 1 tablespoon minced ginger
- 1 fresh chile pepper of your choice, minced
- $1/2$ red bell pepper, seeded and diced small
- $1/2$ green bell pepper, seeded and diced small
- 3 ripe mangoes, peeled, pitted, and diced medium
- 1 cup white vinegar
- $1/2$ cup sugar
- Salt and freshly cracked black pepper to taste

For Chris's Extra-Special Meat Sauce

$^1/_3$ cup Heinz 57 sauce

$^1/_3$ cup Worcestershire sauce

$^1/_3$ cup A.1. steak sauce

For the Asian-Flavored Sauce

$^1/_2$ cup soy sauce

$^1/_4$ cup sesame oil

2 tablespoons rice vinegar

2 tablespoons minced ginger

3 scallions (white and green parts), minced

2 tablespoons sesame seeds, toasted in a sauté pan over medium heat, shaking frequently, until golden brown, 3 to 4 minutes

3 large red onions, peeled and quartered

3 red bell peppers, quartered and seeded

3 green bell peppers, quartered and seeded

3 large ripe but firm tomatoes, cored and quartered

$^1/_2$ pound sweetbreads

$^1/_2$ pound chicken livers

$^1/_2$ pound chicken hearts

8 bone-in chicken thighs

8 baby lamb chops

$^1/_2$ cup vegetable oil

Salt and freshly cracked black pepper to taste

1 pound precooked sausages of your choice (see page 33)

1 loaf crusty French bread or other bread of your choice

1. Make the vinegar-shallot sauce: In a small bowl, combine all the ingredients, mix well, and set aside.

2. Make the mango chutney: In a small saucepan over medium heat, heat the oil until hot but not smoking. Add the onions and sauté, stirring occasionally, until transparent, 5 to 7 minutes. Add the ginger and chile and sauté, stirring occasionally, for 1 minute. Add the bell peppers and sauté, stirring occasionally, for another 2 minutes. Reduce the heat to low, add the mangoes, vinegar, and sugar, and cook, stirring occasionally, for 10 to 15 minutes, or until the mixture becomes slightly thick. Remove from the heat and set aside.

3. For Chris's extra-special meat sauce, just mix all the ingredients in a small bowl and set aside.

continued

4. For the Asian-flavored sauce, combine all of the ingredients in a small bowl, mix well, and set aside.

5. Thread the onions, bell peppers, and tomatoes onto skewers, alternating them however you like, and set aside.

6. Rinse the sweetbreads well, place them in a medium saucepan with enough salted water to cover, and bring to a boil over medium heat. Reduce the heat to low and simmer for 12 to 15 minutes, or until the sweetbreads are firm to the touch; they should feel like the base of your thumb when you press your finger against it. Drain and allow them to cool.

7. Once the sweetbreads have cooled, clean them by gently prying the pieces from the whole (they should separate easily into uniform bite-sized pieces). Wash these nuggets well, thread them onto skewers, and set aside. Thread the livers onto skewers.

8. Now you are ready to start grilling. You may want a partner to help you with this, or you can just stand by the grill throughout the meal, grilling things as people eat them. Set out your sauces where the guests can get at them, then rub everything—the vegetable skewers, sweetbreads, livers, hearts, thighs, and lamb chops—lightly with the vegetable oil and sprinkle generously with salt and pepper. You want **a medium-hot fire** for this marathon session. Place the sausages off to the side of the fire, with low heat. They will heat up nicely while you are grilling the rest of your meats. Place the vegetable skewers directly on the grill and cook for 3 to 5 minutes per side, or until they are well browned. Place the sweetbreads on the grill and cook for 3 to 4 minutes per side, or until they are golden brown. Place the skewered livers and the hearts (which you can just toss on the grill without skewering) on the grill and cook for 4 to 5 minutes per side. Grill the chicken thighs skin side down until the skin is crispy, 8 to 10 minutes, then flip them over and cook for an additional 4 to 6 minutes, or until a peek inside shows no redness. Last but not least, grill the lamb chops for 5 to 6 minutes per side for medium-rare. Take a deep breath and give yourself a pat on the back when you finish this one!

If you need anything else with this extravaganza, try serving it with
Bridget's Couscous Salad for a Crowd (page 320), and follow it up
with a light dessert like Grilled Bananas and Pineapple
with Rum-Molasses Glaze (page 357).

churrasco, brazilian for meat

ONE OF THE GREAT celebrations of meat and live fire is the Brazilian culinary ritual known as churrasco (say "shoo-RAS-koo"). It was born hundreds of years ago in the pampas of southern Brazil, the first place in Latin America where cattle were raised. Out in the open and constantly on the move, the gauchos who watched over the giant herds had little or no access to vegetables, seafood, or exotic spices, but they had plenty of two things: beef and salt. So a custom began of building a giant fire and grilling up prodigious amounts of beef, simply seasoned with salt.

OVER THE YEARS THIS practice spread to northern Brazil and, on the way, was expanded to include not only every part of the cow, but just about every kind of meat known to humankind. Today a typical Brazilian churrasco may offer pork, chicken, duck, turkey, lamb, and spicy sausage along with the steaks, heart, liver, kidney, and ribs of beef. The pork and the various fowl may be marinated in a lime-garlic marinade, but the beef is usually served just as it was in the original days of this ritual feast—encased in salt, which is knocked off after the beef is properly grilled. It's a true walk on the carnivore wild side.

It's only relatively recently that Americans have started
grilling seafood, so to many people it still seems a little bit unusual. But if you
want proof of the beautiful, longstanding relationship between sea creatures and
grilling, all you have to do is check out the beaches of the warm-weather world.
Whether it's grilling red snapper on the beaches of Mexico's Yucatán Peninsula,
tossing giant shrimp onto a hibachi on the waterfront of Singapore, or firing up a
brazier to grill squid on the Mediterranean shores of Tunisia, seafood and live fire
have long been on intimate terms.

STRICTLY ENTRÉES

fire and water: grilled fish and other water-dwellers

While seafood and grilling make an excellent match, however, not everything that swims in the sea is an appropriate candidate for the
grilling fire. Since this is a somewhat rigorous cooking method, you want to avoid
delicate specimens like sole and flounder, which simply fall apart over the fire.
Firm-textured fish like tuna, shark, salmon, and snapper are much more suitable

candidates. Finless seafood like shrimp, squid, scallops, lobster, and clams are also excellent.

Whatever type of fish or seafood you are grilling, there are four steps you should take to avoid the *bête noire* of the process, which anyone who has grilled fish more than a few times has probably experienced: having the fish stick to the grill.

To sidestep this annoying and potentially meal-destroying phenomenon, first make sure your grill rack is super-clean; any residue from previous cooking will provide a natural sticking point for fish. Second, the rack should be very hot before you place the fish on it. The easiest way to accomplish this is simply to put the rack over the fire as soon as you light it and leave it there as the fire heats up to the proper temperature.

You should also coat seafood with a very thin film of oil just before cooking it. Be sure, though, that you just moisten the skin, since if you use too much oil, it will drip into the fire and cause flare-ups. Finally, when you put the fish on the grill, leave it in its original position for at least a couple of minutes before you move it. This allows a sear to develop between metal and flesh, which helps avoid sticking.

If sticking to the grill rack is the greatest danger in grilling seafood, then overcooking may be the worst mistake. To avoid this, remember that seafood calls for only a medium-hot fire, rather than the very hot fire you often use for meat. Also, I recommend that you start checking the interior of the fish for doneness as soon as you approach the recommended grilling time.

Fortunately, checking fish for doneness is easy. Just do what most professional chefs do, and take a peek inside. Fish is generally quite pliable, so you can easily pick it up with your tongs and bend or twist it to get a good view of the interior. Or if you want, you can slip a knife blade into the center of the fish and lift slightly.

Relatively thin fish, along with shrimp and lobster, should be grilled until they are completely opaque in the interior. With thicker fish, however, you want to leave a trace of translucency, since residual heat will do the final bit of cooking after you remove the fish from the grill. It is also best to grill fish in pieces of at least eight ounces or so, then cut them into smaller serving portions after grilling; if you try grilling smaller pieces, they will be too thin to stay moist in the center.

In addition to these general rules, there are specific tips for different types and cuts of seafood. Fish steaks, which include the backbone, may take a bit longer to cook than other types of seafood and should be turned once, about halfway through the estimated grilling time. Thin fillets, which have no bone, will usually cook through without turning. If the fillets you are cooking taper sharply, it is a good idea to tuck the thin end under to ensure even cooking.

Shrimp and scallops can be threaded onto skewers for easy grilling, and clams, oysters, and mussels provide their own built-in timers: Just wash them, put them directly on the grill rack, and cover—when the shells pop open, they are ready to eat.

Last but not least, there is the apex of grilled seafood, the whole fish. Many people recommend using a wire fish basket when grilling whole fish, and that certainly is an acceptable option. In my opinion, however, it is much more challenging and therefore rewarding to cook the fish directly on the grill—it's sort of like doing a trapeze act without the net or shooting an apple off your mate's head without the blindfold. Prepare your fire and your grill rack properly and check the interior for doneness periodically after the initial cooking time has elapsed, and you will be fine. It really isn't that difficult, it's fun to meet the challenge, and your guests will go wild when you bear the beautiful seared whole fish dramatically to the table.

One final word of advice before you head out to the grilling fire—make sure that you have the freshest possible fish you can find. This, in fact, may be the most important tip of all. The primary key to the fantastic seafood meals I've had on tropical beaches all over the world is that the food made the journey from ocean to stomach in about ten minutes. You may not be able to achieve this level of freshness when grilling in your backyard, but if you start with the freshest possible seafood, you're giving yourself the best chance of success.

Grilled Scallops and
Plums with Sweet Mirin
Barbecue Sauce

Soft-Shell Crab with
Grilled Asparagus, Sweet
Pickled Corn Relish, and
Tabasco Tartar Sauce

Almond-Crusted Grilled
Salmon with Garlic
Sauce

Grilled Orange-Cumin
Mahi Mahi with Smoky
Summer Vegetable Hash

Sweet-Crusted Grilled
Bluefish with Avocado-
Corn Vinaigrette

Grilled Swordfish with
Artichokes, Tomatoes,
and Olives

Grilled Swordfish Steaks
with Red Potato Puree

Your Basic Whole
Grilled Fish Strategy

Grilled Trout in a
Smoked Salmon Suit
(aka Grilled Stuffed
Trout with Horseradish-
Dill Sauce)

Pepper-Grilled Tuna
Steak with Parsley-
Garlic Butter

Chile-Ginger Grilled
Tuna with Korean-Style
Salad

Bridget's Alternative
Cold Tuna Plate for a
Hot Summer Day

Grilled Halibut with
Fried Green Apples,
Bacon, and Horseradish
Sour Cream

Grilled Halibut with
Bacon–Red Onion Relish
and Roasted Red Pepper
Mayonnaise

Grilled Monkfish with
Sherry, Raisins, and
Grilled Asparagus

Herb-Crusted Grilled
Monkfish with Roasted
Red Pepper Relish

Grilled Mackerel with
Expensive Olive Oil,
Lemon, and Oregano

Grilled Red Snapper
Palapas-Style with Vera
Cruz Relish

BBQ-Rubbed Grilled
Skate with Mango-Chile
Dressing

Grilled Shad Roe with
Minted Snap Peas

Grilled Scallops and Plums with Sweet Mirin Barbecue Sauce

SERVES 4

When I grill scallops, I like to use the largest kind. People may frown and say that smaller ones taste better, but to me the big ones taste great—and they're a lot cheaper, too. Not only that, but the size really helps us in grilling because the sea scallop is able to spend enough time over a hot fire to catch a flavorful sear without overcooking. I also like to blanch them just briefly to firm them up slightly so they don't stick to the grill.

Here we put a Japanese spin on scallops, with some grilled plums and a sweet mirin sauce. If you can get dead-on fresh scallops, a bit of undercooking is appropriate here.

2 pounds sea scallops (the largest you can find), cleaned

For the Sauce

2 tablespoons minced ginger

1 tablespoon minced garlic

$^1/_2$ cup mirin (or substitute sweet vermouth or sweet sherry)

$^1/_2$ cup rice wine vinegar (or substitute $^1/_4$ cup each water and white vinegar)

$^1/_4$ cup soy sauce

6 to 10 dashes Tabasco sauce

1 tablespoon vegetable oil

Salt and freshly cracked black pepper to taste

4 plums, halved and pitted

1 lime, quartered

1. In a medium saucepan, bring 2 quarts salted water to a boil over high heat. Drop in the scallops and blanch for 1 minute. Drain and thread onto skewers.

2. Make the sauce: In a small bowl, combine all the ingredients and mix well. Set aside.

3. Rub the scallops with the oil, sprinkle with salt and pepper to taste, and grill over **a medium-hot fire** for 2 to 3 minutes per side, or until brown and slightly crisp on the outside. *To check for doneness:* Cut into one of the scallops; it should be just opaque all the way through. Be careful not to overcook, or they will toughen.

4. As the scallops are cooking, place the plums cut side down on the grill and cook for about 3 minutes per side, until slightly seared. Just as the scallops and the plums are almost finished cooking, brush both generously with the sauce.

5. Remove the scallops and plums from the grill and slide the scallops off the skewers. Serve each person 2 plum halves and one quarter of the scallops, garnished with a lime wedge. Pass the remaining sauce separately.

To keep the Asian spirit going with this Japanese-inspired dish, I might try an appetizer portion of Grilled Lamb Satay with Peanut-Mint Relish (page 120) up front, serve K. C.'s Bengali-Style Spinach (page 292) as a side dish, and finish up with Coconut Pancakes with Caramelized Bananas (page 369).

mirin: making rice nice

IT'S HARD TO OVEREMPHA-SIZE the importance of rice in the Japanese diet. Not only does this grain form a part of almost every meal, it also is used to make several other products essential to Japanese cuisine. Among these is sake, the rice wine that might be called the national alcoholic drink. Fermented rice is also used to make a less powerful wine known as mirin. Sweet, golden in color, and low in alcohol content, mirin is used almost exclusively for cooking, adding sweetness and a subtle note of alcohol to a wide variety of dishes. If you can't locate it, you can substitute sweet vermouth or sweet sherry.

Soft-Shell Crab with Grilled Asparagus, Sweet Pickled Corn Relish, and Tabasco Tartar Sauce

SERVES 4 AS ENTRÉE, 8 AS APPETIZER

Anyone who grows up around the Chesapeake Bay (for me it was Tidewater, Virginia) is forced at a young age to sign an agreement that if he ever writes a cookbook, he will include a fried soft-shell crab recipe. Now, I know this is a grilling book and some people claim that you can grill soft-shells, but to me that is heresy; if I were to put a grilled soft-shell recipe here, I would have to renounce my Tidewater roots.

In order to fulfill my legal obligation but at the same time keep the recipe in line with the general concept of the book, I'm going to fry the soft-shells and then call on the classic crab-asparagus combination to bail me out. So here we have crunchy fried soft-shell crabs and some nice, crispy grilled asparagus, both of which work well with the spicy tartar sauce and the corn relish. I believe this not only discharges my obligation but also provides a spring and early summer ritual that can't be topped.

For the Relish

1 ear corn, husked, desilked, blanched in boiling salted water for 2 minutes, drained, and kernels cut off the cob (about 1/2 cup kernels)

1/2 red bell pepper, seeded and diced small

1/3 cup cider vinegar

1/3 cup sugar

1 tablespoon celery seeds

Salt and freshly cracked black pepper to taste

2 cups cornmeal

1 cup all-purpose flour

2 cups buttermilk

8 soft-shell crabs, cleaned

1/2 cup olive oil

1/4 cup unsalted butter

24 spears asparagus, woody ends trimmed, blanched in boiling salted water for 3 minutes, plunged into ice water, and drained

Tabasco Tartar Sauce (recipe follows)

4 lemons, quartered

1. In a small bowl, combine all the ingredients, mix well, and set aside.

2. In a medium bowl, combine the cornmeal and flour and mix well. Place the buttermilk in another medium bowl and drop the crabs in, tossing them around a bit so they get covered, but not so vigorously that you break off their legs. Remove the crabs from the buttermilk and toss them in the cornmeal mixture; again making sure they get completely covered but being careful not to dismember them.

3. In a large frying pan, heat the oil and butter over medium-high heat until hot but not smoking. Drop in just enough of the breaded crabs to fill the pan without crowding it and cook for 3 to 4 minutes per side, or until the crabs are golden brown and crispy. Place the crabs on a paper towel to drain, and cook the remaining crabs.

4. Place the asparagus on the grill over **a medium-hot fire** and cook, rolling them around, for 3 to 4 minutes, until well browned.

5. Place several tablespoons of the relish on each plate, top with one crab per person for an appetizer or two for an entrée, and place the asparagus alongside the crab. Serve with the Tabasco Tartar Sauce and lemon quarters for squeezing.

TABASCO TARTAR SAUCE

> 1 cup mayonnaise (jarred or homemade, see page 344 for recipe)
> $^1/_4$ red onion, peeled and diced small
> $^1/_4$ cup sweet pickles, diced small
> 12 to 18 dashes Tabasco sauce
> Salt and freshly cracked black pepper to taste

In a small bowl, combine all the ingredients and mix well. Cover and refrigerate.

I might serve this with Grilled Spicy New Potato Salad (page 313) and try Mai Tai Pie (page 380) for dessert.

beautiful swimmers

THE LATIN NAME FOR blue crabs means "beautiful swimmers," a moniker they earned because of the fact that their back claws are actually flat paddles with which they propel themselves through the water in quick, short bursts. These are the best eating crabs in the universe, no question about it. I have argued this point with West Coasters, with their Dungeness; Floridians, with their stone crabs; Northeast-erners, with their Jonah crabs; and even Singaporeans, with their awesome spider crabs. After all this, I remain steadfastly convinced of blue crab superiority.

ONLY BLUE CRABS BECOME soft-shells, and in this guise they are in season only from May 15 to September 15, with the height of the season being the first six weeks. In order to grow, these crabs shed their shells, or molt. Crabbers have a keen eye to spot the "peelers," which they put into a special tank, hold until they completely shed their shells, and then sell.

CRABS NEED TO BE alive to be eaten safely. Don't let anyone tell you they are just sleeping—if they aren't moving, don't be buying.

Almond-Crusted Grilled Salmon with Garlic Sauce

SERVES 4

Here's a simple but interesting new way to deal with salmon. In this Spanish-inspired dish, the fish is grilled and then sprinkled with toasted almonds and cumin, followed by a thick garlic-bread sauce. If you're feeling adventurous, you can add some halved green grapes to the sauce after it's been pureed. You can substitute trout or char for salmon in this recipe.

4 8-ounce salmon fillets

3 tablespoons vegetable oil

Salt and freshly cracked black pepper to taste

For the Sauce

1 cup 1-inch cubes stale bread (crusts removed)

10 cloves garlic, peeled

$1/3$ cup red wine vinegar

1 cup extra virgin olive oil

Salt and freshly cracked black pepper to taste

$1/2$ cup blanched almonds, toasted in a 350°F oven until golden brown, about 5 minutes, then roughly chopped

$1/4$ cup cumin seeds, toasted if you want, or 2 tablespoons ground cumin

1. Rub the salmon fillets lightly with the oil and sprinkle with salt and pepper to taste. Place them on the grill over **a medium-hot fire** and cook for 6 to 8 minutes per side. *To check for doneness:* Cut into one of the fillets; it should be opaque all the way through.

2. While the salmon is cooking, make the garlic sauce: Put the bread cubes, garlic, and vinegar in a food processor or blender and puree until smooth. With the motor running, add the olive oil in a steady stream, processing just until incorporated. Season the sauce to taste with salt and pepper.

3. Remove the salmon from the grill. In a small bowl, combine the almonds and cumin and mix well. Sprinkle this mixture over the salmon, drizzle generously with the garlic sauce, and serve.

I might serve this with a double appetizer kind of thing, with Grilled Corn Chowder with Bacon and Thyme (page 25) and Barbecued Oysters in Their Shells (page 70).

SALMON IS PROBABLY THE single most popular fish in America, and for good reason. The meat of salmon is moist, delicate, and distinctive in flavor and, thanks to the fact that it is widely raised on fish farms, this paragon of a fish is available in good quality just about every day of the year in just about every market in the country. There are few other fish about which that can be said. Another advantage of salmon to the griller is that the farm-raised version is actually better for grilling than the more expensive wild salmon, because it has a higher fat content that helps prevent it from overcooking.

Grilled Orange-Cumin Mahi Mahi with Smoky Summer Vegetable Hash

SERVES 4

Mahi mahi, aka dolphinfish (but *no* relation to the Flipper variety of dolphin) is a true grilling fish. The slightly pink flesh is sweet and mild, and the large-flaked texture holds up extremely well to the grilling process. Although mahi is thought of as a tropical fish, many are landed along the East Coast during summer months. This independent fish doesn't travel in schools, and it is caught with hook and line rather than nets.

In this recipe, the cumin helps form a crusty, flavorfully crisp exterior, which is set up by the tender vegetables that are grilled and then chopped up in a hashlike concoction. If you can't locate mahi mahi, you can substitute steaks of mackerel, tuna, bluefish, mako shark, pompano, or swordfish, adjusting the cooking time accordingly.

2 ears corn, husked, desilked, blanched in boiling salted water
    for 2 minutes, and drained

2 medium zucchini, cut lengthwise into 1-inch planks

2 medium summer squash, cut lengthwise into 1-inch planks

1 red onion, peeled and cut into 1-inch rings

1 red bell pepper, halved and seeded

2 tablespoons extra virgin olive oil

Salt and freshly cracked black pepper to taste

1 tablespoon minced garlic

2 tablespoons roughly chopped fresh cilantro

1 tablespoon roughly chopped fresh oregano

2 tablespoons fresh lime juice (about 1 lime)

5 to 7 dashes Tabasco sauce

4 8-ounce mahi mahi steaks, about 1 inch thick

Zest of 1 orange (orange part only), removed in strips and minced

2 tablespoons ground cumin

2 tablespoons vegetable oil

1. Put the corn, zucchini, summer squash, onion, and bell pepper into a medium bowl along with the olive oil and salt and pepper to taste and toss well to coat the vegetables. Lay the vegetables out on the grill over **a medium-hot fire** and, as they brown, flip them over; turn the corn several times. When each vegetable is nicely browned and cooked through, pull off the grill. You should count on 3 to 4 minutes per side for the bell pepper; 4 to 5 minutes per side for the zucchini, summer squash, and onions; and 5 to 7 minutes for the corn.

2. As soon as the vegetables are cool enough to handle, cut the corn kernels off the cob and cut all the other vegetables into bite-sized chunks. Combine all of the vegetables in a bowl, add the garlic, cilantro, oregano, lime juice, and Tabasco, toss well, and set aside.

3. Sprinkle the mahi mahi with salt and pepper to taste. In a small bowl combine the orange zest, cumin, and vegetable oil and mix well. Coat the mahi generously with this mixture and grill over **the medium-hot fire** for 5 to 6 minutes per side. *To check for doneness:* Cut into one of the mahi steaks and peek inside; it should be opaque with no pink. Remove the fish from the fire. Put a generous helping of the vegetable hash on each plate, top with a mahi steak, and serve warm.

For a starter with this, I might try an appetizer portion of Grilled Vietnamese-Style Beef Skewers with Green Mango Slaw (page 124), then Grilled Artichoke and White Bean Salad (page 51) as a side dish, and Caramelized Banana and Lime Tart (page 374) for a super-sweet ending.

Sweet-Crusted Grilled Bluefish with Avocado-Corn Vinaigrette

I think bluefish has an undeserved bad reputation. Because of its high oil content, it loses its freshness quickly and doesn't freeze well, and between those two dynamics, it hasn't gotten a fair shake. But if you can get hold of one that's really fresh—not that hard a task from Cape Cod to the Carolinas from spring through fall—its flavor is rich and strong and its texture soft and tender.

Bluefish is a favorite of mine for two reasons. First, I am fortunate enough to live near a fishmonger who buys the catch of recreational fishers, which means I can get bluefish less than twenty-four hours old. Second, its distinct flavor can stand up to other strong flavors. It's not the easiest fish to grill, since it gets very flaky as it nears doneness. So start flesh side down on a clean hot grill, don't fool with it until you're ready to flip it, and flip it only once. In fact, this is one of the few cases where I might recommend using a spatula instead of tongs.

The rub here is strong and the dressing is earthy and mellow, with just a bit of a kick. If you're one of the nonbelievers and you have access to really fresh bluefish, try this recipe—you'll be a bigger person for it. On the other hand, if you can't get hold of fresh blue, this recipe also works very well with fillets of striped bass, mahi mahi, or mackerel, or steaks of tuna or swordfish.

For the Vinaigrette

1 ear corn, husked, desilked, blanched in boiling salted water for
   2 minutes, drained, and kernels cut off the cob (about $1/2$ cup kernels)
1 avocado, peeled and pitted
4 cloves garlic, peeled
1 tablespoon minced fresh chile pepper of your choice
$3/4$ cup olive oil
$1/4$ cup fresh lime juice (about 2 limes)
$1/4$ cup red wine vinegar
$1/4$ cup roughly chopped fresh cilantro (or substitute parsley)
Salt and freshly cracked black pepper

For the Rub

$1/4$ cup cumin seeds, toasted if you want, or 2 tablespoons ground cumin
$1/4$ cup coriander seeds, toasted if you want, or 2 tablespoons ground
   coriander
$1/4$ cup paprika
$1/4$ cup packed brown sugar
Salt and freshly cracked black pepper to taste

4 8-ounce bluefish fillets, $1^1/2$ to 2 inches thick

1. Make the vinaigrette: Place the corn, avocado, garlic, and chile pepper in a food processor and puree until smooth. With the motor running, slowly drizzle in the oil. Add the remaining vinaigrette ingredients and pulse to mix. Cover and refrigerate. (If you don't have a food processor, you can mash the corn, avocado, and garlic together with a large wooden spoon, as if you were creaming butter and sugar, then just stir in the remaining ingredients.)

2. Make the rub: In a small bowl, combine all the ingredients and mix well.

3. Rub the bluefish fillets well with the spice rub, place on the grill, skin side up, over **a medium-low fire,** and cook for 5 minutes. Flip and cook for an additional 5 to 8 minutes. *To check for doneness:* Cut into one of the fillets to be sure it is opaque all the way through. Serve hot off the grill, drizzled with the chilled vinaigrette.

As a starter, I'd serve an appetizer portion of Grilled Sirloin and Apricot Skewers with Pomegranate Vinaigrette (page 126), then try Grilled Black Pepper Flatbread (page 48) and Grilled Eggplant and Bread Salad for a Crowd (page 311) on the side.

Grilled Swordfish with Artichokes, Tomatoes, and Olives

SERVES 4

Along with tuna, swordfish is probably the preeminent grilling fish, because the tight texture of its flesh approximates that of meat. Swordfish freezes better than any fish I know. I hesitate to say this, but there is some pretty high quality frozen swordfish referred to as "clipper sword," because it is caught and quick-frozen within hours. Freezing technology has advanced a great deal over the years, and I think a lot more of our seafood than we know is frozen and then thawed before we eat it.

But back to cooking. Here we accent the steaklike quality of swordfish with a collection of Mediterranean ingredients mixed together in a free-form chunky relish/salad type of preparation. The poached, then grilled artichokes are excellent all by themselves, but they are even better mixed with the other ingredients, and I think they complement the swordfish very well.

You can substitute steaks of tuna, mahi mahi, or salmon in this recipe.

2 large artichokes
$^1/_4$ cup vegetable oil
Salt and freshly cracked black pepper to taste
1 large tomato, cored and diced large
$^1/_2$ cup pitted brine-cured black olives
$^1/_4$ cup roughly chopped fresh parsley
1 teaspoon minced garlic
1 teaspoon red pepper flakes
$^1/_3$ cup extra virgin olive oil
$^1/_4$ cup fresh lemon juice (about 1 lemon)
4 8-ounce swordfish steaks, about $1^1/_2$ inches thick

1. Cut off the top third of each artichoke, snip off the sharp tips from the remaining leaves, and trim the bottom slightly so that it is even.

2. In a small stockpot, bring 3 quarts of lightly salted water to a boil. Add the artichokes and boil for about 20 minutes, or until the outer leaves pull away easily with a sharp tug. Drain the artichokes, immediately plunge them into ice and water to stop the cooking process, and then drain again.

3. Cut the artichokes in half lengthwise, brush them lightly with 2 tablespoons of the vegetable oil, and sprinkle with salt and pepper to taste. Place the artichokes on the grill over **a medium-hot fire,** cut side down, and cook them for about 10 minutes, or until the cut sides are well browned. Remove the artichokes and cut each half in half.

STRICTLY ENTRÉES

4. In a medium bowl, combine the artichokes, tomato, olives, parsley, garlic, red pepper flakes, olive oil, and lemon juice and mix well. Set aside.

5. Check to be sure the fire is still at the **medium-hot** level. If it is not, add a bit of fuel and wait until it is caught. Rub the swordfish steaks with the remaining 2 tablespoons olive oil, sprinkle with salt and pepper to taste, and place on the grill. Cook for 5 to 7 minutes per side, turning only once. *To check for doneness:* Cut into one of the steaks; it should be just opaque throughout. Remove from the grill and serve, topped with the artichoke mixture.

> For a big blow-out dinner, serve this with an appetizer portion of Grilled Lamb Skewers with Apricots (page 116) to start, Grilled Artichoke and White Bean Salad (page 51) or Fava Bean Salad with Lemon and Shaved Pecorino Romano Cheese (page 318) on the side, and Caramelized Banana and Lime Tart (page 374) for dessert.

Grilled Swordfish Steaks with Red Potato Puree

SERVES 4

Swordfish is big in the Mediterranean region, so here we pair the fish with a North African–inspired spice rub and a potato puree of the type popular in parts of southern France. I usually like my swordfish pretty straight up, but the spice rub is not super-strong, and it plays well with the lemony potato puree. If you prefer, you can skip either the puree or the rub—the dish will still be outstanding with one or the other. If you can't get good swordfish, substitute steaks of tuna, salmon, or mahi mahi.

For the Puree

5 red potatoes about the size of golf balls, peeled

$^1/_4$ cup fresh lemon juice (about 1 lemon)

1 teaspoon kosher salt

Freshly cracked black pepper to taste

$^1/_2$ cup extra virgin olive oil

$^1/_4$ cup roughly chopped fresh parsley

For the Rub

2 tablespoons cumin seeds, toasted if you want, or 1 tablespoon ground cumin

2 tablespoons coriander seeds, toasted along with the cumin seeds if you want, or 1 tablespoon ground coriander

Salt and freshly cracked black pepper to taste

$^1/_4$ cup olive oil

4 8-ounce swordfish steaks, about $1^1/_2$ inches thick

1 lemon, quartered, for garnish

1. Make the puree: Cook the potatoes in boiling water until they are easily pierced with a fork but still offer some resistance, 15 to 18 minutes. Drain the potatoes, rinse well with cold water, and place in a food processor. Add the lemon juice, salt, and pepper and pulse just to mix. With the motor running, drizzle in the oil. Remove the puree from the food processor, stir in the parsley, cover, and set aside.

2. Make the rub: In a small bowl, combine all the ingredients and mix well.

3. Rub the swordfish steaks generously with the rub and grill over **a medium-hot fire** for 5 to 7 minutes per side. *To check for doneness:* Cut into one of the steaks and peek to see if it is opaque throughout.

STRICTLY ENTRÉES

4. Remove the swordfish from the grill and serve each steak with a spoonful of the puree and a wedge of lemon.

This goes well with **Raw Beef with Parsley, Capers, and Hard Cheese (page 79)** as an appetizer, **Grilled Black Pepper Flatbread (page 48)** and **Romaine and Bulgur Salad (page 319)** to accompany, and maybe **Peach Sour Cream Pie (page 378)** for dessert.

Your Basic Whole Grilled Fish Strategy

SERVES 4

Extremely difficult but basically very easy—it seems that's the way it is whenever you're at the outermost edges of any skill. Cooking a whole fish (sans the rookie basket) is a prerequisite for your advanced License to Grill. There is nothing quite like the sight of a whole fish cooking on an open fire, and if you think it looks good, the taste is even better. But how do we reach the top of that mountain, you ask; where is the path?

Well, the path is littered with the bodies of broken whole grilled fish, for experience is the only key. So don't get bummed out if your first couple of attempts end up looking like stir-fries. Try again, and you will eventually reach the goal. To assist in the journey, check out my Nine-Step Path to Grilled Whole Fish Nirvana (page 175). Believe me, this is one pilgrimage that is definitely worth the journey.

> 4 1½-pound whole fish, scaled and gutted (choices include red snapper, trout, ocean perch, bluefish, tilapia, mackerel, hybrid striped bass, tautog, and scud)
> ¼ cup vegetable oil
> Salt and freshly cracked black pepper to taste
> 2 lemons, quartered

1. Make several diagonal slashes about 1 inch deep along the sides of each fish. Rub the fish lightly with the oil and sprinkle generously with salt and pepper inside and out.

2. Make sure that your grill grid is very clean, and place it on the fire at least 10 minutes before you are ready to cook; the easiest thing is just to put the grid over the coals right after you light them.

3. Place the fish directly on the grill over **a medium-hot fire** and grill for 4 to 5 minutes without moving them. It's very important not to mess with the fish at this time, because if a sear has not developed on the skin, the fish will stick. (If the fire is too hot and the fish seem to be burning, though, you may have to move them to a spot with less heat.) After 4 or 5 minutes, use your tongs to gently free the fish from the grill grid, but don't turn them yet—continue to cook for another 2 to 3 minutes.

4. Roll the fish over gently, as you would a sleeping bed partner, and let cook for another 10 minutes or so. *To check for doneness:* Cut into one of the fish at the thickest part and check to see that it is opaque throughout.

5. Remove the fish from the grill, squeeze a lemon quarter or two over the top of each, and serve at once. Once you get a little practice in, you can try out different rubs and stuffings.

In front of this I might serve **Raw Beef with Parsley, Capers, and Hard Cheese (page 79)**, then follow up with **Latin-Flavored Root Vegetable Hobo Pack (page 216)** as a side dish.

the nine-step path to
grilled whole fish nirvana

1. CHOOSE THE RIGHT candidate and make sure it's really fresh. If you're grilling one whole fish per person (which is the best plan), you should look for fish that weigh between 1¹/₄ and 2 pounds. Any larger than that, and you'll have trouble flipping them.

2. START WITH A big hot fire and let it die down, catching it just as it turns from medium-high to medium.

3. MAKE SURE YOUR grill grid is hot and clean. The best way to do this is to put the grid over the coals just after you light the fire, scrub it well with your wire brush, and then leave it on as the fire heats up and dies down.

4. OIL THE FISH very lightly before you grill it, and make several horizontal slashes about 1 inch deep in the sides of the fish—these will help it cook more evenly and also make it easier to tell when the fish is cooked properly.

5. LAY THE FISH over the fire and don't fool with it for 4 or 5 minutes. You want a good sear to form between the fish and the grill, which makes it easier to turn when the time comes.

6. AFTER 4 OR 5 minutes, use your tongs to sort of worry the fish free of the grill surface. Don't turn it at this point, just clear it from the grill.

7. CONTINUE TO COOK on that first side as long as possible, until it's just in danger of getting overdone on that side. At that point, roll it over gently—don't flip it, just roll it, as you would a sleeping bed partner. This is the only time you'll be turning the fish.

8. IF THE FISH should rip apart when you are moving it, it's time to bail. Get a spatula, lift the pieces off the grill and onto a baking sheet, and finish it in a 350°F oven. It will still taste great, but the presentation is going to suffer.

9. TO CHECK FOR doneness, probe around in the slits you made in the side of the fish. The flesh should be almost completely opaque with just a hint of translucence. Remove from the grill and eat immediately. You have arrived.

Grilled Trout in a Smoked Salmon Suit
(aka Grilled Stuffed Trout with Horseradish-Dill Sauce)

SERVES 4

I like trout a lot. It's pretty easy to find, and whole fish always tastes better to me. There are lots of different freshwater kinds—brown, golden, brook, rainbow, lake, and steelhead, to name just a few—and each of them has a different taste. Of course, few of us are familiar with the flavor of wild trout anymore, since most of the trout we get in restaurants and stores is the farmed variety. Some people say there is a huge difference between the two, favoring the wild, but I have also heard of hatcheries that feed their fish better-tasting stuff than they would get in the wild, so I'm not so sure.

In this preparation, we combine some classic accompaniments to smoked salmon—capers, onions, dill, horseradish, sour cream, and lemon—and use them with the trout. Or, as we say in the restaurant kitchen, we put the grilled trout in a smoked salmon suit. It works pretty well (and it's also a lot of fun to say).

You will find trout in a variety of states of boned-ness: bone totally in, some bones out, or all bones removed. For this recipe, you need boneless or semiboned trout, which you then stuff and grill, being careful as you always must be with whole fish. For example, when it comes to turning it on the grill, just kind of gently roll it over. Treat it right, and trout will become one of your favorite dishes.

1 large red onion, peeled and thinly sliced

2 tablespoons minced garlic

1 cup red wine vinegar

$^1/_4$ cup minced capers

Salt and freshly cracked black pepper to taste

4 10- to 12-ounce trout, cleaned and totally boned or
    semiboned, heads and tails left on

$^1/_4$ cup olive oil

For the Sauce

$^1/_2$ cup sour cream

3 tablespoons prepared horseradish

$^1/_4$ cup roughly chopped fresh dill

$^1/_4$ cup fresh lemon juice (about 1 lemon)

Salt and freshly cracked black pepper to taste

2 lemons, quartered

1. In a small bowl, combine the onion, garlic, and vinegar. Cover, refrigerate, and allow to soak for 5 hours, so the onion becomes slightly pickled.

2. Drain the onion and garlic, add the capers and salt and pepper to taste, and mix together well.

3. Spread each trout open, stuff each cavity with one quarter of the onion-caper mixture, and fold back over. Lightly coat the trout with the olive oil and sprinkle with salt and pepper to taste. Grill over **a medium-hot fire** for 4 to 5 minutes per side. *To check for doneness:* The skin should be crisp and a peek inside should show that the fish are opaque all the way through.

4. While the trout are grilling, make the sauce: Combine all the ingredients in a medium bowl, mix well, and set aside.

5. Remove the trout from the grill and serve hot with a generous spoonful of the sauce over each fish and lemon quarters for squeezing.

Try this with an appetizer portion of Grilled Lamb and Fig Skewers with Quince-Ginger Chutney (page 118), serve Chipotle Mashed Sweet Potatoes (page 282) on the side, and finish up with Grilled Bananas and Pineapple with Rum-Molasses Glaze (page 357).

lake trout lesson

WHEN I WAS A kid, our family often visited my Great-Aunt Ethel at her home in Copper Harbor, the northernmost town of Michigan's Upper Peninsula—and that's way, way up there. So remote is this town that in winter it had only thirteen inhabitants.

IN THE SUMMER, THOUGH, we would gather huckleberries, swim in ice-cold Lake Superior, and go out fishing for the giant lake trout, as sweet and succulent a fish as I have ever tasted. Unfortunately, progress put a stop to that. When the St. Lawrence Seaway was opened, connecting the Great Lakes to the Atlantic Ocean via Canada's St. Lawrence River, down from the north came the lamprey, a gross, snakelike creature that fastens itself to lake trout and kills it.

SO DEVASTATED WAS THE lake trout population that for years only the Native Americans who lived in the area were allowed to fish for them, and even they caught precious few. Today, after years of treating the Great Lakes with chemicals, the lamprey population is pretty much gone and the trout are coming back. But it just goes to show—you never know what will happen when you fool around with Mother Nature.

Pepper-Grilled Tuna Steak with Parsley-Garlic Butter

SERVES 4

I've cooked and served countless tuna steaks in my day and seen many whole tunas at markets, but I never really appreciated the fish until one day last summer when I was fortunate enough to go tuna fishing myself. Along with my pal Bill Russell, owner of Westport Rivers Vineyards in Westport, Massachusetts, I set out at 4 A.M. with Captain Al on the *Prowler* out of Snug Harbor, Rhode Island. I was happy to be out on the ocean, and we passed a pleasant enough morning, hooking a couple of sharks and the occasional albacore. But the real excitement came at about two in the afternoon, when we got a call on the radio from a friend of Captain Al's, directing us to a spot not far from where we were.

When we got there, we found about twenty other charter boats locked in fierce battle with a school of yellowfin tunas. In just a couple of minutes I had hooked one, and experienced for the first time the total commitment and intense hard work required to fight the fish for fifteen minutes under constant pressure. It was quite an experience. We caught a bunch of tuna that day, kept one sixty-pounder each, and tagged and released the others.

It was a ritual that forever changed my relationship to this fish. Now when I see one I have much more respect and appreciation for it. I buy it differently, handle it differently, and pay more attention to it than any other fish, with the possible exception of striped bass. I recommend this experience to anyone who has ever enjoyed eating tuna.

This recipe re-creates the dinner we had the night of the tuna expedition. We arrived home late and dead tired, but with enough energy to fire up the grill, roll the bright red steaks in freshly cracked black pepper, throw them on the fire, and triumphantly eat them with just a bit of compound butter—definitely the best tuna I've ever eaten.

You can substitute other fish for the tuna in this recipe, but out of respect for my gallant foe, I'm not going to tell you what they are.

For the Butter

$^1/_2$ cup (1 stick) unsalted butter, softened

1 teaspoon minced garlic

2 tablespoons fresh lemon juice (about $^1/_2$ lemon)

$^1/_4$ cup roughly chopped fresh parsley

2 tablespoons kosher salt

1 cup freshly cracked black pepper

4 8-ounce tuna steaks, about 2 to 3 inches thick

2 tablespoons olive oil

STRICTLY ENTRÉES

1. Make the butter: In a small bowl, combine all the ingredients and mix well. Cover and refrigerate.

2. In a second small bowl, combine the salt and pepper and mix well. Press the tuna steaks into the mixture to coat on all the sides. Drizzle the tuna lightly with the olive oil and grill over **a medium-hot fire** for 4 to 5 minutes per side for medium rare. *To check for doneness:* Cut into one of the steaks and check to see that it is just a bit translucent at the center.

3. Remove the tuna from the grill and serve with a large spoonful of the butter on top of each steak.

I think this goes well with Grilled Mussels Johnson (page 72) and Grilled Pita Bread Salad with Cucumbers and Feta Cheese (page 54), with Grilled Pineapple with Sweet Lime–Black Pepper Sauce (page 358) for dessert, and The Hanker (page 351) as the beverage to start the whole thing out right.

Chile-Ginger Grilled Tuna with Korean-Style Salad

SERVES 4

Up until about ten years ago, tuna might have been considered an underutilized species—we ate lots of it, but only the mushy canned stuff, which bears about the same resemblance to fresh tuna as K-rations do to a prime steak. During the big restaurant push of the eighties, though, tuna emerged as a chef's favorite menu item. In this it was aided not only by its reasonable price and availability, but also by its adaptability to grilling and sautéing and its strength of character, which allows it to hold up to lots of bold flavors.

Undercooking tuna is popular because the meat is so similar to steak that it just seems like a natural way to cook it. One word of caution: If you're looking for tuna to undercook, make sure you get #1 grade. Freshness is always paramount. Fish are graded by color, texture, and freshness, and with #1 grade you are sure to get fish that is free of parasites. Look for meat that is red, gleaming, and moist.

You can substitute steaks of grouper, mahi mahi, swordfish, or salmon in this recipe, but in that case you will probably want to cook the fish a couple minutes more.

$^1/_2$ cup shredded Napa (Chinese) cabbage

$^1/_4$ cup bean sprouts of your choice (radish, alfalfa, etc.)

1 cucumber, peeled, seeded, and thinly sliced

For the Dressing

$^1/_4$ cup soy sauce

$^1/_4$ cup rice vinegar

1 tablespoon minced ginger

1 tablespoon minced garlic

1 fresh chile pepper of your choice, minced

2 tablespoons sugar

2 tablespoons roughly chopped fresh basil

For the Rub

2 tablespoons fresh chile pepper of your choice, minced

2 tablespoons minced ginger

$^1/_4$ cup roughly chopped fresh cilantro

$^1/_4$ cup sesame oil

Salt and freshly cracked black pepper to taste

4 8-ounce tuna steaks, about 2 inches thick

1. In a medium bowl, combine the cabbage, bean sprouts, and cucumber.

2. Make the dressing: In a small bowl, combine all the ingredients and whisk together well. Add just enough dressing to the cabbage-cucumber mixture to moisten the ingredients, toss well, and refrigerate.

3. Make the rub: In a small bowl, combine all the ingredients and mix well.

4. Rub the tuna steaks generously with the spice rub, place them on the grill over **a hot fire,** and cook for about 4 minutes on each side for medium-rare. *To check for doneness:* Cut into one of the steaks and check to see that it is just translucent in the center. Remove from the grill and serve with the chilled vegetable salad.

For a nice Asian-flavored meal, I might try this with Ginger-Scallion Fried Rice (page 301), Pungent Carrot and Cucumber Salad with Ginger and Garlic (page 308), and Grilled Plums with Spicy Hoisin Glaze (page 296).

which tuna?

TUNA INHABIT WARM WATERS around the world, are constantly on the move (the larger ones travel up to seventy-five thousand miles in a year), and have been used as food by humans since before written history. A member of the mackerel family, tuna comes in many shapes and sizes. In the United States, we see mostly yellowfin (twenty to one hundred pounds) and bigeye (about the same size), along with the odd bluefin (up to fifteen hundred pounds). On the West Coast, people often insist that the best tuna is a variety known as ahi, but that is actually just a Hawaiian term for the bigeye and in itself does not connote quality.

Bridget's Alternative Cold Tuna Plate for a Hot Summer Day

SERVES 4

This dish was designed by Bridget Batson, former chef at The Blue Room. Bridget started out at the cold station in the restaurant, putting together salads and plating desserts, and after three years of hard work, dedication, study, and practice, she was running the whole kitchen. She was twenty-three at the time, and this is a good example of the kind of rigor with which young people are approaching the trade of cooking these days. It's quite different from the way it was in my own youth, when many people got into working in restaurants because they couldn't think of anything else they wanted to do. In any case, it's good to see a new guard forming, bringing with them a new set of ideas and fresh ways of looking at things.

Bridget always did a lot of reading about the cuisine of southern France, and here is one of the results. Now, anybody who has been to Nice will recognize the ingredients as a salade Niçoise, with the tuna grilled and a couple of other changes here and there. As usual, though, the success of the dish lies not in its conception but in its execution. It's a first-rate classic summer preparation, for which you should use only the very freshest fish.

For the Aïoli

    2 teaspoons minced garlic

    3 large egg yolks

    1¼ cups olive oil

    2 tablespoons fresh lemon juice (about ½ lemon)

    Salt and freshly cracked black pepper to taste

    8 new potatoes, cleaned and quartered

    3 tablespoons vegetable oil

    Salt and freshly cracked black pepper to taste

    4 8-ounce tuna steaks, about 2 to 3 inches thick

    2 large tomatoes, cored and quartered

    8 radishes, cleaned and quartered

    ½ cup fresh fava beans, blanched in boiling water for 3 minutes, cooled in an ice-water bath, and skins removed (or substitute blanched green beans)

    ¼ cup Niçoise or other brine-cured black olives

    ¼ cup capers, rinsed

    1 bunch watercress, tough stems removed, washed, and dried

    1 bunch flat-leaf parsley, stemmed, washed, and dried

    2 lemons, halved

    ¼ cup olive oil

1. Make the aïoli: Place the garlic and egg yolks in a small bowl and whisk until the mixture is pale yellow. Start to add the oil drop by drop while continuing to whisk. After one third of the oil has been added, add the lemon juice. Continue adding the olive oil in a very fine drizzle, still whisking. Add salt and pepper to taste, cover, and refrigerate until ready to use.

2. In a small bowl, combine the potatoes, 1 tablespoon of the vegetable oil, and salt and pepper to taste and toss well. Place the potatoes on a small baking sheet and roast in a preheated 375°F oven until you can easily pierce them with a fork but they still offer some resistance, 15 to 20 minutes. Remove from the oven and set aside.

3. Lightly rub the tuna steaks with the remaining 2 tablespoons vegetable oil, sprinkle with salt and pepper to taste, and grill over **a hot fire** for 3 to 4 minutes per side. *To check for doneness:* Bend back one of the steaks and peek inside: The center should be dark pink for medium-rare, which is the way I like tuna; if you prefer it more well done, keep cooking it until it reaches the stage you like.

4. Divide the potatoes, tomatoes, radishes, fava beans, olives, capers, and greens among four plates. Place the tuna steaks on the plates, squeeze the lemons all over the top, and sprinkle with the olive oil and salt and pepper to taste. Serve with the aïoli on the side.

This makes a nice lunch served with Grilled Artichoke and White Bean Salad (page 51).

those raw eggs

ALTHOUGH IT IS RELA-TIVELY minor, there is some danger of salmonella from eating uncooked egg yolks. Pregnant women, the elderly, infants, and people whose immune systems are compromised should avoid raw eggs. For others, it is simply a matter of balancing the risk versus the pleasure. If you want aïoli without risk, cook the yolks with 1 tablespoon of water in a saucepan over very low heat, stirring constantly until the mixture bubbles in one or two places. Let stand for 4 minutes, then proceed as described in step #2.

Grilled Halibut with Fried Green Apples, Bacon, and Horseradish Sour Cream

S E R V E S 4

Most halibut is caught around Alaska and British Columbia, but there is a smaller East Coast catch as well. The mild white meat of this fish can hold up to the rigors of grilling, but it is tender and will break, so be a little gentle when you're moving it around on the grill. No body slamming this fish, please. In this prep we get into a northern European mode, with the combination of horseradish, apples, and bacon. The crunchy fried apples contrast with the tender texture of the fish, and the horse-radish sour cream helps perk it up without overpowering its mild flavor.

If you can't get halibut, you can substitute grouper, monkfish, swordfish, or red snapper in this recipe.

8 slices bacon, diced medium

1 red onion, peeled, halved, and thinly sliced

4 Granny Smith or other green apples, peeled, halved, cored,
    and thinly sliced

1 tablespoon minced garlic

$^1/_4$ cup sugar

3 tablespoons cider vinegar

3 tablespoons roughly chopped fresh thyme (or substitute parsley)

Salt and freshly cracked black pepper to taste

4 8-ounce halibut steaks, about $1^1/_2$ inches thick

2 tablespoons vegetable oil

$^1/_2$ cup sour cream

2 scallions (white and green parts), minced

1 tablespoon fresh lemon juice

$1^1/_2$ tablespoons prepared horseradish

1. In a large sauté pan over medium heat, cook the bacon until just crisp, about 6 minutes. Remove the bacon and place on paper towels or a brown paper bag to drain. Pour off all but about 3 tablespoons of the fat from the pan and return the pan to the heat. Add the onion and sauté, stirring occasionally, until just beginning to brown, 6 to 8 minutes. Add the apples and toss them around a bit, then add the garlic and cook, stirring occasionally, for 1 minute. Add the sugar and vinegar and cook for 3 to 5 minutes, or until the apples are crisp-tender but not soggy. Add the thyme and stir to combine. Remove from the heat and season to taste with salt and pepper. Cover to keep warm and set aside.

2. Rub the halibut lightly with the vegetable oil and sprinkle with salt and pepper to taste. Grill over **a medium-hot fire** for 5 to 6 minutes per side. *To check for doneness:* Cut into the thickest part of one of the fillets and peek to be sure it is opaque all the way through.

3. In a small bowl, combine the sour cream, scallions, lemon juice, and horseradish and mix well. Serve the halibut over the apples, topped with the bacon and a big spoonful of the sour cream.

I like this with Grilled Chicken Livers with Green Grape Sauce (page 75) to start, Romaine and Bulgur Salad (page 319) on the side, and Coconut Flan (page 364) for dessert.

Grilled Halibut with Bacon–Red Onion Relish and Roasted Red Pepper Mayonnaise

SERVES 4

Halibut is some of the finest-eating white-fleshed fish around. The largest of the flat-fish, these babies hang out in very deep water and can grow as large as seven hundred pounds. Most that are sold commercially, however, are in the thirty- to fifty-pound range. Like many sea creatures, halibut has a life cycle that includes a strange metamorphosis, which it shares with other flatfish like flounder and sole. A halibut starts out with an eye on either side of its body. Then, when the fish is still a baby, one eye "migrates" to the other side. The side with two eyes becomes dark, and the blind side goes white. Strange fish, but very good eating. If you can't get halibut, you can substitute cod, grouper, swordfish, or even red snapper in this recipe.

For the Relish

> 6 slices bacon, diced small
>
> 2 medium red onions, peeled and thinly sliced
>
> $^1/_4$ cup balsamic vinegar
>
> $^1/_2$ cup roughly chopped fresh parsley
>
> Salt and freshly cracked black pepper to taste

> 4 8-ounce halibut fillets or 10-ounce halibut steaks, about 2 inches thick
>
> 2 tablespoons olive oil
>
> Salt and freshly cracked black pepper to taste
>
> Roasted Red Pepper Mayonnaise (recipe follows)

1. Make the relish: In a medium sauté pan over medium heat, sauté the bacon pieces just until they begin to crisp, about 5 minutes. Drain off all but 3 table-spoons of the bacon fat. Add the onion slices and cook, stirring occasionally, until lightly browned, 5 to 7 minutes. Add the vinegar and cook, stirring a few times, for another 3 minutes, or until most of the liquid has evaporated. Remove from the heat, add the parsley, mix well, and season to taste. Set aside.

2. Rub the halibut with the olive oil and sprinkle with salt and pepper to taste. Place on the grill over **a medium-low fire,** cover with a pie tin or aluminum foil, and cook for about 7 minutes per side for fillets, 8 minutes per side for steaks. *To check for doneness:* Cut into one of the pieces of fish and peek inside; it should be opaque all the way through. Remove the halibut from the grill and serve with the relish and the Roasted Red Pepper Mayonnaise.

ROASTED RED PEPPER MAYONNAISE

1 roasted red pepper (see page 54 for homemade, or use jarred, rinsed), diced small

1 cup mayonnaise (yours or ours, see page 344 for recipe)

1 teaspoon minced garlic

1 tablespoon fresh lemon juice

Salt and freshly cracked black pepper to taste

In a small bowl, combine all the ingredients and mix well. Cover and refrigerate.

Try this with Grilled and Chilled Mediterranean-Style Gazpacho (page 27) in front of it, Sesame Green Beans with Crispy Fried Shallots (page 281) as a side dish, and Gingered Mango Mousse (page 363) for dessert.

Grilled Monkfish with Sherry, Raisins, and Grilled Asparagus

SERVES 4

Of all the cities I've visited, there are a handful that I consider world class in terms of their appreciation of superior-quality seafood. Walking through the local fish market in these cities, seeing the quality and variety, is a real treat. Number one on this short list is Singapore, number two is Hong Kong, and number three has got to be Barcelona. This seaport city takes full advantage of its site on the Mediterranean, home to a rich array of sea creatures such as squid, octopus, and shrimp, as well as all kinds of finfish, laid out in the market with red gills, clean eyes, and a fresh smell.

There is one stand in La Boqueria, Barcelona's main market, where you can take fresh seafood that you have just bought and the owner—a marathon runner whom everyone calls Juanito, or Johnny—will cook it for you. One afternoon we bought some monkfish and he served it up to us with sherry and vinegar, a common combination in Spain. I've added some asparagus to the dish, a good way to welcome spring, since asparagus season is usually pretty close to "dust off the grill" season. If you can't get hold of good-quality monkfish for this recipe, you can substitute swordfish, mako shark, grouper, or wolffish.

For the Sauce

    2 tablespoons olive oil

    1 large onion, peeled and diced small

    1 cup sherry of your choice

    $1/3$ cup raisins

    1 teaspoon red pepper flakes

    3 tablespoons unsalted butter

    16 spears asparagus, woody ends trimmed

    2 tablespoons vegetable oil

    2 tablespoons minced garlic

    $1/4$ cup roughly chopped fresh parsley

    2 pounds monkfish, cleaned

    Salt and freshly cracked black pepper to taste

1. Make the sauce: In a small sauté pan, heat the olive oil over medium heat until hot but not smoking. Add the onion and sauté, stirring occasionally, until transparent, 5 to 7 minutes. Add the sherry, bring to a boil, and simmer vigorously until it has reduced by half, about 10 minutes. Remove from the heat, stir in the raisins and red pepper flakes, and set aside.

2. Fill your sink or a large pot with ice and water. In a large pot of boiling salted water, blanch the asparagus for 2 minutes. Drain, plunge into the ice-and-water bath to stop the cooking, and drain again.

3. In a small bowl, combine the vegetable oil, garlic, and parsley and mix well. Rub the monkfish all over with this mixture, sprinkle lightly with salt and pepper, and grill over **a medium-hot fire** for 6 to 8 minutes per side. *To check for doneness:* Cut into the fish and peek to see that it is opaque all the way through.

4. Just before the monkfish finishes cooking, toss the asparagus on the grill and roll it around until it is slightly browned, 3 to 4 minutes.

5. Place the sauce back on the stove over medium heat, add the butter, and stir until the butter has melted and is incorporated into the sauce. Remove the sauce from the heat and serve the monkfish and asparagus with a drizzle of the sauce.

I might try an appetizer portion of Grilled Pork, Pineapple, and Jalapeño Skewers with Guava-Lime Sauce (page 238) as a spicy starter with this, serve Latin-Flavored Root Vegetable Hobo Pack (page 216) and Clove-Pickled Peaches (page 332) as side dishes, and finish up with Saffron-Cardamom Poached Pears with Cranberry-Currant Relish (page 359).

asparagus, the edible spring lily

ASPARAGUS IS ONE OF those "love it or hate it" vegetables. Those who like it can't wait for the first spears to come poking up through the ground in spring. Those who dislike it—a camp that seems to include almost everyone under the age of thirteen— can't understand why anyone would want to eat the stuff. This controversial veggie is actually a member of the lily family, which means that it is a perennial; once you get a bed started, it will keep producing for up to twenty years. That, in addition to its unique and delicate flavor, helps explain why gardeners are partial to it. But I'm not sure what explains why the French (who to my mind have a tendency to make things culinary a bit more difficult than they really need to be) like to cover their asparagus with dirt so that, when harvested, it is white rather than green. To my taste, the green version actually has more flavor. But then, like everything else involving this odd lily, it's all a matter of taste.

Herb-Crusted Grilled Monkfish with Roasted Red Pepper Relish

SERVES 4

The meat of the ugly monkfish, which comes from the tail, is more similar to pork loins in both size and shape than it is to the fillets of other fish. It even has an outer membrane like the silverskin on meat. And the similarities don't stop there, as its texture is firm and it is often cut into medallions and sautéed.

I'd like to do my small part by encouraging you to try this fish, which is still abundant in the waters of Georges Bank off the Massachusetts coast. If you can, though, try to get the fish guy to take off the outer membrane for you, since it's a pain to deal with. If you get a whole tail, it might not be of uniform thickness to cook evenly, so just put the thinner part over the cooler part of the fire.

In this prep, the herb rub helps create a flavor-packed, crispy crust that complements the sweet, subtle flavor of the monk. If you can't find good-quality monkfish, you can substitute swordfish, mako shark, grouper, or wolffish.

For the Relish

    3 roasted red peppers (see page 54 for homemade, or use jarred, rinsed),
       diced large

    1 small red onion, peeled and diced medium

    1 teaspoon minced garlic

    $^1/_4$ cup roughly chopped fresh basil

    $^1/_4$ cup extra virgin olive oil

    $^1/_4$ cup balsamic vinegar

    Salt and freshly cracked black pepper to taste

For the Rub

    $^1/_2$ cup roughly chopped mixed fresh herbs: parsley, sage, rosemary,
       thyme, oregano, basil, and/or marjoram

    2 tablespoons minced garlic

    $^1/_4$ cup olive oil

    $^1/_4$ cup fresh lemon juice (about 1 lemon)

    1 tablespoon red pepper flakes

    Salt and freshly cracked black pepper to taste

    2 pounds monkfish, cleaned

1. Make the relish: In a small bowl, combine all the ingredients. Toss well and set aside.

2. Make the rub: In a second small bowl, combine all the ingredients and mix well.

3. Rub the monkfish generously with the rub and grill over **a medium fire** for 6 to 8 minutes per side. *To check for doneness:* Cut into the fish and check to see that it is opaque all the way through. Remove from the grill and serve warm, topped with the relish.

> **Grilled Lamb and Red Onion in Grape Leaves (page 80) works well as an appetizer with this dish. Chickpea Salad with Cumin and Mint (page 316) makes a nice side dish, and Grilled Pineapple with Sweet Lime–Black Pepper Sauce (page 358) is a good choice for dessert.**

jerry lewis fish?

THE MONKFISH IS A truly odd-looking creature, with a hideously ugly head that makes up more than half its body weight. Like a number of other comestibles that are grotesque in their raw state but flat-out delicious when cooked, the monkfish has never really been appreciated in this country but is loved in France. French cooks, who call this fish *lotte,* praise it for its subtle flavor and its versatile nature.

NOW, I KNOW WHAT you're thinking—these are the same people who think that Jerry Lewis is subtle and versatile too. But don't hold that against them. They may have odd taste in comedians, but when it comes to the monkfish, they are singing off the right page of the hymn book.

Grilled Mackerel with Expensive Olive Oil, Lemon, and Oregano

SERVES 4

Fall is the start of the mackerel season where I live, and I've become quite fond of the fish. It is in the same family as tuna, with meat that is perhaps a level richer but still relatively light with a delicate but pronounced flavor. Its high oil content also makes it excellent for grilling. There are many types of mackerel, with the most popular types for eating being the King, Atlantic, Pacific, and Spanish. As usual with fish, freshness is the key.

Here I have borrowed a sardine preparation common in Portugal, using garlic, lemon, olive oil, and oregano. For this one, make sure you get a very high quality, fruity olive oil so the flavor shines through.

> $^1/_3$ **cup good-quality extra virgin olive oil**
>
> **Juice of 1 lemon**
>
> $^1/_4$ **cup roughly chopped fresh oregano**
>
> **4 8-ounce mackerel fillets (or substitute tuna, striped bass, mahi mahi,**
>   **or large whole sardines)**
>
> **2 tablespoons vegetable oil**
>
> **1 tablespoon finely minced garlic**
>
> **Salt and freshly cracked black pepper to taste**
>
> **1 lemon, quartered, for garnish**

1. In a small bowl, combine the olive oil, lemon juice, and oregano, mix well, and set aside.

2. Rub the mackerel fillets lightly with the vegetable oil and garlic and sprinkle with salt and pepper to taste. Grill over **a medium-hot fire** for 3 to 4 minutes per side. Watch carefully, since mackerel has a tendency to overcook quite quickly. *To check for doneness:* Peek inside one of the fillets to be sure it is opaque all the way through.

3. Remove the mackerel from the grill and serve, drizzled with the olive oil–herb mixture and garnished with the lemon wedges.

Grilled Shrimp and Cucumber Salad(page 56) makes a nice appetizer with this, Cornmeal Mush with Okra and Tomatoes (page 305) is good as a side dish, and Grilled Bananas and Pineapple with Rum-Molasses Glaze (page 357) is an excellent ending.

Grilled Red Snapper Palapas-Style with Vera Cruz Relish

SERVES 4

Catching fish and cooking them within an hour, less than a hundred yards from where they were caught, seems to be a Mexican tradition. After hanging around for a while in the hutlike beach shacks called *palapas,* with their makeshift kitchens, tables, chairs, hammock, and coolers for ice-cold beverages, you begin to feel that a *palapa* can provide everything you need from life. This dish is based on a method that I observed one morning in a *palapa* near Vera Cruz. The cook hooked a couple of beautiful snappers, walked up to the kitchen, cleaned them, soaked them in some garlic and lime, and grilled them up for lunch. I don't need to go into the inherent beauty of ultra-fresh fish cooked so simply. Suffice it to say that fresher is better and the most important part of any fish recipe is the freshness of your fish.

$1/2$ cup fresh lime juice (about 4 limes)

$1/4$ cup olive oil

2 tablespoons minced garlic

4 8- to 10-ounce red snapper fillets

Salt and freshly cracked black pepper to taste

Vera Cruz Relish (recipe follows)

1. In a shallow pan that can hold the fillets in a single layer, combine the lime juice, olive oil, and garlic and mix well. Add the snapper fillets, cover, and refrigerate for 1 to $1^1/_2$ hours, turning once or twice during this time.

2. Remove the snapper from the lime juice mixture and discard mixture. Dry the snapper with paper towels, then grill over **a medium fire** for 5 minutes per side. *To check for doneness:* Cut into one fillet to make sure it is just opaque throughout.

3. Remove the snapper from the grill, serve at once, with Vera Cruz Relish.

VERA CRUZ RELISH

2 medium tomatoes, cored and diced medium

1 green bell pepper, halved, seeded, and diced small

$1/4$ cup chopped (green and white parts) scallion

2 tablespoons minced fresh chile pepper of your choice

1 tablespoon minced garlic

$1/3$ cup olive oil

$1/4$ cup roughly chopped fresh oregano

In a medium bowl, combine all the ingredients and mix well.

For a Mexican fiesta, serve this with Basic Black Beans (page 299), Jícama-Apple Salad with Orange-Mustard Dressing (page 308), and Grilled Shrimp and Black Bean Salad with Papaya-Chili Dressing (page 57).

BBQ-Rubbed Grilled Skate with Mango-Chile Dressing

Skate is quickly losing its standing in the family of underutilized, underappreciated seafood. What has been known in Europe for years is finally getting through to the American public—the things look damned odd, but they sure taste good.

Part of the reason for the sweet, firm, distinctive taste of this fish is that it feeds almost entirely on crustaceans and mollusks, a rich and delicious diet if there ever was one. In fact, old cooks used to promote the taste of skate by claiming that unscrupulous fishmongers would punch out scallop-shaped rounds from the wings and sell them as scallops. To me the taste and texture of the two are totally different, so I don't see how you could trick anybody. Besides, I think skate stands on its own, with no need of specious tales to confirm its quality.

Skate is usually served sautéed or poached in Europe, but I find that it takes to the grill well, too. In this preparation, the fish is rubbed with a heavy, sweet, barbecue-style rub, grilled, then finished with a mango-chile dressing. An unusual fish, a spicy preparation, and a neat surprise to spring on unsuspecting dinner guests.

For the Dressing

- 1 ripe mango, peeled and pitted
- $1/4$ cup fresh lime juice (about 2 limes)
- $1/4$ cup vegetable oil
- $1/4$ cup roughly chopped fresh cilantro
- 2 tablespoons minced fresh chile pepper of your choice
- Salt and freshly cracked black pepper to taste

For the Rub

- $1/4$ cup paprika
- $1/4$ cup ground cumin
- 2 tablespoons ground coriander
- 1 tablespoon brown sugar
- $1/4$ cup freshly cracked black pepper
- 3 tablespoons kosher salt
- $1/4$ cup olive oil

4 12-ounce skate wings, cleaned and skinned

1. Make the dressing: Place the mango, lime juice, and oil in a food processor and puree until smooth. Pour out into a small bowl, add the cilantro, chile, and salt and pepper to taste and mix well. Set aside.

STRICTLY ENTRÉES

194

2. Make the rub: In a small bowl, combine all the ingredients and mix together thoroughly. Cover the skate generously with the rub, then grill the fish over **a medium-hot fire** for 6 to 8 minutes per side. Don't move the skate around on the grill too much while you're cooking it, because it tears apart easily. *To check for doneness:* Just probe the flesh, which gets tender and stringy (not in a bad way) when done. You should also be able to easily stick your tongs between the flesh and the bone.

3. Remove the skate from the grill and serve it with the dressing drizzled over the top.

Try this with Seared Spinach with Fried Garlic Chips (page 293), Indian-Style Sweet Potato Salad (page 315), or Grilled Tomato Halves with Cheesy Bread Crumbs (page 298).

skate, the winged fish

SKATE IS RELATED TO shark, and some people recommend soaking it in a half-gallon of water combined with $1/4$ cup salt and $1/4$ cup vinegar for a couple of hours before cooking to remove any possible ammonia smell. I think this is optional, but the skin should definitely be removed from the wings, the only part of the fish usually sold. The best way to do this is to get some pliers and kind of rip it off. An even better way is to buy your skate wings already skinned, which is how they are appearing more and more often in markets these days.

Grilled Shad Roe with Minted Snap Peas

Winter is a tough time for cooks. The quality and variety of the winter larder are limited, and while working with root vegetables and braises can be rewarding, when the first foods of spring arrive it is always cause for a renewed sense of wonder. Those first tender spears of asparagus, bright green peas, and succulent soft-shell crabs are a very welcome sign of the plentifulness of seasons to come.

So, without being too corny, this dish is a tribute to spring. It's very simple, but it features the freshness and brightness of the season—the shad are running, the peas are fine, and the bounty of summer is just around the corner.

2 cups snap peas, trimmed

$^1/_4$ cup roughly chopped fresh mint

$^1/_2$ red onion, peeled and thinly sliced

$^1/_2$ red bell pepper, seeded and diced small

Juice of 1 lemon

3 tablespoons extra virgin olive oil

Salt and freshly cracked black pepper to taste

4 pairs shad roe, 6 to 8 ounces each

3 tablespoons vegetable oil

1. Fill a large bowl with water and ice. Bring about 2 quarts of salted water to a boil over high heat, add the peas, and blanch for 1 minute; the peas should turn very bright green. Drain, immediately plunge into the ice-and-water bath to stop the cooking process, and drain again.

2. In a medium bowl, combine the peas with the mint, red onion, bell pepper, lemon juice, olive oil, and salt and pepper to taste and mix well. Set this salad aside while you grill the shad roe.

3. Rub the shad roe lightly with the vegetable oil and sprinkle with salt and pepper to taste. Place them on the grill (make sure the grill is super-clean) over **a medium fire** and grill, turning once, for 3 to 4 minutes per side. Remove from the grill and serve with the salad.

For a spring dinner, Grilled Asparagus with Garlic Mayonnaise or Simple Vinaigrette (page 279) and new potatoes substituted in Fancy Ash-Roasted Potatoes (page 69) go well with this as side dishes. Espresso Black Bottom Pie (page 376) is excellent as a dessert.

At your traditional American backyard cookout, chicken comes in a high fourth in popularity, right after hot dogs, hamburgers, and steaks. Unfortunately, it is often grilled after being dunked in a tomato-based barbecue sauce. This is a mistake, because these sauces contain sugar, which burns when it spends any significant amount of time over the fire. But as long as you avoid that error, chicken is an excellent choice for the grill. It soaks up the flavor of the fire quickly, and its familiar, relatively neutral taste makes a nice foil for other, more aggressive flavors.

STRICTLY ENTRÉES

winged entrées

The dishes in this chapter make use of flavor footprints from many regions, from the Moroccan slant of Grilled Chicken and Eggplant with North African Flavors to the Chinese influences in Hoisin Chicken Breasts with Grilled Peppers and Onions to the Mediterranean taste of Basil-Garlic Chicken Breasts with Grilled Balsamic Peaches. I've also included a couple of recipes for duck breast, which has tremendous flavor when grilled, as long as you're careful to avoid flare-ups, and even a recipe for game hen, which I particularly enjoy as an entrée because it means each person gets a whole bird to eat.

Grilled Chicken and
Eggplant with North
African Flavors

Hoisin Chicken Breasts
with Grilled Peppers and
Onions

Exotic-Flavored Chicken
Thighs with Tomato-
Mint Salad

Slow-Grilled Game Hens
with Garlic-Lemon-
Herb Rub

Basil-Garlic Chicken
Breasts with Grilled
Balsamic Peaches

Slow-Cooked Chicken
Legs with Lime, Olive Oil,
and Garlic

Grilled Duck Breast with
Summer Cherry–
Orange Sauce

Neo-Postmodern
Polynesian Grilled
Chicken

Grilled Duck Breast with
Peach–Green Grape
Chutney

Hoisin Chicken Breasts with Grilled Peppers and Onions

SERVES 4

I love hoisin sauce. I'm not quite as fanatic about it as my nephew Tommy, who slathers the stuff on everything from pasta to toast, but I always have a jar hanging out in the refrigerator ready for use. Here we thin the hoisin sauce with lime juice, spice it up a bit with ginger and chile peppers, then brush it on grilled chicken, peppers, and onions for an easy, healthy meal that's also full of flavor.

For the Sauce

1 tablespoon vegetable oil

2 tablespoons minced ginger

1 tablespoon minced garlic

1/3 cup hoisin sauce

1/4 cup fresh lime juice (about 2 limes)

1/2 cup roughly chopped fresh basil

1 teaspoon red pepper flakes

Salt and freshly cracked white (or black) pepper to taste

4 whole boneless chicken breasts (each 10 to 12 ounces)

Salt and freshly cracked black pepper to taste

2 red bell peppers, halved and seeded

1 large red onion, peeled and sliced into rings about 1 inch thick

1 tablespoon olive oil

1. Make the sauce: In a small saucepan, heat the oil over medium heat until hot but not smoking. Add the ginger and garlic and sauté, stirring occasionally, for 2 minutes. Add the hoisin sauce and lime juice and simmer for 5 minutes. Remove from the heat, stir in the basil, red pepper flakes, and salt and pepper to taste, and set aside (do not refrigerate).

2. Sprinkle the chicken breasts with salt and pepper to taste and place on the grill, skin side down, over **a medium-hot fire.** Cook for 8 to 10 minutes, at which point the skin should be crispy. Turn the breasts over and cook for another 5 to 6 minutes. *To check for doneness:* Cut into the thickest part of one of the breasts and check to be sure that there is no pink color and the flesh is consistently opaque.

3. Meanwhile, rub the bell pepper halves and onion rings with the olive oil, sprinkle with salt and pepper to taste, and place on the grill. Cook for 2 to 3 minutes per side; you want them to have color and to be fairly firm. Remove from the grill and, as soon as they are cool enough to handle, dice them large.

continued

4. Place the chicken breasts on a platter, arrange the diced peppers and onions around the breasts, drizzle the sauce over everything, and serve.

I might add some fire to the dinner by serving these with Ginger-Soy Marinated Grilled Shrimp with Most-Hot Lime-Chile Booster (page 229) as an appetizer, then serve a side dish of Hobo Pack of Winter Vegetables with Many Fresh Herbs (page 221) to bring the heat back down.

Basil-Garlic Chicken Breasts with Grilled Balsamic Peaches

SERVES 4

I'll make any excuse to grill peaches. In the summer, when these luscious fruits are ripe and juicy, their flavor is strong enough to stand up to the slight smoky char they take on after a few minutes on the grill, along with a little sweet-sour balsamic and molasses glaze. Add a garlic- and basil-rubbed chicken breast and you've got a quick, easy, healthy, creative, and tasty summer combination. Brushing the molasses-balsamic mixture on the peaches just before they come off the grill helps promote caramelization, which adds a deep but not overpowering sweetness. If the peaches are underripe or very firm, leave them on the grill a little bit longer.

By the way, since the balsamic glaze needs to spend about twenty minutes on the stove to reduce, you might want to whip up a double or triple batch and stash it in the refrigerator—it keeps forever, and it is very tasty when brushed on any kind of grilled meat during the last minute or two of cooking.

1 cup balsamic vinegar

$^1/_4$ cup molasses

2 to 3 tablespoons freshly cracked black pepper

$^1/_2$ cup roughly chopped fresh basil

3 tablespoons minced garlic

$^1/_4$ cup olive oil

4 whole boneless chicken breasts (each 10 to 12 ounces)

Salt and freshly cracked black pepper to taste

4 peaches, halved and pitted

1. In a small saucepan over medium-high heat, bring the vinegar to a boil and cook until it is reduced by half, 20 to 25 minutes. Stir in the molasses and black pepper, remove from the heat, and set aside.

2. Meanwhile, in a small bowl, combine the basil, garlic, and olive oil and mix well. Rub the chicken breasts with this mixture, sprinkle lightly with salt and pepper, and grill over **a medium fire,** skin side down, until the skin is crispy, 8 to 10 minutes. Turn the breasts over and grill for another 6 minutes. *To check for doneness:* Nick one of the breasts at the fattest point; the meat should be fully opaque with no traces of pink.

3. As the chicken breasts are finishing up, place the peaches on the fire, cut side down, and grill until they are nicely browned, about 2 minutes. Flip them over, brush the cut side with the balsamic glaze, and continue to cook for another 2 minutes. Remove the peaches from the grill, give them another coat of glaze, and serve whole or sliced with the chicken breasts.

To get some Mediterranean flavors going, try this with Lisa White's White Gazpacho (page 30) as a starter, Grilled Artichoke and White Bean Salad (page 51) as a side dish, and Spanish Olive Oil and Wine Cake (page 372) for dessert.

Neo-Postmodern Polynesian Grilled Chicken

When I was a kid, my family drove to the beach every Friday night. Each week we would stop at a different restaurant for dinner, but my input was always the same: Let's stop at Blue Hawaii. To me, this place was the ultimate. They had leis and pupu platters with live fire (I loved cooking stuff over the nasty blue sterno flames), and Mom and Dad always seemed to enjoy their funny drinks. So here is my small tribute to the chefs at Blue Hawaii, a grilled version of the sweet-and-sour Polynesian chicken I adored as a child. My rendition is particularly aromatic, making use of the Southeast Asian herb trilogy of mint, basil, and cilantro in conjunction with lime juice and chiles, which gets a lot of flavor action going. The prep is simple; just cook, toss it all together, and serve.

For the Dressing

> $^{1}/_{2}$ cup fresh lime juice (about 4 limes)
>
> $^{1}/_{4}$ cup sesame oil
>
> $^{1}/_{4}$ cup soy sauce
>
> 1 tablespoon brown sugar
>
> 2 tablespoons chile-garlic paste (or substitute 1 tablespoon minced garlic and 1 tablespoon minced fresh chile pepper of your choice)
>
> 2 tablespoons minced ginger
>
> Freshly cracked white pepper to taste

> 4 whole boneless chicken breasts (each 10 to 12 ounces)
>
> $^{1}/_{4}$ cup olive oil
>
> Salt and freshly cracked black pepper to taste
>
> 1 red bell pepper, halved and seeded
>
> 1 green bell pepper, halved and seeded
>
> 1 red onion, peeled and cut into 1-inch-thick rings
>
> 2 cups fresh pineapple chunks (about $^{1}/_{2}$ small pineapple)
>
> $^{1}/_{4}$ cup roughly chopped fresh mint
>
> $^{1}/_{4}$ cup roughly chopped fresh cilantro
>
> $^{1}/_{4}$ cup roughly chopped fresh basil

1. Make the dressing: In a small bowl, combine all the ingredients and mix well. Cover and refrigerate.

2. Sprinkle the chicken breasts lightly with some of the olive oil (use about 2 tablespoons) and salt and pepper to taste and grill over **a medium-hot fire** for 7 to 9 minutes per side. *To check for doneness:* Cut into one breast at its thickest part and peek inside to be sure it is opaque all the way through with no pink.

3. Meanwhile, sprinkle the bell peppers and onions with the remaining olive oil and salt and pepper to taste, place on the grill, and cook for 3 to 4 minutes on each side, or just until browned.

4. Remove the chicken, onions, and peppers from the grill. Once they are cool enough to handle, cut them into large chunks and place them in a large bowl along with the pineapple chunks, mint, cilantro, and basil. Add enough dressing to moisten, toss well, and serve warm or chilled.

For an Asian-flavored spread, I would serve this with an appetizer portion of Grilled Lamb Satay with Peanut-Mint Relish (page 120), K. C.'s Bengali-Style Spinach (page 292) and Indian-Style Sweet Potato Salad (page 315) as side dishes, and Coconut Flan (page 364) for dessert.

Grilled Chicken and Eggplant with North African Flavors

SERVES 4

The "bowl technique" used in this dish is a favorite of mine. It's about as simple as you can get—you grill some meat or chicken or vegetables and toss them together in a bowl with some raw vegetables and flavorings to mix them up. It's fun, and it opens up new ideas as far as teaming up meat or fish and vegetables.

For this dish, I like to set up a cutting board next to the grill and have everything but the grilled chicken and vegetables already in a big mixing bowl. Then, as the chicken and vegetables are done, I just pull them off the grill, cut them up, and add them to the bowl, tossing the whole lot at the end.

> 4 whole boneless chicken breasts (each 8 to 12 ounces)
> Salt and freshly cracked black pepper to taste
> 1 red bell pepper, halved and seeded
> 1 green bell pepper, halved and seeded
> 1 red onion, peeled and cut into rings about $1/2$ inch thick
> 1 medium eggplant, cut lengthwise into planks about $1/2$ inch thick
> $1/4$ cup vegetable oil
> $1/3$ cup fresh lemon juice (about $1^{1/2}$ lemons)
> $1/3$ cup olive oil
> 1 large tomato, cored and diced large
> $1/2$ cup good-quality green or black olives, pitted
> 2 tablespoons minced garlic
> 2 tablespoons minced fresh chile pepper of your choice
> $1/2$ cup roughly chopped fresh parsley
> $1/4$ cup cumin seeds, toasted if you want, or 2 tablespoons ground cumin

continued

1. Sprinkle the chicken breasts with salt and pepper to taste and grill over **a medium-hot fire,** skin side down, for 8 to 10 minutes. Flip and grill for an additional 5 to 6 minutes. *To check for doneness:* Cut into one of the breasts at the thickest point and check to see that it is opaque all the way through with no redness.

2. Meanwhile, in a small bowl, combine the bell peppers, onion, eggplant, vegetable oil, and salt and pepper to taste and toss to coat the vegetables. Place the vegetables on the grill and cook until browned and softened, 3 to 4 minutes per side.

3. When the chicken and vegetables are done, remove them from the grill and, as soon as they are cool enough to handle, cut them into large chunks. Place in a large bowl, add all the remaining ingredients, and toss well. Season to taste with salt and pepper and serve.

This goes well with Salt-Crusted Grilled Shrimp in Their Shells (page 68) as an appetizer and Macumber Turnip Cakes with Bacon and Onions (page 294) as a side dish. Espresso Black Bottom Pie (page 376) is a good choice for dessert.

cardamom, the chameleon spice

PEOPLE HAVE BEEN USING cardamom for almost three thousand years. Over that time, this seed of a bushy herb in the ginger family has seen many different uses. The ancient Chinese, for example, used it as a breath sweetener, while medieval German doctors mixed it with honey and applied it to the skin to treat bruises. Even today, when it is used almost exclusively as a flavoring, this sweet, pungent spice has not settled down to a single use. In India, it is a primary ingredient in curries as well as in the mixture with which betel leaves are filled before chewing; in Saudi Arabia and other parts of the Middle East, it is flavoring for strong coffee; in northern Europe, its principal task is to add spiciness to certain pastries.

SO INSTEAD OF TAKING anybody's word for it, I recommend that you explore the unique character of this spice and decide for yourself what its best uses are; once you get to know it, I'm pretty sure you'll be using it frequently. If you can find them, it's much better to buy cardamom seeds in the pod, rather than the pre-ground variety. Once the seeds are taken out of the pods, they lose their volatile oils very quickly—as much as half within a week, and all within three months. So while it's somewhat of a pain to extract the seeds from the pods and grind them up, this is one case in which the effort is definitely worthwhile.

STRICTLY ENTRÉES

Exotic-Flavored Chicken Thighs with Tomato-Mint Salad

SERVES 4 AS ENTRÉE

Chicken thighs are outstanding on the grill. The ratio of crisp outside to juicy inside is high, which I like, and the meat on the thigh, to my mind, has a superior flavor to the breast. They are small enough to get done quickly, and, as if all that's not enough, you also get a nice bone to gnaw on.

The exotic aspect of this particular chicken thigh dish comes from the cardamom. Used by Western cooks mostly in breads and sweets, this spice adds a unique flavor—slightly sweet, slightly pungent, and very aromatic—to savory dishes like this one. The fresh tomato-mint salad adds another floral quality, embodying the notion that food can have a tremendous amount of flavor without being what most people think of as "spicy."

> 2 teaspoons crushed cardamom
>
> 3 tablespoons kosher salt
>
> 2 tablespoons freshly cracked black pepper
>
> 12 bone-in chicken thighs

For the Salad

> 3 medium tomatoes, cored and quartered
>
> 1 red onion, peeled, halved, and thinly sliced
>
> $1/3$ cup roughly chopped fresh mint
>
> 2 tablespoons fresh lime juice (about 1 lime)
>
> $1/4$ cup extra virgin olive oil
>
> Salt and freshly cracked black pepper to taste
>
> 2 limes, cut into wedges, for garnish (optional)

1. In a small bowl, combine the cardamom, salt, and pepper and mix well. Sprinkle the thighs generously with this mixture, then place them on the grill, skin side down, over **a medium-low fire** and grill for 8 to 10 minutes, or until the skin is crispy. Flip them over and cook for an additional 4 to 6 minutes. *To check for doneness:* Cut one thigh down to the bone; there should be no redness.

2. While the chicken thighs are cooking, make the salad: Combine all the ingredients in a medium bowl, toss well, and refrigerate.

3. When the thighs are cooked, serve them with the salad, garnished with lime wedges if you want.

Try this with an appetizer portion of Grilled Shrimp and Bacon Skewers with Pickled Onion and Avocado Salad (page 104) in front and Grilled Garlicky Eggplant Planks with Yogurt-Mint Sauce (page 286) on the side. End the meal with Espresso Black Bottom Pie (page 376).

Slow-Cooked Chicken Legs with Lime, Olive Oil, and Garlic

SERVES 4

The method used for this dish is slow-and-low direct cooking. The key is to build a very small fire, spread it out over the bottom of the grill, and then take your time. I don't like to cover the grill for this dish, because with cooking times under an hour, you get a kind of ashy, metallic taste if you put on the cover; after an hour or more, the smoky flavor will predominate. If you're in a hurry, though, you can throw some foil or a tin pie plate over the chicken to create some radiant heat and cut down on the cooking time a bit. We rub the chicken with a fair amount of cumin here, but that's one spice whose earthy flavor is strong but not overwhelming. Toasting the cumin in a sauté pan for a couple of minutes before you rub it on the chicken helps both to bring out its flavor and to reduce the slight harshness of the raw spice.

> 8 large chicken legs, including thigh and drumstick
>   (about 8 ounces each)
> Salt and freshly cracked black pepper to taste
> $^1/_2$ cup cumin seeds, toasted if you want, or $^1/_4$ cup ground cumin
> $^1/_3$ cup olive oil
> $^1/_3$ cup roughly chopped fresh oregano
> $^1/_4$ cup fresh lime juice (about 2 limes)
> 1 tablespoon minced garlic

1. Sprinkle the chicken legs with salt and pepper to taste, rub with the cumin, and grill over **a medium-low fire** for 12 to 15 minutes per side. Watch the chicken particularly carefully when it is fat side down, because danger of flare-up lurks. *To check for doneness:* Cut inside the joint and peek to see that there is no redness next to the bone.

2. While the legs are cooking, combine the olive oil, oregano, lime juice, and garlic in a small bowl and mix well. Remove the legs from the grill, drizzle the olive oil mixture over the top, and serve at once.

I might complement this by starting out with Tortilla Sandwiches of Grilled
Shrimp and Corn with Goat Cheese and Pickled Red Onions (page 40),
serving Simple Latin-Style Rice and Beans (page 300) on the side,
and finishing up with Gingered Mango Mousse (page 363) for dessert.

Slow-Grilled Game Hens with Garlic-Lemon-Herb Rub

SERVES 4

I like game hens because everyone gets themselves a whole bird, a prospect that has always appealed to me. This is a simple yet flavor-packed preparation, especially flavorful because of both the rub and the relatively long cooking time. If you have some chunks or branches of hardwood, this is a good place to use them, because the hen spends a fair amount of time on the grill and will gain some flavor from the wood smoke. A low-temperature, spread-out fire is the key here. Be wary of flare-ups caused by dripping fat, a particular danger when the bird is cooking skin side down. It's pretty easy to butterfly game hens, but if you can get your butcher to do it for you, of course that's even easier.

For the Rub

$^1/_4$ cup minced garlic

$^1/_4$ cup grated lemon zest (about 2 large lemons)

$^1/_2$ cup roughly chopped fresh parsley

2 tablespoons roughly chopped fresh thyme

2 tablespoons roughly chopped fresh rosemary

2 tablespoons roughly chopped fresh sage

$^1/_2$ cup olive oil

4 Rock Cornish game hens

Salt and freshly cracked black pepper to taste

1. Make the rub: In a small bowl, combine all the ingredients and mix together well. The mixture should be fairly pasty.

2. Butterfly the hens and remove the backbone. Rub the hens generously with the rub, sprinkle with salt and pepper to taste, and place on the grill, skin side down, over **a medium-low fire.** You want to cook the hens for considerably longer than most grilled foods—about 15 minutes per side. It's hard not to burn something that is cooked on the grill for this long, even over a low fire, so you have to keep an eye on the hens. You may need to shift them around a bit, moving them to the sides of the grill, where the heat is less intense, if they start to get too dark on the outside. *To check for doneness:* Cut into one of the hens in the thigh or where the wing meets the breast; there should be no pink. Remove from the grill and serve one hen to each person.

These little beauties go very well with Romaine and Bulgur Salad (page 319), Grilled Goat Cheese Tortilla Sandwiches with Mango-Lime Salsa (page 38), or Grilled Regular Mushrooms with Sherry (page 62).

WHEN WE GO TO the store to buy a chicken, we look for just that—a chicken, not a specific breed of chicken. But there is actually a wide variety among the various breeds. Take, for example, the Rock Cornish game hen. This exotic-sounding bird is in fact a cross of two types of chicken, the White Rock and the Cornish. The distinguishing characteristic of this hen, bred specifically for early slaughter, is its size. Most game hens are 4 to 6 weeks of age and weigh around 1½ pounds. This diminutive fowl is very similar to the French poussin, which is a broiler-type chicken of about the same age but even smaller, weighing in at anywhere from 12 to 20 ounces. The advantages of these young chickens for the cook are that they are very tender and that you can serve each person a whole bird, which seems both decadent and celebratory.

Grilled Duck Breast with Summer Cherry–Orange Sauce

SERVES 4

If you can get your hands on some duck breasts and fresh summer cherries, you will have a dish that is simple, elegant, and serene. Be very careful, though, because flare-ups can char the duck in a heartbeat. If you can't locate duck breasts, boneless chicken breasts are also very nice with this sauce.

> 1 cup balsamic vinegar
> 1 cup fresh orange juice (about 2 oranges)
> ¼ cup molasses
> ¼ cup sugar
> 2 tablespoons minced ginger
> Pinch of ground cinnamon
> Pinch of ground allspice
> 1 cup pitted fresh cherries
> Salt and freshly cracked black pepper to taste
> 4 10- to 12-ounce boneless duck breasts

1. In a small saucepan, combine the vinegar and orange juice and bring to a boil over high heat. Reduce the heat to low and let simmer until the mixture has reduced by about half, 35 to 45 minutes. Add the molasses, sugar, ginger, cinnamon, and allspice and continue to cook for 3 minutes, stirring occasionally, to dissolve the sugar. Add the cherries and cook, stirring occasionally, for another 10 minutes. Season to taste with salt and pepper, remove from the heat, and set aside.

2. Build a small fire in one side of your grill, using about enough coals to fill a shoe box. Season the duck breasts well with salt and pepper and place them on the grill, skin side down, off to the edge of **the medium fire.** Cook for 6 minutes, being careful of flare-ups caused by fat dripping into the fire. If flare-ups do occur, move the breasts so that they are not directly over the flames; you want them to cook slowly, allowing the fat to drip off at an even pace and giving the skin time to crisp. Flip the breasts and cook for an additional 5 to 7 minutes. *To check for doneness:* When the duck breasts are nicely browned and as firm to the touch as the heel of your hand, they are medium-rare.

3. Pull the duck breasts off the fire, allow to cool for about 4 minutes, and then thinly slice them on the bias. Serve the duck breasts with the sauce, which can be warm or cold.

I might serve this with August Tomato and Cucumber Soup (page 26),
Grilled Corn with Lime and Chinese Roasted Salt (page 278), and
Gingered Mango Mousse (page 363) for dessert.

Grilled Duck Breast with Peach–Green Grape Chutney

SERVES 4

Duck does take a bit of management over the fire. It's another dish that requires "grilling on the edge," where the key is to cook the duck just around the edges of the fire so the fat doesn't drip right into the flames and cause flare-ups, which can render you dinnerless in the wink of an eye. Cooking with the fatty side down is the most hazardous, but even when grilling the other side, danger lurks. So you want to cook on the outskirts of a hot fire, moving the breasts in and out of range and cooking by both direct and indirect heat. Take it slow and avoid using the grill cover—I feel strongly that something as small as a duck breast gets overwhelmed by the "covered" flavor. When you take the duck off the grill, let it repose (sit) for a while, then slice it thin on the bias, as you would a flank steak. The chutney is pretty quick to make and sets off the duck really nicely; it also goes very well with pork.

> 4 8- to 10-ounce boneless duck breasts
> Salt and freshly cracked black pepper to taste
> Peach-Green Grape Chutney (recipe follows)

1. Build **a small medium fire** in one side of your grill, using about enough coals to fill a shoe box. Season the duck breasts well with salt and pepper and place them on the grill, skin side down, off to the edge of the fire. Cook for 6 minutes, being careful of flare-ups caused by fat dripping into the fire. If flare-ups do occur, move the breasts so that they are not directly over the flames; you want them to cook slowly, allowing the fat to drip off at an even pace and giving the skin time to crisp. Flip the breasts and cook for an additional 5 to 7 minutes. *To check for doneness:* When the duck breasts are nicely browned and as firm to the touch as the heel of your hand, they are medium-rare.

2. Pull the duck breasts off the fire and allow to cool for about 4 minutes, then thinly slice them on the bias and serve with the Peach–Green Grape Chutney.

PEACH-GREEN GRAPE CHUTNEY

> 2 tablespoons olive oil
>
> 1 large red onion, peeled and diced small
>
> 3 peaches, pitted and diced medium
>
> 1 cup seedless green grapes, halved
>
> 1 cup cider vinegar
>
> $^1/_2$ cup packed brown sugar
>
> Pinch of ground allspice
>
> Pinch of ground mace
>
> 1 tablespoon roughly chopped fresh basil
>
> Salt and freshly cracked black pepper to taste

1. In a medium sauté pan, heat the oil over medium heat until hot but not smoking. Add the onion and sauté, stirring occasionally, until transparent, 5 to 7 minutes.

2. Add the peaches and grapes and cook, stirring, until the peaches are a bit browned, about 4 minutes; be careful not to burn the onions here.

3. Add all the remaining chutney ingredients, bring just to a boil, reduce the heat to low, and simmer for 10 minutes. Remove from the heat and set aside.

> **I might try this with Lime Soup with Grilled Cumin Chicken (page 31), Grilled Garlicky Eggplant Planks with Yogurt-Mint Sauce (page 286), and Coconut Pancakes with Caramelized Bananas (page 369).**

elusive duck breasts

BONELESS DUCK BREASTS ARE an outstanding item, but they can be difficult for home cooks to locate. Some butchers carry them, but if yours does not, you have several options. If he has whole ducks (and most do), you can buy one and ask him to cut it up and bone the breasts. A duck is actually easier to bone than a chicken, so the butcher most likely won't mind. A second choice is to buy the duck and bone it yourself. Since there are lots of good uses for duck legs, you'll be setting yourself up for two excellent meals instead of one. Finally, if you don't mind spending a fair amount of money, you can mail order very good duck breasts from D'Artagnan (800–327–8246).

When it comes to cooking methods, you can't get much simpler than sticking stuff in the coals and leaving it there until it's done. In fact, this technique was probably devised even before some cave-dwelling genius thought of threading food on a stick and suspending it over flames.

FOOD FROM THE ASHES

hobo pack cookery

So it seems somehow appropriate that this is the method I used the first time I ever cooked for other people. It was during my initial camping trip with the Longhorn Patrol of Boy Scout Troop 103, when I was elected as cook. I would like to think that my fellow scouts selected me because they somehow glimpsed a hidden talent, but I think the actual reason was that, as the newest member of the patrol, I got stuck with the most disliked task.

In any case, since I knew how to cook only two things and one of them was tuna fish sandwiches, I went with the other option, the old Boy Scout standard known as the hobo pack. This basically consists of some carrots and onions, a bunch of hamburger, and a ton of catsup all wrapped up in foil and stuck in the ashes to cook.

I was a little nervous when I pulled the fire-blackened packets out of the ashes, but when the other scouts proceeded to wolf down my food with great pleasure, I felt for the first time the thrill that comes from having people appreciate your cooking efforts.

I've cooked a lot of food for a lot of people since those days, but I still have a special affection for hobo pack cookery. In addition to fond memories, there are several reason for this. First, the process is incredibly easy. Second, this is a very adaptable cooking method, equally suitable for the backyard grill, the fireplace in your living room, or a driftwood fire on the beach.

Even more important than ease or adaptability, though, is the fact that, like other techniques involving live fire, this is a cooking method with character. Every time you set out to prepare an ash-cooked meal, it's the beginning of a true culinary adventure, with the looming threat of the ruination of dinner providing a built-in drama.

The risk and the fun of ash-roasting come from a single fact: The food is being cooked by a combination of convection and conduction, separated from direct contact with a very intense heat source only by about one-sixteenth of an inch of foil. As a result of this combination of high heat and minimal separation, food cooked in ashes gets real, direct browning, which creates a fantastic caramelized flavor.

As you might expect, some of the food that bumps up against the foil walls of the packet may tip over the edge of browning into burnt. But this is easily remedied: For insurance against fire damage, just start out with about twenty-five percent more food than you actually need.

Hobo pack cookery also provides a great vehicle for personal expression. Since the process consists of little more than cutting up food and putting it together inside a foil wrapper, the sky's the limit when it comes to selecting ingredients. And as you practice your hobo pack skills, you'll find that you can create all sorts of new flavors by combining various ingredients inside the foil.

One aspect of ash cooking that needs some special attention is the wrapping of the food. In this department, I pay homage to my friend Jeff Singleton, aka Smiley, a knowledgeable fellow with a Ph.D. in American history who was also a bartender at the East Coast Grill for twelve solid years.

Each spring and autumn for the past fifteen years, Smiley has performed the same culinary pilgrimage: a day-long trip to the beach, where he inaugurates and then, at the end of the summer, bids farewell to the live fire cooking season with a meal cooked in ashes. The wrapping style described in each of the recipes in this chapter is the one perfected by Smiley over the years. It requires a fair amount of heavy-duty foil, but don't be tempted to skimp or improvise, or you are likely to end up with a higher proportion of burned food than you want.

If you try this method, I know you'll get to like it for its ease, for its flavor, and for the moment of drama when the package that has been hidden in the mysteries of the fire is retrieved and brought to the table. Tension is at a peak as the blackened foil is set before the guests and the skeptics among them remark negatively on the prospect of actually eating what is inside. Then the packets are opened, the wonderful smells emerge, and the cook is instantly transformed from a foolhardy adventurer into a culinary hero—or goat, depending on how much of the food is burned. Either way, though, there is no denying the intrinsic appeal of this method to the primitive cook in each of us and, like meals cooked over a campfire, fire-roasted food somehow just tastes better.

Authentic Hobo Pack, Old Style

Eggplant and Tomato Hobo Pack with Lemon and Garlic

Latin-Flavored Root Vegetable Hobo Pack

Pearl Onion Hobo Pack with Raisins and Sage

Orange–Sweet Potato Hobo Pack

Hobo Pack of Winter Vegetables with Many Fresh Herbs

All-Purpose Ash-Roasted Garlic

Hobo Pack Italiano

Chicken Hobo Pack with Garlic, Lemon, and Herbs

Sausage Hobo Pack with Onions, Peppers, and Green Grapes

Authentic Hobo Pack, Old Style

We've taken a lot of creative license in this book when it comes to hobo packs. But if we were to be purists about it and honor the true "oldways" of the dish, this would be the one. We Boy Scouts did cook other ingredients in our hobo packs, but no combination was as memorable or as popular. You would never have seen herbs or garlic—no fancy roots or intricate spicing here. This was fuel for hungry kids. I have taken the liberty of reducing the catsup from the original, for if my memory serves me correctly the amount that my patrol and I used was absurd; but then again, we figured we could put in fewer vegetables that way. Put this classic into the ashes before the grown-up dinner goes on the grid.

> 1 pound ground beef
>
> 1 red onion, quartered but not peeled
>
> 1 large baking potato, washed and quartered lengthwise
>
> 1 large carrot, unpeeled, quartered
>
> 1 large tomato, quartered
>
> 1 cup catsup
>
> Salt and freshly cracked black pepper to taste

1. In a medium bowl, combine all the ingredients and toss gently.

2. Lay out two sheets of heavy-duty foil, each about 2 feet long, one on top of the other. Place the ingredients in the center, then lay a third length of heavy-duty foil over the top. Fold the edges of the sheets together on all sides, closing the pack, then roll them up until they bump into the food, forming a ridge around its perimeter. Place the pack right side up in the center of a fourth length of foil and fold the four sides over the top of the packet, one after another.

3. Now the package is ready for the coals. The fire should have passed its peak of intensity and be dying down, so that it consists primarily of glowing coals covered with a thin film of gray ash but very few flickering flames—in other words, you want **a medium to low dying fire.** Clear a place for the foil packet, leaving a thin layer of coals. Place the packet on the cleared area and heap up coals all around, but not directly on top. Cook, shifting the packet as needed so it is continuously in contact with glowing coals, for 25 to 30 minutes.

4. Remove from the coals, unroll the foil, and serve at once.

For the full Boy Scout experience, eat this with a S'more, a Coke, and a peanut butter cup for dessert.

Eggplant and Tomato Hobo Pack with Lemon and Garlic

SERVES 4 TO 6 AS SIDE DISH

Eggplant gets kind of mushed up as it cooks in a hobo pack, which actually turns out to be a good quality, particularly if it's getting mushed up with tomatoes and garlic. In this dish, the lemons soften, turn a little brown, and give off some aromatic flavor, as well as acting as a heat shield of sorts for the other ingredients.

- 2 lemons, sliced into thin rounds
- 2 small eggplants, cut lengthwise into quarters
- 4 plum tomatoes, halved
- 2 heads garlic, halved horizontally
- 7 large sprigs fresh oregano or rosemary
- ¼ cup olive oil
- Salt and freshly cracked black pepper to taste

1. Lay out two sheets of heavy-duty foil, each about 2 feet long, one on top of the other. Place the lemon slices in the center, then put the eggplant quarters on top. Follow with the tomatoes and garlic, add the herbs, and drizzle with the olive oil. Lay a third length of heavy-duty foil over the top. Fold the edges of the sheets together on all sides, closing the pack, then roll them up until they bump into the food, forming a ridge around its perimeter. Place the pack right side up in the center of a fourth length of foil and fold the four sides over the top of the packet, one after another.

2. Now the package is ready for the coals. The fire should have passed its peak of intensity and be dying down, so that it consists primarily of glowing coals covered with a thin film of gray ash but very few flickering flames—in other words, you want **a medium to low dying fire.** Clear a place for the foil packet, leaving a thin layer of coals. Place the packet on the cleared area and heap up coals all around, but not directly on top. Cook, keeping watch and shifting the packet as needed so it is continuously in contact with glowing coals, for 20 to 30 minutes, depending on the intensity of the coals.

3. Remove from the coals, unroll the foil, and serve at once.

> Try this Mediterranean-flavored dish with an appetizer portion of Grilled Sausage and Corn over Fettuccine with Tomatoes and Basil (page 99) to start, Grilled Asparagus with Garlic Mayonnaise or Simple Vinaigrette (page 279) on the side, and Grilled Bananas and Pineapple with Rum-Molasses Glaze (page 357) for dessert.

Latin-Flavored Root Vegetable Hobo Pack

This is a play on the popular Latin American combination of yucca, lime, garlic, and olive oil. Here we substitute potato for the yucca and put it in a hobo pack instead of boiling it. But we do follow the Cuban/Puerto Rican tradition of putting lime and cilantro on the vegetables after cooking, as a quick flavor booster. This preparation works well not only with potatoes or yuccas, but with any other exotic roots or tubers you might come across in your supermarket.

3 large Idaho potatoes, washed and cut into 2-inch rounds
2 yellow onions, halved but unpeeled
2 heads garlic, loose skin rubbed off, top $1/4$ inch sliced off
$1/3$ cup olive oil
Salt and freshly cracked black pepper to taste
2 tablespoons cumin seeds
$1/4$ cup roughly chopped fresh cilantro (or substitute parsley)
2 limes, halved

1. Rub the potatoes, onions, and garlic with the oil and sprinkle with salt and pepper to taste.

2. Lay out two sheets of heavy-duty foil, each about 2 feet long, one on top of the other. Place the ingredients in the center, then lay a third length of heavy-duty foil over the top. Fold the edges of the sheets together on all sides, closing the pack, then roll them up until they bump into the food, forming a ridge around its perimeter. Place the pack right side up in the center of a fourth length of foil and fold the four sides over the top of the packet, one after another.

3. Now the package is ready for the coals. The fire should have passed its peak of intensity and be dying down, so that it consists primarily of glowing coals covered with a thin film of gray ash but very few flickering flames—in other words, you want **a medium to low dying fire.** Clear a place for the foil packet, leaving a thin layer of coals. Place the packet on the cleared area and heap up coals all around, but not directly on top. Cook, keeping watch and shifting the packet as needed so it is continuously in contact with glowing coals, for 25 to 30 minutes, depending on the intensity of the coals.

4. While the hobo pack is cooking, place the cumin seeds in a small sauté pan over medium heat and toast, shaking frequently, until you see the first hint of smoke, 2 to 3 minutes. Remove from the heat.

5. Remove the hobo pack from the fire and unroll the foil. Sprinkle the vegetables with the cilantro and toasted cumin seeds, squeeze the limes over the top, and you're ready to serve.

Try serving this one with Grilled Delmonico Steak Adobo with
Charred Spring Onions and Sweet Corn Relish (page 131) as your entrée
and Peach Sour Cream Pie (page 378) for dessert.

venezuelan roots

TRAVELING ALONG THE CARIBBEAN coast of Venezuela, near the small colonial town of Rio Caribe, I was fortunate enough to be invited to lunch at a club for workers from the area's cacao plantations. This turned out to be a small compound nestled in a grove of banana and breadfruit trees, complete with a concrete water tank where children could swim, a rectangular dirt court where men played continuous games of bocce, and a roof suspended over tables long enough to seat forty or fifty diners. At the back of the eating area was the "kitchen," basically a sink and a giant wood-burning grill set in concrete.

ON THIS DAY, THE men at the grill were preparing the specialty of the region, a fish stew called *sancocho de mero*. Simmering away in a giant metal pot on the grill, it smelled wonderful, and when they brought it to the table, it tasted even better. In a thin but flavorful broth spiked with tiny chiles and *culantro* (wild cilantro) were large chunks of ultrafresh grilled grouper, along with a profusion of roots and tubers including yucca, malanga, boniato, and several others I couldn't identify. The starchy consistency of the tubers provided a perfect contrast to the fish.

BUT THIS WAS JUST the beginning of my introduction to the skillful use of root vegetables by Venezuela's cooks. As I continued to travel through the country, I found that, over centuries of experience, home cooks had learned to take advantage of the distinct qualities of a vast variety of roots and tubers, creating a whole palette of flavors and textures from foods that are plentiful and inexpensive in the tropical climate. These simple, homey preparations were among the best things I had eaten in a long time.

SO I RECOMMEND THAT, whenever you find a root or tuber in a market that you're not familiar with, buy it, take it home, and try it out—maybe in a hobo pack, which is a great way to treat these vegetables. There's a whole world of root vegetables out there and, after all, you never know when you'll find something that you like as much as that old favorite, the potato.

Pearl Onion Hobo Pack with Raisins and Sage

SERVES 4 AS SIDE DISH

When I make this dish, I like to leave the skins on the onions for several reasons. First, they help protect these little pearls, which is a definite plus, because anything in a hobo pack is prone to burning. Second, it's a pain to peel them all yourself, and much easier just to let your guests do it after they are cooked. Finally, I actually think the cooked skins taste pretty good.

Think of this dish in your creamed onion slot. A perfect holiday go-along, and very festive when pulled from the burning embers and taken straight to the holiday table.

20 pearl onions about the size of golf balls, trimmed but not peeled
$^1\!/_2$ cup raisins
$^1\!/_2$ cup roughly chopped fresh sage
$^1\!/_2$ cup olive oil
Salt and freshly cracked black pepper to taste

1. In a large bowl, combine all the ingredients and toss well.

2. Lay out two sheets of heavy-duty foil, each about 2 feet long, one on top of the other. Place the onions and raisins in the center, sprinkle the sage over them, and drizzle with the oil. Season with salt and pepper to taste and lay a third length of heavy-duty foil over the top. Fold the edges of the sheets together on all sides, closing the pack, then roll them up until they bump into the food, forming a ridge around its perimeter. Place the pack right side up in the center of a fourth length of foil and fold the four sides over the top of the packet, one after another.

3. Now the package is ready for the coals. The fire should have passed its peak of intensity and be dying down, so that it consists primarily of glowing coals covered with a thin film of gray ash but very few flickering flames—in other words, you want **a medium to low dying fire.** Clear a place for the foil packet, leaving a thin layer of coals. Place the packet on the cleared area and heap up coals all around, but not directly on top. Cook, keeping watch and shifting the packet as needed so it is continuously in contact with glowing coals, for 15 to 25 minutes, depending on the intensity of the coals.

4. Remove the pack from the coals and unroll the foil. At this point you can either serve the onions as they are and allow your guests to squeeze the meat out of the peels themselves, which is what I prefer, or you can peel the onions first, then serve them, topped with the raisins and juices.

This goes well with Grilled Lamb Chops with Pomegranate-Eggplant Relish (page 144) as an entrée, Arugula with Pancetta, Grilled Asparagus, and White Beans (page 50), and Maple Bread Pudding with Oven-Dried Pears and Homemade Raisins (page 367) for dessert.

Orange–Sweet Potato Hobo Pack

SERVES 4 AS SIDE DISH

Although sweet potatoes originated in Central America, they were brought to the United States by African slaves, who in turn had been introduced to them by European slave traders. These rich, flavorful tubers, which have a remarkably high sugar content for a vegetable, have remained embedded in the cooking of the South ever since. There they turn up not only by themselves as a side dish, but also as an ingredient in everything from soup to custard pies.

Here we use the heat of the coals to make a kind of fire-roasted version of candied sweet potatoes, complete with oranges, onions, and raisins, then drizzle them with a mixture of honey, lemon juice, and parsley. You won't beat this as a side dish for an autumn or winter dinner, or as a snack by the fire on a cold Sunday afternoon.

> 4 medium sweet potatoes, washed but not peeled, cut into rounds
>   about 2 inches thick
> 1 orange, thinly sliced (including peel)
> 1 large red onion, peeled and quartered
> $^1/_3$ cup raisins
> $^1/_4$ cup olive oil
> $^1/_4$ cup unsalted butter, cut into small bits
> Salt and freshly cracked black pepper to taste
> $^1/_3$ cup fresh lemon juice (about 1 large lemon)
> $^1/_3$ cup honey
> $^1/_3$ cup roughly chopped fresh parsley

1. In a large bowl, combine the sweet potatoes, orange, onion, raisins, olive oil, and butter. Toss lightly, sprinkle with salt and pepper to taste, and toss lightly again.

2. Lay out two sheets of heavy-duty foil, each about 2 feet long, one on top of the other. Place the sweet potato mixture in the center, then lay a third length of heavy-duty foil over the top. Fold the edges of the sheets together on all sides, closing the pack, then roll them up until they bump into the food, forming a ridge around its perimeter. Place the pack right side up in the center of a fourth length of foil and fold the four sides over the top of the packet, one after another.

3. Now the package is ready for the coals. The fire should have passed its peak of intensity and be dying down, so that it consists primarily of glowing coals covered with a thin film of gray ash but very few flickering flames—in other words, you want **a medium to low dying fire.** Clear a place for the foil packet, leaving a thin layer of coals. Place the packet on the cleared area and heap up coals all around, but not directly on top. Cook, keeping watch and shifting the packet as needed so it is continuously in contact with glowing coals, for 30 to 35 minutes, depending on the intensity of the coals.

4. While the hobo pack is cooking, combine the lemon juice, honey, and parsley in a small bowl and mix well to combine.

5. Remove the foil pack from the coals, unroll the foil, drizzle the vegetables with the lemon-honey mixture, and serve at once.

This is a fantastic side dish with Hoisin Chicken Breasts with Grilled Peppers and Onions (page 199), Grilled Veal Chops with Expensive Mushrooms (page 138), or Slow-Grilled Game Hens with Garlic-Lemon-Herb Rub (page 207).

the paradoxical sweet potato

UNLIKE MOST PRODUCE, SWEET potatoes are usually better if bought in the winter, rather than in the autumn months when they are harvested. This is because those bought "out of season" have usually been cured, while those bought fresh-dug have not.

IN THE OLD DAYS, Southern farmers used to cure their sweet potatoes by stacking the tubers in specially constructed "sweet potato houses," where they were dried over the course of several days by the smoke and heat from a wood fire, usually oak. As the potatoes cured, the white sap found in newly dug potatoes dried out, a process that somewhat paradoxically resulted in potatoes with creamier flesh. In addition, the long, low heating converted some of the starch in the potatoes to sugar, so they were sweeter when eaten.

TODAY, SWEET POTATOES ARE often marketed without being cured from August through October. Most sweet potatoes found in stores after November, however, have been cured, although the process is now accomplished in giant industrial kilns rather than rustic sweet potato houses.

Hobo Pack of Winter Vegetables with Many Fresh Herbs

SERVES 4 AS SIDE DISH

Maybe it's the rough-and-ready heritage of the hobo pack that urges me not to peel food that's going down the hobo trail. Or maybe because the food is likely to burn I want all the protection possible. Whatever the reason, I prefer to leave root vegetables unpeeled in hobo packs; if they are properly roasted, the skins of all but onions will be soft enough to eat, or you can peel the flesh out of them quite easily if you prefer.

The root vegetables of winter are not always the most popular, but fire-roasted turnips and beets are hard to beat. To boost their flavor quotient even more, here we combine them with lots of fresh herbs and garlic. If you have any leftovers, they are ideal for late-night refrigerator raids.

> 2 beets the size of baseballs, unpeeled, trimmed and halved
> 1 large carrot, unpeeled, trimmed and quartered
> 1 red onion the size of a baseball, unpeeled, halved
> 2 turnips the size of baseballs, unpeeled, halved
> 1 head garlic, loose peel rubbed off, halved horizontally
> 1 tablespoon roughly chopped fresh rosemary
> 1 tablespoon roughly chopped fresh thyme
> 1 tablespoon roughly chopped fresh oregano
> 1 tablespoon roughly chopped fresh parsley
> 1/3 cup olive oil
> Salt and freshly cracked black pepper to taste

1. In a large bowl, combine all the ingredients and toss well to coat the vegetables with the oil and herbs.

2. Lay out two sheets of heavy-duty foil, each about 2 feet long, one on top of the other. Place the ingredients in the center, then lay a third length of heavy-duty foil over the top. Fold the edges of the sheets together on all sides, closing the pack, then roll them up until they bump into the food, forming a ridge around its perimeter. Place the pack right side up in the center of a fourth length of foil and fold the four sides over the top of the packet, one after another.

3. Now the package is ready for the coals. The fire should have passed its peak of intensity and be dying down, so that it consists primarily of glowing coals covered with a thin film of gray ash but very few flickering flames—in other words, you want **a medium to low dying fire.** Clear a place for the foil packet, leaving a thin layer of coals. Place the packet on the cleared area and heap up coals all around, but not directly on top. Cook, keeping watch and shifting the packet as needed so it is continuously in contact with glowing coals, for 25 to 35 minutes, depending on the intensity of the coals.

4. Remove from the coals, unroll the foil, and serve at once.

Try this with an appetizer portion of Grilled Shrimp and Asparagus Skewers with Lime-Soy Dipping Sauce (page 108) as a starter and Grilled Flank Steak "in the Style of Pastrami" with Spicy Tomato-Horseradish Relish (page 134) as your entrée.

All-Purpose Ash-Roasted Garlic

SERVES 4 AS SIDE DISH

If you want the real thing, this is it—real roasted garlic. It has dozens of uses. Serve it with toast and let each guest squeeze his or her own; use it as a condiment with grilled steak or lamb chops; squeeze it into mashed potatoes; use it in dressings and mayonnaise; or mix it with fresh herbs, lemon, and olive oil and use it as a sauce for vegetables. It's one of the world's great flavors, and it's fun to squeeze besides.

4 large heads garlic, loose peel rubbed off, top $1/4$ inch sliced off
$1/4$ cup olive oil
Salt and freshly cracked black pepper to taste

1. Place the garlic heads in the center of a sheet of heavy-duty aluminum foil about 1 foot long. Pour the oil over the garlic and sprinkle with salt and pepper to taste, then cover with a second sheet of foil and roll the edges of the two sheets together on all sides, closing the pack. Place the pack in the center of another 1-foot length of foil and fold this length up around the pack.

2. Lay the packet in the dying embers of **a medium to low fire** and pile coals up on all sides. Cook for 35 minutes, moving it around occasionally to keep it in contact with glowing coals. Remove the pack from the coals and unroll the foil. Your garlic is ready to use.

As its name suggests, this dish is all-purpose.

Hobo Pack Italiano

SERVES 4 TO 6 AS SIDE DISH

This substantial Italian-flavored side dish is sure to impress your guests when it is retrieved from the burning embers. Fashioned on the tried-and-true bacon-mushroom pairing, it gets a lot of juice from the mushrooms, which become soft and tender and give up a lot of liquid as they cook. It doesn't take all that long to cook this dish, so be careful and check it early; the mushrooms are done when a peek inside shows them to be moist throughout.

> 1 pound mushrooms of choice, trimmed and cleaned
>
> 2 red onions, quartered but unpeeled
>
> 1/4 pound thinly sliced prosciutto, cut into thin strips
>
> 1 head garlic, cloves separated but not peeled
>
> 1/4 cup chopped fresh herbs: any one or a combination of parsley, sage, rosemary, or thyme
>
> 1/3 cup olive oil
>
> Salt and freshly cracked black pepper to taste
>
> 10 leaves mustard greens, kale, or other slightly bitter leafy green

1. In a medium bowl, combine all the ingredients except the greens and toss together well.

2. Lay out two sheets of heavy-duty foil, each about 2 feet long, one on top of the other. Place the tossed ingredients in the center, lay the greens on top, then lay a third length of heavy-duty foil over the top. Fold the edges of the sheets together on all sides, closing the pack, then roll them up until they bump into the food, forming a ridge around its perimeter. Place the pack right side up in the center of a fourth length of foil and fold the four sides over the top of the packet, one after another.

3. Now the package is ready for the coals. The fire should have passed its peak of intensity and be dying down, so that it consists primarily of glowing coals covered with a thin film of gray ash but very few flickering flames—in other words, you want **a medium to low dying fire.** Clear a place for the foil packet, leaving a thin layer of coals. Place the packet on the cleared area and heap up coals all around, but not directly on top. Cook, keeping watch and shifting the packet as needed so it is continuously in contact with glowing coals, for 15 to 20 minutes, depending on the intensity of the coals.

4. Remove from the coals, unroll the foil, and serve at once.

This dish goes on the side, and I like it with Lamb Shish Kebobs over Fettuccine (page 100) as an entrée and, if I'm feeling a little ambitious, Little Chèvre Cheesecakes with Guava-Lime Sauce (page 370) for dessert.

Chicken Hobo Pack with Garlic, Lemon, and Herbs

I generally don't like to cook the individual components of a dish together, since I prefer to taste the flavors of each ingredient clearly. But the hobo pack is an exception. Encouraged by both direct heat and convection cooking, the flavors blend together in an outstanding fashion. In this dish, for example, the garlic cloves are mellowed and their flavor spreads throughout the entire dish; the juice that is created is not to be missed.

As with other hobo packs, the coals don't have to surround the packet totally, and the packet should be moved around a bit to avoid burning in the places where it is directly up against the coals. It takes a try or two to get this part down right, but once you have it, the hobo pack provides a ready blank canvas for your creative use of whatever's in the fridge.

6 bone-in chicken thighs (about 1¹/₂ pounds total)

2 heads garlic, separated into cloves but not peeled

1 lemon, thinly sliced

¹/₄ cup roughly chopped fresh herbs: any one or a combination
   of parsley, oregano, rosemary, thyme, sage, or basil

1 teaspoon red pepper flakes

¹/₄ cup olive oil

Salt and freshly cracked black pepper to taste

1. In a medium bowl, combine all the ingredients and toss gently.

2. Lay out two sheets of heavy-duty foil, each about 2 feet long, one on top of the other. Place the ingredients in the center, then lay a third length of heavy-duty foil over the top. Fold the edges of the sheets together on all sides, closing the pack, then roll them up until they bump into the food, forming a ridge around its perimeter. Place the pack right side up in the center of a fourth length of foil and fold the four sides over the top of the packet, one after another.

3. Now the package is ready for the coals. The fire should have passed its peak of intensity and be dying down, so that it consists primarily of glowing coals covered with a thin film of gray ash but very few flickering flames—in other words, you want **a medium to low dying fire.** Clear a place for the foil packet, leaving a thin layer of coals. Place the packet on the cleared area and heap up coals all around, but not directly on top. Cook, shifting the packet as needed so it is continuously in contact with glowing coals, for 25 to 30 minutes, depending on the intensity of the coals. *To check for doneness:* Unwrap the packet and peek inside one of the thighs; there should be no redness next to the bone.

4. Remove from the coals, unroll the foil, and serve at once.

You might want to serve this with Red Snapper Cocktail (page 73) as an appetizer and Grilled Bananas and Pineapple with Rum-Molasses Glaze (page 357) for dessert.

Sausage Hobo Pack with Onions, Peppers, and Green Grapes

SERVES 4 AS ENTRÉE

It's a Sunday in October, the first cold weather is coming in, and I'm cranking up the first fire of the season. Maybe there's a big football game on the tube or the fall classic is on and I've got some pals coming over. In a situation like that, I like to stick this hobo pack in the fire. Then, when I download the mixture into a sub roll, I never have to miss a pitch or a pass. Just like at the ball park—except for the green grapes, of course. Add more red pepper flakes if you like more heat.

> 1½ pounds fresh sausage (hot or sweet or mixed), cut into small chunks
> 2 red onions, peeled and thinly sliced
> 1 green bell pepper, halved, seeded, and thinly sliced
> 1 red bell pepper, halved, seeded, and thinly sliced
> ½ cup seedless green grapes, halved if large
> 1 tablespoon red pepper flakes
> ¼ cup chopped fresh herbs: any one or a combination of parsley, thyme, oregano, sage, rosemary, or basil
> ¼ cup olive oil
> Salt and freshly cracked black pepper to taste

1. In a medium bowl, combine all ingredients and toss gently.

2. Lay out two sheets of heavy-duty foil, each about 2 feet long, one on top of the other. Place the ingredients in the center, then lay a third length of heavy-duty foil over the top. Fold the edges of the sheets together on all sides, closing the pack, then roll them up until they bump into the food, forming a ridge around its perimeter. Place the pack right side up in the center of a fourth length of foil and fold the four sides over the top of the packet, one after another.

3. Now the package is ready for the coals. The fire should have passed its peak of intensity and be dying down, so that it consists primarily of glowing coals covered with a thin film of gray ash but very few flickering flames—in other words, you want **a medium to low dying fire.** Clear a place for the foil packet, leaving a thin layer of coals. Place the packet on the cleared area and heap up coals all around, but not directly on top. Cook, keeping watch and shifting the packet as needed so it is continuously in contact with glowing coals, for about 20 minutes, depending on the intensity of the coals.

4. Remove from the coals, unroll the foil, and serve at once.

I like this with **Chickpea Salad with Horseradish-Yogurt Dressing** (page 317) as a starter, **Latin-Flavored Coleslaw with Grilled Avocados** (page 309) on the side, and **Grilled Bananas and Pineapple with Rum-Molasses Glaze** (page 357) for dessert.

The recipes in this chapter are not for everybody. They're for you knuckleheads out there who have to do the "heat thing." Maybe it's not good for you, but the demons inside draw you to it.

FOR HEAT FANATICS
way hot

Fortunately for me, I'm a recovering heat fanatic and no longer feel the unrelenting pull to always search out and eat the hottest. This is not to say, however, that I am completely recovered or repentant. I will unapologetically ask the waitperson in any restaurant regardless of the quality of the linen to bring me Tabasco sauce (one of the world's top four hot sauces, along with El Yucateco, Saigon Paste, and of course Inner Beauty Real Hot Sauce, Original Formula), fill any Asian broth with chiles until my head sweats, and, if challenged, I will never back down. Come to think of it, maybe I've fallen off the wagon after all.

But that's not so bad, because it means that a kinship still exists between us, and I know you heat freaks need a chef who understands your needs—a chef who says the culinary arguments describing very hot food as one-dimensional are spurious, who refutes the old argument that heat covers the delicate nature of seafood. If we heat admirers needed anything more than our taste buds to justify us, we could point out that both arguments are Eurocentric and become specious when viewed from a global perspective.

Well, I am your chef. And I don't ask you to trust me without bona fides; I come armed with my résumé of more than fifteen "Hotter than Hell Night" experiences at the East Coast Grill. On those nights, as I look out over a room filled with customers panting and perspiring, their flushed faces plastered with that silly grin you get when you're on a heat high, I know the true joy of the fellowship of heat. The customers are asking each other for advice, shouting back and forth across the restaurant, passing plates from table to table, and generally acting as if they are truly at the gathering of a giant family.

So I am ready for the task. I'm your man for recipes that combine deep flavors and intense heat, and here they are. From Chipotle-Rubbed Grilled Skirt Steak, for a blazing meat experience, to Grilled Jerk Shark, for a variation on the classic Jamaican habanero encounter, to Chile-Coated Grilled Summer Squash and Zucchini, for a vegetarian conflagration, these are recipes that will bring the sweat to your brow and a smile to your face.

Ginger-Soy Marinated Grilled Shrimp with Most-Hot Lime-Chile Booster

Grilled Jerk Shark with Pineapple Salsa

Chile-Grilled Squid on Sesame Spinach

Chile-Coated Chicken Thighs with Couscous and Tomato-Raisin Relish

Chipotle-Rubbed Grilled Skirt Steak with Grill-Roasted Bananas

Grilled Pork, Pineapple, and Jalapeño Skewers with Guava-Lime Sauce

Chile-Coated Grilled Summer Squash and Zucchini with Honey-Lime Dressing

Really Hot Purple Pickled Eggs

Chile-Garlic in Vinegar

Ginger-Soy Marinated Grilled Shrimp with Most-Hot Lime-Chile Booster

SERVES 4 AS APPETIZER

In this dish we use shrimp that are small enough so the flavors of the garlic, ginger, and cilantro in the marinade can come through clearly. The sugar provides a little sweetness and encourages some caramelization on the exterior. To put the shrimp into the heart of hotness, we add a chile-laced "booster," which should be served only to folks who have been properly warned of its incendiary properties. Jalapeños work well here but, as always, it's best to use a chile pepper that you know and love.

16 medium shrimp (about 1 pound), peeled, deveined, and butterflied

Freshly cracked white pepper to taste (or substitute black)

2 tablespoons minced ginger

1 tablespoon minced garlic

1 teaspoon sugar

3 tablespoons soy sauce

2 tablespoons sesame oil

$^1/_4$ cup chopped fresh cilantro (or substitute parsley)

For the Booster

$^1/_3$ cup minced fresh chile peppers of your choice

$^1/_4$ cup roughly chopped fresh mint

2 tablespoons minced ginger

$^1/_4$ cup fresh lime juice (about 2 limes)

1 tablespoon molasses

1 tablespoon grated lime zest (green part only) (optional)

1. Sprinkle the shrimp with white pepper to taste. In a medium bowl, combine the ginger, garlic, sugar, soy sauce, sesame oil, and cilantro and mix well. Toss the shrimp into the marinade and let them sit for an hour, refrigerated.

2. While the shrimp are marinating, make the booster: Combine all of the ingredients in a food processor or blender and puree until smooth. Cover and refrigerate until ready to use.

3. Drain the shrimp, discarding the remaining marinade, and thread the shrimp onto skewers. Grill over **a medium-hot fire** for 3 to 4 minutes per side. *To check for doneness:* Cut into one of the shrimp and check to see that it is opaque all the way through. Serve the shrimp hot or cold and pass the booster separately for people to use as much as they dare.

I might serve this along with Barbecued Oysters in Their Shells (page 70) and maybe a bowl of Basic Black Beans (page 299) to cool the heat a bit.

Grilled Jerk Shark with Pineapple Salsa

The jerk technique, first practiced by escaped Maroon slaves in the Blue Hills of Jamaica, has become one of the most inspiring, fully evolved, borrowed, redone, and ripped-off cooking methods of the decade. Throw some chiles on it and grill it, and people are willing to call it "jerk." Of course, it's hard to say exactly who is wrong and right in this area; there are no Jerk Police around to protect the true, original process, and even on the island of Jamaica the quality and ingredients of jerk vary wildly.

Not one to buck a trend, I was also inspired to borrow, evolve, and spin off a bastard jerk preparation of my own, jerk shark. I feel that shark, with its firm texture and bland flavor, is a perfect volunteer to stand up not only to the smoke of the jerk process, but also to the dynamic heat and ultra-aromaticity of the Scotch bonnet.

The pineapple salsa provides some relief from the heat. If you want even more action, add grill-roasted bananas (see page 357) to the mix.

For the Jerk Rub

> 10 Scotch bonnet or habanero chile peppers , minced
>   (or substitute 15 of your favorite milder fresh chile peppers)
> 2 tablespoons roughly chopped fresh parsley
> $1/2$ cup dried herbs: any one or a combination of rosemary, basil,
>   thyme, or oregano
> 2 tablespoons ground coriander
> 3 scallions (white and green parts), finely chopped
> 2 tablespoons ground allspice
> 2 tablespoons salt
> $1/4$ cup freshly cracked black pepper
> Juice of 2 limes
> $1/2$ cup cheap yellow mustard
>
> 4 8- to 10-ounce shark steaks
> 2 limes, quartered
> Pineapple Salsa (recipe follows)

1. Make the rub: In a small bowl, combine all the ingredients and mix together well.

2. Cover the shark steaks generously with the rub, place them on the grill over **a medium fire,** and cook for 4 to 5 minutes per side. *To check for doneness:* Cut into one of the steaks and peek to see that it is opaque all the way through.

3. Serve the steaks with the lime wedges and a generous helping of Pineapple Salsa.

PINEAPPLE SALSA

MAKES ABOUT 3 CUPS

$^1/_2$ small pineapple, peeled, cored, and cut into bite-sized chunks

$^1/_2$ red bell pepper, seeded and diced small

$^1/_2$ green bell pepper, seeded and diced small

$^1/_2$ cup roughly chopped fresh cilantro

1 tablespoon minced ginger

1 tablespoon ground cumin

1 tablespoon curry powder

1 tablespoon red pepper flakes

$^1/_4$ cup fresh lime juice (about 2 limes)

Salt and freshly cracked black pepper to taste

In a small bowl, combine all the ingredients and mix well. This salsa will keep, covered and refrigerated, for 3 or 4 days.

> I might serve a starter of Grilled Scallop–Stuffed Avocados with
> Papaya Vinaigrette (page 58) with this, then accompany it with
> Simple Latin-Style Rice and Beans (page 300).

the real jerk

MY FIRST EXPERIENCE WITH jerk was at the jerk epicenter of the universe, Boston Bay. This spot, on the northeast coast of Jamaica, also happens to be right next to Jamaica's premier surf spot. So one day, on my way back to the town of Port Antonio after an afternoon surf session, I stopped off at a couple of the roadside stands to guzzle some Red Stripe beers and check out the "cue." From my first look at these stands, I had the deal pretty much wired. They related directly to the barbecue dives of my youth—a cinder-block rig, a small hut dispensing Cokes or beers, and a bunch of guys basically just standing around watching meat smoke and passing this off as work. These jerkmasters were the direct equivalent of the pitmasters I had admired so much as a kid.

EACH DAY AFTER SURFING, I'd stop by a different stand and sample the pork or chicken. (The original jerk preparation was pork rubbed with a spicy paste and slowly smoked to preserve it. Now chicken has been added to the basic repertoire, but the key ingredients remain the Scotch bonnet paste and a lot of smoke.) I'd hang out with the guys, watching them make their spice pastes and homemade jerk sausages, and from my vantage point it seemed as if the same guy never made the stuff the same way two days in a row. Not only that, but the list of ingredients used in the different huts up and down Boston Bay also differed significantly. So much for ever truly winning the "What is real jerk?" debate.

IN ANY EVENT, I think the jerk phenomenon is a good one, because it has encouraged a lot of people to try food of another culture that they might never have tried otherwise. But if you're ever down in Jamaica, don't let the other versions of jerk you might find around the island fool you—the real thing is at Boston Bay. Between the jerk and the peaceful, beautiful surroundings (the movie *Blue Lagoon* was filmed nearby), it's well worth a drive.

Chile-Grilled Squid on Sesame Spinach

SERVES 4 AS ENTRÉE

First let me say that the sesame spinach is wonderful on its own, so even if you don't like squid or hot food, you should check out this way of preparing spinach.

Grilling is an excellent way to deal with the peculiar texture of squid. Cooking tradition decrees that you have to cook this water dweller either slow and low or quick and hot; anything in between, and it will be so rubbery that you'll find your jaw getting tired trying to chew it. Here we use an unusual cooking tool, a foil-wrapped brick, to ensure quick cooking by keeping the squid flat against the grill. The heat is in the crust and is nicely balanced by the cool, fresh sesame spinach.

For the Rub

    1 tablespoon red pepper flakes

    1 tablespoon minced garlic

    1 tablespoon minced ginger

    2 tablespoons peanut or other vegetable oil

    1 teaspoon freshly ground white pepper (or substitute black)

    1 pound squid, cleaned, tentacles and bodies separated

    10 ounces spinach, trimmed, washed, and dried

    $1/4$ cup soy sauce

    2 tablespoons sesame oil

    $1/4$ cup rice vinegar

    1 teaspoon minced ginger

    Salt and freshly cracked black pepper to taste

    $1/2$ cup sesame seeds, toasted in a 350°F oven until golden brown, 5 to 7 minutes

    2 limes, quartered, for garnish (optional)

1. Make the rub: In a small bowl, combine all the ingredients and mix together well. Coat the squid bodies and tentacles generously with the rub and set aside.

2. Fill your sink or a large stockpot with ice and water. In a large saucepan, bring 1 quart of salted water to a boil over high heat. Add the spinach and blanch very briefly, only about 15 seconds. Drain and immediately place in the ice-and-water bath to stop the cooking process; the spinach should remain bright green. After 30 seconds, drain the spinach and place it in a large mixing bowl.

3. In a medium bowl, combine the soy sauce, sesame oil, rice vinegar, and ginger and mix well. Pour this dressing over the spinach, toss well, and season to taste with salt and pepper. Cover and refrigerate until ready to serve.

continued

4. Place the squid bodies on the grill over **a very hot fire** and cover with a clean (or foil-wrapped) brick. The size of your squid will determine how many bodies go on the grill per round; if you bought squid with 4- to 5-inch bodies, you can get 3 or 4 on at once. You want to cook the bodies about 2 minutes per side, then remove the brick and use your tongs to roll them around on the grill for 30 seconds more. Remove from the grill, set aside, and repeat this process with all of the bodies. Next place the tentacles on the grill and cook for about 2 minutes, using the tongs to roll them around on the grill so they are evenly cooked; you are looking for the tentacles to get brown and crispy.

5. Place the spinach on a platter, arrange the squid over the spinach, sprinkle with the sesame seeds, and garnish with the lime wedges if you want. Serve warm.

**This goes really well with Ginger-Scallion Fried Rice
(page 301) to cool down the heat a bit.**

four uses for a brick on the grill

MOST PEOPLE DON'T CON-SIDER a brick to be a cooking tool, but it is very useful to the griller. A very clean brick—or one wrapped in foil, if you don't feel like scrubbing it—is handy for holding certain ingredients flat against the grill grid so they cook quickly and evenly. Here, for example, are four items that cook better if you top them with a brick:

1. Squid bodies
2. Thin pork chops
3. Butterflied quail
4. Flatbreads that you want to turn into crackers

Chile-Coated Chicken Thighs with Couscous and Tomato-Raisin Relish

SERVES 4 AS ENTRÉE

For the heat-loving, thrill-seeking, more-hotter-more-better crowd, here are smoky grilled chicken thighs liberally coated with chiles, then served over couscous with a slightly sweet tomato relish. This dish combines a collection of North African flavors, with the rub being a distant cousin of fiery harissa, the hot sauce of choice for the region. The couscous helps balance the heat, while the relish offers a little relief.

Take it slow when you grill the thighs; because of the rub, there is an increased risk of their burning on the outside. So watch them particularly carefully and move them off the direct fire if they start to blacken or if you have flare-ups. This is yet another case when it helps to have a space on your grill that is not over any part of the fire.

For the Rub

> 1/2 cup minced fresh chile peppers of your choice
>
> 1/4 cup minced garlic
>
> 1/4 cup olive oil
>
> Salt to taste

> 8 bone-in chicken thighs
>
> 2 cups instant couscous, soaked in a medium bowl in 2 1/3 cups warm
>   water for about 10 minutes, or until soft
>
> 1/4 cup fresh lemon juice (about 1 lemon)
>
> 1/4 cup olive oil
>
> 1/2 cup roughly chopped fresh parsley
>
> Salt and freshly cracked black pepper to taste
>
> Tomato-Raisin Relish (recipe follows)

1. In a large bowl, combine all the rub ingredients and mix well. Add the chicken thighs to the bowl and toss well to coat thoroughly with the rub. Grill the thighs over **a medium fire** for 8 to 10 minutes per side. *To check for doneness:* Cut into the thickest part of one of the thighs and check to see that there is no redness near the bone.

2. While the chicken is cooking, gently rub the couscous between your hands to break it up. Toss the couscous with the lemon juice, olive oil, and parsley, and season to taste with salt and pepper.

3. Place the couscous on a platter or individual serving plates and top with the chicken thighs. Serve the Tomato-Raisin Relish on the side.

continued

TOMATO-RAISIN RELISH

3 tomatoes about the size of baseballs, cored and diced small

$^1/_3$ cup raisins

$^1/_4$ cup pine nuts, toasted in a 350°F oven until golden brown,
about 7 minutes

$^1/_4$ cup roughly chopped fresh mint

$^1/_4$ cup fresh lemon juice (about 1 lemon)

$^1/_4$ cup extra virgin olive oil

1 teaspoon ground cinnamon

1 tablespoon sugar

Salt and freshly cracked black pepper to taste

In a small bowl, combine all the ingredients. Mix well, cover, and refrigerate.

**I like this with Cornmeal Mush with Okra and Tomatoes (page 305)
and K. C.'s Bengali-Style Spinach (page 292).**

Chipotle-Rubbed Grilled Skirt Steak with Grill-Roasted Bananas

SERVES 4 AS ENTRÉE

Skirt steak is a reasonably priced cut of meat that is outstanding on the grill. Here I use a super-strong chipotle rub to create a dangerously hot crust, then provide some heat relief with the simple yet sublime roasted bananas.

4 ripe bananas, unpeeled

For the Rub

$1/4$ cup canned chipotle peppers, mashed or chopped

1 tablespoon minced garlic

2 tablespoons cumin seeds, toasted if you want,
   or 1 tablespoon ground cumin

$1/2$ cup roughly chopped fresh cilantro

$1/4$ cup fresh lime juice (about 2 limes)

$1/4$ cup peanut or vegetable oil

$2^1/2$ pounds skirt steak

Salt and freshly cracked black pepper to taste

1. Build **a hot fire** in your grill. Place the bananas around the edge of the grill so they are not over the flames. The bananas will slowly roast as you prepare the rest of the dish. They are done when the skin is brown and they are soft to the touch, which should take 12 to 15 minutes.

2. Make the rub: In a medium bowl, combine all the ingredients and mix well.

3. Sprinke the skirt steak with salt and pepper, rub generously with the rub, and grill over **a hot fire** for 3 to 4 minutes per side for medium-rare. *To check for doneness:* Nick the steak and peek inside; if you like it more well done, simply continue to cook until it looks one degree less done than you like it.

4. Remove the steak from the grill and thinly slice it against the grain. Slice the bananas open so you can eat them right out of the skins and serve them along with the steak.

Try this with Grilled and Chilled Mediterranean-Style Gazpacho (page 27), Grilled Apple and Bread Salad with Arugula, Blue Cheese, and Grapes (page 49), and Simple Spicy Grilled Tomato Salsa (page 330) on the side.

Grilled Pork, Pineapple, and Jalapeño Skewers with Guava-Lime Sauce

SERVES 2 AS ENTRÉE, 4 AS APPETIZER

This pork skewer is definitely one for the diehard heat-heads. If the hot sauce–soaked pork doesn't get you, the charred jalapeños will. So ice down a slew of cold ones; they don't do any good against the heat, of course, but who cares? They taste great anyway.

By the way, you can substitute pineapple or even orange juice for the guava juice called for in this recipe, but you won't get the same rich, deep flavor. If your city or town has any sizable Latin population, it is a sure bet that there will be a shelf full of Goya products in the "ethnic" section of the supermarket. Guava juice will probably be there, along with tamarind nectar, mango nectar, and a host of others. Give these juices a try—they provide an easy way to get some of the flavors of the tropics in our colder climate.

For the Rub

$1/4$ cup cumin seeds, toasted if you want, or 2 tablespoons ground cumin

2 tablespoons minced garlic

$1/2$ cup Inner Beauty Hot Sauce or your favorite hot sauce

2 tablespoons olive oil

Salt and freshly cracked black pepper to taste

1 pound boneless pork loin, cut into 16 pieces

$1/2$ small pineapple, peeled, cored, and cut into 16 large chunks

8 jalapeño peppers, halved

$1/3$ cup guava juice (or substitute pineapple juice)

$1/3$ cup fresh lime juice (about 2 large limes)

1 tablespoon minced ginger

Salt and freshly cracked black pepper to taste

1. In a small bowl, combine all the rub ingredients and mix together well. Add the pork chunks and toss well to coat, then thread the pork, pineapple chunks, and halved jalapeños sequentially onto 4 large skewers and set aside while you make the sauce.

2. In a small saucepan, bring the guava juice, lime juice, and ginger to a boil over high heat. Reduce the heat to low and simmer for about 20 minutes, stirring every once in a while; the sauce should thicken enough to coat the back of a spoon. Remove from the heat, season to taste with salt and pepper, and set aside.

3. Grill the pork skewers over **a medium-hot fire** for 5 to 6 minutes per side. *To check for doneness:* Cut into a piece of the pork—it should be just pink at the center. Remove the skewers from the grill, put on a platter or individual plates, and drizzle lightly with the sauce. Pass the rest of the sauce separately.

Like many hot and spicy dishes, this matches up well with the smooth and soothing taste of Simple Latin-Style Rice and Beans (page 300). I also like it with Latin-Flavored Coleslaw with Grilled Avocados (page 309).

Chile-Coated Grilled Summer Squash and Zucchini with Honey-Lime Dressing

SERVES 4 AS SIDE DISH

In the summer it's always fun to try to figure out new ways to cook all the zucchini and yellow squash that's around. This was last summer's idea, and I'm still happy with it. The understated flavor of the squashes provides a good vehicle for heat, which is both cut and accentuated by the sweet-and-sour lime-honey dressing. If you have chipotle peppers in your pantry, this is a good place to use them. Of course, if you are not a big fan of heat, you can always cut the chiles way down, or even leave them out, and still have an excellent dish.

For the Dressing

$^{1}/_{4}$ cup olive oil

$^{1}/_{3}$ cup fresh lime juice (about 2 large limes)

3 tablespoons honey

$^{1}/_{4}$ cup roughly chopped fresh cilantro (or substitute parsley)

Salt and freshly cracked black pepper to taste

$^{1}/_{4}$ cup olive oil

1 tablespoon minced garlic

$^{1}/_{4}$ cup minced fresh chile pepper of your choice

2 tablespoons cumin seeds, toasted if you want,
    or 1 tablespoon ground cumin

Salt and freshly cracked black pepper to taste

2 medium zucchini, cut lengthwise into $^{1}/_{2}$-inch planks

2 medium summer squash, cut lengthwise into $^{1}/_{2}$-inch planks

continued

1. Make the dressing: In a small bowl, whisk together all of the ingredients and set aside.

2. In a medium bowl, combine the olive oil, garlic, chile pepper, and cumin and mix well. Add the squash and zucchini planks and toss well so the squashes are completely covered with the mixture.

3. Place the squashes on the grill over **a medium-hot fire** and cook for about 3 minutes on each side, or until well browned. Remove the squashes from the grill, place on a platter, drizzle with the dressing, and serve.

This dish goes with just about anything. I particularly like it with fish for some reason (maybe because it helps banish that old axiom that heat and seafood don't go together), but it also goes well with meat.

Really Hot Purple Pickled Eggs

MAKES 1 DOZEN EGGS

I got into eating pickled eggs when I was a student at the Culinary Institute of America in Hyde Park, New York. Occasionally we would take breaks from our arduous studies and head up to Gafney's, where we would shoot some pool and hang out. The meal of choice there for budding Escoffiers—twenty-five-cent hot dogs, draft beer, and pickled eggs—provides a true insight into the mind of a cook, for it is a truism that chefs are appreciative of not only the best food but also the worst.

These are not Pat Gafney's eggs, but a souped-up version that is fun to have in the refrigerator for those special occasions. I think the sweet spices really help set up the heat here.

1 dozen large eggs

1 quart cider vinegar

1 beet about the size of a baseball, peeled and thinly sliced

$^1/_2$ cup sugar

10 small fresh hot chile peppers of your choice, halved

$^1/_3$ cup Tabasco sauce

3 tablespoons cayenne pepper

2 tablespoons coriander seeds

1 whole nutmeg, smashed into pieces with a hammer,
    or 1 tablespoon ground nutmeg

1 teaspoon ground cinnamon

Pinch of ground mace

Salt and freshly cracked black pepper to taste

1. Cook the eggs in boiling salted water for 10 minutes. Drain, plunge into ice water to stop the cooking process, drain again, and peel. Place in a medium bowl.

2. In a medium saucepan, combine all of the remaining ingredients and bring to a boil over high heat. Reduce the heat to medium and simmer vigorously until the beet slices are tender, about 15 minutes.

3. Pour the hot liquid over the eggs and refrigerate. You can eat them as soon as they cool, but they will be better in a day or two. These will last, covered and refrigerated, for about 1 month.

These are an excellent snack with beers before the game, or with a collection of cocktails like Henry's Cuban Rum Julep (page 354), Ken's Vodka Gimlet (page 349), and Blue-Green Mangoritas (page 350).

Chile-Garlic in Vinegar

One of my late August/early September tasks is to harvest my mixed crop of chile peppers (I usually grow four kinds), cut them up, and put them in empty liquor bottles along with garlic and some spices for use in the coming year. This is my variation on the hot-and-spicy vinegar that graces tables all over the hot-weather world. It's an outstanding condiment, for a shot of this stuff is to many dishes as a new haircut is to a person's face—it provides a fresh perspective without changing the basic concept. In small containers, like the cafeteria-type oil and vinegar dispensers with the silver tops, this also makes a nice gift, and it's substantially cheaper than the versions you buy in stores. The colors are bright, and it's easy to make it last by simply adding more vinegar to the bottle as you use it up. Of course, you total chile-heads can also eat the pickled peppers.

3 pints white vinegar

20 garlic cloves, peeled

2 tablespoons kosher salt

3 tablespoons freshly cracked black pepper

$1/4$ cup coriander seeds, toasted if you want,
    or 2 tablespoons ground coriander

3 tablespoons cumin seeds, toasted with the coriander seeds if you want,
    or $1^1/_2$ tablespoons ground cumin

3 cups fresh chile peppers of your choice, preferably of several colors,
    halved

Place all of the ingredients except the chile peppers in a medium saucepan and bring to a boil over high heat. Remove from the heat and add the chile peppers. Let the mixture cool to room temperature, then ladle it into jars or other small containers, cover tightly, and refrigerate. You can use the vinegar as soon as it cools, but it's better in a day or two. The vinegar—and chiles—will keep, covered and refrigerated, forever.

This is a great condiment to have around, just sitting out on the table for folks to use as they will. I particularly like to squirt some of the vinegar on greens of any kind.

When you talk barbecue, you're not just talking about a cooking method, you're talking about a way of life. You're talking about the ability to spend all night sitting around a smoldering pit fire, drinking beer and trading stories and occasionally slipping a chunk of wood on the fire to justify your presence. You're talking about the willingness to drive sixty, a hundred, two hundred miles just to find out the secret behind some pulled pork that you found particularly outstanding. You're talking about having the sheer gall to defend to the death the drop-dead superiority of your Secret Family Heirloom Moppin' Sauce, even though you know damned well you just made it up last week.

SLOW AND LOW

barbecuing and smoke-roasting

What you are *not* talking about, though, is grilling. As you know by now, grilling is a quick, high-heat cooking method most suitable for relatively tender foods. Barbecue is on the other end of the live fire cooking spectrum—it consists of cooking tough cuts of meat for a very long time over the heat and smoke from a very low fire.

In other words, when you barbecue, you are putting a whole pig or a large, tough cut of meat such as beef brisket or pork shoulder in an enclosed space and allowing it to cook indirectly by the smoke from a hardwood fire. The temperature is kept below 220°F, and the very slow cooking process causes the meat's stringy connective tissues, called collagen, to dissolve into gelatin, so you end up with a richly smoky, tender, juicy treat. When you're talking barbecue, you're talking cooking with real wood, real slow, for a real long time.

In the South, where this unique American cooking technique originated, barbecue was traditionally cooked in "pits" composed of cinder blocks and wire mesh and often enclosed with corrugated tin. Over the years, ingenious pitmasters have rung every possible variation on this simple arrangement. If you go to the Memphis in May International Barbecue Festival, for instance, you will see everything from portable "pits" in the shape of hogs to mammoth devices that took days to erect, even though they will be used only once. But all of these contraptions have two things in common: They are large enough to hold hardwood logs, and they are designed so the meat is situated not directly above the flames, but off to the side, so it cooks by smoke and indirect heat.

Of course, only the dedicated few will care to dig a barbecue pit in their backyard large enough to hold whole logs. So for most of us, it's not possible to duplicate authentic barbecue at home. But with a little adjusting, we can approximate the real thing by using a covered grill with a low fire off to one side, mimicking the indirect cooking of a barbecue rig.

What this technique requires, though, is a great deal of patience. When you're making backyard barbecue, the key element is the pace at which you feed wood to the fire. The aim is to keep the fire just smoldering, so that the smoke does most of the cooking and the temperature inside the covered grill never gets above 220°F. After a while you will figure out your own personal refueling policy, but you might want to do what I do, and add a handful of coals or wood chunks every twenty to thirty minutes—or, if you prefer, every time you finish a beer. If this gets tedious and you are tempted to add larger amounts of fuel to speed up the process, repeat to yourself the barbecue mantra: "Slow and low, slow and low." Believe me, when the barbecued meat comes off the grill and you taste the contrast between the crusty, chewy exterior and the tender, moist inner meat, you will be well rewarded. Plus, you will have had the added benefit of honing your ability to talk about absolutely nothing in a convivial fashion for hours on end.

There's one more thing to keep in mind when barbecuing. Part of the point is to cook the meat right on through doneness until you reach tenderness. In other words, the food is ready to come off the grill not when it is cooked all the way through, but at the point well beyond that when it has become truly tender. When you're barbecuing brisket, for example, the best test for doneness is to stick a large fork directly down into the brisket, perpendicular to the grill surface, and try to pick the brisket up. If you can't because the brisket won't hold the fork, then it's done.

We have also included some recipes in this chapter that use a technique somewhere between barbecuing and grilling. I think the best name for it is "smoke-roasting." It is designed to impart the deep, smoky flavor of live fire cooking to foods such as a whole duck, a large pork roast, or a big sirloin of beef, all of which are too large to grill but not so tough that they need the barbecue treatment.

As with barbecue, the idea behind smoke-roasting is to cook in a covered grill but not directly over the coals. The difference is that with smoke-roasting you are using a slightly larger fire, so the food cooks faster. In other words, it's kind of like cooking in a very smoky wood-fired oven at relatively low heat. The resulting foods are not as fully smoke-infused as barbecue, but they are still plenty tasty, and they come off the grill faster.

Whether you are barbecuing or smoke-roasting, you need to pay particular attention to the fuel. Smoke consists largely of unburned particles of fuel, so when you cook in a closed, live fire environment for a long period of time, the fuel that you use begins to make a real difference in the flavor of the finished product. I would make a concerted effort to use a combination of some lump hardwood charcoal for convenience and some wood for flavor. The wood can be in the form of either small logs or large chunks. As to the type of wood, I would put oak, hickory, or any fruitwood up there as the top choices. If you want more information about this, call my buddy Don Hysco at People's Woods in Rhode Island (401–725–2700); he'll tell you more than you ever wanted to know about the virtues and drawbacks of every type of hardwood.

Because barbecue is a unique American folk-cooking phenomenon, explaining the "how to" is really only part of the story. For those of you who have not read our previous book *The Thrill of the Grill,* here is some information on the indispensable rhetoric of barbecue, along with a glossary of some of the key terms to master if you want to become a pitmaster.

THE RHETORIC OF BARBECUE

Giving cooking instructions for barbecue is only providing half of what you need to know. Anyone familiar with the rites and rituals of barbecue knows that almost equal in importance to the actual taste of the 'cue is the amount and quality of the mumbo jumbo you put out while barbecuing. I have therefore prepared for you a primer on the subject, in which I provide the basic vocabulary essential to mastering this other, more mystical aspect—the Zen of Barbecue, as it were. Learn it well and practice it often, because only when you can go off on rants and unintelligible sermons on your preferred style of barbecue will you be a true pitmaster. Pick yourself a *nom de barbecue,* grab your cooler, and head off into the deepest recesses of your yard to practice the vocabulary below. The essence of stubborn individuality and backwoods primitivism await you.

Types of Barbecue

EASTERN NORTH CAROLINA STYLE: My personal favorite, this is no doubt the real original. It consists of either whole pig or pork shoulder cooked over hickory, then chopped or minced or pulled (depending upon which particular part of eastern North Carolina you hail from) and mixed with a light vinegar-based sauce—mention a tomato-based sauce east of Raleigh, and you had better be prepared to do some quick explaining. This style of 'cue is eaten on a cheap white bun with sweet coleslaw.

WESTERN NORTH CAROLINA STYLE: This is also pork barbecue, but the meat is dressed with a tomato-based sauce with a heavy vinegar accent. Not much different from eastern North Carolina style, right? Wrong. In the world of barbecue, even something this small becomes a serious bone of contention.

TEXAS STYLE: When you talk barbecue in Texas, you are talking beef brisket. This is one of the toughest, gnarliest cuts of meat known to humankind, but ten to twenty hours of slow cooking over mesquite or oak will turn it into one of America's original regional foods. The sauce used here is a catsup-based blend limited only by the imagination of the cook. Chili powder and cumin are very popular additions.

KANSAS CITY STYLE: The raging debate as to whether Memphis or Kansas City is the barbecue capital of the world is as endless as it is heated. (Personally, I believe it's eastern North Carolina, but that's another story.) Barbecue is deeply embedded in the daily lives of people who live in K. C. It is a big sparerib town but also ranks high in the beef brisket department. A preparation that they think is truly unique to Kansas City, though, is "burnt ends." This is the top section of the beef brisket, which is removed from the leaner bottom and cooked even longer. The surface of the meat becomes very crispy and almost black, and the flavor is intense. Sauces in Kansas City are tomato-vinegar–based and generally pungent, strong, and assertive. The variety of sauces is immense, and some restaurants are known more for their distinctive sauce than for the actual barbecue.

MEMPHIS STYLE: If it's spareribs and brisket in Kansas City, it's ribs and shredded pork in Memphis. Home of the Memphis in May International Barbecue Championship, the city is practically synonymous with barbecue. Memphis ribs come wet or dry, but this town is best known for its amazing variety of dry rubs. The shredded pork is mixed with a sweet tomato-based sauce. Not content to rest on its reputation, however, Memphis is constantly on the cutting edge of culinary development, with new menu items ranging from barbecued bologna (surprisingly awesome) to barbecue pizza and barbecue spaghetti.

Other Terms You Need to Know

BASTING SAUCE (aka mopping sauce): This is a sauce used during the long cooking process, applied with a brush or a mop, depending on the size of the piece of meat involved. The sauce can range in content from complicated concoctions of spices, herbs, and vinegar to just plain old warm beer—its purpose is to keep the meat moist. Sugar and catsup are not generally included, because they will burn during cooking. A typical recipe might be: ½ gallon white vinegar, 2 warm beers, ¼ cup cayenne pepper, and 2 secret ingredients of your choice.

FINISHING SAUCE: Now, after you've explained to your guests about your mopping sauce and the meat is ready to eat, it's time to whip out your finishing sauce. This sauce—never used during the actual cooking—varies in complexity from plain vinegar with salt and pepper to elaborate potions of over thirty ingredients. I know people who swear by a certain sauce, while others will just doctor a bottle of store-bought. In any case, it's a good condiment and should complement rather than hide the smoky flavor. Unless it is a light vinegar-based sauce, it should be served on the side, so that each individual can decide how much he or she wants.

RIBS: I may occasionally smoke-roast beef ribs, but real barbecue calls for pork ribs. An old butcher I know speaks of a time when butchers gave away pork ribs because of their high fat content, toughness, and lack of meat. But then along came barbecuing, which gave these formerly unpopular pork parts a unique niche in culinary society. Songs, stories, and some very bad poems have been written about perfectly cooked pork ribs.

There are three types of pork ribs: 1. Country ribs, which come from the hard end of the pork loin and aren't really ribs at all but fatty pork chops. These are for grilling, not barbecuing. 2. Loin or baby back ribs, which are smaller and daintier than spareribs. This fairly tender cut does not have the fat content needed to stand up to the long cooking of proper barbecuing, although it is good for shorter cooking. 3. Spareribs, which come from the belly of the hog. To my mind these are the only ribs for barbecuing. They have a good amount of meat on them, but more important, this is the cut on top of which the bacon sits. We're talking serious flavor here, along with plenty of fat to keep it juicy. Spareribs come in slabs with thirteen bones. The slabs vary in size according to the weight of the pig, the most popular size being "3 and down." This means that a full thirteen-bone slab with chine bone and brisket flap still on will weigh three pounds or less. There is also a variation of the full slab called "St. Louis cut" or "Chinese cut," in which the slab is trimmed of the chine bone and brisket flap to form a slab that is of uniform size and similar in appearance to a slab of baby backs.

PORK SHOULDER: This cut is really the front leg of the pig. It is very popular for barbecue because of its low price, which in turn results from the fact that it is the most unwanted cut of pork for everything other than barbecue. Filled with fat and riddled with connective tissue, this cut is impossible to ruin unless you torch it by putting it directly over a flame. For home barbecue, I recommend the pork butt, which is a section of the shoulder which weighs four to seven pounds.

LINKS: This is a common name for sausage that is barbecued. Links are popular in Oklahoma and Texas.

MUTTON: Meat from an old sheep, this has a very distinctive flavor, and when you say "barbecue" in certain parts of Kentucky, it is mutton that you are talking about. Some folks say that its age, its strong flavor, and its general lack of popularity make it ideal for barbecue.

PITMASTER: This is a term that dates back to the time when one man would stay with the barbecue pit at all times. Today's new pit designs, however, have made the eighteen- to twenty-hour days of this tireless artisan a thing of the past.

OPEN PIT: In this barbecue technique, used in some parts of North Carolina, the meat to be barbecued is placed on a grill directly over a very low fire, although four or five feet above it. This technique is tricky, demanding a very watchful eye, because flare-ups are common whenever cooking is done by direct heat. Most open pits are simple affairs, consisting of cinder blocks piled six or seven high with a mesh grill laid across the top. Coals are shoveled into the bed, and sometimes corrugated tin is put on top of the meat to create an ovenlike effect.

CLOSED PIT: Despite its name, this is not a hole in the ground. This is the most common technique for cooking barbecue. The meat is cooked in an enclosed space, ranging from a fifty-five-gallon drum to a two-car garage, in which smoke is forced to mingle with the meat. A closed pit can use either direct or indirect fire, although indirect is far preferable because there is no danger of flare-ups.

LOG BURNER: I know it's hard to believe, but in some parts of this great land of ours people are cooking barbecue over charcoal. So when barbecuers gather, one of the standard questions is "Are you a log burner?" If you want to be taken at all seriously, answer in the affirmative.

DRY RUB: A mixture of dry spices, this is at the very heart of barbecue. Rubbed on the meat before it is cooked, it helps form a crust on the outside that contains a tremendous amount of concentrated flavor.

PIG PICKIN': This is a gathering of people, originally for political purposes, at which a whole pig is barbecued and laid out for guests to pull apart, thus the term "pulled pork." This ritual is very popular in North Carolina and Virginia.

Sweet-Spicy Barbecued Spareribs with Green Chile Sauce

Chinese-Style Baby Back Ribs with Ginger-Scallion Barbecue Sauce

Jeff's Smoked Bones

Mediterranean-Style Slow-Roasted Beef Brisket

Horseradish-and-Cumin-Crusted Whole Smoke-Roasted Sirloin with Mustard Aïoli

Herb-Crusted Pork Loin Roast with Creamy Polenta and Roasted Tomato-Garlic Sauce

Puerto Rican–Style Barbecued Pork Butt with Two Sauces and Corn Bread

Barbecued Whole Game Hens with Orange, Oregano, and Cumin Seed

Jake's World-Famous Deep-Fat-Fried Whole Turkey

Barbecued Whole Turkey with Mexican-Style Stuffing

Chinese-Spiced Whole Duck with Orange–Green Peppercorn Sauce

Corn Bread–Stuffed Barbecued Game Hens with Bourbon-Shallot Sauce

Sweet-Spicy Barbecued Spareribs with Green Chile Sauce

SERVES 4 AS ENTRÉE

This recipe is for the real thing: "3 and down" pork spareribs. This term refers to the weight of the ribs, in this case three pounds or a little bit under for each slab of ten to twelve ribs. By comparison, baby back ribs weigh about half as much. So here you'll be working with regulation barbecue-contest ribs, without a doubt the #1 eating ribs—and, unfortunately, something of a problem for the home cook.

Because of their large surface area and the amount of time they need to cook, you need professional equipment to do these ribs in classic barbecue style. I usually cook a slab of 3/downs in our professional barbecue pit, at about 200°F for around four hours. The long, slow cooking is necessary because, although it looks small and thin, the rib is actually pretty tough and needs plenty of time to break down and get tender. This is difficult to do at home, though, because on a standard grill you only have room to cook one slab at a time using indirect heat.

So I've come up with a variation of the "easy" method. I know that some folks recommend parboiling the ribs, but in my experience that is a total disaster. I know that may sound snobbish, but I'm a chef, so every once in a while I've got to cop an attitude. But seriously, parboiling toughens the ribs, removes flavor, and does very little else. So I have resorted to a kind of "parbaking" method, in which the ribs are basically cooked slow and low in the oven and then put over a very low grilling fire to add some smoky flavor and a fresh sear at the end of the cooking process.

In this recipe we take a Latin approach, with a sweet-spicy cumin rub and a hot green chile sauce. Relatively mild chile peppers such as the Anaheim, poblano, or banana are fairly easy to find, but if you're having a hard time getting hold of them, substitute any fresh green chile that you like, or just spice up your favorite tomato-based barbecue sauce with some lime juice and Tabasco sauce and use that instead. Either way, you're going to have some great smoky ribs under that sauce.

For the Rub

 2 tablespoons ground cumin

 2 tablespoons ground coriander

 $^1/_4$ cup paprika

 $^1/_4$ cup minced garlic

 $^1/_4$ cup roughly chopped fresh cilantro (or substitute parsley or oregano)

 $^1/_4$ cup lightly packed brown sugar

 2 tablespoons kosher salt

 2 tablespoons freshly cracked black pepper

 2 full racks 3/down pork spareribs (see above)

For the Sauce

    3 tablespoons olive oil

    2 yellow onions, peeled and diced small

    2 tablespoons minced garlic

    1 16-ounce can tomatillos, drained, or 1 pound (12 to 15)

        fresh tomatillos, husked, rinsed, blanched in boiling salted water

        for 4 minutes, and halved

    4 fresh Anaheim (New Mexico) or poblano chile peppers

        (or substitute $1/4$ cup diced fresh green chile pepper of your choice)

    $1/4$ cup fresh lime juice (about 2 limes)

    $1/2$ cup roughly chopped fresh cilantro (or substitute parsley or oregano)

1. In a small bowl, combine all the rub ingredients and mix well. Coat the ribs thoroughly with the rub, place them on baking sheets, and roast in a 200°F oven for $3^1/2$ hours. Don't bother to turn them, because all you are doing is slow cooking and infusing them with spices.

2. While the ribs are cooking, make the sauce: In a medium saucepan, heat the oil over medium heat until hot but not smoking. Add the onions and sauté, stirring occasionally, until transparent, 5 to 7 minutes. Add the garlic and sauté, stirring occasionally, for 1 minute. Add the tomatillos, chiles, and lime juice and simmer for about 5 minutes; if you are using fresh tomatillos, you want them to just start to break down. Remove the sauce from the heat and puree in a food processor or blender, a bit at a time, until smooth. Stir in the cilantro and set aside; if you want to serve it warm, return it to the saucepan. Just before serving, rewarm over low heat.

3. Remove the ribs from the oven. They can stand out for a while, can be refrigerated at this point for up to 2 days, or can go right onto the grill. (If you do refrigerate them, bring them to room temperature before the final grilling.) When you're ready to put them on the grill, put them over **a low fire** and leave them there for 7 to 10 minutes, turning once or twice. Since they are already cooked through at this point, what you are looking for is to give them some color and a good sear. When they have achieved this, remove them from the grill and serve them accompanied by the sauce.

These are fantastic when combined with Simple Latin-Style Rice and Beans (page 300) and Latin-Flavored Coleslaw with Grilled Avocados (page 309). For dessert, try Minted Melon with Caribbean Elixir (page 361).

those hot pods

MORE RAPIDLY THAN JUST about any other ingredient, chile peppers have made the change from an exotic rarity to an essential ingredient for cooks all over the United States. Nothing could please me more, since I love the heat and flavor of these little pods. There are over two thousand varieties of chile that we know of, and undoubtedly there are hundreds more local varieties known only to those who grow and eat them. Each type has its own individual heat level and flavor, and it's a lot of fun to check them out as you run across them. There are many excellent books that deal with chiles in detail, of which we particularly recommend *The Whole Chile Pepper* (Little, Brown, 1990) by Dave Dewitt and Nancy Gerlach, *The Great Chile Book* (Ten Speed Press, 1991) by Mark Miller with John Harrison, *Rick Bayless' Mexican Kitchen* (Scribner's, 1996) by Rick Bayless, and *Red Hot Peppers* (Macmillan, 1993) by Jean Andrews.

Chinese-Style Baby Back Ribs with Ginger-Scallion Barbecue Sauce

SERVES 4 AS ENTRÉE, 8 AS APPETIZER

Where I come from, we don't really call baby back ribs barbecue. I was appalled, for example, when they allowed them to be entered in the Rib Division of the Memphis in May International Barbecue Championship. Baby backs are cut from a different place on the hog than real ribs, closer to the spine and therefore more tender. And, in my humble opinion, they don't have nearly the flavor of the spareribs that lie under the belly, from which bacon is made.

But, tirades aside, I must admit that baby backs can be seriously delicious food, if not true barbecue. The best baby backs I've ever had have been in Chinese restaurants, so here I put them through a rigorous Asian flavor treatment, with a sweet and aromatic soy-spice rub and a dipping sauce that reminds me of the thick quasi-Polynesian teriyaki-style sauces of Chinese restaurants.

$^1/_2$ cup soy sauce

$^1/_2$ cup white vinegar

$^1/_4$ cup lightly packed brown sugar

3 tablespoons freshly cracked white pepper (or substitute black pepper)

2 tablespoons five-spice powder

4 racks baby back ribs (each rack about $1^1/_2$ pounds)

For the Sauce

      $^1/_2$ cup white vinegar

      1 cup soy sauce

      2 tablespoons minced ginger

      $^1/_3$ cup lightly packed brown sugar

      $^1/_2$ cup minced scallions (white and green parts)

1. Build a small fire in one half of a covered grill. Let the fuel become completely engulfed in flames, then wait a few minutes for the fire to burn down somewhat.

2. In a small bowl, combine the soy sauce, vinegar, brown sugar, pepper, and five-spice powder and mix well. Generously coat the ribs with this mixture and place them on the half of the grill without the fire under it. Put the cover on the cooker and vent slightly. Cook for 45 minutes, feeding the fire once in the middle of this period to keep it going. Flip the ribs and cook them an additional 45 minutes, again feeding the fire once. *To check for doneness:* Cut into one of the ribs; there should be no pink in the center.

3. While you are cooking the ribs, make the sauce: In a small saucepan, combine all of the ingredients except the scallions and bring to a boil over high heat. Reduce the heat to low and simmer for 30 to 45 minutes, or until the sauce is reduced by about one half; it should be thick enough to coat the back of a spoon. Remove the sauce from the heat, cool for a few minutes, and stir in the scallions.

4. Remove the ribs from the fire and serve brushed with the sauce, or with the sauce on the side for dipping.

> Try this with some Asian-flavored side dishes like Ginger-Scallion
> Fried Rice (page 301), Pungent Carrot and Cucumber Salad with
> Ginger and Garlic (page 308), and/or Grilled Plums with
> Spicy Hoisin Glaze (page 296). For dessert, try Mai Tai Pie (page 380).

Jeff's Smoked Bones

When I was living and working in South Florida years ago, Monday night was "bone night" over at the local steak house. This was a restaurant that served an astronomical amount of prime ribs, which meant they had a lot of unused beef rib bones, which were not really popular. So on the slow night, they tried to unload all their excess in something they promoted as an all-you-can-eat kind of thing. Now, these ribs have a very high ratio of bone to meat and are largely unappreciated outside the state of Texas. It takes a doglike approach to get the most out of eating "dem bones"—I know guys who will hang on to one bone for over ten minutes, gnawing and tearing at it to get all the meat. I could eat my share, though, and they've become a favorite of Jeff Unger, the chef at the East Coast Grill, who loves to smoke bones over hickory wood.

So here's an adaptation of Jeff's flavored bones. These things are so monstrous that unless you have commercial grilling equipment, you're going to have to cheat a little bit. Here we rub the ribs, put them in the oven, and slow-cook them to get them tender, then roll them around on the grill to impart some smoke and char. The bourbon-shallot barbecue sauce is a high-minded combination that suits beef well, so you have a kind of uptown/downtown thing going on here. This is a prehistoric kind of dining experience, so I would recommend serving it only to folks you know pretty well.

For the Rub

$^1/_2$ cup freshly cracked black pepper

$^1/_4$ cup lightly packed brown sugar

$^1/_4$ cup paprika

$^1/_4$ cup ground cumin

$^1/_4$ cup kosher salt

5 pounds beef ribs

For the Sauce

1 cup bourbon

1 cup minced shallots (or substitute red onion)

1 tablespoon minced garlic

$^1/_2$ cup catsup

$^1/_3$ cup molasses

$^1/_2$ cup cider vinegar

Salt and freshly cracked black pepper to taste

SLOW AND LOW

254

1. Make the rub: Combine all of the ingredients in a small bowl and mix well. Rub the ribs generously with this mixture.

2. Lay the ribs on a baking sheet that has been covered with foil and bake them in a 200°F oven for 5 hours.

3. While the ribs are cooking, make the sauce: Heat the bourbon in a small saucepan over medium-low heat for just 1 minute to warm it up. Now, be careful for this next part: Roll a piece of paper up into a tube or get one of those long fireplace matches, light it, and hold it inside the pan right over but not touching the bourbon; the bourbon should ignite. Once the bourbon has stopped flaming (about 1 minute), add the shallots and cook for 3 to 4 minutes, stirring occasionally, until the shallots are soft.

4. Add the rest of the sauce ingredients, reduce the heat to low, and simmer for 15 minutes; the sauce should be slightly thickened. Remove it from the heat, cover to keep warm, and set aside.

5. Remove the ribs from the oven, cut them into individual ribs, and grill them over **a medium-hot fire** for 3 to 5 minutes, or until the rub develops a crusty appearance. Remove from the fire, brush generously with the warm bourbon sauce, and serve.

I might serve this with Seared Spinach with Fried Garlic Chips (page 293) or, if you have more people over, with Smoky Ratatouille for a Crowd (page 288). Peach Sour Cream Pie (page 378) is a good dessert choice.

Mediterranean-Style
Slow-Roasted Beef Brisket

Cooking a beef brisket is perhaps the zenith of barbecuing skill, much more difficult than pork ribs or pork butt or even a whole pig. But to qualify for my Ph.B. (Doctor of Barbecue), I had to master the challenge of the noble beef brisket. Noble because while it is one of the lowliest cuts of beef, riddled with gristle and connective tissue, it hides within a true nobility of intense flavor. The challenge is to bring out that flavor while transforming the gnarly meat into a tender treat.

Some folks (particularly those from Texas) say that brisket is the meaning of the word barbecue. While others might disagree (no question, barbecue actually means pork), all would agree that a brisket cooked for ten hours over a slow-smoldering fire is a nectarous gastronomic experience.

Here I take the brisket out of its barbecue context a bit by resituating it in the Mediterranean. It's still rubbed in the traditional manner, and it still has a rich finishing sauce, but both rub and sauce have a different flavor orientation from classic barbecue.

1 10- to 14-pound beef brisket
Salt and freshly cracked black pepper to taste

For the Rub

$^1/_4$ cup ground cumin
$^1/_4$ cup ground coriander
$^1/_4$ cup crushed fennel seeds
$^1/_4$ cup red pepper flakes
1 cup dried basil
$^1/_2$ cup olive oil
$^1/_4$ cup minced garlic

For the Sauce

$^1/_4$ cup olive oil
2 yellow onions, peeled and diced medium
2 tablespoons minced garlic
3 large tomatoes, cored and diced medium
$^1/_4$ cup sugar
$^1/_4$ cup grainy mustard
$^1/_2$ cup red wine vinegar
1 cup balsamic vinegar
$^1/_2$ cup roughly chopped fresh basil
Salt and freshly cracked black pepper to taste

1. Sprinkle the brisket generously with salt and pepper.

2. Make the rub: In a small bowl, combine all the ingredients and mix well. Rub the brisket thoroughly on all sides with the rub and allow it to come to room temperature.

3. Build a very small fire in one side of a covered grill, as close to the side as possible, using about enough charcoal to fill half of a shoe box. Place the brisket on the grill on the side away from the fire so that none of the meat is directly over the flame. Put the lid on the cooker, pull up a chair, and grab the cooler.

This is where a person learns about the Zen of Barbecue. You have keep the fire going steadily, but very quietly. If you've got a thermometer on your covered grill, you want to keep the temperature between 180° and 220°F. Remember, "slow and low is the way to go." You have to figure out your own personal refueling policy. The one I like is one handful of coals or wood chunks to every beer. This goes on for 8 to 10 hours, or however long you can make it, the longer the better. Don't be scared by the darkening of the exterior of the brisket—it should be super-dark, and that's my personal favorite part. *To check for doneness:* Stick a large fork directly down into the brisket, perpendicular to the grill surface, and try to pick it up. If you can't because the brisket won't hold the fork, then it's done.

4. While the brisket is cooking, make the sauce: In a medium saucepan over medium heat, heat the oil until hot but not smoking. Add the onions and sauté, stirring frequently, for 7 to 9 minutes, or until browned. Add the garlic and cook, stirring, for 1 minute. Add the tomatoes, sugar, mustard, and vinegars, reduce the heat to low, and simmer for 1 hour; the sauce will thicken.

5. In a food processor or blender, puree the sauce until smooth. Stir in the basil and salt and pepper to taste and set aside.

6. Upon completion, pull the brisket off the grill, trim off the excess fat, and slice it thin. Serve with the sauce on the side.

This dish goes very well with **Tomato Risotto with Toasted Pine Nuts** (page 302), **Romaine and Bulgur Salad** (page 319), or **Seared Spinach with Fried Garlic Chips** (page 293).

Horseradish-and-Cumin-Crusted Whole Smoke-Roasted Sirloin with Mustard Aïoli

SERVES 10 TO 15 AS ENTRÉE

Save this one for a real banquet. It's big and it's expensive, but the taste and texture of a whole roasted sirloin is both impressive and unique, as you would expect from this cut which is almost always cut into sirloin strip steaks. Because the piece of meat is so large, achieving the proper state of doneness can be something of an issue. I advise you to get a good meat thermometer (the small instant-read ones about the size of a pen are the most convenient), because this cut of meat is best—depending on your taste, of course—when cooked on the rarer side. I pull mine off the grill when it's anywhere from 118° (way rare) to 124°F (starting to get medium-rare). Make sure you're taking the temperature down in the middle of the meat, or you're not going to get the reading that you're looking for. If you take the sirloin off the grill and then find that it's rarer than you like it, you can cut it into thickish slices (one to two inches), grill them as you would steaks, and tell your guests you're serving them unique "smoke-roasted then grilled" steaks. I would definitely have some toasted crusty bread with the beef and the mustard mayo, a combination that gives a whole new meaning to the term "roast beef sandwich."

> 1 10- to 11-pound whole beef sirloin (ask your favorite butcher)

For the Spice Paste
> 1½ cups grated fresh horseradish (or substitute 1 cup prepared horseradish)
> ½ cup cumin seeds, toasted if you want, or ¼ cup ground cumin
> ½ cup minced garlic
> 1 cup olive oil
> ½ cup kosher salt
> ½ cup freshly cracked black pepper

For the Aïoli
> 4 large egg yolks
> 6 tablespoons fresh lemon juice (about 1½ lemons)
> ½ cup Dijon mustard
> 2 cups olive oil
> Salt to taste

> 4 bunches watercress, trimmed and washed

1. Start a small fire in one half of a large covered grill, using about enough charcoal to fill a shoe box. Let the fuel become completely engulfed in flames, then wait a few minutes for the fire to burn down a bit.

2. While the fire is getting going, trim any areas of thick fat off the sirloin—but don't remove every speck of fat, because you will want to leave some to add flavor to the meat.

3. Make the spice paste: In a small bowl, combine all the ingredients and mix well. Rub the sirloin generously with this mixture, then place it on the grill over the side with no fire, being careful that no part of the sirloin is over the coals. Put the lid on the kettle with the vents open about a quarter of the way and cook for about 1$\frac{1}{2}$ hours, adding charcoal as necessary to keep the fire going. At the 40-minute mark, turn the sirloin around, changing the side that is closest to the fire.

4. At the 1$\frac{1}{2}$-hour point, begin checking the sirloin with an instant-read thermometer: Remove from the fire at 118°F for very rare, 122°F for rare, 126°F for medium-rare, and so on, adding 4 degrees for each level of doneness. Let the sirloin rest for 30 minutes before slicing.

5. Meanwhile, make the aïoli: Combine all of the ingredients except the oil in a food processor or blender and blend well. With the motor running, slowly drizzle in the oil until just incorporated. Place the aïoli in a small bowl and refrigerate until ready to serve.

6. Make a bed of the watercress on a platter or individual plates, slice the sirloin, and place on the watercress. Serve with the aïoli on the side.

For a feast for a lot of folks, I might serve this with Bridget's Couscous Salad
for a Crowd (page 320) and Smoky Ratatouille for a Crowd (page 288).
For a light but interesting dessert, go with a double recipe of
Papaya Ice with Sweet Hot Pepper Sauce (page 362).

getting the real horseradish buzz

HORSERADISH IS ONE OF those flavorings that we have gotten so used to in its prepackaged form—in this case, little jars of grated horseradish mixed with vinegar—that we have almost lost track of how it tastes fresh. The first time I tried grating fresh horseradish over a steak, I was amazed at its full, mustardy flavor. Without the sourness of the vinegar, the freshly grated root actually has a kind of sweetness along with its pungent bite. So next time you see one of these odd-shaped roots in a produce bin, pick it up and take it home. Pare off the brown outer skin, use a hand grater to finely shred the inner white flesh over a steak or some oysters on the half-shell, and I'm betting that you'll quickly become a fresh horseradish fan. Sometimes a little extra work is definitely worth the effort.

Herb-Crusted Pork Loin Roast with Creamy Polenta and Roasted Tomato-Garlic Sauce

The cut of pork we use here is mostly free of connective tissue, which means we don't have to worry about cooking it at very low temperatures to melt that tough, gristly tissue. But we still want to keep the heat indirect and the temperature fairly low—about 225° to 280°F—so the roast cooks all the way through without burning on the outside. That means it's going to take a little longer to cook than it would in a 350°F oven, but this is more than compensated for by the fantastic smoky flavor it soaks up while cooking. If I had a chunk of hardwood or a green fruit tree branch, I would definitely use it to supplement the coals here and generate some flavoring smoke.

Make sure the butcher removes the chine bone from the roast. This will allow you to cut full chop slices straight through the roast, an impressive display if you carve it in front of your guests. The sauce is a quick and easy tomato-herb job that gets additional flavor from roasting at a high temperature.

So serve the creamy polenta, lay the roasted chops right on top, spoon over some sauce, and you and your friends will be enjoying one of life's small pleasures—slow-cooked, herb-crusted, smoky roast pork loin, oh yeah!

1 cup roughly chopped mixed fresh herbs: any combination of parsley, thyme, sage, rosemary, basil, oregano, and/or marjoram

$^1/_4$ cup minced garlic

1 to 2 tablespoons red pepper flakes, depending on your taste for heat

$^1/_4$ cup kosher salt

$^1/_4$ cup freshly cracked black pepper

$^1/_4$ cup olive oil

1 3- to 4-pound bone-in center-cut pork loin roast, chine bone removed

4 cups water

2 cups cornmeal

Salt and freshly cracked black pepper to taste

For the Sauce

6 plum tomatoes, halved

1 medium red onion, peeled and cut into eighths

12 cloves garlic, peeled

$^1/_3$ cup extra virgin olive oil

Salt and freshly cracked black pepper to taste

$^1/_4$ cup roughly chopped fresh basil

$^1/_4$ cup balsamic vinegar

1. Build a small fire in one half of a covered grill, using about enough charcoal to fill a shoe box. Let the fuel become completely engulfed in flames, then wait a few minutes for the fire to burn down a bit.

SLOW AND SLOW

2. In a small bowl, combine the herbs, garlic, red pepper flakes, salt, pepper, and olive oil and mix well. Rub the pork loin generously with the herb mixture and place on the grill, fat side down, over the side of the grill with no fire. Cover and cook for 45 minutes. Add a handful of coals to the fire, flip the pork loin over, cover again, and cook for another 45 minutes. *To check for doneness:* Cut into the roast and peek inside to make sure the meat is just a bit pink in the center. (If you're using a meat thermometer, the temperature should be 150°F.) Remove the pork from the grill and allow it to sit for about 10 minutes.

3. While the pork is cooking, make the polenta: In a medium saucepot, bring the water to a rapid boil over high heat. Add the cornmeal in a slow, steady stream, whisking constantly to prevent it from becoming lumpy. Once all the cornmeal is added, turn down the heat to low and cook for about 45 minutes, stirring frequently, until the polenta pulls away from the side of the pan in a mass and, when tasted, has a smooth rather than a grainy texture. Season to taste with salt and pepper.

4. Make the sauce: Combine the tomatoes, onion, garlic, olive oil, and salt and pepper to taste in a medium bowl and toss to combine. Spoon these ingredients onto a small cookie sheet and roast in a preheated 450°F oven until the onion and tomatoes start to brown, 15 to 20 minutes. Remove from the oven and, as soon as the tomatoes, onion, and garlic are cool enough to handle, roughly chop them. You want them to be chunky. Place in a medium bowl, add the basil and vinegar, mix well, and set aside.

5. Carve the roast into full-chop slices. Spoon a serving of polenta onto each individual serving plate, lay a pork chop on top, top with the tomato-garlic sauce, and serve.

Try this rich dish with a relatively straightforward side dish like Seared Spinach with Fried Garlic Chips (page 293) or Grilled Tomato Halves with Cheesy Bread Crumbs (page 298). Saffron-Cardamom Poached Pears with Cranberry-Currant Relish (page 359) is an excellent dessert choice here.

Puerto Rican–Style Barbecued Pork Butt with Two Sauces and Corn Bread

SERVES ABOUT 6 AS ENTRÉE

Barbecue as we know it is a homegrown product of the American South, but other cultures have very similar traditions. Spend some time driving around the island of Puerto Rico, for example, and you'll see plenty of makeshift smokers set up on the side of the road, slow-cooking pork by the indirect heat and smoke of a wood fire—a pretty fair description of barbecuing.

As always with the barbecue process, aka smoke-roasting, the idea is to keep the temperature between 180° and 222°F and to go slow. The #1 goal is to tenderize this cut of meat, which is at once very flavorful and incredibly tough. The second goal is to add some deep, smoky flavor. If you have some chunks of wood or some green branches lying around, this is the time to use them, since they generate a lot of smoke. I'm not crazy about wood chips, but they are passable here.

This is a long process, so take it slow. It doesn't take too long before the butt gets really dark on the outside, as if it's finished cooking, but be patient. As in stewing or braising, the meat is done not when it reaches a certain temperature, but when it is tender. A good way to determine this is to stick a big fork straight into the pork butt and try to lift it up. If it falls off the fork, it's done. Otherwise, keep cooking. If you get really bored, you can always finish the butt in the oven.

Here I've provided sauces both sweet and sour to keep everybody happy, plus some corn bread to round out the dish.

1 4- to 5-pound boneless pork butt

For the Rub

2 tablespoons ground cumin

2 tablespoons minced garlic

2 tablespoons roughly chopped fresh oregano or cilantro

2 tablespoons freshly cracked black pepper

2 tablespoons salt

2 tablespoons white vinegar

2 tablespoons yellow mustard

2 tablespoons minced fresh chile pepper of your choice

2 tablespoons olive oil

For the Sour Sauce

$^1/_4$ cup white vinegar

$^1/_4$ cup fresh lime juice (about 2 limes)

1 tablespoon minced garlic

1 tablespoon minced fresh chile pepper of your choice

$^1/_4$ cup roughly chopped fresh oregano or cilantro

Salt and freshly cracked black pepper to taste

For the Sweet Sauce

> ¹/₂ cup catsup
>
> 3 tablespoons molasses
>
> 1 tablespoon red wine vinegar
>
> 1 tablespoon of your favorite steak sauce
>
> 1 tablespoon rum
>
> 2 teaspoons ground allspice
>
> Salt and freshly cracked black pepper to taste
>
> 1 recipe Your Basic Corn Bread (recipe follows)

1. Set the pork butt in a large roasting pan. Make the rub: In a small bowl, combine all the ingredients and mix well. Rub the pork butt generously with this mixture.

2. Build a small fire in one side of a covered grill, using about enough charcoal to fill a shoe box. Let all the charcoal become completely ignited, then wait a few minutes for the fire to die down a bit. Place the butt on the grill on the side away from the fire.

3. Cover the grill, vent slightly, and cook the pork for 5 to 7 hours, adding a bit of charcoal every 30 to 40 minutes, or as needed to keep the fire going. *To check for doneness:* The meat should be tender and the internal temperature should be between 165° and 170°F on a meat thermometer. To test, stick a big fork into the butt and try to lift it up off the grill; if it falls off the fork, it's done.

4. Meanwhile, make the sour sauce: Combine all of the ingredients in a small bowl and mix well. Cover and refrigerate until ready to use.

5. Make the sweet sauce: In a small saucepan, combine all the ingredients and bring to a boil over high heat. Reduce the heat to low and simmer for 10 minutes, stirring occasionally, to blend all the flavors. Remove from the heat, let cool, and refrigerate until ready to use.

6. When the pork butt is done, remove from the grill and chop or shred it, whichever you prefer. Cut about half the pan of corn bread into slices about ¹/₂ inch thick and lay on a platter or individual serving plates. (Reserve the rest for corn bread croutons or pass separately.) Spoon the pork over the corn bread, and let your guests pick their favorite sauce to finish.

continued

YOUR BASIC CORN BREAD
MAKES 12 LARGE PIECES

4 cups all-purpose flour

2 cups yellow cornmeal

$1^1/_4$ cups sugar

2 tablespoons baking powder

1 teaspoon salt

4 large eggs

3 cups milk

$2^1/_2$ tablespoons vegetable oil

$^1/_2$ cup (1 stick) unsalted butter, melted

1. Preheat the oven to 350°F. Lightly grease an 8" × 12" baking pan.

2. Sift together the flour, cornmeal, sugar, baking powder, and salt into a large bowl. In another bowl, whisk together the eggs, milk, and oil.

3. Pour the wet ingredients over the dry ingredients, then add the melted butter and stir until just barely mixed. Pour the batter into the greased pan and bake for 1 hour, or until the top of the corn bread is golden brown and a cake tester inserted in the center comes out clean.

This makes an excellent meal when combined with Simple Latin-Style Rice and Beans (page 300) and a few condiments like Spicy Lime-Marinated Cabbage and Onion (page 331), Clove-Pickled Peaches (page 332), and Pickled Pineapple (page 335).

smoke rings

A WELL-COOKED PORK BUTT or other piece of barbecued meat should have a pinkish ring about a quarter-inch to an inch thick at the exterior. Inexperienced folks sometimes think the ring means the meat is not fully cooked around the outside, but in fact it is a sign of good barbecue. The ring, which represents the depth to which smoke has penetrated into the meat, is known in the trade as "smoke ring," as in, "Wow, that's an awesome smoke ring on that pork butt."

Barbecued Whole Game Hens with Orange, Oregano, and Cumin Seed

SERVES 2 AS ENTRÉE

These birds have a triple layer of seasoning. First some oranges go into the cavity, then we push a garlic-oregano mixture between the skin and meat—by the way, this is a super technique to use for any whole chicken dish, because putting the seasonings under the skin spreads their flavor through more of the bird—and then the outside of the bird is rubbed with salt, pepper, and cumin to enhance the flavor of the crispy skin. Again, as with all covered-grill cooking, you should start with your fire slightly hotter, then let it rachet down during the cooking process.

> 2 oranges, unpeeled, cut into $1/2$-inch-thick slices
>
> 1 yellow onion, peeled, halved, and cut into thick slices
>
> 1 tablespoon olive oil
>
> Salt and freshly cracked black pepper to taste
>
> $1/4$ cup roughly chopped fresh oregano
>
> 2 tablespoons minced garlic
>
> 2 Rock Cornish game hens
>
> $1/4$ cup cumin seeds, toasted if you want, or 2 tablespoons ground cumin

1. In a small bowl, combine the oranges, onion, olive oil, and salt and pepper to taste and mix well. Divide this mixture in half and stuff it into the cavities of both of your birds.

2. In a small bowl, combine the oregano and garlic and mix well. Starting at the tip of the breastbone, loosen the skin from the breasts of the birds, being careful not to tear it. Gently rub the oregano and garlic under the skin, pushing it as far down the breasts as you can. Sprinkle the outside of the chicken with the cumin and salt and pepper to taste.

3. Build a small fire off to one side in a covered grill, using about enough charcoal to fill a shoe box. Let all of the fuel become completely engulfed in flames and then, when the flames have died down and you are left with flickering coals, place the hens on the grill over the side with no fire. It is important that the hens not come in contact with the flames at any time during cooking.

4. Cover the grill and vent slightly. You will need to check the fire every 15 minutes or so as the hens cook, adding a bit more fuel as necessary to keep the fire going. The hens will take 45 minute to an hour. *To check for doneness:* Prick the thigh with a fork at the thickest part; when the juices run clear, the birds are done. Remove from the grill, discard the stuffing, carve the birds, and serve.

You might try serving these with Grilled and Chilled Mediterranean-Style Gazpacho (page 27), Grilled Spicy New Potato Salad (page 313), or Sweet-Potato Steak Fries with Your Own Catsup (page 284).

Jake's World-Famous Deep-Fat-Fried Whole Turkey

SERVES 8 TO 10 AS ENTRÉE

Okay, I know you're going to say, "What the hell is going on here? What is deep-fat-fried whole turkey doing in a barbecue chapter?" And I'll tell you—it's here because I know the people who actually read the barbecue chapter, and they're the type of people who think nothing of spending twelve hours cooking pork butts. And I know that these are the folks who really appreciate the odd craft that cooking is, and who enjoy the ritual of friends and family as much as the food. So don't look at this recipe as an anomaly, but instead as a kind of extra bonus for buying the book. I figure if you've reached this point, it means that we have developed some level of trust, that you've taken that leap of faith, perhaps with a little skepticism, and have been rewarded and maybe somewhat surprised with results better than you expected.

So here is your opportunity to be the first in your sphere of culinary influence to deep-fat-fry a whole turkey. Picture your friends as they arrive and you tell them that they will be having deep-fried whole turkey—now you know how Columbus felt when trying to convince potential backers that he could get to the East by sailing west. But to the thrill-seeking cook goes the glory, as fifty minutes later (notice that it's less than an hour's cooking time for a sixteen-pound turkey!) the crispy, golden-brown turkey is retrieved from the pot and sliced into juicy meat. This turkey is a bona fide mind-blowing experience.

I first experienced this when my friend Kenton "Jake" Jacobs, the true living legend of Northeast barbecue, winner of titles, holder of medals, and all-around good guy, cooked one for me. It's not greasy, it's moist and crisp, and it's fast. What more could you ask?

Of course, when working with this much hot fat, precautions need to be taken. This is a *very dangerous* technique. Two gallons is a lethal amount of hot oil, and, speaking from experience, I can tell you that a hot fat burn is the worst burn of all. So be very careful. Turn your face away from the pot when lowering the turkey, lest it drop and splatter hot oil in your face. And when the turkey comes out, don't stop being diligent. Put the fat somewhere to cool where it can't be spilled or touched. I think this is best done outside on a portable burner. I'd certainly *never* do it on live fire. Also, having a big enough pot is key, so that when the turkey is completely submerged in oil, the oil is not close to overflowing.

> 2 gallons peanut oil
>
> 1 16- to 19-pound turkey
>
> Salt and freshly cracked black pepper to taste

1. In a very large pot (at least 4 gallons) set over a portable burner, preferably in the backyard far away from where anyone is hanging out, heat the oil to 375°F.

2. Rub the turkey generously inside and out with salt and pepper. If you have a wire basket large enough for the turkey, put the bird in the basket and lower it into the hot fat. Otherwise, tie a length of very sturdy string across the back of the turkey, connecting it on either side to one of the wings, to serve as a handle. Lower the turkey into the fat, turning your face away in case you slip and the turkey drops in and splatters the hot oil.

3. Cook for 50 minutes. Pull the turkey out and allow it to sit for 10 minutes (making sure to move the fat to some safe location to cool down), then carve and serve.

You might enjoy this with a couple of Southern-inspired dishes like Cornmeal Mush with Okra and Tomatoes (page 305) and Green Apple and Celery Root Salad with Bacon-Buttermilk Dressing (page 306). Espresso Black Bottom Pie (page 376) is a perfect dessert here.

Barbecued Whole Turkey with Mexican-Style Stuffing

SERVES 6 AS ENTRÉE

Roasting a turkey in a covered grill is both challenging and rewarding; if you've done it before without any stuffing, allow a little extra time for this version. The corn bread stuffing stays moist when cooked this way, and the apple, sausage, and smoke is a nice flavor mix. I like to start with a relatively hot fire and then try to keep it steady during the whole cooking time. It's not crucial, but try not to let the temperature drop too far, or the cooking time will be a little off.

1 10-pound turkey
Salt and freshly cracked black pepper to taste

For the Stuffing

1 tablespoon vegetable oil

1 large yellow onion, peeled and diced small

2 tablespoons minced garlic

1 jalapeño or other small fresh chile pepper of your choice, minced

1 pound chorizo or other sausage of your choice, sliced

2 Granny Smith or other green apples, cored and diced small

6 cups $^1/_2$-inch corn bread cubes, stale or lightly toasted
(see page 264 for corn bread recipe)

$^1/_4$ cup roughly chopped fresh cilantro (or substitute parsley)

1 cup milk

Salt and freshly cracked black pepper to taste

For the Rub

$^1/_4$ cup olive oil

2 tablespoons minced garlic

2 tablespoons ground cumin

Salt and freshly cracked black pepper to taste

1. Remove the innards from the turkey. Rub the turkey inside and out with a generous amount of salt and pepper, and set aside.

2. Make the stuffing: In a large sauté pan over medium heat, heat the oil until hot but not smoking. Add the onion and sauté, stirring occasionally, until transparent, 5 to 7 minutes. Add the garlic and jalapeño and sauté, stirring occasionally, for 1 minute. Add the sausage and sauté for another 5 minutes to render out some of the fat. Remove from the heat, pour off the fat, and place in a medium bowl. Add the apples, croutons, and cilantro and mix well, then add the milk, season to taste, and mix well again.

3. Build a small fire in one half of a covered grill, using about enough charcoal to fill a shoe box. Let the fuel become completely engulfed in flames, then wait a few minutes for the fire to burn down a bit.

4. Fill the cavity of the bird three-quarters full with the stuffing. (Cook any remaining stuffing in a greased ovenproof bowl for about 1$^1/_2$ hours.)

5. Make the rub: In a small bowl, combine all the ingredients and mix well. Cover the entire bird with the rub.

6. Place the turkey on the grill over the side with no fire. It is important that the turkey not come into contact with the flames at any time during the cooking process. Cover the grill and vent slightly. You will need to check on the fire often as the turkey cooks, adding a handful or two of fuel as necessary to keep the fire going. You should also turn the turkey around at least twice during the cooking time, or more often if the side facing the fire seems to be getting too done. The turkey will take about 3 hours. *To check for doneness:* Pierce the thigh with a fork. When the juices run clear, the turkey is done. Remove from the grill and allow to rest at least 15 minutes before carving. Serve accompanied by the stuffing.

This is a celebratory dish, so serve it with several substantial side dishes like Bridget's Couscous Salad for a Crowd (page 320), Grilled Eggplant and Bread Salad for a Crowd (page 311), and maybe a double batch of Chipotle Mashed Sweet Potatoes (page 282).

Chinese-Spiced Whole Duck with Orange–Green Peppercorn Sauce

Whole barbecued duck is a transcendental happening. The combination of the rich, semi-gamy meat and woodsy smoke is truly exceptional.

When cooking ducks, I've always struggled to get the skin as crispy as possible. Recently I was eating Peking duck in an excellent Chinese restaurant and was fortunate enough to meet the owner. Under intense interrogation, he started to give me some details of the method. Turns out that it's a complicated process that has to do with steaming the duck and then drying it, the key being to separate the fat from the meat so that during subsequent cooking the fat will drop out more easily. We do a variation on this method at my restaurants, and you can do it at home, too. Just put about five quarts of water in a large stockpot along with a cup of vinegar and a quarter cup of honey. Bring the mixture to a rolling boil, dunk the duck in for ninety seconds, then go on with the preparation described below. Marinating the duck in the salt and sherry also helps to dehydrate the skin, so the longer you let it sit like this, the better, but if you don't have time for this step, it's no big deal.

The sauce we use here is an orangy Chinese type that I think goes well with the pungent ginger–green pepper rub.

1 4- to 5-pound duck
$^1/_4$ cup kosher salt
$^1/_2$ cup dry sherry
2 yellow onions, peeled and quartered
2 oranges, unpeeled, quartered

For the Rub

$^1/_3$ cup freshly cracked white pepper (or substitute black)
$^1/_3$ cup finely chopped scallions (white and green parts)
$^1/_4$ cup minced ginger
$^1/_4$ cup sesame oil

For the Sauce

2 cups fresh orange juice (4 to 5 juice oranges)
$^1/_2$ cup white vinegar
$^1/_4$ cup soy sauce
$^1/_4$ cup molasses
$^1/_4$ cup rinsed canned green peppercorns
Salt and freshly cracked white pepper (or substitute black) to taste

1. Trim all the excess fat from the duck tail and remove the innards. Rub the duck all over with the salt and sherry and place on a rack, uncovered, in the refrigerator for as long as you have before cooking, or up to 4 days.

2. Turn the duck on its back and prick the skin just below the breast and legs with a fork a few times to allow the fat to escape as the duck cooks, so the skin will crisp. Flip the duck back over and stuff the cavity with the onions and oranges.

3. Make the rub: In a small bowl, combine all the ingredients and mix well. Rub the outside of the duck generously with this mixture.

4. Build a fire off to one side in a covered grill, using enough charcoal to fill about one and a half shoe boxes. Let all of the fuel become completely engulfed in flames and then, when the flames have died down and you are left with flickering coals, place the duck on the grill over the side with no fire. It's okay to have the fire a little hot at this point and then let it slow down as the cooking goes on. We're not cooking to tenderize here, so slow and low is not important—what is important is that the duck not come in contact with the flames at any time during cooking.

5. Cover the grill, vent slightly, and cook for about 2¹⁄₂ hours. You will need to check the fire every 20 minutes or so, adding a bit more fuel as necessary to keep the fire going. Each time you do this, move the duck to a slightly different position—this helps promote even cooking. *To check for doneness:* After 2¹⁄₂ hours, insert an instant-read thermometer in the middle of the thigh, without touching the bone; if the thermometer reads 160°F, the duck is done.

6. Meanwhile, make the sauce: In a small saucepan, combine the orange juice, vinegar, and soy sauce and bring to a boil over high heat. Reduce the heat to medium-low and simmer vigorously until the liquid is reduced to about a cup, 40 to 50 minutes. Remove from the heat, stir in the molasses and peppercorns, and season to taste with salt and pepper.

7. When the duck has reached 160°F, remove it from the grill. Discard the onions and oranges and carve the duck. Serve hot, accompanied by the sauce, which can be either hot or at room temperature.

Try this one with a couple of side dishes with Asian roots, like Ginger-Scallion Fried Rice (page 301), Sesame Green Beans with Crispy Fried Shallots (page 281), and Grilled Corn with Lime and Chinese Roasted Salt (page 278).

Corn Bread–Stuffed Barbecued Game Hens with Bourbon-Shallot Sauce

Game hens are neat because everybody gets his or her own bird. Here we kind of roast them on the grill, then serve them with a brothy sauce flavored with bourbon to help keep everything moist.

Again, this is smoke-roasting as opposed to barbecuing, the difference being one of method. When you are barbecuing, the temperature must remain very low. Here it's all right if the temperature gets a little hotter, because we're not trying to tenderize, we just don't want to burn the birds on the outside. To ensure that goal, I still prefer indirect cooking, even with the cover on the grill.

For the Stuffing

> $1/2$ cup (1 stick) unsalted butter
>
> 1 large onion, peeled and diced small
>
> 2 Granny Smith or other green apples, peeled, halved, cored, and diced small
>
> 2 cups corn bread crumbled into small chunks (see page 264 for corn bread recipe, or substitute any bread of your choosing)
>
> $1/4$ cup roughly chopped fresh sage, oregano, and/or marjoram
>
> 1 cup milk
>
> Salt and freshly cracked black pepper to taste

For the Rub

> $1/4$ cup paprika
>
> $1/4$ cup freshly cracked black pepper
>
> $1/4$ cup lightly packed brown sugar
>
> $1/4$ cup kosher salt
>
> 4 Rock Cornish game hens

For the Sauce

> 2 tablespoons olive oil
>
> $1/2$ cup minced shallots
>
> 1 tablespoon minced garlic
>
> 2 cups chicken stock
>
> 1 cup bourbon
>
> $1/4$ cup fresh lemon juice (about 1 lemon)
>
> Salt and freshly cracked black pepper to taste

SLOW AND LOW

1. Make the stuffing: Place the butter and onion in a medium sauté pan over medium heat and sauté, stirring occasionally, until the onions are transparent, 5 to 7 minutes. Add the apples and sauté, stirring occasionally, for 5 minutes more. Transfer to a medium bowl, add the corn bread, herbs, milk, and salt and pepper to taste, and mix well.

2. Make the rub: In a small bowl, combine all the ingredients and mix well. Divide the stuffing into 4 portions and stuff each bird, then cover the birds well with the rub.

3. Build a small fire off to one side in a covered grill, using about enough charcoal to fill a shoe box. Let all of the fuel become completely engulfed in flames and then, when the flames have died down and you are left with flickering coals, place the hens on the grill surface over the side with no fire. It is important that the hens not come in contact with the flames at any time during cooking.

4. Cover the grill and open the vents slightly. You will need to check the fire every 20 minutes or so as the hens cook, adding a bit more fuel as necessary to keep the fire going. They will take 1 to 1^1/$_2$ hours. *To check for doneness:* Pierce the thigh of a hen with a fork. If the juices run clear, the hens are done.

5. While the hens are cooking, make the sauce: In a medium saucepan over high heat, heat the oil until hot but not smoking. Add the shallots and garlic and sauté, stirring occasionally, until soft, 3 to 5 minutes. Add the stock and bourbon and bring to a boil, then turn the heat to low and simmer until the liquid has reduced by about half, 30 to 45 minutes. Add the lemon juice and salt and pepper to taste, cook for 10 more minutes, and remove from heat.

6. When the hens are done, remove them from the grill and serve warm with the sauce.

I like these little guys served with Seared Pumpkin with Cumin, Lime, and Molasses (page 289). Try Minted Melon with Caribbean Elixir (page 361) for dessert with this one.

I'm partial to side dishes. When I hear the term, it conjures up the old-fashioned vegetable dishes that were passed around our family dinner table when I was a child: rich corn pudding, crunchy salads, silken scalloped potatoes, thick-sliced August tomatoes with onions, molasses-laced baked beans, and on and on. While I always ate my share of the meat, fish, or chicken at those dinners, I remember the outstanding tastes and the constant variety of the side dishes more vividly.

GREAT WITH GRILLED FOOD

something on the side

These days, side dishes are still high on my list. I'm fond of the old Southern tradition of "meat and three"—the classic diner meal, consisting of a plate of meat and three side dishes of your choice—and often try to re-create the concept in more sophisticated restaurants by ordering three or four sides to go along with my entrée.

In fact, while each of the dishes in this chapter is excellent served on the side, every one also has enough dynamic flavors and culinary interest to be suitable for the center of the plate, with no need to take second billing to an entrée. Used in this way, they are ideal for those who are trying to cut down on red meat consumption for health reasons. A couple of the recipes here, such as Macumber Turnip Cakes with Bacon and Onions, rely on small amounts of meat for flavoring. But most, like the side dishes of my childhood, are entirely vegetarian, with many of the vegetables having gained some nice smoky flavor from spending time over the grilling fire.

Some of these recipes, such as K.C.'s Bengali-Style Spinach or Grilled Eggplant Rounds with Sweet Chile Sauce, are influenced by the spicy cuisines of the hot-weather world. Others, including Fava Bean Salad with Lemon and Shaved Pecorino Romano Cheese, are inspired by the flavors of the Mediterranean. Many others, like Grilled Spicy New Potato Salad, Grilled Corn with Lime and Chinese Roasted Salt, and Sweet-Potato Steak Fries with Your Own Catsup, are old standbys with a new outlook.

For all their variety, the dishes here share certain characteristics: They are all casual, pretty straightforward, and full of interesting textures and flavors, and they all go great with grilled food. I encourage you to use them any way you want, whether as a side dish or a meal in themselves, but to use them early and often.

Grilled Corn with Lime
and Chinese Roasted Salt

Grilled Asparagus
with Garlic Mayonnaise
or Simple Vinaigrette

Sesame Green Beans
with Crispy Fried
Shallots

Chipotle Mashed
Sweet Potatoes

Grilled Potatoes with
Yogurt-Parsley Sauce

Sweet-Potato Steak
Fries with Your Own
Catsup

Grilled Garlicky
Eggplant Planks with
Yogurt-Mint Sauce

Grilled Eggplant
Rounds with Sweet
Chile Sauce

Smoky Ratatouille
for a Crowd

Seared Pumpkin with
Cumin, Lime, and
Molasses

Kohlrabi Puree with
Lemon and Olive Oil

K. C.'s Bengali-Style
Spinach

Seared Spinach with
Fried Garlic Chips

Macumber Turnip Cakes
with Bacon and Onions

Grilled Plums with Spicy
Hoisin Glaze

Grilled Tomato Halves
with Cheesy Bread
Crumbs

Basic Black Beans

Simple Latin-Style Rice
and Beans

Ginger-Scallion
Fried Rice

Tomato Risotto with
Toasted Pine Nuts

Simple Lentils

Cornmeal Mush with
Okra and Tomatoes

Green Apple and Celery
Root Salad with Bacon-
Buttermilk Dressing

Jícama-Apple Salad
with Orange-Mustard
Dressing

Pungent Carrot and
Cucumber Salad with
Ginger and Garlic

Latin-Flavored Coleslaw
with Grilled Avocados

Grilled Eggplant and
Bread Salad for a Crowd

Grilled Spicy New
Potato Salad

Grilled Sweet Potato
Salad with Sweet-Sour
Bacon Dressing

Indian-Style Sweet
Potato Salad

Chickpea Salad with
Cumin and Mint

Chickpea Salad with
Horseradish-Yogurt
Dressing

Fava Bean Salad with
Lemon and Shaved
Pecorino Romano Cheese

Romaine and
Bulgur Salad

Bridget's Couscous
Salad for a Crowd

Grilled Corn with Lime and Chinese Roasted Salt

Here's another entry in the growing family of grilled corn recipes. The Chinese technique of roasting salt with whole spices produces a unique flavor, as the salt gathers in the other tastes. Add a squeeze of lime and you're talking a grilled corn approach that you'll probably be the first one on your block to try—but definitely not the last, once your friends get a taste.

>   2 tablespoons Szechuan peppercorns
>   1 tablespoon star anise
>   1 teaspoon ground cinnamon
>   1 cup kosher salt
>   12 ears corn, husked, desilked, blanched in boiling water for 2 minutes,
>   and drained
>   4 limes, cut into wedges

1. In a small sauté pan over low heat, combine the peppercorns, star anise, cinnamon, and salt and cook, stirring constantly, until the salt starts to smoke slightly and becomes fragrant, 2 to 3 minutes. Pour the salt through a strainer or small-holed colander to remove the anise and peppercorns, then set aside.

2. Grill the corn over **a medium-hot fire** for 3 to 4 minutes, rolling often, until golden brown. Remove from the grill, sprinkle liberally with the roasted salt, and serve with the lime wedges for squeezing.

This is a fantastic all-purpose side dish that you can serve with just about anything as long as the corn is good.

Grilled Asparagus with Garlic Mayonnaise or Simple Vinaigrette

SERVES 4

In the part of the country where I live, the arrival of the first asparagus and the liberation of the grill from winter storage happen at about the same time, so grilling asparagus seems like a natural. Actually, the blanching process is even more important here than the grilling. It's the kind of seemingly simple technique that makes a tremendous difference in the end result of your cooking, a truism that was pounded into me at an early age by a French chef at the Culinary Institute of America. Make sure your water is at a rolling boil, blanch the asparagus in batches so it cooks quickly, and immediately after blanching, plunge it into ice water to stop the cooking process. Your guests will marvel at the bright green and the crisp snap of your wonderful grilled "grass" in this simple prep, which showcases the inherent flavor and texture of this unique vegetable. For those who are avoiding mayonnaise, I have also provided a simple vinaigrette option for dressing the asparagus.

For the Mayonnaise

> 2 large egg yolks
>
> 1 cup extra virgin olive oil
>
> 1 teaspoon minced garlic
>
> 2 tablespoons fresh lemon juice (about $^1/_2$ lemon)
>
> 1 tablespoon roughly chopped fresh basil
>
> Salt and freshly cracked black pepper to taste

> OR

For the Vinaigrette

> $^1/_2$ cup extra virgin olive oil
>
> $^1/_4$ cup fresh lemon juice (about 1 lemon)
>
> 1 tablespoon minced garlic
>
> Salt and freshly cracked black pepper to taste

> 25 to 30 spears asparagus, bottom $^1/_4$ inch trimmed
>
> 2 tablespoons olive oil
>
> Salt and freshly cracked black pepper to taste

1. Make the mayonnaise: In a food processor, combine the egg yolks, garlic, and lemon juice and puree for about 10 seconds to blend well. With the motor running, add the oil in a steady stream; turn off the motor as soon as the oil is just incorporated. It is important not to overbeat the mixture, because it should remain light. Add the basil and salt and pepper to taste, pulse to combine, cover, and refrigerate. Or, if you prefer the vinaigrette, simply whisk all the ingredients together in a small bowl.

2. Fill your sink or a large stockpot with water and ice. In a small stockpot, bring 6 quarts of water and a pinch of salt to a boil. Drop half of the asparagus in the water and cook for 3 minutes; it should remain bright green and firm. Immediately transfer the asparagus in the ice-water bath to stop the cooking process. Repeat the process with the remaining asparagus.

3. Drain the asparagus and toss it in a medium bowl with the olive oil and salt and pepper to taste. Grill the asparagus over **a medium-hot fire** for 3 to 4 minutes, turning several times, until it is nicely browned. Remove to a platter, spoon the mayonnaise or vinaigrette over the top, and serve.

I like this with a fish dish such as Grilled Mackerel with Expensive Olive Oil, Lemon, and Oregano (page 192), Grilled Orange-Cumin Mahi Mahi with Smoky Summer Vegetable Hash (page 166), or Herb-Crusted Grilled Monkfish with Roasted Red Pepper Relish (page 190).

mayonnaise safety

THERE IS SOME DANGER OF salmonella from eating uncooked egg yolks, although it is relatively minor. This danger is reduced by the acid content of mayonnaise, but it still exists. Pregnant women, the elderly, infants, and people whose immune systems are compromised should avoid raw eggs. For others, it is simply a matter of balancing the risk versus the pleasure. Only you can decide. If you want mayonnaise without risk, you can lightly cook the egg yolks prior to making your mayonnaise, as described on page 344.

Sesame Green Beans with Crispy Fried Shallots

SERVES 4

For many people, green bean recipes are like movies: You always think there are lots of good ones around until you're ready for one, then you can't find any you really like. Here's an outstanding one, which combines the crunchy crispness of fried shallots with lightly blanched green beans and a dressing packing lots of Asian flavors.

1¹/₂ pounds green beans, trimmed

¹/₄ cup vegetable or peanut oil

5 shallots, peeled, halved, and thinly sliced

Salt and freshly cracked black pepper to taste

For the Dressing

¹/₂ cup soy sauce

¹/₄ cup sesame oil

¹/₄ cup rice vinegar

2 tablespoons minced ginger

1 tablespoon minced garlic

1 bunch scallions (white and green parts), chopped

¹/₄ cup sesame seeds, toasted in a 350°F oven until golden brown,
    about 7 minutes

1. Fill your sink or a large pot with ice and water. Bring about 3 quarts of salted water to a boil over high heat. When the water reaches a full boil, throw about half the green beans in and blanch for 2 to 3 minutes, or until the beans turn bright green and are tender but still have some snap to them. Remove the beans, plunge them into the ice water to cool, then remove from the ice-water bath and set aside. Repeat with the remaining beans.

2. Put the oil in a medium saucepan and bring just to a simmer over medium heat. Add the shallots and fry until golden brown, 7 to 10 minutes. Remove them from the oil with a slotted spoon, lay them out on a paper towel or brown paper bag to drain, and sprinkle with salt and pepper to taste.

3. Make the dressing: In a small bowl, combine all the ingredients and whisk together until blended. Place the green beans in a medium bowl, add the dressing and toss well. Sprinkle the shallots over the top and serve.

I like this dish so much that I would have to put it in the "all-purpose side dish" category. It goes particularly well with Asian-flavored preps.

Chipotle Mashed Sweet Potatoes

People often ask me how I come up with ideas, and this dish is a good example of one type of inspiration. A while ago, I was fortunate enough to have Bobby Flay, chef of Mesa Grill and Bolo in New York, cook at the Blue Room as a guest chef. As part of his menu, Bobby made scalloped sweet potatoes flavored with chipotles, which are dried smoked jalapeño peppers. Well, we went overboard and prepared way too many potatoes and too much chipotle cream, so for dinner the following night, we made them into chipotle mashed sweet potatoes, which turned out to be outstanding. This kind of "borrowing" is very common, and is a constant source of good-natured ribbing whenever chefs gather together. Since just about everything has already been made at one time or another at some place in the world, no cook can really claim anything as totally original. Food is always in a constant state of evolution, and that's part of the fun of cooking.

> 4 medium sweet potatoes, peeled and diced large
> 2 tablespoons mashed canned chipotle peppers
> 1 cup light cream
> 1 to 4 tablespoons unsalted butter, your choice
> Salt and freshly cracked black pepper to taste

1. In a small pot, bring 2 quarts of water and a pinch of salt to a boil over high heat. Add the sweet potatoes and cook for about 10 minutes, or until they are easily pierced by a fork but still offer some resistance.

2. While the potatoes are cooking, combine the chipotles, cream, and butter in a small saucepan and cook over medium heat for about 5 minutes, stirring, until the butter has melted and the cream has thickened slightly.

3. Drain the potatoes and place them in a medium bowl. Add the cream mixture and mash the potatoes with a fork until the cream is mixed in and the potatoes are fairly smooth. Add salt and pepper to taste and serve.

What are regular mashed potatoes good with? Just about anything—
and I would say the same for these. They are nice with hearty meat
dishes, but you can also serve them with chicken, seafood, or a
vegetarian platter.

Grilled Potatoes with Yogurt-Parsley Sauce

SERVES 4

This simple dish takes its inspiration from the flavors of the Middle East. Yogurt, lemon, cumin, parsley, and garlic all blend together with potatoes that gain a little smokiness from the fire. Be sure that you leave the potatoes on the grill long enough to get a good crust on the outside, since that gives the dish some texture.

4 medium potatoes of your choice, cut into rounds about 1 inch thick

¼ cup olive oil

Salt and freshly cracked black pepper to taste

1 cup plain yogurt

¼ cup fresh lemon juice (about 1 lemon)

2 tablespoons cumin seeds, toasted if you want, or 1 tablespoon ground cumin

1 cup fresh parsley leaves

4 cloves garlic, peeled

⅓ cup extra virgin olive oil

1. In a medium saucepan, bring a quart or so of salted water to a boil over high heat. Add the sliced potatoes and boil for 8 to 10 minutes—you want the potatoes to reach the point where you can easily stick a fork through them but still feel some resistance; the slices should not break apart easily. Drain and cool to room temperature.

2. Toss the cooled potato slices in a medium bowl with the olive oil and salt and pepper to taste, then place the potatoes on the grill over **a medium fire.** Cook for about 3 minutes on each side, or until nicely browned.

3. Remove the potatoes from the grill and put them in a medium bowl. Add the yogurt, lemon juice, and cumin, toss well, and set aside.

4. Place the parsley and garlic in a food processor and puree until smooth. With the motor running, slowly drizzle in the olive oil just until incorporated. Just before serving, drizzle this mixture over the potatoes.

Try this to chill down a hot and spicy dish like Chile-Coated Chicken Thighs with Couscous and Tomato-Raisin Relish (page 235) or Chipotle-Rubbed Grilled Skirt Steak with Grill-Roasted Bananas (page 237).

Sweet-Potato Steak Fries with Your Own Catsup

Growing up in the South and eating lunch in the elementary school cafeteria, I became a big fan of sweet potatoes, which were always served so sweet that I thought they were a dessert instead of a vegetable. This unassuming root vegetable is an outstanding example of a humble ingredient that can be used in all kinds of different ways. Here the whole potatoes are baked, then cut into quarters, browned up in a pan, and seasoned well with salt and pepper to create meaty, flavorful steak fries. Be sure to keep a close eye on the potatoes while they're in the oven so they don't get overdone, and don't crowd them in the sauté pan, or the temperature of the oil will drop too much.

The homemade catsup is not essential for the fries (you can use bottled catsup if you want), but it is very tasty. The recipe makes about six cups, which is no doubt more than you will use on the fries, but it will keep up to three weeks covered and refrigerated—so you might as well make a big batch while you're at it.

> 4 medium sweet potatoes, washed but not peeled
> 1 cup vegetable oil
> Salt and freshly cracked black pepper to taste
> Your Own Catsup (recipe follows)

1. Place the sweet potatoes on a small baking sheet and bake in a preheated 400°F oven for about 45 minutes. You should start checking after 25 minutes, because the moisture content of sweet potatoes varies a lot, and some potatoes will be done much faster than others. *To check for doneness:* Poke the potatoes with a fork or skewer; they should pierce easily but with some resistance, firm but not hard in the center. Remove the potatoes from the oven and allow to cool. As soon as they are cool enough to handle, cut them lengthwise into quarters.

2. In a large sauté pan over medium-high heat, heat the oil to 350°F. (If you don't have a thermometer, test the oil temperature by dropping in a small piece of potato; it should drop to the bottom, then immediately surface and start bubbling.) Once the oil is hot, carefully add 4 potato quarters and cook for 4 to 6 minutes, turning occasionally, until they turn a deep golden brown. Remove to paper towels or brown paper bags to drain, sprinkle with salt and pepper to taste, and repeat with remaining quarters. Serve with the catsup on the side.

YOUR OWN CATSUP

2 tablespoons vegetable oil

1 yellow onion, peeled and diced small

2 tablespoons minced garlic

2 medium tomatoes, cored and diced medium

1 cup tomato puree

1 cup white vinegar

$\frac{1}{2}$ cup water

$\frac{1}{3}$ cup raisins

$\frac{1}{2}$ cup molasses

$\frac{1}{4}$ cup lightly packed brown sugar

1 tablespoon ground allspice

14 to 16 dashes Worcestershire sauce

Pinch of ground cloves and/or mace

Salt and freshly cracked black pepper to taste

1. In a medium saucepan, heat the vegetable oil over medium heat until hot but not smoking. Add the onion and cook, stirring occasionally, until transparent, 5 to 7 minutes. Add the garlic and cook, stirring a few times, for 1 minute. Add all the remaining catsup ingredients and bring to a boil. Reduce the heat to low and simmer uncovered for 1 hour, stirring occasionally.

2. Remove from the heat and puree in a food processor or blender until smooth. Cover and refrigerate.

Serve these with anything grilled, or with anything that you're serving to kids—they love 'em.

aroma of the west indies

I HAD ALWAYS THOUGHT of allspice as a kind of second-rate seasoning, mainly used in baking, until I spent some time in Jamaica, where this spice—which is the dried unopened but mature berry of an ever-green tree native to the island—is used to its full advantage. In fact, many Jamaicans treat allspice (which is called *pimienta* everywhere but in the United States) pretty much as we do pepper—they put it in a grinder and set it on the table for use on just about everything. Although it is often described as having the combined flavors of nutmeg, cloves, and cinnamon, allspice has a unique taste all its own, well worth getting to know.

One Jamaican night, after tasting red beans and rice heavily flavored with this aromatic, slightly peppery spice and then tucking into a grilled whole red snapper stuffed with habanero peppers, sautéed callaloo, and whole allspice berries, I became a convert and I've been using the spice far more often ever since.

Grilled Garlicky Eggplant Planks with Yogurt-Mint Sauce

SERVES 4

Vegetables used to be pretty much an afterthought in American cooking, with meat the star attraction. But these days, more and more people are paying attention to vegetables, a trend that I definitely favor. Cooks often turn to the Mediterranean for inspiration, where there is a long tradition of excellent vegetable dishes, and where the cozy relationship of eggplant to live fire is well known.

When grilling eggplant, be careful that it browns but doesn't get black on the outside, and that the inside gets moist but not quite mushy.

If you have saffron around and pomegranates are in season, this dish, rich with the flavors of the southern Mediterranean, becomes something that not only tastes great, but is rather exotic as well. If you have any left over, you can simply cut up the eggplant, add it to the yogurt, and stuff it into some pita for lunch—or you can grill the pita and use the eggplant-yogurt mixture as a dip with drinks tomorrow night.

> 1 teaspoon saffron threads (optional)
> 1/2 cup plain yogurt
> 3 tablespoons finely chopped fresh mint
> 2 tablespoons pomegranate seeds (optional)
> Salt and freshly cracked black pepper to taste
> 2 medium eggplants, cut lengthwise into planks about 1/2 inch thick
> 1/4 cup vegetable oil
> 2 tablespoons minced garlic
> 1 tablespoon red pepper flakes

1. If using the saffron, bring about 2 tablespoons of water to a boil in a small saucepan. Remove from the heat, add the saffron, and let cool to room temperature.

2. In a small bowl, combine the yogurt, mint, the pomegranate seeds if you have them, the saffron if you're using it, and salt and pepper to taste and mix well. Set aside.

3. In a medium bowl, combine the eggplant, oil, garlic, red pepper flakes, and salt and pepper to taste and toss well so the eggplant planks are coated with the other ingredients.

4. Grill the eggplant over **a hot fire** for 2 to 3 minutes per side, or until golden brown and soft. *To check for doneness:* Cut into one of the eggplant planks and peek inside; it should look moist all the way through. Remove from the grill and serve hot with the yogurt sauce on the side.

This Middle Eastern–inspired dish is very nice alongside Grilled Lamb and Fig Skewers with Quince-Ginger Chutney (page 118).

Grilled Eggplant Rounds with Sweet Chile Sauce

SERVES 4

This is one of my oldies but goodies, simple but with a lot going on. The richly flavored, smoky, tender eggplant goes really well with the sweet-sour glaze and the sprinkle of spiciness on top. Be sure you cook the eggplant all the way through but without overcooking it; you are looking for it to be browned outside and moist-appearing all the way through the inside, but not mushy.

For the Sauce

2 tablespoons sesame oil

1 tablespoon minced garlic

1 teaspoon minced ginger

$^1/_2$ cup fresh lime juice (about 4 limes)

2 tablespoons catsup

2 tablespoons brown sugar

2 teaspoons minced fresh chile peppers of your choice

2 medium eggplants, cut into rounds about 1 inch thick

$^1/_4$ cup vegetable oil

Salt and freshly cracked black pepper to taste

8 scallions (white and green parts), thinly sliced on the bias

3 tablespoons coriander seeds, toasted if you want, or 1$^1/_2$ tablespoons ground coriander

1 tablespoon red pepper flakes

1. Make the sauce: In a medium saucepan, heat the sesame oil over medium heat until hot but not smoking. Add the garlic and ginger and sauté, stirring occasionally, for 3 minutes. Add the lime juice, catsup, brown sugar, and chile peppers and bring to a boil, stirring occasionally. Reduce the heat to low and simmer, stirring once in a while, for 20 minutes, or until the sauce is thick enough to coat the back of a spoon. Remove from the heat and set aside.

2. Put the eggplant rounds into a medium bowl along with the vegetable oil and salt and pepper to taste, and toss to coat. Place the eggplant on the grill over **a medium-hot fire** and cook until browned and soft, about 4 minutes per side. *To check for doneness:* Cut into the eggplant and check to be sure the interior looks moist (raw eggplant is dry, cooked is moist). Brush the eggplant on both sides with the chile sauce, leave it on the grill for about 10 seconds, and then remove it from the grill. Sprinkle with the scallions, coriander, and red pepper flakes, and serve warm.

This goes well with Asian-flavored preps like Grilled Scallops and Plums with Sweet Mirin Barbecue Sauce (page 161).

Smoky Ratatouille for a Crowd

This is a good dish to prepare when you have a crowd coming over. I like to make it while everyone is having drinks and hanging out. The layout is visually pleasing, with all the different colors and shapes on the grill, and the process of putting the dish together is fun to watch and pretty easy, so you can cook, drink, and talk all at the same time. Keep a big cutting board out by the grill so you can cut the vegetables up as they are ready, throw them into a giant bowl, and then lay on the vinegar, oil, herbs, and garlic.

2 medium yellow squash, cut lengthwise into planks about 1 inch thick

2 medium zucchini, cut lengthwise into planks about 1 inch thick

2 medium eggplants, cut lengthwise into planks about 1 inch thick

2 red onions, peeled and cut into rings about 1 inch thick

6 plum tomatoes, halved

3 red bell peppers, halved and seeded

1 pound large white mushrooms, trimmed and cleaned

³/₄ cup vegetable oil

Salt and freshly cracked black pepper to taste

³/₄ cup balsamic vinegar

¹/₂ cup olive oil

2 tablespoons minced garlic

1 cup roughly chopped fresh herbs: any combination of parsley, basil,
    oregano, rosemary, thyme, and/or sage

1. In a large bowl, combine all of the vegetables with the vegetable oil and salt and pepper to taste and toss well.

2. Place the vegetables on the grill over **a medium-hot fire** and cook until they are golden brown and tender. You will have to keep a careful eye on the grill, because with all of the different shapes and sizes, the vegetables are going to be finishing at different times: It will take 6 to 9 minutes total for the tomatoes; 4 to 5 minutes per side for the squash, zucchini, onions, and eggplant; 5 to 7 minutes per side for the bell peppers; and 8 to 10 minutes total for the mushrooms.

3. As you remove the cooked vegetables from the grill, set them aside to cool a bit. As soon as they are cool enough to handle, cut them into bite-sized pieces and place in a large bowl. Add the vinegar, olive oil, garlic, and herbs and toss gently. Season to taste with salt and pepper and serve warm or cold.

This is unbelievable in combination with BBQ-Rubbed Grilled Skate with Mango-Chile Dressing (page 194).

eggplant menagerie

THE LARGE PURPLE GLOBES that we see in our supermarkets are just the tip of the eggplant iceberg. Asian varieties, in particular, are wild—they can be as small as plums or as large as cantaloupes, shaped like anything from an egg to a long curly snake, and covered with skin that may be various shades of white, green, pink, yellow, black, or violet, or even striped. Eggplants have been eaten for thousands of years around the world, and have also been put to other nonculinary uses. In the imperial court of fifth-century China, for example, women made a dye from the skins of black eggplant, which they then used to stain their teeth gray, a practice that apparently made them look particularly fetching.

Seared Pumpkin with Cumin, Lime, and Molasses

SERVES 4 TO 6

Although we tend to think of pumpkins mainly as carving material for jack-o'-lanterns, they actually make very good eating. They are also totally healthful, with very high levels of beta-carotene, a substance that seems to be helpful in preventing cancer. There are literally hundreds of varieties of pumpkins, but the general rule is that the smaller ones known as "sugar pumpkins" are the most tender and sweetest. If you can't get small pumpkins (or just don't feel like using them), you can substitute Hubbard, banana, acorn, or butternut squash in this recipe.

$1/4$ cup olive oil

2 red onions, peeled and cut into thin slices

$1^1/2$ pounds pumpkin flesh (from about 1 3-pound pumpkin),
   peeled and cut into large dice (4 to 5 cups diced pumpkin)

1 tablespoon minced garlic

2 tablespoons ground cumin

$1/2$ cup water

$1/4$ cup molasses

$1/4$ cup orange juice

$1/4$ cup red wine vinegar

2 limes, halved

$1/2$ cup roughly chopped fresh parsley

1. In a large sauté pan over medium heat, heat 2 tablespoons of the olive oil until hot but not smoking. Add the onions and sauté, stirring occasionally, until transparent, 5 to 7 minutes. Remove from the pan and set aside.

continued

2. Add the remaining 2 tablespoons oil to the pan and heat until hot but not smoking. Add the diced pumpkin and sauté, stirring occasionally, until browned, 3 to 4 minutes.

3. Add the reserved onions to the pan along with the garlic and cumin and sauté, stirring frequently, for 1 minute. Add the water, molasses, orange juice, and vinegar and bring the mixture to a simmer. Simmer, stirring occasionally, for 10 minutes, or until the pumpkin is tender but not mushy.

4. Remove from the heat, squeeze the juice from the limes into the mixture, and stir well. Serve sprinkled generously with the parsley.

This makes an excellent side dish with any pork prep, such as Chuletas:
Thin Grilled Pork Chops with Simple Tomato Relish (page 147),
Grilled Double-Thick Pork Chops with Grilled Peaches and Molasses-Rum
Barbecue Sauce (page 148), or Spice-Crusted Pork Tenderloins
with Banana-Date Chutney (page 150).

pumpkin dissection

WE ALL REMEMBER WHAT a pain it was to reach inside and laboriously scrape all the seeds out of a pumpkin that we were planning to make into a jack-o'-lantern. The idea of first doing that, then cutting the pumpkin into sections, then removing the peel, is enough to deter most cooks from pumpkin cookery.

FORTUNATELY, THERE IS a far easier way to clean pumpkin. First, slice about one inch off both the top and the bottom. Then slice off the skin from top to bottom in sections, working your way around the pumpkin as if you were removing the peel from an orange. Once all the peel is removed, cut the pumpkin into quarters, scrape off the seeds, and then cut the flesh into chunks. It really makes the whole thing much easier.

Kohlrabi Puree with Lemon and Olive Oil

SERVES 4 TO 6

When I was growing up, there were quite a few vegetables in my father's garden that were normal back then but have come to seem oddities these days. Among the oddest of these were Cape gooseberries (which we called ground cherries) in their papery, lantern-shaped husks, and the strange purple globelike vegetables known as kohlrabi. A member of the turnip family, they taste kind of like really sweet turnips. Look for small ones, not much bigger than a tennis ball; older ones tend to get a little tough.

> 4 kohlrabi, peeled and cut into large chunks
> 2 tablespoons vegetable oil
> 1 yellow onion, peeled and diced small
> 2 tablespoons minced garlic
> $1/4$ cup fresh lemon juice (about 1 lemon)
> $1/4$ cup olive oil
> Salt and freshly cracked black pepper to taste

1. In a large saucepan, bring 2 quarts of salted water to a boil over high heat. Add the kohlrabi chunks and simmer for about 15 minutes, or until very tender. You should be able to pierce the kohlrabi very easily with a fork.

2. While the kohlrabi is cooking, place the vegetable oil in a small sauté pan and heat over medium heat until very hot but not smoking. Add the onions and sauté, stirring occasionally, until transparent, 5 to 7 minutes. Add the garlic and sauté, stirring occasionally, for 1 minute. Set aside.

3. Drain the kohlrabi and place it in a medium bowl. Add the onions, garlic, lemon juice, and olive oil. Use a fork to mash the kohlrabi until it is creamy but still has some chunks; be careful not to overmix, or the kohlrabi will become too starchy and sort of gluey. Season to taste with salt and pepper and serve hot.

The smooth flavors of this dish go well with rich meat dishes like Grilled Lamb Chops and Sausage on Arugula and Mint (page 142).

K. C.'s Bengali-Style Spinach

SERVES 4

K. C. O'Hara, an alumnus of the East Coast Grill, used to make this as a quick and tasty side dish for simple grilled fish. The idea is to use your biggest sauté pan, get the oil smoking hot, and then throw in the well-dried spinach and stir as if your life depended on it. As soon as the greens start to wilt, add the ginger and garlic and stir furiously for another thirty seconds. The speed of stirring is essential here to keep the spinach green and prevent it from overcooking. This is the kind of cooking that I really like: quick and hot, and you need to be fast and well organized to make it work just right. Multiply this action by three or four hundred pans over a five-hour period, and you have the job description of a sauté cook in a restaurant on a busy Saturday night.

2 tablespoons sesame oil

2 tablespoons olive oil

1 pound spinach, trimmed, washed, and well dried

1 tablespoon minced garlic

1 tablespoon minced ginger

$^1/_4$ cup red wine vinegar

2 teaspoons brown sugar

1 tablespoon red pepper flakes

2 tablespoons coriander seeds, toasted if you want,
   or 1 tablespoon ground coriander

$^1/_4$ cup chopped almonds, toasted in a 350°F oven until golden brown,
   8 to 10 minutes

1. In a large sauté pan over medium-high heat, combine the olive and sesame oils and heat until very hot but not quite smoking. Add the spinach and toss very quickly and continuously for about 1 minute; the spinach should wilt slightly but remain bright green. (Tongs are great for this action.) Add the garlic and ginger and toss wildly for another 30 seconds. Remove from the heat, transfer to a medium bowl, and refrigerate until chilled.

2. Add the vinegar, sugar, red pepper flakes, and coriander to the chilled spinach and mix well. Serve cold, sprinkled with the toasted almonds.

> This is an excellent side dish with any fish dish like BBQ-Rubbed
> Grilled Skate with Mango-Chile Dressing (page 194), Grilled Swordfish
> with Artichokes, Tomatoes, and Olives (page 170), or
> Grilled Swordfish Steaks with Red Potato Puree (page 172).

Seared Spinach with Fried Garlic Chips

SERVES 4

When I'm working and get home late, this dish plus a simple pasta is my meal of choice. It's quick, easy, tasty, and a good way to get those greens that everybody needs. As with other dishes of this type, the key is to use a large sauté pan, heat the oil really hot, and get the spinach in and out quickly so it preserves its flavor and texture. Perk it up with red pepper flakes, a squeeze of lemon, and some crispy garlic chips and you've got a dish that I never get tired of. The garlic chips can be used in lots of other ways too; try them on grilled steak or fish or as a flavor booster to other vegetables.

6 tablespoons extra virgin olive oil

8 cloves garlic, peeled and thinly sliced

20 ounces spinach, trimmed, well washed, and dried

1 lemon, halved

Generous pinch of red pepper flakes

Salt and freshly cracked black pepper to taste

1. Place ¼ cup of the olive oil in a small sauté pan, add the garlic slices, and bring the oil to a simmer over medium heat. Fry the chips until golden brown, 7 to 10 minutes, then remove with a slotted spoon and place on a paper towel to drain.

2. Pour the oil remaining in the pan into a large sauté pan, add the 2 remaining tablespoons oil, and heat over high heat until almost smoking hot. Add the spinach and cook, stirring furiously, for about 1 minute; the spinach should turn bright green and wilt slightly.

3. Remove the spinach from the heat, squeeze the lemon over the top, and add the red pepper and salt and black pepper to taste. Toss well and serve, garnished with the fried garlic chips.

This is a dish that goes great with anything, anytime, anywhere.

Macumber Turnip Cakes
with Bacon and Onions

These days, I am fortunate enough to be able to spend a fair amount of time in the town of Westport in southern Massachusetts. This town serves as the proud home to, among other things, the macumber turnip. The citizenry here is as proud of this turnip (actually a type of rutabaga) as the folks in Vidalia, Georgia, are of their sweet onion. Every year around Christmastime, a group of local farmers, businesspeople, fishermen, and neighbors are invited to the home of Carol and Bob Russell, owners of Westport Rivers Vineyards, for a covered dish celebration, to which each person brings his or her favorite turnip creation. Along with classics like clam and turnip chowder and pickled turnips, I have tried such dishes as turnip ice cream (quite good) and turnip coladas (need work).

In any event, last year I was lucky enough to be invited to this turnip tribute, and I borrowed a recipe from my pal Steve "Maurice" Johnson. It was my first time making turnip cakes and they didn't work out so well, but here they are in perfected form. The secret is to squeeze the grated turnips really hard to get as much moisture as possible out of them before mixing them with the other ingredients.

If you live in the Northeast, it will be well worth your time to seek out the macumber at your local produce market or supermarket. (If you want to find out about this, call Coastal Growers Cooperative at 617–636–2222.) I guarantee you'll love these tubers.

6 slices bacon, diced small

1 large yellow onion, peeled and diced small

3 cups grated turnips, preferably macumber

$\frac{1}{3}$ cup all-purpose flour

1 large egg, lightly beaten

Salt and freshly cracked black pepper to taste

$\frac{1}{4}$ cup olive oil

1. Place the bacon in a small sauté pan over medium heat. As soon as the bacon has rendered a couple of tablespoons of fat, add the onions and sauté, stirring occasionally, until the bacon is crisp and the onions are soft and lightly browned, 5 to 7 minutes. Remove from the heat and set aside.

2. Squeeze the grated turnips very well to remove as much moisture as possible. Then squeeze them again. In a medium bowl, combine the turnips with the onions, bacon, and flour and mix well. Add the egg to this mixture, season to taste with salt and pepper, and mix well.

3. In a small sauté pan over medium heat, heat the olive oil until hot but not smoking. Form the turnip mixture into small ovals about 2 inches long and $1/2$ inch thick. Place 3 or 4 cakes in the pan and cook for about 5 minutes, or until the edges of the cakes turn golden brown and they are loose in the pan. Flip and cook for another 5 minutes, or until golden brown and crispy. Put the cakes on a paper towel–lined cookie sheet in a warm oven and repeat the process with the remaining turnip mixture. Serve warm.

I like these little cakes as an accompaniment to fish dishes.
For some reason they seem particularly good with halibut, so try them
with Grilled Halibut with Fried Green Apples, Bacon, and Horseradish
Sour Cream (page 184) or Grilled Halibut with Bacon–Red Onion Relish
and Roasted Red Pepper Mayonnaise (page 186).

Grilled Plums with Spicy Hoisin Glaze

SERVES 4

Putting fruit over the grilling fire gives it a slight smoky char that not only enhances the inherent sweetness of many fruits, but also deepens their flavors.

Because the purpose of grilling fruit is not really to cook it so much as to flavor it, doneness is not an issue. Therefore, the cooking time does not need to be exact, and it is easily regulated by visual clues. Added flavor is indicated by color, so go for darkness, making sure that you get a slight char on the fruit. When light grill marks or lightly blackened edges appear, the fruit is just about ready.

At this point, the sugar from the fruit has burned slightly, adding a faint caramel flavor. Now it is time to add another flavor dimension by brushing on a sugar-based glaze, such as the hoisin-based glaze we use here. When the sugar in the glaze melts, a new taste is added to the mix, along with the flavors of the glaze ingredients themselves. This is where it all comes together, so keep a sharp eye on the grill; allow the glaze to darken just slightly, which usually takes about thirty seconds to one minute, then pull the plums off the fire before the sugar is burned black.

1/4 cup hoisin sauce

2 tablespoons soy sauce

2 tablespoons white vinegar

2 tablespoons catsup or tomato puree

1 tablespoon minced fresh chile pepper of your choice

Salt and freshly cracked black pepper to taste

6 plums, halved and pitted

2 tablespoons vegetable oil

1. In a small bowl, combine the hoisin sauce, soy sauce, vinegar, catsup, chile pepper, and salt and pepper to taste and mix thoroughly.

2. Rub the plum halves lightly with the oil and place them on a grill, cut side down, over **a medium-hot fire.** Cook until the plums have acquired a bit of a sear, about 2 minutes, then flip them over, coat lightly with the glaze, and grill for another 30 seconds. Remove from the heat and serve, drizzled with any remaining glaze.

You've got to try these with Chinese-Style Baby Back Ribs with Ginger-Scallion Barbecue Sauce (page 252) or, for that matter, with any other Asian-style entrée you happen to be making.

tips for grilling fruit

THE FRUIT CHUTNEYS OF India, the banana stews of Africa, and the green mango salads of Thailand provide ready examples of spicy, savory uses for fruit, and from these dishes, it is only a short hop to grilling.

THE RANGE OF FRUIT that is amenable to grilling is virtually unlimited, from mangoes to apples to peaches. As a general rule, though, fruits that come from bushes and ground-hugging plants—such as berries—are often too delicate to stand up to grilling, while those that grow on trees have the requisite sturdiness.

AS BEFITS A CATEGORY of food that basically comes ready to eat, there is very little pre-grilling preparation necessary for fruits. Most fruits— bananas, pineapples, peaches, plums, apples, pears, and so on—can simply be halved and then pitted and/or cored before grilling. Larger fruits, such as pineapples, and very juicy fruits, such as oranges and other citrus, should be cut into thick slices. Generally it is best to leave the skin or peel on, since it helps the fruit retain its integrity over the fire.

TO PREVENT FRUIT FROM sticking to the grill, oil it before placing it on the grill grid. But use a very light hand; too much oil will not only interfere with the taste of the fruit, it may also cause flare-ups, which will give the fruit an ashy taste.

Grilled Tomato Halves with Cheesy Bread Crumbs

SERVES 4

When those late-summer tomatoes are heavy on the vine and you're looking for new ways to use them, try this. Fast and easy, it is excellent with grilled meat. Stale bread is best for the bread crumbs, but you can use fresh; you'll just need to leave them in the oven longer to get really dry. Since the bread crumbs will keep about two weeks when stored in an airtight container, I recommend you make a double batch while you're at it and keep them for next time you want this dish.

> 2 slices stale or fresh bread of your choice
> $^1/_4$ cup roughly chopped fresh parsley
> $^1/_4$ cup freshly grated Parmesan cheese
> 1 tablespoon finely grated lemon zest (yellow part only)
> Salt and freshly cracked black pepper to taste
> 4 tomatoes about the size of baseballs, cored and halved
> $^1/_4$ cup olive oil

1. Break the bread up into small pieces, discarding the crust. Place the pieces on a small baking sheet and toast in a preheated 200°F oven for about 1 hour, or until the pieces are dried and golden brown. Roughly crumble into small crumbs—you should have about $^1/_2$ cup.

2. In a small bowl, combine the bread crumbs with the parsley, cheese, lemon zest, and salt and pepper to taste. Mix well and set aside.

3. In a small bowl, combine the tomatoes, olive oil, and salt and pepper to taste and toss well. Place the tomatoes on the grill, cut side down, over **a medium-hot fire** and cook for 2 to 3 minutes, or until well browned. Remove from the grill, sprinkle generously with the crumbs, and serve.

I think these are particularly nice with any roasted red meat dish. Try them, for example, with Mediterranean-Style Slow-Roasted Beef Brisket (page 256) or Horseradish-and-Cumin-Crusted Whole Smoke-Roasted Sirloin with Mustard Aïoli (page 258).

Basic Black Beans

SERVES 6 TO 8

Also called turtle beans, these tasty and nutritious legumes are a staple in much of the world. They store very well, so it makes sense to make a double batch and keep them in the refrigerator. I think the beer adds a nice depth of flavor to the mix, particularly if you use an amber beer. However, if you prefer to keep your malt beverages for drinking straight, you can always just use water.

2 cups dried black beans

$^1/_4$ cup vegetable oil

2 large yellow onions, peeled and diced small

2 tablespoons minced garlic

$^1/_4$ cup white vinegar

2 cups water

1 bottle of your favorite beer

1 teaspoon chili powder

1 teaspoon ground cumin

4 dashes Tabasco sauce

1 teaspoon sugar

Salt and freshly cracked black pepper to taste

1. Soak the beans in cold water overnight, or for at least 5 hours, then drain and rinse well.

2. In a saucepan, heat the oil over medium-high heat until hot but not smoking. Add the onions and sauté, stirring occasionally, until transparent, 5 to 7 minutes. Add the garlic and sauté, stirring, for another minute. Add the vinegar, water, beer, chili powder, cumin, Tabasco, and sugar, and bring to a simmer.

3. Add the beans and return the mixture to a simmer, then reduce the heat to low, cover well, and cook for 3 hours, or until the beans are soft to the bite. If you think that additional liquid is needed, add more beer. Finish the dish by seasoning with salt and pepper to taste.

You can't go wrong serving these with any spicy hot dish.

Simple Latin-Style Rice and Beans

SERVES 4

Let's face it, a billion people can't be wrong—rice and beans is a great combination. Eaten all over the world, this perfect complement of proteins is innately satisfying and goes with just about anything. Our Latin-style version features black beans, cooked separately from the rice, and then mixed in at the end. If you're in a hurry, canned beans are perfectly acceptable here. I like to make up a double or triple batch of this stuff and keep it on hand in the refrigerator to heat up as a side dish or a snack. Make it a staple of your diet; you'll never get tired of it.

1 tablespoon vegetable oil

1 small yellow onion, peeled and minced

1 tablespoon minced garlic

$^1/_2$ jalapeño or other fresh chile pepper of your choice, minced

1 teaspoon cumin seeds (optional)

1 cup rice

$1^2/_3$ cups water

1 teaspoon kosher salt

1 cup cooked black beans (see page 299) or 1 16-ounce can black beans, drained and rinsed

$^1/_2$ cup roughly chopped fresh cilantro

Salt and freshly cracked black pepper to taste

1. In a medium saucepan, heat the oil over medium heat until hot but not smoking. Add the onion and sauté, stirring occasionally, until soft, 3 to 5 minutes. Add the garlic, chile pepper, and cumin seeds if you are using them and continue to sauté, stirring occasionally, for another 2 minutes.

2. Add the rice and sauté for 1 minute more. Add the water and salt and bring just to a simmer, then reduce the heat to medium-low, cover, and cook until the water is absorbed and the rice is tender, about 15 minutes.

3. When the rice is cooked, add the beans, mix well, and cook for about 5 minutes, stirring occasionally, to heat the beans through. Add the cilantro and salt and pepper to taste, stir well, and you're ready to serve.

Far be it from me to tell you exactly what to serve this with—it's a staple of the Latin world, and to my mind it goes with just about anything, particularly any dish with Latin flavor influences.

Ginger-Scallion Fried Rice

SERVES 4

This simple (and eggless) version of classic fried rice is flavorful but still plain enough to serve with many different types of grilled food. A full bunch of scallions might seem like a lot to use with this amount of rice, but try it and you may find a new appreciation for this pungent and slightly sweet member of the onion family.

Timing is important on the rice—you want to make sure it is dry but not burned, because cooking it until dry helps create those separated grains for which fried rice is known. It also helps if, after the rice is cooked, you put a tea towel over the pan and fit the lid on over the tea towel before you set the rice aside to sit for a few minutes. The towel absorbs a lot of the moisture that would otherwise keep the rice grains together.

2 tablespoons vegetable oil

3 tablespoons minced ginger

1 tablespoon minced garlic

1 cup rice

$1^3/_4$ cups water

$^1/_4$ cup sesame oil

$^1/_2$ red bell pepper, seeded and diced large

$^1/_2$ green bell pepper, seeded and diced large

6 medium mushrooms, trimmed, cleaned, and thinly sliced

1 bunch scallions (white and green parts), thinly sliced

$^1/_4$ cup soy sauce

Salt and freshly cracked black pepper to taste

1. In a medium saucepan, heat the vegetable oil over medium heat until hot but not smoking. Add the ginger and garlic and sauté, stirring occasionally, for 2 minutes. Add the rice and sauté, stirring occasionally, for 3 minutes. Add the water, cover, reduce the heat to low, and cook until the water is absorbed and the rice is tender, 15 to 20 minutes. Remove from the heat and set aside for a few minutes.

2. In a large sauté pan, heat the sesame oil over medium heat until hot but not smoking. Add the bell peppers and mushrooms and sauté, stirring occasionally, for 2 minutes. Add the cooked rice and sauté for a few minutes to heat through, stirring occasionally. Add the scallions and soy sauce and stir until thoroughly mixed. Season to taste with salt and pepper and serve.

This is another of those all-purpose dishes, an excellent accompaniment to any dish with Asian flavors.

top ten grilled things to add to risotto

- Grilled shrimp
- Grilled eggplant
- Grilled mushrooms
- Grilled sliced pork tenderloin
- Grilled sliced chicken tenderloin
- Grilled figs and ham
- Grilled quail
- Grilled fennel
- Grilled peppers and onions
- Grilled squid or octopus

Tomato Risotto with Toasted Pine Nuts

SERVES 4

Risotto is easy to make, it just takes a little watching and tending. Basically it's rice that you cook by adding liquid in relatively small batches, allowing the grain to absorb each batch before you add the next. The rich, creamy texture that results makes it an outstanding side dish for grilled foods.

> 2 cups chicken stock
> 1 large tomato, cored and diced small
> 1 cup white wine
> 2 tablespoons unsalted butter
> $1/2$ yellow onion, peeled and diced medium
> 1 tablespoon minced garlic
> 1 cup arborio rice
> 1 cup pine nuts, toasted in a 350°F oven until golden brown,
>   7 to 10 minutes
> 2 tablespoons freshly grated good-quality Parmesan cheese
> Salt and freshly cracked black pepper to taste

1. In a medium saucepan, combine the chicken stock, diced tomato, and white wine. Bring to a boil over high heat, then reduce the heat to low and allow to simmer gently while you proceed with the recipe.

2. Melt the butter in a large sauté pan over medium heat. Add the onion and garlic and sauté, stirring occasionally, until the onion is transparent, 5 to 7 minutes.

3. Add the rice and stir for a minute or so, just to coat the grains. Pour in 1 cup of the hot liquid, reduce the heat to low, and cook, stirring frequently, until the liquid is almost completely absorbed. At that point, add $1/2$ cup more of the hot liquid. Repeat this process, adding the liquid in $1/2$-cup doses and tasting frequently to monitor the texture, until the rice is creamy and firm, neither hard nor mushy. Stir in the pine nuts and cheese, season to taste with salt and pepper, and serve at once.

This is a really nice side dish to serve with any Mediterranean-flavored entrée, such as Grilled Swordfish with Artichokes, Tomatoes, and Olives (page 170) or Grilled Veal Chops with Expensive Mushrooms (page 138).

the ancestral grain

THROUGHOUT THE WORLD, THE most common source of food is not vegetables or fish or even meat, but cereal grains. In fact, four specific grains—corn, rice, wheat, and sorghum—provide the large majority of the calories consumed by human beings. Recently, in the kind of discovery that makes science seem as weird as science fiction, researchers at Texas A&M University uncovered evidence that three out of four of these mega-important grains share a common ancestor.

THE ANCESTRAL GRAIN, WHICH flourished some sixty-five million years ago, was a kind of grassy weed, with long blades for leaves and small flowers at the stem tips, similar to those of the sorghum plant. As the earth's land masses separated, this proto-grain evolved differently on each of three continents. In Asia, it became rice; in the Americas, corn; and in Africa, sorghum. But even after sixty-five million years, and despite the fact that these three descendants now seem like completely separate plants, all share common genes at the DNA level.

Simple Lentils

SERVES 4

Because of their shape and size, lentils don't have to be presoaked before cooking, making them the most convenient members of the healthful pulse family, which also includes chickpeas and beans of all types. These disk-shaped little legumes, with a rich, earthy flavor, come in a number of colors. For this dish, you can use brown lentils, green lentils, or the smaller gray-green ones known as *de Puy,* which are harder to find but have a wonderful flavor. Red and yellow lentils, which are actually hulled versions of the darker varieties, don't work as well here because they don't hold their shape when cooked.

$^1/_2$ pound (about 1 cup) green, brown, or de Puy lentils

3 cups water

Salt and freshly cracked black pepper to taste

1 small red onion, peeled and diced small

2 tomatoes about the size of baseballs, cored and diced small

1 cup roughly chopped fresh parsley

$^1/_3$ cup olive oil

$^1/_4$ cup fresh lemon juice (about 1 lemon)

$^1/_4$ cup pine nuts, toasted in a 350°F oven for 8 to 10 minutes, or until golden brown (optional)

1. In a medium saucepan, combine the lentils, water, and salt and pepper to taste. Bring to a rapid boil over high heat, reduce the heat to medium, and simmer until the lentils are tender to the bite but not mushy, about 30 minutes. Drain and set aside to cool to room temperature.

2. In a medium bowl, combine the onion, tomatoes, and parsley. Add the cooled lentils and mix well.

3. In a small bowl, whisk together the oil and lemon juice. Add this to the lentil mixture, toss well, and stir in the pine nuts if using them. (This dish will keep, covered and refrigerated, for 3 to 4 days.)

> You might try this as a side dish alongside a meat dish that has a lot of flavors going on, such as Grilled Vietnamese-Style Beef Skewers with Green Mango Slaw (page 124) or Grilled Sirloin and Apricot Skewers with Pomegranate Vinaigrette (page 126). It's also nice with Almond-Crusted Grilled Salmon with Garlic Sauce (page 165).

Cornmeal Mush with Okra and Tomatoes

SERVES 4

Because of the rage for Italian cooking in this country, we Americans are most likely to know cornmeal mush as polenta, but the technique of slowly cooking cornmeal in hot water is used in many cultures. Here we borrow a page from Southern cooks, adding some tomatoes and okra to the mush to make an outstanding side dish for roasted or grilled meats or any really spicy food.

4 cups water

1 teaspoon salt

1 cup yellow cornmeal

Salt and freshly cracked black pepper to taste

1 tablespoon olive oil

$^1/_2$ medium yellow onion, peeled and diced small

1$^1/_2$ teaspoons minced garlic

1 cup $^1/_4$-inch-thick slices okra

2 large tomatoes, cored and diced large

2 tablespoons roughly chopped fresh parsley

1. Combine the water and salt in a medium saucepan and bring to a boil over high heat. Add the cornmeal in a slow, steady stream, whisking constantly to prevent it from clumping. Once all the cornmeal has been added, reduce the heat to low and cook for 30 minutes, stirring very frequently. If the mush begins to get too thick, add a bit of warm water. *To test for doneness:* Look for the mush to pull away from the sides of the pan and to have a creamy consistency with no graininess when tasted. When it has reached this stage, remove from the heat and season to taste with salt and pepper.

2. Meanwhile, heat the olive oil in a small sauté pan over medium heat until hot but not smoking. Add the onion and sauté, stirring occasionally, until transparent, 5 to 7 minutes. Add the garlic and sauté, stirring a few times, for 1 minute to soften. Add the okra and tomatoes and cook for 5 to 7 minutes, or until the vegetables are slightly softened.

3. Pour the mush out onto a platter or individual serving plates, top with the okra mixture, sprinkle with the parsley, and serve at once.

This slightly unusual dish provides an unbelievable flavor balance for Puerto Rican–Style Barbecued Pork Butt with Two Sauces and Corn Bread (page 262).

Green Apple and Celery Root Salad with Bacon-Buttermilk Dressing

Along with parsley root, celery root—also called celeriac—is an almost-forgotten, deeply underappreciated vegetable. Knobby and brown on the outside and white on the inside, it comes from a variety of celery grown specifically for this purpose. Although we call it celery root, it is actually not a root at all, but the lowest part of the stem of the plant, which grows under the ground. Knobs of celeriac, which may be as small as an apple or as large as a cantaloupe, have a firm, crunchy texture and a fresh, aromatic flavor reminiscent of the taste of celery ribs, with a kind of grassy undertone like parsley. Like many other vegetables that we now consider somewhat exotic, celeriac was once quite popular and is now beginning to come into favor again as our national vegetable consciousness expands. Here we combine it with crunchy green apples and dress it with a rather assertive bacon-buttermilk dressing, which celery root has both the texture and the flavor to stand up to.

For the Dressing

> 6 slices bacon
>
> 2 scallions (white and green parts), minced
>
> 1 tablespoon minced garlic
>
> 2 tablespoons sour cream
>
> 2 tablespoons mayonnaise
>
> $^1/_2$ cup buttermilk
>
> 1 tablespoon fresh lemon juice
>
> 2 dashes Tabasco sauce
>
> $^1/_4$ cup roughly chopped fresh parsley
>
> Salt and freshly cracked black pepper to taste
>
> 3 Granny Smith apples, cored and cut into matchsticks
>
> $1^1/_2$ pounds celery root (celeriac), peeled, cored, and cut into matchsticks
>
> 1 red onion, peeled, halved, and thinly sliced
>
> 1 head radicchio, thinly sliced (optional)

1. In a sauté pan over medium heat, cook the bacon until crisp, 6 to 8 minutes. Drain on a paper towel or brown paper bag, then roughly chop.

2. In a medium bowl, combine the remaining ingredients for the dressing. Add the bacon pieces and mix well.

3. In another medium bowl, combine the apples, celery root, and onions. Add the dressing, mix well, and refrigerate. Serve as is or on a bed of radicchio.

I would serve this with a pork entrée like Chuletas: Thin Grilled Pork Chops with Simple Tomato Relish (page 147).

Jícama-Apple Salad with Orange-Mustard Dressing

SERVES 4 TO 6

When asked to describe jícama, I usually say that it's like a cross between an apple and a potato, which is pretty close. Its crisp, juicy texture is its most distinctive characteristic. Here we add some apples and a red onion and toss the mixture with a light mustard-mint-orange juice dressing for a bright, fresh, crispy salad.

For the Dressing

$1/2$ cup orange juice

2 tablespoons fresh lime juice (about 1 lime)

2 tablespoons cider vinegar

2 tablespoons grainy mustard

2 tablespoons brown sugar

$1/4$ cup roughly chopped fresh mint

Salt and freshly cracked black pepper to taste

1 jícama, peeled and cut into matchsticks

3 Red Delicious apples, cut into matchsticks

1 red onion, peeled, halved, and thinly sliced

1. Make the dressing: In a small bowl, combine all the ingredients and whisk together well.

2. In a medium bowl, combine the jícama, apples, and onion. Add the dressing, toss well to coat, and serve. (This salad will last, covered and refrigerated, for 3 days.)

This goes really well with Mexican-flavored dishes like Barbecued Whole Game Hens with Orange, Oregano, and Cumin Seed (page 265).

Pungent Carrot and Cucumber Salad
with Ginger and Garlic

Fresh and clean-tasting, this slightly sweet, slightly hot combination packs a lot of punch. Plus, the little trick of melting a couple of ice cubes in the salad right before serving makes the carrots and cucumbers amazingly crisp and refreshing. This salad will keep for a while, but it is best when mixed as close to serving as possible.

2 medium carrots, peeled and sliced into $^1/_2$-inch rounds

2 medium cucumbers, peeled, halved lengthwise, seeded,
    and cut into $^1/_2$-inch slices

2 tablespoons minced ginger

1 tablespoon minced garlic

1 tablespoon minced fresh chile pepper of your choice

2 tablespoons sugar

$^1/_3$ cup rice vinegar (or substitute white vinegar)

2 tablespoons fish sauce (optional)

Salt and freshly cracked white pepper to taste
    (or substitute black pepper)

2 ice cubes

1. Fill a small pot with cold water and a tray of ice cubes. In a small saucepan, bring 1 quart of salted water to a boil over high heat. Throw the carrots into the boiling water and cook for 30 seconds. Drain, immediately plunge into the ice water to stop the cooking process, and drain again.

2. In a medium bowl, combine the carrots with all the remaining ingredients except the ice cubes and toss well to combine. Chill until ready to serve.

3. About 10 minutes before you're going to serve the dish, toss on the ice cubes and stir occasionally. When the cubes have melted, you're ready to serve.

This salad goes well with any Asian-flavored entrée like Hoisin Chicken
Breasts with Grilled Peppers and Onions (page 199) or Neo-Postmodern
Polynesian Grilled Chicken (page 202).

Latin-Flavored Coleslaw with Grilled Avocados

SERVES 4 TO 6

The mixture of cabbages and carrots is most colorful, the creamy, sweet-hot dressing has lots of flavors going for it, and to top it all off, the avocados are grilled. Now, just as you may be, I was a little skeptical of this unusual dish at first. But Mark Hall, aka Big Red, chef of the Blue Room, first tried putting avocados over the fire to make a garnish for a Mexican dish, and it turned out to be a real winner. Aided by the chili powder and cumin, the cut side of the avocado should acquire a well-seared flavorful coating. Ripe but firm is the ideal texture for the avocado, but that's always tough to find; in this dish, you can get away with very firm, mushy, or basically anything except rock-hard.

For the Dressing

$^1/_2$ cup mayonnaise (jarred or homemade, see page 344 for recipe)

$^1/_3$ cup olive oil

$^1/_3$ cup fresh lime juice (about 2 large limes)

$^1/_4$ cup red wine vinegar

2 ears corn, husked, desilked, blanched in boiling salted water for
   2 minutes, drained, and kernels cut off the cob (about 1 cup kernels)

2 tablespoons sugar

2 tablespoons catsup

4 to 10 dashes Tabasco sauce, depending on your taste for heat

Salt and freshly cracked black pepper to taste

2 cups shredded green cabbage

1 cup shredded red cabbage

1 cup shredded carrots (about 1 medium carrot)

3 ripe but firm avocados, halved and pitted but not peeled

2 tablespoons olive oil

1 tablespoon chili powder

1 tablespoon ground cumin

Salt and freshly cracked black pepper to taste

1. Make the dressing: In a food processor or blender, combine all the ingredients and puree until smooth.

2. In a medium bowl, combine the green cabbage, red cabbage, and carrots. Add the dressing, mix well, cover, and refrigerate.

3. Sprinkle the avocados with the olive oil, chili powder, cumin, and salt and pepper to taste. Place them on the grill over **a medium-hot fire,** cut side down, and cook for 3 to 5 minutes, or until seared—you are looking for some real color here. Pull the avocados off the grill and, as soon as they are cool enough to handle, turn them out of their skins, slice them, and serve them on top of generous helpings of the slaw. (If the avocados don't slip out of their skins easily, just spoon out chunks on top of the slaw.)

This is excellent with any Latin-flavored dish. I particularly like it with Sweet-Spicy Barbecued Spareribs with Green Chile Sauce (page 250).

avocado heritage

WHEN I WAS A child I hated avocados, but I always felt slightly guilty about it. That was because I didn't like to disappoint my father, who invariably purchased avocados whenever they appeared in our local supermarket, brought them home to ripen in a paper bag, and then served them up as a special treat.

I REFUSED TO EAT them, but he didn't give up. He valiantly kept trying to convince me that I should enjoy the rich taste of this rather odd fruit, which he served in thin slices, perched on a slab of iceberg lettuce and laced with the sweet, bright-orange bottled concoction known as "French dressing." But to no avail—like many kids, I found the unctuous fruit just this side of disgusting.

SOME YEARS LATER, ON a trip to Mexico, I was served an avocado dish that was kind of like a very chunky, super-spicy guacamole. Since I was a guest in the house, I went ahead and ate it despite misgivings. As my teeth slid through the smooth flesh of the avocado and my mouth was filled with its rich, herby, buttery flavor, I finally understood my father's mania. In fact, I couldn't understand how I could ever have found this taste unappealing, and ever since, I have considered avocados a special treat.

SO THE MORAL IS, don't worry if your kids won't eat something that you really like. Just keep on telling them how wonderful it is and, when they get to be adults, they will undoubtedly become fanatics just as you are today. As an added advantage, whenever they eat this food they will think of you, just as I never eat an avocado without thinking of my father.

Grilled Eggplant and Bread Salad for a Crowd

SERVES 8

This is another version of the classic bread salad. The twist here is that we grill some onions and tomatoes and then puree them to make a dressing with a tasty smoky dimension. But we're not done with the grill after that—we also grill up the eggplant and some bread. Then the eggplant and bread are combined with a number of other Mediterranean flavors in a multidimensional salad. This is an excellent dish when you are serving a crowd of people on a summer afternoon.

For the Dressing

4 plum tomatoes, halved

1 large red onion, peeled and cut into rings about 1 inch thick

3 tablespoons vegetable oil

Salt and freshly cracked black pepper to taste

2 tablespoons minced garlic

1/2 cup balsamic vinegar

1/4 cup fresh lemon juice (about 1 lemon)

3 tablespoons grainy mustard

3/4 cup olive oil

2 large eggplants, cut lengthwise into planks about 1 inch thick

1/3 cup vegetable oil

Salt and freshly cracked black pepper to taste

4 thick slices crusty bread

4 plum tomatoes, diced large

1 medium red onion, peeled and diced small

1/2 cup Kalamata or other brine-cured black olives, pitted

1/2 cup roughly chopped fresh basil

1 tablespoon minced garlic

1. Make the dressing: Rub the tomatoes and onions with the vegetable oil, sprinkle with salt and pepper to taste, and place on the grill over **a medium-hot fire.** Cook for 4 to 5 minutes per side, or until nicely browned. Remove them from the fire and, as soon as they are cool enough to handle, cut into small chunks and put in a food processor or blender. Add the garlic, balsamic vinegar, lemon juice, and mustard and pulse until the mixture is pureed but still somewhat chunky. With the machine running, drizzle in the olive oil just until incorporated. Transfer to a bowl, cover, and refrigerate.

continued

2. Rub the eggplant planks with the vegetable oil and sprinkle with salt and pepper to taste. Grill over **a medium-hot fire** for 4 to 5 minutes per side, or until well browned. At the same time, place the bread on the grill around the edges of the fire, where the heat is low, and toast until fairly dry and golden brown, 4 to 5 minutes. Remove the eggplant and bread from the grill as they are done and, when cool enough to handle, cut them into medium chunks.

3. In a large bowl, combine the eggplant, tomatoes, red onion, olives, basil, and garlic, season to taste with salt and pepper, and toss well. Just before serving, add the bread to the mixture, stir the dressing well, and add just enough dressing to moisten the ingredients. Toss well and serve at once to prevent the bread from becoming soggy.

> I like this with substantial, rather rich meat dishes like
> Herb-Crusted Pork Loin Roast with Creamy Polenta and
> Roasted Tomato-Garlic Sauce (page 260).

Grilled Spicy New Potato Salad

SERVES 4

Served hot, this dish is like grilled hash browns; served cold, it's a flavorful and unusual potato salad. The deep flavor of well-browned potatoes is the star here, so make sure you leave them on the grill long enough to get well seared. You can use any small potatoes you want—Yukon Golds are excellent—and if you don't have mustard seeds, don't let that stop you, just substitute a couple of tablespoons of prepared mustard.

> 16 new potatoes about the size of golf balls
> $^1/_4$ cup olive oil
> Salt and freshly cracked black pepper to taste
> $^1/_3$ cup extra virgin olive oil
> $^1/_4$ cup mustard seeds, toasted if you want
> $^1/_4$ cup roughly chopped fresh parsley
> 1 tablespoon minced garlic
> 2 tablespoons fresh lemon juice (about $^1/_2$ lemon)
> 6 to 16 dashes Tabasco sauce, depending on your taste for heat

1. In a large saucepan, bring 2 quarts of salted water to a rapid boil over high heat. Toss in your potatoes and cook for about 15 minutes, or until the potatoes can be pierced with a fork but still offer considerable resistance—you want them to be firm but not crunchy. Drain, run under cold water, and drain again.

2. Halve the potatoes and thread them onto skewers, with the cut sides all facing the same way. Rub them lightly with the olive oil, sprinkle with salt and pepper to taste, and place them on the grill over **a medium-hot fire.** Cook for 3 to 5 minutes, or they are until golden brown.

3. Slide the potatoes off the skewers into a medium bowl and add all the remaining ingredients. Season to taste and toss well. This dish can be served warm or cold; it will keep, covered and refrigerated, for 3 to 4 days.

This salad goes great with any beef dish, such as Horseradish-and-Cumin-Crusted Whole Smoke-Roasted Sirloin with Mustard Aïoli (page 258).

Grilled Sweet Potato Salad with Sweet-Sour Bacon Dressing

SERVES 4

This version of hot German potato salad uses the more flavorful sweet potato in place of the traditional white potato. The key to success with this dish is the proper blanching of the sweet potatoes—too little and they are hard, too much and they fall apart on the grill. Start checking the potato slices after about eight minutes in the boiling water, and take them out as soon as you can easily stick a fork through them without having them break apart.

3 medium sweet potatoes, peeled and cut into rounds about 1 inch thick

3 tablespoons vegetable oil

Salt and freshly cracked black pepper to taste

4 slices bacon, diced medium

1 medium red onion, peeled and thinly sliced

1 tablespoon minced garlic

$^1/_2$ cup white vinegar

$^1/_3$ cup olive oil

$^1/_4$ cup sugar

$^1/_3$ cup chopped fresh parsley

1. Blanch the sweet potatoes in a large pot of boiling salted water until they are tender but not mushy, 8 to 10 minutes. You should be able to stick a fork through the potatoes easily but still feel some resistance, and the slices should not break apart easily. Drain and cool to room temperature.

2. In a small bowl, combine the potatoes, vegetable oil, and salt and pepper to taste and toss well to coat the potatoes. Place the potatoes on the grill over **a hot fire** and cook until well browned, 3 to 5 minutes. Remove from the grill, place in a medium bowl, and set aside.

3. In a large sauté pan over medium heat, cook the bacon pieces until they just start to crisp, about 6 minutes. Remove the bacon to paper towels to drain.

4. Pour out all but about 2 tablespoons of the bacon fat from the pan. Add the onion slices and cook for 2 minutes, stirring occasionally, then add the garlic and cook for another 2 minutes. Remove the pan from the heat and stir in the vinegar, olive oil, sugar, reserved bacon, and salt and pepper to taste.

5. Add the bacon mixture to the grilled potatoes and toss well. Sprinkle with the parsley and serve.

I like this as a side dish with a giant, thick steak like Grilled Delmonico Steak Adobo with Charred Spring Onions and Sweet Corn Relish (page 131) or Pepper-Crusted Grilled Filet Mignon with Blue Cheese Butter and Roasted Garlic Mash (page 133).

Indian-Style Sweet Potato Salad

SERVES 4

Next time you're thinking of making potato salad, trot this one out. It's not like Mom used to make, but this Indian-inspired version is easy to put together and has a lot of interesting flavors going on. A nice addition if you have some around the house is a handful of toasted sesame seeds sprinkled over the salad just before you serve it. Also, if you're one of those people who is not a fan of cilantro, you can substitute parsley here.

> 3 medium sweet potatoes, peeled and cut into 1-inch cubes
>
> $^1/_3$ cup red wine vinegar
>
> $^1/_3$ cup fresh lime juice (about 3 small limes)
>
> $^1/_4$ cup molasses
>
> $^1/_4$ cup catsup
>
> 2 tablespoons Dijon mustard
>
> 1 tablespoon curry powder
>
> $^1/_4$ cup raisins
>
> 1 teapoon minced fresh chile pepper of your choice
>
> $^1/_4$ cup roughly chopped fresh cilantro
>
> Salt and freshly cracked black pepper to taste

1. In a large pot, bring 2 quarts of salted water to a rapid boil over high heat. Throw your sweet potatoes in and cook until they can be pierced fairly easily with a fork but still offer a good amount of resistance, 8 to 10 minutes. Drain the potatoes, rinse with cold water, and refrigerate until chilled, at least 30 minutes.

2. In a medium bowl, combine all the remaining ingredients and mix well. Add the chilled sweet potatoes, toss well to coat, and serve. (This salad will keep, covered and refrigerated, for 3 to 4 days.)

I might serve this alongside Chinese-Style Baby Back Ribs with Ginger-Scallion Barbecue Sauce (page 252) or Chinese-Spiced Whole Duck with Orange–Green Peppercorn Sauce (page 270).

yam i am?

YOU KNOW ALL THOSE yams that occasionally show up in the produce bins at the supermarket, the ones with the odd shapes, wild colors, and great names like Jewel, Garnet, and Beauregard? Well, the fact is they are not really yams at all; they are varieties of sweet potato. Real yams are starchier tubers, grown in most tropical countries of the world but seldom available in the United States. They are somewhat sweeter and moister but less nourishing than sweet potatoes. Does it make any difference? Only to a botanist. Those fancy sweet potatoes are still outstanding even if you do want to call them yams.

Chickpea Salad with Cumin and Mint

Here's a Middle Eastern–inspired salad that's tasty, flavorful, healthy, and easy to make. If you haven't eaten chickpeas before, try substituting this for the pasta salad on your next summer buffet, and I believe you'll be a convert. Canned chickpeas are perfectly acceptable to my taste buds, and they are far easier to deal with than the dried version, so they might actually be your first choice here.

> 1 cup dried chickpeas or 1 15-ounce can chickpeas
>
> 1 tablespoon salt
>
> $^1/_3$ cup olive oil
>
> $^1/_4$ cup fresh lemon juice (about 1 lemon)
>
> 1 tablespoon minced garlic
>
> 1 red bell pepper, halved, seeded, and diced medium
>
> $^1/_2$ cup roughly chopped scallions (white and green parts)
>
> $^1/_4$ cup roughly chopped fresh mint
>
> 2 tablespoons cumin seeds, toasted if you want, or 1 tablespoon ground cumin
>
> 1 tablespoon minced jalapeño or other fresh chile pepper of your choice (optional)
>
> 2 bunches watercress, trimmed, washed, and dried

1. If you are using dried chickpeas place them in a large pot, cover with water, and let soak overnight, or for at least 5 hours. Drain and rinse two or three times.

2. Return the chickpeas to the pot, cover with water again, add salt, and bring to a boil over high heat. Immediately reduce the heat to medium and simmer for 1 hour to 1 hour and 15 minutes, or until the chickpeas are tender but not mushy. Drain and rinse thoroughly with cold water. If you are using canned chickpeas, simply drain and rinse them.

3. Place the chickpeas in a medium bowl, add all the remaining ingredients except the watercress, and toss well. Cover and refrigerate until well chilled, at least 30 minutes. When chilled, place the watercress on a platter or individual serving plates, top with the chickpea mixture, and serve.

This is nice with Peach and Chicken Skewers with Middle Eastern Shake and Simple Raisin Sauce (page 112).

Chickpea Salad with Horseradish-Yogurt Dressing

SERVES 4

When I think of cold vegetable salads, I think of the southeastern Mediterranean, where there is an awesome vegetable tradition. These preparations are simple in terms of ingredients but complex in terms of flavor. Please don't let any hang-ups you have about chickpeas turn you off to this recipe. Try it, and I bet you will add it to your summer salad repertoire. If you have any leftovers, they're easy to deal with the next day—just puree and thin out a bit with water for a hummus-like concoction for dipping or stuffing pita bread. As always with chickpeas, it's much easier to use the canned variety here.

1 cup dried chickpeas or 1 15-ounce can chickpeas

1 cucumber, peeled, seeded, and diced small

1 tomato about the size of a baseball, cored and diced small

1 small red onion, peeled and diced small

$^{1}/_{4}$ cup roughly chopped fresh dill

For the Dressing

$^{1}/_{2}$ cup plain yogurt

$^{1}/_{4}$ cup fresh lemon juice (about 1 lemon)

$^{1}/_{4}$ cup olive oil

$^{1}/_{4}$ cup prepared horseradish

Salt and freshly cracked black pepper to taste

1. If you are using dried chickpeas, place them in a large pot, cover with water, and let them soak overnight, or for at least 5 hours. Drain and rinse two or three times.

2. Return the chickpeas to the pot, cover with water again, add 1 tablespoon salt, and bring to a boil over high heat. Immediately reduce the heat to medium and simmer for 1 hour to 1 hour and 15 minutes, or until the chickpeas are tender but not mushy. Drain and rinse thoroughly with cold water. If you are using canned chickpeas, simply drain and rinse them.

3. In a medium bowl, combine the chickpeas, cucumbers, tomatoes, onion, and dill and toss well.

4. Make the dressing: In a small bowl, combine all the ingredients and mix well.

5. Pour the dressing over the chickpea mixture, toss, and chill before serving.

I think this is an excellent combination with Grilled Lamb Skewers with Apricots (page 116).

Fava Bean Salad with Lemon and Shaved Pecorino Romano Cheese

SERVES 4

I really enjoy fresh fava beans. Over the past couple of years I've even taken to grow-ing them in my garden to be sure I have a good supply in the summer. This simple salad features the mellow flavor of the fava spiked with a little lemon and garlic. There is some labor involved in dealing with this bean—you first shuck it as you would green peas, then peel off the inner lining—but it's well worth it. If you're not feeling ambitious, this recipe also works very well with lima beans or just about any other fresh pea or bean.

2 tablespoons salt

4 cups shucked fresh fava beans

$^1/_4$ cup extra virgin olive oil

2 tablespoons minced garlic

$^1/_4$ cup fresh lemon juice (about 1 lemon)

Salt and freshly cracked black pepper to taste

$^1/_2$ cup shaved pecorino romano, Asiago, or Parmesan cheese

2 tablespoons roughly chopped fresh parsley, for garnish

1. Fill the sink or a large bowl with ice and water. In a medium saucepan, bring 2 quarts of water and the salt to a rolling boil. Drop the fava beans into the water and blanch for 4 minutes. *To check for doneness:* Just eat one of the beans—it should be tender but not mushy. Drain the favas and immediately drop them into the ice water for a few minutes to stop the cooking process. Drain again and slip off the outer skins.

2. In a small bowl, combine the beans with the olive oil, garlic, lemon juice, and salt and pepper to taste and toss well. Add the cheese, sprinkle with the parsley, and serve.

This salad is nice with a pasta dish like Linguine with Grilled Shrimp and Black Olives (page 87).

fava pharmacy

ALTHOUGH STILL A RARITY in America, the fava is perhaps the single most popular bean in the world. Also known as broad beans, these subtly flavored legumes are among the most ancient of cultivated foods and today are favorites from China to India to the Middle East to Italy. Throughout North Africa street vendors selling freshly cooked favas as snacks are a common sight, and in Egypt, the national dish is a version of fava bean salad. Favas are also reputed to have antimalarial properties, and contain high concentrations of a chemical effective in treating, among other things, Parkinson's disease.

Romaine and Bulgur Salad

SERVES 4

Here we have the ingredients of the classic Middle Eastern dish tabboulleh, retrofitted into a more familiar salad form. The bulgur acts as a sort of substitute for croutons. I like the contrast of the crisp romaine and the tender bulgur, and the lemon and mint in the dressing help to spritz it all up.

For the Dressing

$^1/_2$ cup olive oil

$^1/_4$ cup fresh lemon juice (about 1 lemon)

1 teaspoon minced garlic

1 tablespoon ground cumin

2 tablespoons roughly chopped fresh mint

Salt and freshly cracked black pepper to taste

1 cup bulgur

$1^1/_2$ cups boiling water

Pinch of salt

1 head romaine lettuce, washed, dried, and torn into medium-sized pieces

2 tomatoes, cored and quartered

1 cucumber, peeled, halved, seeded, and thinly sliced on the bias

1 red onion, peeled and sliced into thin rings

8 radishes, cleaned and thinly sliced

1. Make the dressing: In a small bowl, combine all the ingredients and mix well. Cover and refrigerate.

2. In a small bowl, combine the bulgur, boiling water, and salt and set aside to steep for about 20 minutes. When the bulgur is done, it should be tender but not mushy.

3. In a large bowl, combine the romaine, tomatoes, cucumbers, onion, and radishes. Stir the dressing well, add just enough to moisten all the ingredients, and toss well. Place the salad on a platter or individual serving plates, sprinkle generously with the bulgur, and serve.

I like this with all kinds of dishes, but particularly with Mediterranean-influenced preps like Grilled Mackerel with Expensive Olive Oil, Lemon, and Oregano (page 192).

Bridget's Couscous Salad for a Crowd

Although some people think couscous is a grain, it is actually a form of pasta. if you have ever seen the painstaking method of making it by hand, you'll really appreciate the instant version. Here we add nuts, dried fruit, and seasonings to create a dish that is excellent all by itself. It also works beautifully as a bed for grilled chicken, pork, lamb, seafood, or, in fact, just about anything. The best strategy is to prepare the couscous first, then pull the food right off the grill and set it onto the couscous so the juices can drip down and mingle with the tiny pasta.

$3^1/_2$ cups "instant" couscous (about 2 boxes)

$4^1/_2$ cups boiling water

About 1 tablespoon olive oil

1 cup slivered blanched almonds, toasted in a 400°F oven until lightly
    browned, about 5 minutes, then roughly chopped

1 cup dried apricots, thinly sliced

1 cup golden raisins

$^1/_4$ cup grated orange zest (orange part only; about 1 large orange)

$^1/_4$ cup roughly chopped fresh mint

2 tablespoons ground cumin

6 tablespoons extra virgin olive oil

6 tablespoons fresh lemon juice (about $1^1/_2$ lemons)

Salt and freshly cracked black pepper to taste

1. In a large bowl, combine the couscous and boiling water and allow to stand for about 15 minutes, or until all the water is absorbed and the couscous has expanded and become soft.

2. Fluff the couscous with a fork. As soon as the couscous is cool enough to handle, rub your hands with a little olive oil and gently rub the couscous between your hands to make sure all the lumps are broken up. Add all the remaining ingredients and mix together gently until well combined. Serve warm or cold.

**This is a versatile dish, excellent as an all-purpose starch
backup dish anytime you have a crowd over for a meal.**

couscous à go-go

A FEW YEARS AGO, while in Tunisia, we were taken to view what was billed as the "World's Largest Couscous Factory," the Couscousserie du Sud in the coastal city of Sfax. The visit was remarkable not so much for the rather prosaic factory tour (the highlight of which involved putting on little paper hats and shoes, supposedly to keep the factory clean), but for the demonstration we saw in a courtyard just outside the factory doors. There, on a raised platform, sat four middle-aged Tunisian women in traditional fancy dress, patiently making couscous by hand in the old-fashioned way.

THIS EXACTING AND VIRTUALLY never-ending process involves mixing semolina flour with a bit of water and working it with your fingers to form small lumps; spreading the lumps out in the sun to dry; reworking the lumps with your hands to form smaller lumps; steaming the resulting couscous; and then resteaming it.

WHILE THE WOMEN'S HANDS moved incredibly fast, it was obvious that few people in the modern world could afford the time it takes to make this artisanal product. Our guide explained that many rich urban families deal with this problem by having women from the countryside come to their houses once every few months to make a large supply of couscous. For most other people—and certainly for most people outside North Africa—the solution is to buy instant couscous, which has been precooked and can be reconstituted either by soaking or by steaming.

Different people call them by different names, but the one thing all the recipes in this chapter have in common is that they are power-packed. They are designed, each and every one, to deliver a ton of intense flavor with very little effort.

BIG FLAVORS WITH LITTLE EFFORT

condiments and pickles, spice rubs and pastes

Wherever you go around the world, people use relishes, pickles, and condiments for this purpose. It might be a puckery dill pickle from the American South, an incendiary mango chutney from India, or a salt-laced pickled turnip from the Middle East, but it's going to give you some real taste, and it's going to be something that can be made in advance and kept on hand to spike any meal that needs a lift.

Here you will find such "little dishes" as Sweet-and-Smoky Pickled Corn Relish for spooning over grilled chicken or pork, and Apricot-Ginger

Relish to go with that grilled fish. Grilling a steak? Time to pull out the All-Purpose Basil-Chile Finishing Sauce or the Lime-Pickled Mangoes for a dynamic flavor boost. You'll also find all-purpose condiments to just set out on the table, like Spicy Thai Tomato-Herb Relish, Saigon Paste, or Pickled Ginger Strips. We've included seven individual spice rubs and pastes, too, arranged in order from simplest to most complex. Rub one of these mixtures on whatever you are about to grill, and you'll be rewarded with a slightly crunchy crust on the outside of the food that delivers a fantastic burst of flavor.

So stock up your pantry with a few of these recipes, and in about two minutes you'll be able to turn a simple piece of grilled meat or fish, or even some grilled vegetables, into a meal laced with deep, strong, complex flavors.

Red Grape–Pear Chutney

Lime-Ginger Chutney

Sweet-and-Smoky Pickled Corn Relish

Ginger-Date Chutney

Apricot-Ginger Relish

Spicy Thai Tomato-Herb Relish

Simple Spicy Grilled Tomato Salsa

Spicy Lime-Marinated Cabbage and Onion

Clove-Pickled Peaches

Pickled Ginger Strips

Preserved Limes

Pickled Pineapple

Lime-Pickled Mangoes with Ginger and Chiles

All-Purpose Basil-Chile Finishing Sauce

Saigon Paste

All-Purpose Tamarind Glaze

Seven Spice Rubs and Pastes

Toasted Base Rub

General All-Purpose Barbecue Rub

Easy Tropical Spice Powder

Asian Spice Rub

Mediterranean Wet Spice Paste

Southeast Asian Wet Spice Paste

Complex "Roast-Whole-Seeds-and-Grind-'Em" Spice Mix

Simple Homemade Mayonnaise

Red Grape–Pear Chutney

Like all the best chutneys, this simple mixture is packed with a lot of separate, competing flavors: the mellowness of pears, the sweetness of orange juice and brown sugar, and the sourness of wine vinegar—with some barely cooked seedless grapes to add little bursts of texture and sweet liquid. It takes just a few minutes to make and is particularly good with chicken, pork, or lamb, or just added to some plain rice for a simple lunch dish.

3 tablespoons vegetable oil

1 large red onion, peeled and diced medium

Pinch of ground cloves

2 tablespoons minced ginger

4 pears, halved, cored, and diced small

$^1/_2$ cup fresh orange juice (about 1 large orange)

$^1/_3$ cup red wine vinegar

$^1/_2$ cup lightly packed brown sugar

1 cup seedless red grapes (or substitute green), halved

Salt and freshly cracked black pepper to taste

1. In a medium saucepan, heat the oil over medium heat until hot but not smoking. Add the onion and cloves and sauté, stirring occasionally, until the onions are transparent, 5 to 7 minutes. Add the ginger and sauté, stirring occasionally, for 1 minute.

2. Add the pears, orange juice, vinegar, and sugar and cook, stirring occasionally, until almost all the liquid is gone, 3 to 5 minutes. Add the grapes and cook for 2 minutes, stirring frequently. Remove from the heat and season to taste with salt and pepper. Serve warm or cold. This will keep, covered and refrigerated, for a week to 10 days.

Lime-Ginger Chutney

Since it uses a citrus fruit, rind and all, this is like a marmalade of sorts. But it has a lot more tartness and flavor to it than any marmalade you can buy in a store. It's very easy to make, and it goes well with any kind of grilled meat, particularly pork or chicken.

> 6 limes, sliced into very thin rounds
>
> 3 tablespoons vegetable oil
>
> 1 small red onion, peeled and diced medium
>
> 2 tablespoons minced ginger
>
> ½ cup lightly packed brown sugar
>
> ½ cup fresh lime juice (about 4 limes)
>
> Salt and freshly cracked black pepper to taste

1. In a medium saucepan, bring 1 quart of water to a boil over high heat. Drop the lime slices in and bring back up to a boil, then remove the pot from the heat and drain the lime slices. Refill the pot with water, place it back over high heat, and bring to a boil again. Drop the lime slices back in, bring back up to a boil, and drain. (This will soften and remove the bitterness from the rinds.)

2. In a medium sauté pan, heat the oil over medium heat until hot but not smoking. Add the onion and sauté, stirring occasionally, until it is soft and beginning to brown, 7 to 9 minutes. Add the ginger and limes and cook for 2 minutes, stirring frequently. Add the sugar and lime juice and simmer for about 10 minutes, or until most of the liquid has evaporated. Remove from the heat and serve at room temperature or chilled. This chutney will keep, covered and refrigerated, for about a week.

BIG FLAVORS WITH LITTLE EFFORT

Sweet-and-Smoky Pickled Corn Relish

MAKES ABOUT 4 CUPS

This is an easy relish to make during those late summer days when corn is plentiful. I like it with pork or chicken, but it's also good on sandwiches of any kind.

4 ears corn, husked, desilked, blanched in boiling water for 2 minutes,
    and drained
1 red onion, peeled and diced small
1 red bell pepper, halved, seeded, and diced small
2 cups white vinegar
1 cup sugar
3 tablespoons celery seeds
2 tablespoons mustard seeds
1 teaspoon ground allspice
Salt and freshly cracked black pepper to taste

1. Grill the corn over **a medium-hot fire,** rolling it around occasionally, until golden brown, 5 to 7 minutes. Remove from the grill and, as soon as the ears are cool enough to handle, cut the kernels from the cobs and place in a small bowl. Add the onion and bell pepper to the corn.

2. In a small saucepan, combine the vinegar and sugar and bring to a boil over high heat, stirring occasionally to dissolve the sugar. Add the celery seeds, mustard seeds, and allspice, then pour the mixture over the corn, peppers, and onions. Mix well and season to taste with salt and pepper. This relish, which can be served hot or cold, will keep for 3 to 4 days, covered and refrigerated.

Ginger-Date Chutney

MAKES ABOUT 1 ½ CUPS

The dates in this wickedly strong, rich, and powerful mixture are so sweet that it is almost more of a very spicy jam than a chutney. I would serve this with any roast meat, particularly lamb or pork, or as a complement to ultrahot food.

> 1 cup fresh dates, pitted and roughly chopped
> ⅓ cup golden raisins
> 2 tablespoons minced ginger
> 2 tablespoons minced fresh chile pepper of your choice
> 2 tablespoons brown sugar
> ½ cup white vinegar
> Salt and freshly cracked black pepper to taste

In a small bowl, combine all of the ingredients and mix well. This chutney will keep, covered and refrigerated, for about a week.

Apricot-Ginger Relish

MAKES ABOUT 3 CUPS

If you are ever fortunate enough to find a truly ripe apricot on the tree, pick and eat it immediately. This is one of the great treats of the fruit world—soft, delicate, rich, perfumey, and uniquely flavorful. Though never as wonderful as the tree-ripened fruit, some store-bought apricots do come close. They are best in the summer months, when they are in season in California. Here we combine these succulent fruits with ginger and rice wine vinegar in a light relish that would go well with any fish or pork dish.

> 8 ripe but firm apricots, pitted and diced small (or substitute 4 peaches)
> ½ red bell pepper, seeded and diced small
> ½ cup rice wine vinegar (or substitute white vinegar)
> 2 tablespoons minced ginger
> ¼ cup minced scallions (white and green parts)
> 2 tablespoons sugar
> 4 to 7 dashes Tabasco sauce
> Salt and freshly cracked white pepper to taste

In a small bowl, combine all of the ingredients, mix well, and refrigerate. This relish will keep, covered and refrigerated, for up to a week.

Spicy Thai Tomato-Herb Relish

MAKES ABOUT 2 CUPS

The foursome of Southeast Asian herbs in this relish, along with the ginger and lime, make for a most pungent and aromatic mixture, which goes equally well with grilled fish or meat. If you can't find lemon grass, don't let it stop you from making this relish, since it's still excellent without it. If you do have lemon grass, make sure that you use only the inner part of the bottom third of the stalk—the rest is too hard and fibrous to eat. I also encourage you to get some fish sauce and try it in this relish. It's much more subtle than its aroma would suggest; Thai cooks use it much as we use salt, to add a depth of flavor and bring out other tastes.

$^1/_4$ cup roughly chopped fresh mint

$^1/_4$ cup roughly chopped fresh basil

$^1/_4$ cup roughly chopped fresh cilantro

2 tablespoons roughly chopped lemon grass
   (inner one third of bottom third of stalk only)

1 large tomato, cored and diced small

1 red onion, peeled and diced small

1 tablespoon minced ginger

1 teaspoon minced garlic

3 tablespoons fish sauce (optional)

$^1/_3$ cup fresh lime juice (about 2 large limes)

1 tablespoon sugar

Salt and freshly cracked black pepper to taste

In a small bowl, combine all the ingredients and mix well. This relish is best served cold and will keep, covered and refrigerated, for 3 to 4 days.

Simple Spicy Grilled Tomato Salsa

MAKES ABOUT 2 CUPS

This is a cooked salsa that more closely resembles an ultra-high-quality jarred salsa than the classic salsa fresca. The flavors are a little different too, but the traditional raw and vibrant salsa spicing combination of chile, lime, and cilantro still shows through the smoky onion and tomato base. A quarter-cup of chipotle peppers is a lot, so if you don't like really spicy food, you should probably cut back on it or substitute another milder chile pepper of your choice.

6 tomatoes about the size of baseballs, cored and halved

2 large red onions, peeled and quartered

3 tablespoons olive oil

Salt and freshly cracked black pepper to taste

$^1/_4$ cup canned chipotle peppers

$^1/_2$ cup fresh cilantro leaves

$^1/_4$ cup fresh lime juice (about 2 limes)

1 tablespoon minced garlic

1 tablespoon ground cumin

1. In a large bowl, combine the tomatoes, onions, olive oil, and salt and pepper to taste and toss well to coat the vegetables. Place the tomatoes and onions on the grill over **a medium fire** and cook, turning once or twice. What you are looking for here is to give the vegetables some color and smoky flavor, not to cook them through, so they are done when they have acquired a good amount of color. Depending on your particular fire, this could be anywhere from 3 to 8 minutes for the tomatoes, slightly longer for the onions.

2. Remove the tomatoes and onions from the grill, place them on a small baking sheet, and roast in a preheated 350°F oven for about 5 minutes, or until they are cooked through. This will add a roasted flavor that complements the grilled flavor.

3. Remove the onions and tomatoes from the oven and, as soon as they are cool enough to handle, roughly chop them and place in a large bowl. Add all the remaining ingredients, mix well, and season to taste with salt and pepper. Serve hot or cold. This salsa will keep, covered and refrigerated, for about 3 days.

Spicy Lime-Marinated Cabbage and Onion

MAKES ABOUT 4 CUPS

This condiment is reminiscent of the spicy pickled cabbages of the world, like the *cordito* of El Salvador, the *kim chee* of Korea, and the Szechuan pickled cabbage of China. They are usually set out in small dishes on the table and used to perk up the main course, and I recommend you do the same with this. Its piquant flavor benefits grilled meat or fish.

> 5 cloves garlic, peeled and thinly sliced
> 1 cup white vinegar
> 1 tablespoon sugar
> 3 tablespoons minced fresh chile pepper of your choice (or less to taste)
> 1 cup shredded cabbage
> 1 cup shredded carrots
> 1 red onion, peeled and thinly sliced
> $^1/_2$ cup fresh lime juice (about 4 limes)
> Salt and freshly cracked black pepper to taste

In a medium saucepan, combine the garlic, vinegar, sugar, and chiles and bring to a boil over high heat. Add the cabbage, carrots, and onion, remove from the heat, stir in the lime juice and season to taste with salt and pepper. Cover and refrigerate. This can be used the day it is made, but it is much better after it sits for a day or so. It will keep, covered and refrigerated, for 5 days.

Clove-Pickled Peaches

Fresh peaches are so wonderful that I try to use them in all kinds of ways. Here their mellow sweetness gets a kick from rum, brown sugar, cloves, and ginger, making an excellent picnic-type accompaniment to any grilled dinner.

> 2 cups white vinegar
>
> 1 cup water
>
> 1 cup rum of your choice
>
> 1 pound brown sugar
>
> 1/2 cup whole cloves
>
> A piece of ginger about the size of your index finger, peeled and sliced into thin rounds
>
> 7 peaches, halved, pitted, and peeled

In a large saucepan, combine all of the ingredients except the peaches and bring to a boil over high heat. Put the peaches in a bowl and pour the liquid over them. Let cool to room temperature and refrigerate. You can eat them right away if you want, but they will be better in a day or two. These will keep, covered and refrigerated, for 1 month.

cloves, the most aromatic bud

CLOVES, WHICH ARE THE dried unopened buds of an Asian evergreen tree, are perhaps the most aromatic of all spices. When we were driving through the highland tropical forests of Penang, Malaysia, for example, we could smell the sweet, fragrant spice long before we came to the groves of tall trees on which it grew. This quality has caused cloves to be used for many purposes throughout their history, in addition to cooking. The Chinese of the Han dynasty, for example, held cloves in their mouths to sweeten their breath when in the presence of the emperor, and medieval European physicians prescribed them as an antidote to such disparate afflictions as the plague and impotence.

Pickled Ginger Strips

MAKES ABOUT ¹/₂ CUP

In Japan, this is the famous *gari* that accompanies sashimi and sushi. I like the technique because ginger looks so nice and fresh in the store and I always buy a lot of it, then it always seems to get old before I use it up. So use this method and you will always have ginger on hand when you need it. It is also a special garnish for dishes using ginger, or can just be left on the table as an all-purpose add-in to Asian foods. Try to cut the ginger into strips no larger than matchsticks, since the smaller they are, the quicker they get pickled.

²/₃ cup rice wine vinegar (white vinegar will do)

¹/₃ cup sugar

1 teaspoon salt

2 pieces ginger about three times the size of your index finger, peeled and cut into small very thin strips

In a small saucepan, bring the vinegar, sugar, and salt to a boil over high heat. Add the ginger strips and count to 15, then remove from the heat. Allow to cool to room temperature, then cover and refrigerate. These strips will keep, covered and refrigerated, for up to 3 months.

Preserved Limes

This relatively quick method of preserving limes can also be used with lemons. In the traditional method, the salt is rubbed into the fruit and it is allowed to stand for weeks, creating its own liquid. This method is faster, and it works well. The process softens up the rind and gives some sweetness to the fruit, which can then be thrown into stews, as is done in India and Egypt. The way I like to use it, though, is to clean off the pulp, dice the rind very fine, and use it anywhere I would use lime juice; it adds yet another flavor dimension to a dish.

> **8 limes**
> About $1^1/_2$ cups kosher salt
> About $2^1/_2$ cups water

1. Deeply score the skin of each lime 4 times lengthwise, down to but not into the flesh.

2. Place the limes in a small pot, add enough salt to cover them, and then add water just to cover the limes. The water should taste like very strong sea water. Bring to a boil over high heat, then remove from the heat and let the limes cool to room temperature in the liquid. Don't worry if the salt is not completely dissolved—it will continue to dissolve as the limes sit over the coming days. When the limes are at room temperature, pour them and the salty water into a jar, cover, and refrigerate.

3. Allow to sit for 10 days, turning the jar over every few days. After 10 days the limes will be ready to use, but they should be rinsed off before you use them. They will keep, covered and refrigerated, for about 3 months.

dried limes

ALTHOUGH VERY DIFFICULT TO make at home, dried limes are a great souring agent. You'll find them in Middle Eastern shops either whole or in powdered form. As with any other fruit or vegetable, drying concentrates and intensifies the flavor characteristics of these citrus fruits. Starting off with an intense acidic bite, they ripen in the mouth into a strongly aromatic, almost flowery taste. When used whole, these dried fruits are most often dropped into soups or stews; in powdered form, they are often sprinkled over meat dishes.

Pickled Pineapple

MAKES ABOUT 5 CUPS

When I was a kid eating at my grandma's, the table was always covered with all kinds of flavors—watermelon pickles, cucumber pickles, a bowl of deviled eggs, leftover deviled ham—so that every meal was like a buffet. This is actually a traditional way of eating in many other countries, such as India, Japan, Korea, and Indonesia, where the meal usually consists of a bunch of little pickles and salads as complements to the main course. This pickled pineapple is a new addition to this tradition, and goes well with almost any meal. Just set it out and let people use it as they will.

> 3 cups white vinegar
>
> 2 cups lightly packed brown sugar
>
> 2 cinnamon sticks (or substitute 2 teaspoons ground cinnamon)
>
> 1 tablespoon nutmeg, freshly grated if possible
>
> 10 whole cloves
>
> 1 pineapple, peeled, cooled, and cut into large chunks

In a medium saucepan, combine the vinegar and sugar and bring to a boil over high heat. Remove from the heat, add the spices and pineapple, mix well, cover, cool, and refrigerate. You can eat the pineapple the same day, but it will be better if it can sit a day for the flavors to get acquainted. This will keep, covered and refrigerated, for up to 3 weeks.

Lime-Pickled Mangoes
with Ginger and Chiles

MAKES 1 ½ QUARTS

For this recipe, you are best off using mangoes that aren't super-ripe, since you want them to maintain some firmness throughout the process. In fact, mangoes that are a little underripe work out very well. These pickles are fun to lay out to add a little flavor to any kind of meal; don't save them for the exotic dishes. I personally eat them with a nice big grilled steak and some horseradish.

1 cup fresh lime juice (about 8 limes)

2 cups red wine vinegar

1 cup sugar

3 tablespoons minced ginger

¼ cup thinly sliced fresh chile pepper of your choice

Salt and freshly cracked black pepper to taste

4 semi-ripe mangoes, peeled, pitted, and cut into ½-inch cubes

In a small pot, bring all of the ingredients except the mangoes to a boil over high heat. Put the mangoes in a bowl, pour the hot liquid over them, cool, and refrigerate. You can eat them right away, but they will be better in a day or two. These will keep, covered and refrigerated, for 1 month.

tropical emissary

IN STEAMY SOUTHEAST ASIAN cities like Singapore and Kuala Lumpur, the fruit stands resemble fantasies created by a child with a hyperactive imagination. Here are red-orange rambutans, bristling with pointy spikes; purple-brown mangosteens, their white inner flesh tasting of molasses and cream; nutlike langsat that split open to spill out sections tasting like honeyed grapefruit; and huge orange-yellow jackfruit, mealy and mellow, hinting of vanilla.

MOST OF THESE PHANTASMAGORICAL beauties are too perishable to find their way to American markets and too delicately attuned to their tropical rain forest homes to be grown on our shores. But their rich, deep, succulent, uniquely tropical flavors can be experienced from the mango, which is adaptable enough to be grown in Florida, Mexico, and Haiti. Once you've wrapped your taste buds around a really good mango, you'll be ready to book the next flight to Kuala Lumpur.

All-Purpose Basil-Chile Finishing Sauce

MAKES ABOUT 1 CUP

This is what is known in barbecue-speak as a finishing sauce, which means it goes on after cooking, as opposed to a mopping sauce, which goes on during cooking. This is the condiment I use when I'm having my grilled steak dinner. Just spoon this right over the top of the steak as soon as it's done. It is also good with lamb or with fish that has a strong flavor, such as mackerel, bluefish, or tuna. Come to think of it, it's also excellent spooned over grilled vegetables.

$^1/_4$ cup olive oil
$^1/_4$ cup balsamic vinegar
1 tablespoon minced garlic
3 tablespoons minced fresh chile pepper of your choice
$^1/_2$ cup roughly chopped fresh basil
Salt and freshly cracked black pepper to taste

In a small bowl, combine all the ingredients and mix well. This mixture is best used fresh, but it will keep, covered and refrigerated, for up to 5 days.

Saigon Paste

MAKES ABOUT 1 $^1/_4$ CUP

This is my version of the standard table condiment of Vietnamese restaurants. A Vietnamese waiter once described it to me as "more exciting than Atlantic City." I don't know about that, but it is a handy condiment to have hanging around to add punch to any dish. Not surprisingly, it goes particularly well with Asian soups or noodle preparations.

$^3/_4$ cup roughly chopped fresh chile peppers of your choice
1 clove garlic, peeled
2 tablespoons minced ginger
1 tablespoon sugar
$^1/_2$ cup rice vinegar (or substitute white vinegar)
1 tablespoon kosher salt

Combine all the ingredients in a food processor or blender and puree until smooth. Pour out into a small bowl, cover, and refrigerate. This paste will keep, covered and refrigerated, for up to a month.

All-Purpose Tamarind Glaze

MAKES ABOUT 6 CUPS

We use this all-purpose glaze a lot in the restaurants. We either brush it on food about a minute before it comes off the grill to add a final caramelization or brush it on just prior to serving. Sweet, sour, and a little hot, it provides a dynamic flavor boost for just about anything grilled.

> 1 1-pound package tamarind pulp
> 2 cups water
> 1 8-ounce jar apricot preserves
> 1 cup rice vinegar (or substitute white vinegar)
> 2 tablespoons red pepper flakes
> Grated zest of 1 lemon (yellow part only)
> Grated zest of 2 limes (green part only)
> Grated zest of 1 orange (orange part only)

1. To separate the tamarind seed from the pulp, place the tamarind blocks in a bowl with just enough warm water to cover and let stand for 30 minutes to soften. Once the tamarind has softened, pour the tamarind and liquid into a sieve suspended over a bowl, and push the fruit through the sieve with a wooden spoon. This will take some time and energy. When you're finished, you should have the seeds in the sieve and the pulp and liquid in the bowl.

2. In a medium saucepan, combine the strained tamarind with all the remaining ingredients and bring to a boil over high heat. Reduce the heat to low and simmer, stirring every once in a while, for 20 minutes. Remove from the heat and allow to cool to room temperature, then cover and refrigerate. This glaze will keep, covered and refrigerated, for up to 3 months.

the sweetness of sour

PERHAPS THE MOST WIDELY used souring agent in the world—after lemons and limes—is tamarind. Tamarind trees, which grow up to seventy feet tall, are found throughout the humid tropics, and cooks from India to the Caribbean to equatorial Africa to the Middle East all use the pulp that is found inside the tree's fuzzy, light brown pods. For culinary purposes, the pulp is usually soaked in hot water, then mashed against a sieve to remove the seeds imbedded in it. It has a dark, lingering flavor strongly etched with sourness, which comes from the tartaric acid in the fruit. If you can get hold of tamarind, you should definitely give it a shot—it is one of the world's great flavors. If you can't find it, substitute equal parts molasses and fresh lime juice.

Seven Spice Rubs and Pastes

Want to add intense, deep flavor to your food with an absolute minimum of effort? Want to sample the "flavor footprints" of cuisines from all over the world? Want to make your kitchen smell as exotic and enticing as a Moroccan soup? Then spice rubs are just the ticket for you.

As you have probably figured out, I love spice rubs. I love to rub them on meat, on fish, on vegetables, I love to slip them into stews and soups, I love to use them just about any way.

Rubbing food with mixtures of spices before cooking is an incredibly easy way to add intense flavor to your cooking. I like this technique better than the more traditional approach of marinating food before grilling, for several reasons. For one thing, you are using a more concentrated dose of spices, so you get more intense flavors. Second, you don't have to plan in advance as you do with marinades—just rub the food with the spices and start cooking. Third, rubs adhere better to the surface of foods than marinades, which again gives them the flavor-intensity edge. Fourth, there is no oil to drip into the fire and cause flare-ups, as there is with marinades.

Most important, though, is the flavor dynamic created when food rubbed with spice mixtures is cooked over the direct high heat of a grilling fire. As the food cooks, the rub creates a super-flavorful, slightly crunchy crust on the exterior, while the interior retains the distinct flavor of the food.

The spice blends you use can be as simple as roasted cumin seeds combined with salt and pepper, or as complex as India's garam masala, which may contain a dozen or more individual spices. And the technique for using spice rubs is about as simple as it gets. Just take small handfuls of whatever spice combo you have chosen and rub it over the entire surface of the food you are going to cook, using a bit of pressure to make sure that a good layer adheres to the food (that's why they call it a "rub," after all). Don't bother with brushes or other types of applicators; bare hands are really the best way to apply these mixtures. Once you've started to cook, don't worry if the rub begins to turn dark brown. This is what happens to spices when they are cooked, particularly with a high-heat cooking method like grilling. As long as the spices don't begin to smoke, you are in the clear.

I always have some spice rubs mixed up and ready to use in my kitchen. If you get into the habit of stocking them, just as you do salt and pepper, it will take you only a couple of minutes to put together a dish that is incredibly flavorful, with deep, rich, complex flavors. So, to make your life easier, here are a handful of all-purpose spice rubs, from the very simple to the slightly more complex.

1. Toasted Base Rub

For me, cumin and coriander are the two spices most helpful in creating a canvas onto which other flavors can be painted. Be it Mexico, the Middle East, India, or Southeast Asia, these two spices are integral parts of most any spice mixture. They are good straight up, or as a base for other flavors. For instance, add garlic and basil and a little olive oil for an outstanding Mediterranean-flavored wet spice paste. For this spice mix, you need to toast the seeds first, then crack them (cumin seeds can be used whole if you really want to, but coriander seeds need to be cracked). This spice mix is best on strong-flavored foods like beef, lamb, or bluefish. This recipe makes about 2 cups, and the mixture will keep, covered and stored in a cool dry spot, for up to 3 months.

> $^2/_3$ cup cumin seeds, toasted in a sauté pan over medium heat, shaking,
>   until just fragrant, 2 to 3 minutes, then crushed
> $^2/_3$ cup coriander seeds, toasted with the cumin seeds, then crushed
> $^1/_3$ cup kosher salt
> $^1/_3$ cup freshly cracked black pepper

2. General All-Purpose Barbecue Rub

Sweet, salty, with a blast of cumin, this rub can be used anywhere, any time. Excellent for traditional barbecue flavor profiles, this very simple combination of dry ingredients will keep, covered and stored in a cool dark spot, for up to 3 months. This recipe makes about 2 cups.

$^1/_3$ cup freshly cracked black pepper	$^1/_3$ cup ground cumin
$^1/_3$ cup kosher salt	2 tablespoons cayenne pepper
$^1/_3$ cup lightly packed brown sugar	2 tablespoons ground allspice
$^1/_3$ cup paprika	2 tablespoons ground ginger

3. Easy Tropical Spice Powder

All spices originated in the tropics, a fact that helps explain why the cooking of hot-weather regions is so flavorful. This general-purpose spice mix can be used either as a rub or as a flavoring mixture for other dishes such as soups and stews. A little sweet and a little earthy, it is very easy to make, simply a combination of powdered spices. Just before using this mix I might toast it in a dry sauté pan, stirring, until the aroma is strong, two to three minutes. This recipe makes about 2 cups; the mixture will keep, covered and stored in a cool dry spot, for up to 3 months.

¹/₄ cup ground cumin	2 tablespoons ground ginger
¹/₄ cup ground coriander	2 tablespoons curry powder
¹/₄ cup kosher salt	2 tablespoons ground allspice
¹/₄ cup freshly cracked black pepper	2 tablespoons cayenne pepper
2 tablespoons ground cinnamon	2 tablespoons powdered mustard

4. Asian Spice Rub

This simple rub of Asian flavors is super-aromatic and excels with fish or chicken. If you don't have white pepper, you can substitute black, but you won't get quite the same aromatic flavor. This recipe makes about 1 cup and the mixture will keep, covered and stored in a cool dry spot, for up to 3 months.

¹/₄ cup ground ginger	2 tablespoons red pepper flakes
¹/₄ cup ground white pepper	2 tablespoons ground cinnamon
¹/₄ cup anise seeds	2 tablespoons ground cloves

5. Mediterranean Wet Spice Paste

Wet spice pastes work in the same way as spice rubs. A slight disadvantage is that, unlike the dry rubs, they don't keep for months, but I think this is more than offset by the fact that you can use fresh aromatic herbs as well as spices. For this Mediterranean-flavored paste, which is fantastic slipped under the skin of chicken breasts or thighs before grilling, use whatever Mediterranean herbs you have on hand, in whatever proportion you feel like. This recipe makes about 1¾ cups and will keep, covered and refrigerated, for up to 1 week.

1 cup mixed roughly chopped herbs: any one or a combination of parsley, rosemary, sage, or thyme	1 tablespoon red pepper flakes
3 tablespoons minced garlic	2 tablespoons kosher salt
¹/₄ cup olive oil	2 tablespoons freshly cracked black pepper

6. Southeast Asian Wet Spice Paste

This paste, which combines classic Asian flavors with an accent on ginger, is highly aromatic and just a little hot. It's an excellent choice for any pork product. This recipe makes a little more than 1½ cups and will keep, covered and refrigerated, for up to 1 week.

continued

₁/₄ cup minced ginger

2 tablespoons minced garlic

¹/₂ cup roughly chopped fresh cilantro

¹/₄ cup roughly chopped fresh mint

1 teaspoon minced fresh chile pepper
of your choice

¹/₄ cup sesame oil

3 tablespoons ground white pepper

7. Complex "Roast-Whole-Seeds-and-Grind-'Em" Spice Mix

This is a graduate-level mixture along the lines of garam masala, the leading spice mixture of northern India. Here you start with the spices whole, which is key because it ensures a level of freshness that is not at all certain when using preground spices. Combine all the spices in a large sauté pan, then toast them over medium heat, shaking constantly, until you see the first wisp of smoke, about two to three minutes. At that point, remove the spices from the heat and grind them in a mortar with a pestle, spice grinder, or clean electric coffee grinder. If necessary, this mixture will keep, covered and stored in a cool dark place, for several months, but the point is that you want to toast and grind the spices as close as possible to using them, so storage is not really an issue here. This recipe, which makes about 1¾ cups, is also good as a spice mixture for flavoring soups, stews, or other such dishes.

¹/₄ cup fennel seeds

¹/₄ cup cumin seeds

¹/₄ cup coriander seeds

¹/₄ cup black peppercorns

¹/₄ cup white peppercorns

2 tablespoons cardamom seeds

2 tablespoons star anise

1 tablespoon whole cloves

1 1-inch cinnamon stick

¹/₄ cup kosher salt

killing another spice myth

IT COMES AS A surprise to many Americans to find that the relative lack of spices in Western cooking is a development of comparatively recent vintage. At banquets in medieval France, for example, it was not unusual for foods to be served practically buried in spices, and platters with separate compartments filled with additional spices were passed around like relish trays.

IRONICALLY, WHEN EUROPEANS BEGAN to discover new routes to the lands where spices were grown and these potions therefore became less rare and expensive, they lost some of their cachet and began a slow fade from the culinary vocabulary. As spices have become less prevalent in Western cooking, a bias developed against them. Seemingly bewildered as to why their ancestors would want to spice their food so heavily, modern cooks settled on the notion that this predilection developed as a way of disguising the taste of spoiled meat back in the days before refrigeration.

THIS MYTH, STILL COMMONLY passed around today even by cooking "experts" who should know better, is rather easily disproved. First, aromatic spices were extremely expensive in those days. There were any number of less costly ways to disguise rotten meat, including inexpensive herbs and other flavorings, if that was what people wanted to do. Even more telling is the fact that meat that we would consider totally spoiled (and disgusting) these days was actually highly prized in earlier times. Even as late as 1900, for example, many English cooks insisted that a pheasant was not fit to eat until it had been "hung" so long that the meat turned slightly green and started to fall off the bones.

LET'S FACE IT—THE reason cooks of the Middle Ages used lots of spices is because, when properly employed, they make food taste fantastic. We probably don't want to go so far as to cover our food in spices, but experimenting with mixtures of the world's spices is a quick, easy way to add real flavor to our food. These are some culinary roots it would be good to get back to.

CONDIMENTS AND PICKLES, SPICE RUBS AND PASTES

Simple Homemade Mayonnaise

You can always use prepared mayonnaise, but this is one of the cases when the flavor of the homemade version is so much fresher that it's worth whipping up a batch every once in a while. There's not all that much to it, particularly if you have a food processor or blender. Of course, if you are a purist, you can make mayonnaise using a whisk and bowl.

As always when using uncooked egg yolks, there is a small risk of salmonella. Pregnant women, the elderly, infants, and people whose immune systems are compromised should avoid raw eggs. For others, it is simply a matter of balancing the risk versus the pleasure. If you want mayonnaise without risk, cook the egg yolks and lemon juice, along with a tablespoon of water, in a saucepan over very low heat, stirring constantly, until the mixture bubbles in one or two places. Let stand for four minutes, then proceed with the recipe.

> 2 large egg yolks
> 1 tablespoon fresh lemon juice
> 1 cup extra virgin olive oil
> Salt and freshly cracked black pepper to taste

1. Combine the egg yolks, lemon juice, and 2 tablespoons of the olive oil in the bowl of a food processor or blender and pulse to blend.

2. With the motor running, add the remaining olive oil in a slow, steady stream. Like magic, it will form a thick, creamy emulsion. If the mixture is a little too thick, add about a tablespoon of water to thin it. Season to taste with salt and pepper. This will keep, covered and refrigerated, for 3 days.

There are three tools that are essential for proper grilling—tongs, a wire brush, and your favorite beverage. And if I were forced to choose the most indispensable of them, I might well forego the tongs and the brush. It's hot over the grill, there's a lot of pressure involved, and the right beverage is critical to keep you in a relaxed frame of mind so you do your best work and have fun at the same time.

ALCOHOLIC AND NOT

beverages of choice

Fortunately for you, one of our primary specialties is sampling beverages of the tropical world, and here we have condensed literally hundreds, no thousands, of investigatory sessions into the top nine drinks of the hot-weather regions.

From the Latin-inspired Puerto Viejo Rum Punch to the strange and exotic Blue-Green Mangorita, these beverages are guaranteed to match up well with the smoky, seared flavor of food cooked over live fire. And, for those occasions when for some reason you want to keep all of your wits about you, we've even thrown in a couple of nonalcoholic but still luscious tropical beverages, Ginger Limeade and Chilled Moroccan Mint Tea.

Ginger Limeade

Doc's Chilled
Moroccan Mint Tea

Jimmy's Pink
Greyhound Punch

Ken's Vodka Gimlet

Blue-Green Mangoritas

The Hanker

Puerto Viejo Rum
Punch for a Crowd

Rum and Cokes *Estilo*
Hombre de Negocios

Henry's Cuban
Rum Julep

Ginger Limeade

MAKES 4 DRINKS

If you or any of your friends has ever been to Little Compton, Rhode Island, you are sure to know Olga's Cup and Saucer, located right next to Cole Walker's world-famous vegetable stand. Olga and Becky bake up fine sweet and savory treats, and you can go vegetable shopping, then sit and enjoy a cooling ginger lemonade and a pizza, burrito, or pastry.

That's where I first had the precursor of this drink, ginger lemonade. I changed it to limeade, thinking that if ginger lemonade tasted good, the ginger-lime combo would work too—and sure enough, it did. So drink up, and if you ever drop in at the Cup and Saucer, say hello for me.

1 cup sugar

2 cups water

A piece of ginger about the size of your index finger,
   peeled and cut into thick slices

2 cups fresh lime juice (about 16 limes)

Mint sprigs for garnish (optional)

1. In a small saucepan, combine the sugar and $1/2$ cup of the water and bring to a boil, stirring frequently, over high heat. Boil for 1 minute to dissolve the sugar, then remove from the heat and allow to cool.

2. Put the remaining $1^1/2$ cups water in another saucepan with the ginger and bring to a boil over high heat. Reduce the heat to medium and boil for 20 minutes. Remove from the heat and allow to cool.

3. When both mixtures have cooled, remove and discard the ginger and combine the two liquids. Add the lime juice and mix well, then pour over crushed ice and serve, garnished with mint sprigs if you want.

Doc's Chilled Moroccan Mint Tea

S E R V E S 4

The first time I had mint tea was about twenty years ago on a narrow street in Tangier, Morocco. A man had set up a brazier at the side of the street and was grilling skewers of tiny lamb cubes, which he served up with a dab of hot sauce. When you ordered the skewers, you also got a small glass of mint tea, served in typical dramatic fashion—poured with pinpoint accuracy from a silver teapot held about three feet above the glass, a process that served to both aerate the tea and impress the drinker.

Intensely sweet, wildly aromatic, and dramatically thirst-quenching, this is a world-class drink. I always think of it as the American version of the "sweet tea" of the South, and I like to keep a pitcher of it in the refrigerator all summer. If you've got a patch of mint growing in your yard, there's no better use for it. Plus, if you're looking for a suitably laid-back activity for a summer's afternoon, you can always practice pouring the tea into your glass from three feet up.

> 3 tea bags of your choice
> 1 very large handful of mint sprigs (about 2 cups) washed
> $^2/_3$ cup sugar, or more to taste
> 4 cups cold water
> 1 smaller handful of mint sprigs, washed (optional)

1. Place the tea bags, large handful of mint, and the sugar in a heatproof pitcher or very clean teapot.

2. Bring the water to a boil and pour into the pitcher or teapot. Allow to steep for about 10 minutes, then stir gently and strain into a large pitcher. Pour out a small glass and taste, adjusting the sweetening as needed—remember, this is supposed to be a very sweet tea. The sweetness somehow adds to its thirst-quenching qualities.

3. Place the pitcher in the refrigerator until well chilled, then either serve it as is, or stuff a small handful of mint sprigs into each glass before adding the chilled tea, making it even more aromatic and dramatic.

Jimmy's Pink Greyhound Punch

MAKES 4 DRINKS

Every February I'm fortunate enough to visit my close friends Jim and Bonnie Burke down in the Florida Keys. I look forward to the trip every year, and as soon as I arrive I begin my annual attempt to eat my weight in stone crabs and raw oysters. There's a little bar not far from their place where we like to go to eat the steak and pork chop combo and drink cocktails made with juices freshly squeezed to order. This is my shot at re-creating one of those wonderful beverages, a concoction of vodka and fresh pink grapefruit juice.

> 1¹/₂ quarts fresh pink grapefruit juice (5 to 6 grapefruits)
> 1 pint vodka
> 1 tablespoon grenadine
> 4 ounces Triple Sec
> 16 to 20 ice cubes
> 2 limes, quartered

In a large pitcher, combine the grapefruit juice, vodka, grenadine, and Triple Sec and mix well. Pour over ice, garnish with lime wedges, and serve.

Ken's Vodka Gimlet

The "Goodman," as it is known at the East Coast Grill, is the summer cocktail of choice of our congenial chef d'cuisine, Mr. Ken Goodman. It's easy to make and the sweet lime juice and raspberry vodka blend well. It makes a colorful, potent drink that's easy to be around, just like its creator.

> 1 bottle of vodka
> 1 pint raspberries
> Rose's lime juice
> Ice
> Lime wedges

1. Remove a cup or so of vodka from a full bottle (Ken's personal choice is Absolut) and replace it by dropping in the raspberries.

2. Wait anywhere from 3 days to 2 weeks to get the flavor and color you prefer.

3. Add the flavored vodka in a 4 to 1 ratio with the Rose's lime juice to a cocktail shaker or large glass filled with ice. Strain into martini glasses, add a squeeze of lime, and drink up.

Blue-Green Mangoritas

Not just another blue margarita, this one was specifically designed to match the ocean color in a small lagoon in southern Mexico. The unique green color of this vibrant summer cooler is the result of mixing blue curaçao with mango puree. It looks a little strange, but the flavor is unreal. If you like, you can substitute Triple Sec for the blue curaçao, and all you sacrifice is the bizarre blue-green color. In the summer, when mangoes rock, this drink is fantastic. You can skip the salt-sugar combo on the rim of the glass, but it makes a nice touch.

> 1 cup mango puree (about 1 medium mango)
> 1 1/2 cups tequila of your choice
> 1/2 cup blue curaçao
> 1 cup fresh lime juice (about 8 limes; reserve a few of the juiced limes for salting the rims)
> 3 tablespoons kosher salt
> 3 tablespoons sugar

1. In a pitcher, combine the mango, tequila, curaçao, and lime juice and mix well until you achieve a nice uniform blue-green color.

2. In a small bowl, combine the salt and sugar and mix well. Rub a squeezed lime around the rim of each glass and dip the glasses into this mixture to lightly coat the rims. Add ice cubes, fill with mangorita, and drink up.

mexican hooch

IN EVERY COUNTRY OF THE WORLD, people take a readily available food, soak it, ferment it, and distill it into a colorless, high-octane alcoholic beverage. Brazilians convert sugarcane into *cachaca;* in North Africa, figs end up as *boukha;* Chinese farmers use sorghum to make *maotai;* grappa, the recently trendy Italian drink, is made from the leftovers of the wine-making process; and of course American moonshine is a corn product.

TEQUILA, THE MEXICAN ENTRY into this peasant alcohol vernacular, is made from the agave. Mexican distillers cut the hearts from the plants, roast them to convert the starches to sugars, ferment the resulting liquid twice, and finally distill it to create the powerful beverage we call tequila or mezcal.

LIKE THE GRAPPA OF Italy, tequila is starting to be appreciated and refined. There are now several super-premium versions available in the United States. If you want a powerful sipping beverage with some real flavor, this will fit the bill.

The Hanker

MAKES 2 DRINKS

While walking down the wide avenue known as the Ramblas in Barcelona, Spain, one evening around cocktail time (the civilized hour of 9 P.M.), my companions and I lucked into one of those rare travel occurrences—finding a really cool place without having a clue where you're going.

I was with Michael Schlow, Executive Chef of Cafe Louis in Boston, and our friend Susu Aleward, and the object of our good fortune was the Bar Boadas. *Boadas* is Spanish for "silly," but it was a cocktail drinker's dream. There, in an intimate, wood-paneled atmosphere, two bow-tied master craftsmen of mixology were plying their craft, preparing all the classics in an Art Deco atmosphere that served as a temple to consumers of highballs. Not only could you have the best mint juleps this side of Virginia, you could also have perfect Rob Roys, ideal martinis, or whatever else you fancied. If your drink required pouring, it was done from three feet above the glass, and if shaking was involved, it was like a dance.

The Boadas also offered a "cocktail of the day." Being samplers of the typical, we all opted for that day's offering, the Hanker. We spent quite some time at the Boadas that night, and consumed our share of hankers. I'll always remember this cocktail because of our discovery and the outstanding company in which I first drank it.

4 ounces gin
4 ounces Drambuie
4 ounces Dubonnet (red or white)
Cracked ice
Mint sprigs for garnish

Combine the gin, Drambuie, and Dubonnet in a glass pitcher and stir well. Fill two highball glasses with cracked ice, pour in the mixture, garnish with mint springs, and drink 'em down.

Puerto Viejo Rum Punch for a Crowd

When you travel a lot, you tend to develop a list of places that you go to as soon as you arrive in any new town. For me, one of those places is the market, to check out the food, and the other is a neighborhood bar, to see how my counterparts live. This latter practice has led me to sample some pretty weird concoctions, from fig liquor in a back-street bar in Tunis to snake wine in a little joint in Kuala Lumpur. Some of the most interesting potions I've come across in this way, though, have been in the West Indies and Central America, where rum is the fuel of choice and the mixer is your call from a dizzying array of carbonated beverages.

This particular drink is an attempt to re-create the "rum and whatevers" I came to appreciate while sitting in a bar in the small beach town of Puerto Viejo on the east coast of Costa Rica, about twenty miles from Panama. The huge waves crashing down on the outer reef were a little too big for me that day, so I spent the afternoon viewing the surfing from a comfortable bar stool, enjoying enough rum drinks that the day made a lasting impression. This punch is in the spirit of those drinks. It's an excellent potion for a crowd, and it has the added bonus of giving you an excuse to tell travel stories.

> 1 quart fresh grapefruit juice (about 4 large grapefruits)
> 1/4 cup sugar
> 1 12-ounce can Hawaiian Punch or other mixed fruit juice drink
> 1 12-ounce can orange soda
> 2 cups tonic water
> 1/3 cup fresh lime juice (about 2 large limes)
> 1 bottle of your favorite rum
> A big bucket of ice

In a large punch bowl, combine all of the ingredients except for the ice and mix well. Fill some tall glasses with ice and you are ready to go.

Rum and Cokes *Estilo Hombre de Negocios*

MAKES 4 DRINKS

If you're like I used to be, you frown on rum and Cokes as a relic of bad teenage parties, something that everyone eventually grew out of—or should have. I learned to like rum during one low-budget winter in Barbados, so I guess I was primed for a reappraisal. But it wasn't until I went to a business meeting in Belize that I gained a true appreciation of the king of the tropical drinks, Cuba Libre, otherwise known as a rum and Coke.

The meeting, which concerned buying Scotch bonnet peppers for our hot sauce, was to start around 9 P.M. I had flown all day to get there, the heat was raging, and I was tired and thirsty. We met at a bar, and on the table was a bottle of rum, a couple of Cokes, some limes, and a bowl with a big chunk of ice and a pick. What I really wanted was an ice-cold beer, but I thought better of it; when in Rome, and all that. So I chopped off a lot of ice, filled my glass, added a little rum, a little Coke, and a squeeze of lime, and had a sip—it was incredibly refreshing. It turned out to be a long, complicated meeting, but the rum and Cokes smoothed the way.

The experience has stayed with me, and now in the summer I'll freeze a block of ice, put the fixings out, and allow guests to make their own. Not everybody appreciates the technique, but there are always a few converts in the crowd, and I myself have become a big rum and Coke fan.

    1 block of ice
    1 ice pick
    12 6½-ounce bottles of Coca-Cola
    5 limes, quartered
    1 bottle of good rum

1. Sit down at a table inside or outdoors on a hot day or evening with three friends who are looking to catch up or just hang out.

2. Put four tall glasses on the table along with the block of ice in a large bowl, the ice pick, the Cokes, a bottle opener, the limes, and your bottle of rum.

3. Use the pick to get some ice off the block (a lost art that is fun to relearn), put it in your glass, pour in some rum, add some Coke, squeeze in a lime quarter, and drink. Repeat as many times as needed.

Henry's Cuban Rum Julep

MAKES 4 DRINKS

These days it seems as if lots of restaurants you walk into have their own special cocktail. I think the reason for this is that chefs tend to spend a lot of time at the bar after work, and they have a hard time disengaging themselves from their natural urge to create. My good friends Paul and Lisa O'Connell had just opened their new Cambridge restaurant, Chez Henri, and I was fortunate enough to witness Paul's creative process as he crafted this drink. Of course there were failures, but at the end what emerged was this combination of two time-honored drinks of the New World. One is the mint julep, in which mint and sugar are muddled in tall glasses and strong bourbon is poured over the top. The other is the national cocktail of Brazil, the *capahrina*, in which limes and sugar are muddled and aguadente is poured over. Both are basically straight liquor drinks that pack a punch. This is a sublime drink to relax with while preparing to prepare dinner.

> 1 cup fresh mint leaves
> 2 limes, each cut into 8 chunks
> 2 tablespoons sugar
> About 16 ice cubes
> 6 ounces rum of your choice (I've had good luck with Barbencourt,
>   Ron del Barralito, and Santa Teresa Añejo, a Venezuelan import)

1. Divide the mint, limes, and sugar among four tall glasses.

2. Take a spoon and muddle (bruise) the mint, limes, and sugar in the bottom of each glass for 20 to 30 seconds or so.

3. Wrap the ice cubes in a towel and smash them a couple of times with a hammer or a frying pan. It is crucial that the ice be cracked—not crushed, not cubed, but cracked into pieces about the diameter of a die (that's half a set of dice).

4. Fill the glasses to the top with the ice.

5. Pour in the rum, stir well, and serve.

I'm not so sure that the recipes in this chapter should be called "desserts." I myself am more likely to eat them in midafternoon rather than at the end of a meal, so maybe we should refer to them as "sweet snacks." But then, a friend of mine told me that he has taken to serving one of them, the Minted Melon with Caribbean Elixir, as a summer appetizer, so there goes the snack label, too.

THINGS OF BEAUTY

a few desserts

Whatever we call them, these sweet concoctions all seem to me to go particularly well with grilled food. Since I am partial to the foods of hot-weather countries, many of the recipes here are inspired by the flavors of those regions. Gingered Mango Mousse, for example, features one of the tropic's great flavor duets. Coconut Pancakes with Caramelized Bananas is a takeoff on a sweet sold by street vendors in Singapore, and the light and refreshing Papaya Ice with Sweet Hot Pepper Sauce makes excellent use of the traditional tropical combination of hot and sweet.

Other desserts you'll find here, such as Espresso Black Bottom Pie, Maple Bread Pudding with Oven-Dried Pears and Homemade Raisins, and Peach Sour Cream Pie, are descendants of good old American favorites, either from the South, where I grew up, or New England, where I live and work now.

In any case, whether you eat them at the end of a grilled meal, as an afternoon snack, or even as a decadent breakfast, I think you'll find every one of these sweets a thing of beauty.

Grilled Bananas and
Pineapple with Rum-
Molasses Glaze

Grilled Pineapple with
Sweet Lime–Black
Pepper Sauce

Saffron-Cardamom
Poached Pears with
Cranberry-Currant
Relish

Minted Melon with
Caribbean Elixir

Papaya Ice with Sweet
Hot Pepper Sauce

Gingered Mango Mousse

Coconut Flan

Malaysian-Style Coconut
Pudding

Maple Bread Pudding
with Oven-Dried Pears
and Homemade Raisins

Coconut Pancakes with
Caramelized Bananas

Little Chèvre
Cheesecakes with Guava-
Lime Sauce

Spanish Olive Oil and
Wine Cake

Caramelized Banana
and Lime Tart

Espresso Black
Bottom Pie

Peach Sour Cream Pie

Mai Tai Pie

Grilled Bananas and Pineapple with Rum-Molasses Glaze

SERVES 4

This grilled dessert is a rich combination of sweet bananas and pineapple with a glaze that's like a hot toddy, topped off with your favorite ice cream. As usual when grilling fruit, we leave the peel on until the fruit comes off the grill, since it helps the fruit retain its integrity over the fire. I like to serve the bananas in the peel so people can just scoop them out, but you might want to peel the pineapple before you serve it.

$1/4$ cup dark rum

$1/4$ cup molasses

$1/4$ cup unsalted butter

2 tablespoons fresh lime juice (about 1 lime)

4 bananas, unpeeled, halved lengthwise

$1/2$ ripe pineapple, unpeeled, cut into 4 slices about $1/2$ inch thick

3 tablespoons vegetable oil

1 pint of your favorite ice cream

1. In a small saucepan, combine the rum, molasses, butter, and lime juice. Cook over medium heat, stirring frequently, until the butter is melted and the ingredients are well blended. Remove from the heat.

2. Rub the banana halves and pineapple slices lightly with the oil. Place on the grill, with the bananas cut side down, and grill over **a medium fire** for about 2 minutes, or until the bananas are just golden and the pineapple slices have acquired light grill marks. Flip the fruit over, paint with the rum-molasses glaze, and grill for an additional 1 minute. Remove from the grill.

3. Serve each person 2 banana halves and a slice of pineapple (peeled if you want to make it easy for your guests), topped with a scoop of ice cream. If there is leftover glaze, drizzle it over the ice cream.

Grilled Pineapple with Sweet Lime–Black Pepper Sauce

SERVES 8

Many folks still consider grilling fruit to be a rather bizarre concept. But if you give it a try, you'll find that the slight smoky char of grilling enhances the inherent sweetness and deepens the flavors of many fruits. Pineapple, which combines sweet juiciness with a sturdy texture, is among the very best fruits for grilling. Here we combine it with a peppery sweet-sour mint sauce for an easy but flavorful dessert. It's a good one for those times when you're serving a crowd of people since it holds up well, which means you can grill up a big batch and set it out for people to help themselves.

> A small handful of black peppercorns (about 20), finely crushed
> $1/4$ cup light corn syrup
> $1/4$ cup fresh lime juice (about 2 limes)
> 1 teaspoon dried mint
> 2 pineapples, peeled and cut into 1-inch-thick slices
> (you will need 16 slices)
> $1/4$ cup roughly chopped fresh mint

1. In a small saucepan, combine the pepper, corn syrup, lime juice, and dried mint and cook over medium heat, stirring occasionally, until just warm, about 5 minutes. Remove from the heat and allow to cool to room temperature.

2. Meanwhile, place the pineapple slices on the grill over **a medium fire** and cook until lightly charred, about 4 minutes per side. During the last 30 seconds of cooking, brush with the lime-pepper sauce, then remove from the grill.

3. Stir the fresh mint into the remaining sauce. Serve 2 slices of grilled pineapple per person, topped with several tablespoons of the sauce.

for pineapples, small is good

PINEAPPLES ARE ACTUALLY composed of one to two hundred small fruitlets, known as "eyes," gathered together around a fibrous central core. It takes about eighteen months for a pineapple tree to bear its first fruit, and this initial fruit is also the largest the tree will ever produce. After that, smaller fruits are produced each year. The secret, though, is that the pineapples also get sweeter as they get smaller. So in general, as long as the pineapple you are buying is ripe, the smaller the better.

Saffron-Cardamom Poached Pears with Cranberry-Currant Relish

SERVES 4

Lots of people think that poached fruit is a kind of second-rate, dietetic dessert, suitable only for those who want to watch their weight. I think those people are equating poached fruit with the kind of tasteless canned fruit that many of us were served in our childhood. In fact, poached fruit is an excellent vehicle for all kinds of flavors. It lets you have a tasty, satisfying dessert that doesn't sit heavily in your stomach after a filling meal. Here we poach mellow pears in sweet white grape juice, infuse them with aromatic cinnamon and the distinctive flavor of cardamom, then top them with a slightly tart cranberry relish. If you don't feel like making the relish, you can always serve the pears with a couple of tablespoons of crème fraîche on top instead.

For the Relish

1 12-ounce bag cranberries

1 cup currants (or substitute raisins)

1 cup sugar

1^1/$_2$ cups water

^{1}/$_2$ cup roughly chopped walnuts, toasted in a heavy skillet, shaking frequently, just until fragrant, about 4 minutes

^{1}/$_4$ teaspoon vanilla extract

4 cups white grape juice

^{1}/$_4$ cup sugar

^{1}/$_2$ teaspoon ground cardamom

^{1}/$_4$ teaspoon vanilla extract

1 1-inch cinnamon stick (or substitute ^{1}/$_4$ teaspoon ground cinnamon)

4 ripe but firm pears, peeled, halved, and cored

Generous pinch of saffron threads

1. Make the relish: In a heavy saucepan, combine the cranberries, currants, sugar, and water and cook over medium heat, stirring occasionally, until the cranberries start to pop, 4 to 5 minutes. Reduce the heat to low and simmer gently until slightly thickened, about 3 minutes. Remove from the heat, stir in the walnuts and vanilla, and allow to cool to room temperature.

2. Meanwhile, combine the grape juice and sugar in a medium saucepan and cook over medium heat, stirring a few times, until the mixture just begins to boil. Reduce the heat to low, add the cardamom, vanilla, cinnamon, and pears, and simmer gently until the pears can be pierced with a fork but still offer some resistance, 3 to 8 minutes, depending on the ripeness of the pears. Add the saffron threads, remove from the heat, and allow the pears to cool in the poaching liquid.

3. Place 2 pear halves on each plate, top with a generous dollop of relish, and serve.

those costly spices

SOME FOODS, LIKE TRUFFLES, are expensive because they are rare and must be harvested in the wild. Others, like apricots, are costly because they are very delicate and hard to raise successfully. And then there are the food items that cost a lot because of the way they are gathered. Prominent in this latter category are spices such as saffron and cardamom. Saffron, the most costly of all spices, is actually the stigmas of certain purple crocuses, which must be harvested by hand. Workers have to harvest about seventy thousand flowers to get just one pound of saffron. Cardamom, the world's third most expensive spice (after vanilla), is the dried seed of a willowy bush of the ginger family. This spice also has to be harvested by hand, largely because the seed pods, which are attached to stalks that sprawl along the ground, don't all ripen at once and so must be repeatedly looked over and picked as they ripen individually. After picking, the cardamom pods have to be dried very slowly; if the process is hurried, the pods split open and the seeds inside dry out and lose their flavor. So the next time you wince at the price of one of these costly flavorings, try to think about the process by which it came to you—and it might be less painful to shell out the big bucks.

Minted Melon with Caribbean Elixir

SERVES 6 TO 8

Here's another dessert that takes advantage of that excellent tropical pairing, sweet and hot. This one is light and refreshing, an aromatic, spicy, but still cooling end for a big meal. My friend Carl Taplin, who lives on an island off the coast of Maine but loves the flavors of the Caribbean, has even taken to serving small portions of this dessert as an appetizer. During the late summer months, when good melons are plentiful, you might want to follow Carl's example and make up a triple or quadruple batch of both the elixir and the sugar syrup and refrigerate them (where they will keep indefinitely); that way, you can always be ready to whip up this dessert in about fifteen minutes. For a change, try a scoop of sorbet on top of the salsa, or add some fresh strawberries to the mix.

For the Elixir

> 2 cups water
>
> 1 cup sugar
>
> 1 1-inch piece ginger, peeled and thinly sliced
>
> 1 teaspoon coriander seeds
>
> 2 whole cloves
>
> 1$\frac{1}{2}$ tablespoons dark rum
>
> $\frac{1}{2}$ teaspoon vanilla extract

For the Melon Mixture

> $\frac{1}{2}$ cup sugar
>
> $\frac{1}{2}$ cup water
>
> 1 jalapeño or other fresh chile pepper of your choice, split in half
>
> 2 cups peeled and diced (medium) honeydew melon
>
> 2 cups peeled and diced (small) cantaloupe
>
> 2 tablespoons roughly chopped fresh mint

1. Make the elixir: In a small saucepan, combine the water, sugar, ginger, coriander seeds, cloves, rum, and vanilla. Bring to a boil over medium heat, reduce the heat to low, and simmer for 30 minutes to infuse the syrup with the spices. Strain, discard the spices, cover the liquid, and refrigerate until ready to serve.

2. Make the melon mixture: In a small saucepan over medium heat, combine the sugar, water, and chile pepper. Cook for 10 minutes, stirring occasionally, until the mixture is the consistency of syrup and you can taste the chile flavor. Remove from the heat, cover, and refrigerate.

3. Just before you are ready to serve, combine the melons and mint with the chile syrup and mix well. Divide the melon mixture among serving bowls, pour the chilled elixir on top, and serve.

Papaya Ice with Sweet Hot Pepper Sauce

The combination of hot and sweet is found throughout the warm-weather world, from India to North Africa to the American South (think of barbecue sauce). Here we combine the two in a sweet-and-spicy sauce to spoon over a soothing tropical ice. You don't have to add the vodka to the ice, but the alcohol does make the mixture smoother. This recipe works equally well with a couple of mangoes or four peaches in place of the papaya.

> $^1/_2$ cup sugar
>
> $^1/_2$ cup water
>
> 4 papayas, peeled, seeded, and cut into small chunks
>
> 1 tablespoon fresh lemon juice
>
> 1 tablespoon vodka (optional)

For the Sauce

> 1 jalapeño or red cherry chile pepper, minced
>
> 1 1-inch piece ginger, peeled and minced
>
> $^1/_2$ cup fresh lime juice (about 4 limes)
>
> $^1/_4$ cup honey
>
> $^1/_2$ cup apricot jam

1. In a small saucepan, combine the sugar and water and bring to a simmer over medium heat, stirring frequently to dissolve the sugar. Meanwhile, in a food processor or blender, combine the papayas, lemon juice, and vodka if desired and blend or process until well pureed. Pour in the sugar syrup and pulse to mix well. Pour the mixture into a 9" × 12" baking pan and freeze until solid, at least 3 hours, or overnight.

2. Make the sauce: In a small saucepan, combine the chile pepper, ginger, lime juice, honey, and apricot jam and cook over low heat, stirring, until the mixture just comes to a boil. Remove from the heat and allow to cool to room temperature.

3. Just before serving, remove the frozen papaya mixture from the freezer, break it into chunks, and puree it in a food processor or blender. Place in individual serving bowls or goblets, pour some sauce over each serving, and serve.

Gingered Mango Mousse

SERVES 8

This dessert couldn't be simpler. Basically, you take mango and ginger (a truly great flavor combo) and serve them up in a kind of cloud of sweetened whipped cream. Using the juice from the ginger lets you spread its sweet, distinctive, and slightly pungent taste evenly throughout the whole dish. Light, fluffy, and refreshing, this is an excellent dessert after a spicy meal. If you have pomegranate seeds, they make it more dramatic in appearance and add a nice edge of tartness, but the mousse is just fine without them.

6 ripe mangoes, peeled, pitted, and cut into small chunks

2 tablespoons fresh lime juice (about 1 lime)

1 1¹/₂-inch piece ginger, peeled

2 cups heavy cream

¹/₄ cup sugar

Seeds from 1 pomegranate (optional)

1. In a food processor or blender, combine the mango and lime juice and puree until smooth.

2. Place the peeled ginger (cut into 2 or 3 pieces if easier to handle) into a garlic press and squeeze the ginger juice into the puree, and mix to combine.

3. In a large bowl, whip the heavy cream to soft peaks, adding the sugar as you are whipping. When the cream is at the soft peak stage, add the mango puree and whip until just slightly stiff. Refrigerate until well chilled. Serve in goblets, sprinkled with the pomegranate seeds if you have them.

mango's unsavory relations

IN THE DAYS OF the British Empire, mangoes became a very popular fad food in England. At the same time, though, they acquired a reputation as having an unpleasant resinous flavor. In those days this was often true, because of the rather odd fact that these fragrant tropical fruits come from the same family as poison ivy and poison sumac. The same resin that produces the familiar itchy rash from those noxious plants also produced in some mangoes a resinous underflavor similar to turpentine. Fortunately, this characteristic has been bred out of today's commercially available varieties, leaving only the musky flavor of the fruit's yellow or orange flesh.

Coconut Flan

There's really no such thing as the definitive flan recipe. Every cuisine features a custard of some kind, and every tropical cuisine has one flavored with the ubiquitous coconut. In warm climates, this dish would be made with evaporated milk, since it is difficult to keep fresh milk in hot weather. This version, made with cream, is both less sweet and less dense.

As with all custards, be careful not to overcook the flans. Remove them from the oven when the center is still jiggling a little bit, then let them cool gently by sitting in the hot water bath. If you let them stay in the oven too long, you may get a dish that looks more like scrambled eggs than a smooth, silky custard.

> 1^1/$_2$ cups sugar
> ^{1}/$_4$ cup very hot water
> 2 cups light cream or half-and-half
> 1^1/$_2$ cups unsweetened coconut milk (canned, or
>   see page 368 for homemade)
> ^{1}/$_2$ cup sweetened shredded coconut
> 4 large eggs
> 2 large egg yolks
> 2 tablespoons rum of your choice
> ^{1}/$_2$ teaspoon vanilla extract
> Toasted coconut for garnish (optional)

1. Preheat the oven to 275°F, and put 8 small custard cups or ramekins into a lasagne pan or large roasting pan.

2. In a small heavy skillet, heat ^{3}/$_4$ cup of the sugar and 1 tablespoon of the hot water over very low heat, stirring constantly with a wooden spoon, until the sugar has melted and turned a very light brown. Remove the pan from the heat and *very slowly* stir in the remaining 3 tablespoons hot water—be careful here, because if you add it too quickly, it will spatter and the caramel will boil up and over the pan. Pour the caramelized syrup into the custard cups, adding just enough to each one to thinly coat the bottom. (Be careful not to touch the sugar as you do this— it's incredibly hot. Also, don't worry if the sugar seems to have become hard and brittle after you pour it into the cups—it will soften later after you pour in the custard.) Set the cups aside.

3. In a heavy saucepan, combine the cream, coconut milk, and shredded coconut and cook over medium heat, stirring constantly, until the first tiny bubbles appear along the sides of the pan. Set aside.

4. In a large bowl, combine the eggs, yolks, rum, vanilla, and the remaining $3/4$ cup sugar and whisk together well. Slowly add the cream mixture, whisking constantly. Strain this mixture, then ladle into the custard cups.

5. Carefully pour boiling water into the lasagne pan to come halfway up the sides of the custard cups. Cover the pan with a cookie sheet or aluminum foil, place on the top shelf of the preheated oven, and bake for 45 minutes to 1 hour, or until the custard is just set but still jiggles in the center when you shake the pan gently.

6. Remove the flans from the oven, take off the cover, and let them cool to room temperature while still in their water bath. Then refrigerate until well chilled, at least 1 hour, or up to 24 hours.

7. When you are ready to serve the flans, unmold them by running a knife along the inner edge of each custard cup and inverting onto individual plates. Drizzle with any caramel syrup remaining in the cups, and sprinkle with toasted coconut if you want.

nature's milk bottle

AT THE END OF a quarter-mile dirt road near the little town of San Blas on Mexico's Pacific coast, a white stucco hotel perches on a wide sand beach. The oceanside swimming pool is cracked and empty, the hotel's upper floors more or less permanently unoccupied, but in the cavernous lobby, right next to the grand staircase, a teenage boy sits all day. On his left is a pile of whole young coconuts, on his right are empty, bright green husks, and across his lap is a machete.

FOR A FEW PESOS, the boy will whack the top off one of the green ovals, then hand it to you along with a less-than-pristine spoon. Scoop out the pure white flesh—sweet as jelly, light as mousse, with a texture like vanilla custard—and you will begin to understand why, for the more than one third of the world's population that lives in the humid tropics, coconuts are a major food source. In the fortunate phrase of botanist H. C. Harries, these giant nuts are "a milk bottle left on the doorstep of mankind."

Malaysian-Style Coconut Pudding

SERVES 8

As might be expected in a dessert inspired by the cuisine of a country where nutmeg, mace, and cloves are all grown commercially, this pudding relies on aromatic spices for much of its flavor. If you can get your hands on the dark, semirefined brown palm sugar called jaggery, it adds a strong molasses kind of flavor that is characteristic of Malaysian sweets. If you can't find it, though, brown sugar will do just fine.

As with all custards, it's important not to overcook. Even if you think it's not done yet, go ahead and remove this one from the oven when the center still jiggles, then let it cool in the water bath so it finishes cooking in the gentlest possible manner. This gives the custard a wonderfully smooth, silky texture.

> 6 large eggs, lightly beaten
>
> 2 cups half-and-half
>
> Scant 2 cups unsweetened coconut milk
>
>   (1 14-ounce can, or see page 368 for homemade)
>
> $1/2$ teaspoon ground cardamom
>
> $1/2$ teaspoon ground nutmeg
>
> $1/2$ teaspoon ground mace
>
> 2 teaspoons rose water (optional)
>
> $1/2$ teaspoon vanilla extract
>
> $3/4$ cup lightly packed brown sugar (or jaggery if you can get hold of it)
>
> 2 tablespoons hot water
>
> $3/4$ cup sweetened shredded coconut, toasted in a 350°F oven until lightly browned, 3 to 4 minutes

1. Preheat the oven to 250°F.

2. In a large bowl, combine the eggs, half-and-half, coconut milk, spices, rose water if using it, and vanilla and mix well.

3. In a small saucepan, combine the brown sugar and hot water and cook over medium heat, stirring constantly, until the sugar has melted. Gradually whisk into the egg mixture.

4. Pour the mixture into a 2-quart baking pan. Place the pan in a larger roasting pan, then carefully pour boiling water into the roasting pan to come halfway up the side of the baking pan.

5. Bake for about 1 hour and 45 minutes, or until almost set. *To check for doneness:* Jiggle the pan slightly; the center of the custard should jiggle a bit rather than being completely set. Remove from the oven and allow to cool in the water bath until cool enough to serve. (Or cool to room temperature, remove from the water bath, cover, and refrigerate for later serving.) Just before serving, sprinkle with the toasted coconut.

malaysian mélange

MALAYSIAN CUISINE IS ACTUALLY a wild medley of different cooking styles and traditions. There is the rather intricate cooking of the large immigrant Chinese population, mostly from Fukien province; there is spicy Indian cooking, imported by workers brought from southern India to work on oil palm plantations; there is the more earthy cooking of the indigenous Malay population; there is some European influence from early Portuguese colonizers; and there is the "Baba and Nonya cuisine," the unique cooking style created by the Straits-born Chinese, with one Malay and one Chinese parent. All in all, it's an exhilarating mix.

Maple Bread Pudding with Oven-Dried Pears and Homemade Raisins

SERVES 8 TO 10

Oven-drying fruit may seem like a chore, but in fact it is supremely simple. All you have to do is set your oven to very low, put in the halved or sliced fruit, and go about your business for a few hours. For such a no-brainer, the process delivers big rewards. Removing the moisture from fruit dramatically changes its nature, concentrating sweetness and adding deep complexities of flavor. It is as if when the universal common denominator of water is removed, the inner core of the fruit's particular character is revealed. Here we take advantage of this metamorphosis of flavor by drying pears and grapes, then layering them in a simple, homey bread pudding flavored with maple syrup.

4 ripe pears of your choice, peeled, halved, and cored
$^1/_2$ cup seedless red or green grapes, halved
1 tablespoon vegetable oil
8 large eggs
$^1/_4$ cup all-purpose flour
4 cups half-and-half
$1^1/_2$ cups maple syrup
1 teaspoon vanilla extract
Dash of ground cinnamon
Dash of ground nutmeg
Pinch of salt
1 large loaf stale bread (Italian or French is best),
    crusts removed and bread cut into $^1/_2$-inch-thick slices

1. Preheat the oven to 200 °F. Rub the pears and grapes lightly with the vegetable oil and place on a rack set on a baking pan. Place on the middle rack of the oven and let them dry there for 6 hours. The pears should be somewhat shrunken in size and slightly dry on the outside, but still tender; the grapes should resemble plumped raisins. Remove the fruit from the oven and allow to cool to room temperature.

2. Increase the oven temperature to 350°F. Butter and flour an 8" × 12" × 2" baking dish.

3. In a large bowl, beat the eggs lightly. Add the flour and beat until smooth. Add the half-and-half, maple syrup, vanilla, spices, and salt, and beat until well mixed.

4. Slice the pear halves lengthwise into slices about $1/2$ inch thick. Add the pears and grapes to the custard and mix lightly.

5. Layer the bread lengthwise in the baking dish, in 3 or 4 rows, overlapping it slightly so that it fits snugly into the dish. Ladle the custard evenly over the bread, then let the bread soak in the custard for about 5 minutes, pushing it down if necessary to be sure it is fully submerged.

6. Cover the pan with aluminum foil. Place a second baking dish full of water on the bottom shelf of the oven, and place the pudding on the middle shelf. Bake for 1 hour, turning the pudding around after 30 minutes to ensure even cooking.

7. After 1 hour, remove the foil and continue baking for 15 minutes longer, or until the top is golden brown and the custard is firmly set. Serve at once.

homemade coconut milk

PLACE EQUAL QUANTITIES OF coconut meat and boiling water in a food processor or blender. Puree well, then strain the resulting mixture through cheesecloth, pressing to extract all the liquid. Discard the solids, and what you have left is coconut milk.

Coconut Pancakes with Caramelized Bananas

SERVES 8

I know, pancakes for dessert may seem a little odd. But this is my version of a sweet sold in Singapore by street vendors, who cook up sweet coconut pancakes on black griddles set above portable stoves, then wrap them around meltingly sweet caramelized bananas and hand them to you to eat as you walk around. You can serve them that way, too, or roll the pancakes into cylinders and ladle the bananas over the top, which is a little easier. Just be sure that you don't overbeat the batter for these pancakes, or it will be gluey.

> 2$^1/_2$ cups unsweetened coconut milk (canned or homemade, see page 368)
> $^1/_2$ cup all-purpose flour
> 3 large eggs
> $^3/_4$ cup sugar
> Pinch of salt
> 1 cup sweetened shredded coconut, toasted in a 350°F oven until lightly
> browned, 4 to 5 minutes
> 2 tablespoons unsalted butter
> 3 ripe bananas, peeled and cut into $^1/_2$-inch slices
> Vegetable oil for cooking

1. Preheat the oven to 225°F.

2. In a large bowl, combine the coconut milk, flour, and eggs and mix until well blended. Add $^1/_2$ cup of the sugar, the salt, and $^1/_2$ cup of the toasted coconut and stir to blend; do not overmix or the mixture will become gluey. (If this happens, add a splash of regular milk, stir to blend, and let it rest for 30 minutes.)

3. In a nonstick skillet, combine the butter and the remaining $^1/_4$ cup sugar and cook over medium heat, stirring, until the butter is melted. Add the banana slices and cook, stirring, until lightly browned, 3 to 4 minutes. Pour into an ovenproof bowl and place in the oven to keep warm.

4. Pour about a tablespoon of vegetable oil into the skillet and heat over medium heat until hot but not smoking. Pour a large spoonful of batter into the skillet and cook until little bubbles appear on the top and a peek at the underside shows that it is lightly browned. Flip and cook on the other side until lightly browned. Place in a baking pan lined with a tea towel and keep warm in the oven. Repeat with the remaining batter, stacking the pancakes as you make them.

5. Roll the pancakes into cylinders, top with the banana mixture, and serve, garnished with the remaining toasted shredded coconut.

Little Chèvre Cheesecakes
with Guava-Lime Sauce

Because it uses evaporated milk, this simple custard-type dessert has a kinship to the flans made in tropical climates all over the world. But we give it a different twist by flavoring it with tangy goat cheese (chèvre), adding some cream cheese to give it the texture of cheesecake, and serving it with a sauce featuring the distinctly tropical flavor of guava. If you can't get hold of guava paste, you can serve the cheesecakes without the sauce; they have enough flavor to stand on their own.

$1^3/_4$ cups plus 1 tablespoon sugar

$^1/_4$ cup very hot water

2 8-ounce cans evaporated milk

2 teaspoons grated lemon zest (yellow part only)

1 teaspoon vanilla extract

3 large eggs

1 large egg yolk

4 ounces chèvre (goat cheese), at room temperature

2 ounces cream cheese, at room temperature

For the Sauce

$5^1/_2$ ounces (one quarter of a 22-ounce can) guava paste, cut into small chunks

$^1/_4$ cup water

2 tablespoons fresh lime juice (about 1 lime)

2 tablespoons rum of your choice

1. Preheat the oven to 350°F, and put 6 4-ounce custard cups or ramekins into a lasagne pan or other large baking pan.

2. In a small heavy skillet, heat $^3/_4$ cup of the sugar and 1 tablespoon of the hot water over very low heat, stirring constantly with a wooden spoon, until the sugar has melted and turned a very light brown. Remove the pan from the heat and *very slowly* stir in the remaining 3 tablespoons hot water—be careful here, because if you add it too quickly, it will spatter and the caramel will boil up and over the pan. Pour the caramelized syrup into the custard cups, adding just enough to each one to thinly coat the bottom. (Be careful not to touch the sugar as you do this— it's very hot.) Set the cups aside.

3. In a small saucepan, combine the evaporated milk, lemon zest, and 5 tablespoons sugar and heat over medium-high heat, stirring constantly, until the first tiny bubbles appear along the sides of the pan. Remove from the heat and allow to sit for 15 minutes so the flavor of the lemon is infused into the milk. Then whisk in the vanilla, eggs, and yolk and set aside.

4. In a medium bowl, combine the cheeses and beat until smooth. Add the remaining $3/4$ cup sugar and stir until smooth. Add the milk-egg mixture in 3 portions, stirring until smooth after each addition. Pour the mixture through a fine strainer to remove any lumps, then ladle it into the ramekins.

5. Fill the lasagne pan with enough very hot water to come halfway up the ramekins, cover the pan with a cookie sheet or aluminum foil, and place on the top shelf of the oven. Bake for 40 to 45 minutes, or until the custard is just set. Remove from the oven, take off the cover, and allow the cheesecakes to cool to room temperature while still in their water bath. Then refrigerate until chilled.

6. While the cheesecakes are chilling out, make the sauce: In a small saucepan, combine all of the ingredients and cook over low heat, stirring to break up the guava pieces. You want to heat the mixture just long enough to melt the guava and create a smooth sauce, which should take about 10 minutes. Remove the sauce from the heat and set aside.

7. When you are ready to serve, slide a small knife around the inside rim of each cheesecake to loosen them, flip them over onto individual plates, spoon on the guava sauce, and serve.

tropics in a can

GUAVAS, WHICH ORIGI-NATED IN Brazil but are now found all over the tropical world, have a very distinctive, intense aroma and a sweet-tart taste. Unfortunately, they do not travel well, so it's tough to sample them here in the United States. But you can still enjoy the taste of this tropical fruit by buying the canned guava paste found in many Latin markets. Most brands contain nothing but guava and some sugar and citric acid, so they come reasonably close to the taste of the fresh fruit. Try putting a small dish of the paste out on the tray the next time you serve cheese and crackers; it goes particularly well with a good, strong sharp Cheddar.

Spanish Olive Oil and Wine Cake

MAKES 1 LOAF: SERVES 6 TO 8

In Spain, where olive oil has been produced for thousands of years, cooks are very imaginative in its use, and there are a number of sweets that use it to excellent advantage, as there are in Italy. You don't actually taste the oil in this cake, but it gives it a very nice, slightly crumbly texture. To add to the Spanish theme, the cake is doused with a simple sherry syrup just after it comes out of the oven. The cake is superb on its own, but you might also want to try topping each slice with some fresh fruit and a big spoonful of whipped cream.

> 1 tablespoon unsalted butter, softened, for the pan
>
> $1^1/_4$ cups all-purpose flour plus 2 tablespoons for the pan
>
> 2 teaspoons baking powder
>
> $^1/_2$ teaspoon salt
>
> 1 cup plus 2 tablespoons sugar
>
> $1^1/_4$ cups extra virgin olive oil
>
> 3 large eggs
>
> $1^1/_2$ teaspoons grated orange zest (orange part only)
>
> $^1/_2$ teaspoon vanilla extract
>
> 2 tablespoons white wine
>
> 2 tablespoons dry sherry

1. Preheat the oven to 350°F. Coat an $8^1/_2$" × $4^1/_2$" loaf pan with the tablespoon of butter, sprinkle it with the 2 tablespoons of flour, and set aside. (Don't skimp here—the cake will stick if you don't use enough butter and flour.)

2. Sift the $1^1/_4$ cups flour together with the baking powder and salt and set aside.

3. In a medium bowl, combine 1 cup of the sugar, the olive oil, eggs, orange zest, and vanilla and beat with an electric mixer until smooth and light. Add the flour mixture in two batches, folding it in with a spatula or wooden spoon until just incorporated.

4. Spoon the batter into the prepared loaf pan and bake for 45 to 50 minutes. *To check for doneness:* Stick a cake tester or toothpick into the middle of the cake; if it comes out moist but has no batter sticking to it, the cake is done.

5. Meanwhile, combine the wine, sherry, and the remaining 2 tablespoons sugar in a small saucepan and heat over medium heat, stirring to dissolve the sugar, until the first bubbles appear around the edges. Remove from the heat.

6. Remove the loaf from the oven and spoon the wine-sherry sauce over the top while the cake is still hot. Cool on a rack for 10 minutes, then slide a knife around the sides of the cake and remove. Serve by itself or with fresh fruit of your choice and whipped cream.

Caramelized Banana and Lime Tart

MAKES 1 9-INCH TART: SERVES 8 TO 10

This recipe was developed by Wesley Miyazaki, the talented pastry chef at the Blue Room. Wesley took the unusual career path of earning a Ph.D. in biology at Massachusetts Institute of Technology before turning to the world of pastry, and he brings a sense of fun and experimentation to his tropically inspired desserts. One of Wes's favorite techniques is to make flavored crusts for his pies and tarts, an approach that gives him more components to play around with. Here he combines a sweet coconut crust with the intense sweetness of caramel-coated bananas, then adds a lime-flavored custard for a little contrast. The overall effect is rich and so sweet it's on the edge of candy, with a nice play of tropical flavors.

For the Crust

$^1/_2$ cup (1 stick) unsalted butter, softened

3 tablespoons sugar

Pinch of salt

1$^1/_4$ cups all-purpose flour

$^1/_2$ teaspoon vanilla extract

$^1/_2$ cup sweetened shredded coconut, toasted in a 350°F oven, shaking
once or twice, until browned, 5 to 6 minutes

2 tablespoons ice water

$^1/_4$ cup unsalted butter

$^1/_4$ cup sugar

2 tablespoons water

3 or 4 ripe bananas, peeled and cut into 1-inch slices

3 large egg yolks

1 14-ounce can condensed milk

$^1/_3$ cup fresh lime juice (about 3 small limes)

3 tablespoons fresh lemon juice (about 1 small lemon)

1. Make the crust: Combine the butter and sugar in a medium bowl and cream until the mixture is uniform. Add the salt, flour, and vanilla and mix well. Add the coconut and water and work the dough well with the heel of your hand to incorporate the ingredients.

2. Turn the dough out onto a well-floured surface and roll it into an 11-inch circle. Carefully transfer the circle to a 9-inch tart pan and press the dough into the pan, making sure that the bottom is thin and that the sides are thick (this allows for some shrinkage during baking). Prick the dough all over with a fork and refrigerate for 30 minutes.

3. Preheat the oven to 450°F.

4. Bake the chilled crust for 10 to 15 minutes, or just until golden brown. Remove from the oven and set aside. Turn the oven temperature down to 350°F.

5. In a small saucepan, melt the butter over low heat. Add the sugar and cook, stirring constantly, until the mixture turns a light brown, 8 to 10 minutes. It will look separated and clumpy, but don't worry; add the water—now it should look smooth. Add the bananas and toss a few times to coat with the caramel. Turn off the heat and continue to toss the bananas every couple of minutes or so until the caramel sauce becomes smooth. If there are any undissolved chunks of sugar in the caramel, pull them out. Pour the bananas into the cooled tart shell and refrigerate until chilled, about 30 minutes.

6. In a medium bowl, whisk together the egg yolks, condensed milk, lime juice, and lemon juice. Pour this mixture over the bananas, making sure they are completely covered. Place in the 350°F oven and bake until the custard is lightly set, 15 to 20 minutes. Allow to cool to room temperature before serving.

easy grated coconut

UNLESS IT IS TO be eaten out of hand as a simple snack or used in a relish of some sort, fresh coconut meat is almost always grated before it is used in cooking. In most Asian markets you will find hand-held graters of various shapes and sizes that are used to perform this task. You can approximate the texture of hand-grated coconut, however, by dropping small pieces of the meat into a food processor while the motor is running and processing until the coconut is well grated. The result will not be as fluffy or moist as hand-grated coconut, since the processor does crush the coconut somewhat, but it is close enough for most uses.

Espresso Black Bottom Pie

This very rich pie is an old Southern tradition. In this version, the Oreo cookie crust is practically a dessert all by itself, and when you fill it with a smooth chocolate mousse filling and top that with a soft, flavorful espresso cream, you get what my lyrical friend Bill Cramp was moved to call "a symphony of chocolate flavors." Of course he'd had a few glasses of wine at the time, but I think his assessment was right on the money.

For the Crust

> 1 teaspoon cold unsalted butter
>
> 3 cups Oreo cookies (about 1 pound), crumbled
>
> $1/4$ cup unsalted butter, melted

For the Mousse

> $1/4$ cup unsalted butter, softened
>
> $1/4$ cup sugar
>
> 2 large eggs
>
> 2 tablespoons heavy cream
>
> 8 ounces semisweet chocolate, melted
>
> 1 teaspoon vanilla extract

For the Espresso Cream

> 6 tablespoons sugar
>
> $1^1/_2$ tablespoons cornstarch
>
> 2 large egg yolks
>
> $1^1/_2$ cups milk
>
> 1 teaspoon unflavored gelatin
>
> 2 tablespoons cold water
>
> 6 tablespoons ground espresso beans or
>
>> 2 tablespoons instant espresso powder
>
> 1 cup heavy cream

1. Preheat the oven to 350°F.

2. Make the crust: Butter a 9-inch pie pan with the cold butter. (This will prevent the crust from sticking.) In the bowl of a food processor, pulverize the Oreos. Transfer to a mixing bowl, add the melted butter, and mix well. Pat this mixture evenly into the buttered pie pan and bake for 10 minutes. Remove from the oven, let cool, and refrigerate.

3. Make the mousse: In a medium bowl, cream the butter and sugar together with an electric mixer until light and fluffy. Add the eggs and mix just until they are incorporated. Add the cream, chocolate, and vanilla and mix just until smooth. Place in the shell and chill for 1 hour.

4. Make the espresso cream: In a small bowl, combine the sugar and cornstarch, mix well, and set aside. In a second small bowl, whisk together the egg yolks and $1/4$ cup of the milk. Set aside. In a third small bowl, combine the gelatin and water and set aside.

5. In a small saucepan, combine the remaining $1^1/4$ cups milk and the espresso and heat over medium-high heat until small bubbles just begin to form around the edges of the milk. (This will infuse the flavor of the espresso into the milk.) If you're using ground beans, strain the mixture, discard the grounds, and return the flavored milk to the heat; if you're using instant espresso powder, just continue on with the recipe.

6. Whisk the sugar-cornstarch mixture into the milk. Add a few tablespoons of this mixture to the egg mixture, then add the egg mixture to the milk-sugar mixture, whisking constantly. Let the mixture cook, stirring, until it thickens a bit, 2 to 3 minutes. Add the gelatin-water mixture, mix well, and remove from the heat. Place in a large bowl over an ice bath to cool and thicken more, stirring every couple of minutes to keep it smooth.

7. Whip the heavy cream until soft peaks form. Gently fold the whipped cream into the expresso cream mixture just until incorporated. Refrigerate until chilled, about 30 minutes.

8. Top the mousse with the espresso cream and chill for 2 hours to set up before serving.

melting chocolate

EVERY BAKER SEEMS TO have a favorite way to melt chocolate. The most fail-safe of the traditional methods is to put the chocolate in the top of a double boiler over barely simmering water. If you don't want to mess with setting up a double boiler, you can just chop the chocolate coarsely and melt it in a heavy saucepan over the lowest possible heat, stirring and watching carefully so it doesn't burn. Or you can just put it in a pan in a very low oven. With any of these methods, it's important to be careful that the pan you are using is completely dry; even a little bit of water will cause the chocolate to "seize up" and become stiff and lumpy.

OF COURSE, IF YOU happen to have a microwave in your kitchen, the very easiest way to melt chocolate is to just put it in the microwave for 30 seconds on low power. It's easy, it's foolproof, and it has the added advantage that you have found something other than reheating coffee that the microwave actually does well.

Peach Sour Cream Pie

MAKES 1 9-INCH PIE: SERVES 6

Peaches, which originally came from China, are as close to a tropical fruit as anything that grows in our country north of Florida or California. Rich, luscious, mellow, juicy— you can run out of adjectives trying to describe the virtues of these fruits. Here we combine them with sour cream in a simple Southern-style pie that falls somewhere between a cheesecake and a plain fruit pie. It's just right for those late-summer days when peaches are at their height and you have enough to cook with as well as eat out of hand.

For the Crust

1¼ cups all-purpose flour

¼ teaspoon salt

½ cup (1 stick) cold unsalted butter, cut into small chunks

3 tablespoons ice water

For the Filling

2 large eggs

½ cup sugar

1½ cups sour cream

½ teaspoon grated lemon zest (yellow part only)

Pinch of ground nutmeg

Pinch of ground ginger

Pinch of salt

5 medium peaches, peeled, pitted, and cut into thick slices
(about 2½ cups)

For the Topping

½ cup all-purpose flour

¼ cup lightly packed brown sugar

Generous pinch of ground nutmeg

Generous pinch of ground cinnamon

½ cup (1 stick) cold unsalted butter, cut into small chunks

1. Make the crust: In a medium bowl, combine the flour and salt and mix well. With two table knives or a pastry cutter, cut in the cold butter chunks just until the mixture starts to look like coarse meal. Sprinkle the water over the mixture and mix it in with your hands until the dough just comes together. Pat the dough into a disk, wrap it in plastic wrap, and refrigerate for 30 minutes.

THINGS OF BEAUTY

2. On a floured surface, roll the chilled dough out into a circle 10 inches in diameter. Fit it into a 9" pie tin, crimp the edges, and refrigerate.

3. Preheat the oven to 350°F.

4. Make the filling: In a medium bowl, combine all of the ingredients and mix well. Set aside.

5. Make the topping: In a small bowl, combine all the ingredients and mix with a fork just until the mixture looks crumbly. You don't want it to look like a dough.

6. Now you're ready for the assembly. Place the filling in the pie shell and sprinkle the topping over the top. Bake for 50 to 60 minutes or until the filling is well set. Serve warm or cold.

peach buzz

FRESH PEACHES WERE A constant feature of my summers growing up. Every year from late July through early September, my mother made sure that there was always a "lug"—the name we gave to the balsa wood crates in which twenty-four peaches were sold, each nestled in its pink tissue paper—sitting out on the counter, so my siblings and I could eat as many as we wanted, anytime we wanted. These peaches, which were yellow-fleshed Elbertas, became my personal idea of what fruit should be like.

RECENTLY, THOUGH, I SPENT some time in South Carolina with Dori Sanders, a second-generation peach farmer who is also a novelist and cookbook author. From Dori I learned that my revered Elbertas are in fact only one among more than two thousand (that's right, two thousand) hybrid varieties, each as different from one another as Delicious and McIntosh apples. In addition to the yellow-fleshed types such as the prototypical Elberta and lesser-known varieties like Blake, Glohaven, Redskin, and Biscoe, there are also delicate white-fleshed varieties such as Georgia Belle and Summer Flame, and even red-fleshed peaches, like the Indian Blood.

Whatever the variety, all peaches can be divided into two camps according to the way the flesh relates to the pit. The clingstones, so called because the flesh clings tightly to the pit, are used mostly for cooking or canning; freestones, which get their name from the fact that the flesh practically falls away from the pit when they are cut, are best for eating out of hand.

ALL OF THIS IS good to know, but as long as the peach you are eating is dead-ripe, it is pretty much guaranteed to be delicious, for this is one of nature's great fruits.

Mai Tai Pie

This recipe was first tested at a snowy New Year's Day cookout in Boston. It never made it to the dessert portion of the meal, however, since it was consumed without benefit of plates or utensils by the guys minding the fire out on the back deck. When some of the other guests expressed their dismay at this behavior, I pointed out that, after all, it seemed appropriate for a dessert named after a cocktail.

Make sure to grate the lime before you juice it, and use dark rum if you have it, since it gives the pie a stronger flavor than light rum.

1 20-ounce can crushed pineapple, undrained
$^1/_4$ cup cornstarch
Pinch of salt
$^1/_4$ cup rum, preferably a dark version like Myers's or Bacardi Gold
$1^1/_2$ cups sugar
5 large eggs, separated
1 tablespoon unsalted butter
Finely grated zest (green part only) and juice of 1 lime
1 prebaked 9-inch pie shell

1. Preheat the oven to 350°F.

2. In a medium saucepan, combine the pineapple, cornstarch, salt, rum, and $^3/_4$ cup of the sugar. Cook over medium heat, stirring, until the mixture just comes to a boil, then remove from the heat.

3. Stir a couple of tablespoons of the hot pineapple mixture into the egg yolks, then pour the yolk mixture back into the pineapple mixture and stir to combine thoroughly. Return the mixture to the heat and cook for 1 to 2 minutes more, stirring constantly, until it just begins to simmer. Stir in the butter, lime zest, and lime juice. Remove from the heat and allow to cool almost to room temperature.

4. Beat the egg whites until they hold soft peaks, then sprinkle the remaining $^3/_4$ cup sugar over the top and continue to beat until they form stiff peaks. Fold 1 cup of the beaten whites into the pineapple mixture. Pour the mixture into the pie shell and bake for about 15 minutes, or until set.

5. Spread the remaining stiff egg whites over the top of the baked pie and slip it back into the oven for about 10 minutes, or until the meringue is just browned.

index

North African flavors, grilled chicken and eggplant with, 203–204

O

octopus, grilled, and perciatelli with fennel and lemon, 93–94
okra, cornmeal mush with tomatoes and, 305
olive(s):
    black, linguine with grilled shrimp and, 87
    black, relish, grilled open-faced eggplant sandwiches with fresh mozzarella and, 39
    green, and tomato relish, grilled lamb and potato skewers with, 122–123
    grilled swordfish with artichokes, tomatoes and, 170–171
olive oil:
    expensive, grilled mackerel with lemon, oregano, and, 192
    kohlrabi puree with lemon and, 291
    slow-cooked chicken legs with lime, garlic, and, 206
    and wine cake, Spanish, 372–373
onion(s):
    and cabbage, spicy lime-marinated, 331
    hoisin chicken breasts with grilled peppers and, 199–200
    macumber turnip cakes with bacon and, 294–295
    pearl, hobo pack with raisins and sage, 218–219
    pickled, and avocado salad, grilled shrimp and bacon skewers with, 104–105
    sausage hobo pack with peppers, green grapes, and, 225–226
    spring, charred, grilled Delmonico steak adobo with sweet corn relish and, 131–132
onion(s), red:
    -bacon relish, grilled halibut with roasted red pepper mayonnaise and, 186–187
    and grilled lamb in grape leaves, 80–81
    and grilled shrimp skewers with sour salad and cashew dipping sauce, Tommy's, 106–107
    pickled, tortilla sandwiches of grilled shrimp and corn with goat cheese and, 40–41
    quixotic mixed grill with vegetable skewers and four sauces, 152–154

orange:
    -balsamic glaze, grilled pork and apple skewers with, 128
    barbecued whole game hens with oregano, cumin seed and, 265
    -cherry sauce, summer, grilled duck breast with, 208–209
    -cumin mahi mahi, grilled, with smoky summer vegetable hash, 166–167
    -green peppercorn sauce, Chinese-spiced whole duck with, 270–271
    -mustard dressing, jícama-apple salad with, 307
    -sweet potato hobo pack, 219–220
oregano:
    barbecued whole game hens with orange, cumin seed and, 265
    grilled mackerel with expensive olive oil, lemon, and, 192
oysters, 71
    barbecued, in their shells, 70

P

pancakes, coconut, with caramelized bananas, 369
pancetta, arugula with grilled asparagus, white beans and, 50–51
papaya:
    -chile dressing, grilled shrimp and black bean salad with, 57–58
    ice with sweet hot pepper sauce, 362
    vinaigrette, grilled scallop–stuffed avocados with, 58–59
parsley:
    -garlic butter, pepper-grilled tuna steak with, 178–179
    raw beef with capers, hard cheese and, 79–80
    -yogurt sauce, grilled potatoes with, 283
pasta, 85–100
    grilled sausage and corn over fettuccine with tomatoes and basil, 99
    lamb shish kebobs over fettuccine, 100
    linguine with grilled shrimp and black olives, 87
    linguine with smoky lobster, grilled corn, and roasted pepper–garlic sauce, 88–89
    macaroni with grilled squid, eggplant, and peppers, 91–92
    penne with grilled tuna and crisp-fried capers, 95
    perciatelli and grilled octopus with fennel and lemon, 93–94